U-Boats against Canada

U-Boats against Canada

German Submarines in Canadian Waters

MICHAEL L. HADLEY

McGill-Queen's University Press
Kingston and Montreal

© McGill-Queen's University Press 1985
ISBN 0-7735-0584-9
Reprinted 1985

Legal deposit second quarter 1985
Bibliothèque nationale du Québec

Printed in Canada

This book has been published with the help of a grant
from the Social Science Federation of Canada using
funds provided by the Social Sciences and Humanities
Research Council of Canada. Publication has also
been assisted by the Canada Council and Ontario Arts
Council under their block grant programs.

CANADIAN CATALOGUING IN PUBLICATION DATA

Hadley, Michael L.
  U-boats against Canada

  Bibliography: p.
  Includes index.
  ISBN 0-7735-0584-9.

  1. World War, 1939–1945 – Naval operations –
  Submarine. 2. World War, 1939–1945 – Naval
  operations, German. 3. World War, 1939–1945 –
  Campaigns – Atlantic Ocean. 4. World War, 1939–
  1945 – Naval operations, Canadian. 5. Canada –
  Coast defenses. I. Title.
D781.H32 1985   940.54'5   C85-098078-X

*To the
Craig Campbells
and
Klaus Hornbostels
of the Atlantic War*

Contents

Illustrations

Preface

The suspected presence of German U-boats in Canadian waters has fascinated a broad spectrum of observers since the closing days of the First World War. Popular articles about real or imagined patrols, attacks, sinkings, or landing of spies have aroused considerable curiosity and many questions, but provided few answers. This book gives the first detailed account of what actually happened. During the long and exhausting Battle of the Atlantic, the Canadian Navy achieved much. It provided 48 per cent of the escorts to ocean-going convoys between North America and Europe; it swept mines in United Kingdom and European waters; it supported the bitter Murmansk convoys, the Torch landings in North Africa, the Normandy landings in France; it patrolled the Mediterranean and Caribbean, and assisted the United States in securing the convoy routes between New York and Cuba. It sank U-boats. Historical accounts tend to focus on the exploits of these "Far Distant Ships" to the virtual neglect of Canada's war in home waters.

My account, by contrast, takes its point of departure from German initiatives off Canadian shores. A commander will, of course, usually take initiatives only when he feels he has the upper hand. He strikes where his enemy is weak. The disadvantageous light into which this circumstance occasionally casts Canadian naval policy and practice for the years 1939–45 is therefore unavoidable. How well the Canadian Navy managed against the German U-boat threat of the Second World War reflects not only upon the men at sea, but more especially upon the strategic policy planners who provided – or failed to provide – the sailors with the resources to fulfil their task. A government's defence posture constitutes not only a response to perceived threat; it is also a statement about the priority it accords to national security. This account is, therefore, not without a certain uncomfortable relevance to our present and future maritime plans.

German submersibles of the First World War had extremely limited underwater endurance and consequently operated as surface raiders. They would proceed to their operational zone on the surface, submerge on sighting a distant target, and then surface suddenly at close quarters to effect their attack and withdrawal. The German U-boat skippers sometimes even issued receipts to the merchant captains and fishermen whose boats they had sunk. By the end of 1918, Canada had lost eleven schooners and a trawler to this method. The total loss of 2002 gross tons of shipping ranged from the 107-ton schooner *C.M. Walters* to the 695-ton *Dornfontein*. In all, this was but a token of future losses when a new German admiral, Karl Dönitz, would send out U-boats once again: this time, however, with improved technology and a new tactical doctrine. The confrontations of the First World War held little of the abhorrent ideological freight that encumbered Allied perceptions of German submarine warfare between 1939 and 1945. For in the Second World War the ultimate maritime weapon emerged as a tool of Nazism. It symbolized for the Allies the pernicious Nazi will for world domination, and ultimately for murder. Like the demagoguery and perverted politics they reflected, these "demon machines," as some press reports described them, were perceived as profoundly evil, cunning, vicious, and mean. Allied submarine attacks against Axis shipping, by contrast, were merely a matter of "shooting ducks." Such is the rhetoric of war. The extent to which German submariners were politically motivated, or perceived themselves as instruments of Nazi policies and ideology, forms the subject of separate ongoing studies. Suffice it to say here that their conservative and traditionalist bent inclined them to a nationalist, rather than to a necessarily national-socialist persuasion. The record leaves little doubt, however, that their senior officer, Admiral Karl Dönitz, embraced the Nazi faith. This, of course, goes a long way in explaining how he succeeded Hitler as head of state.

Significantly, however, Canadian public attitudes towards U-boats in the early days of the Second World War, before the enormity of Germany's intentions was fully grasped, remained characteristically ambivalent. Like the tradition of vicarious terror in films and books that engenders the antithetical sensations of repugnance and delight, U-boats provided the armchair observer with a peculiar thrill. U-boat warfare even provided Canadians with heroes – albeit anonymous, enemy heroes – who seemed to exude a certain suave savoir-faire, and sometimes even a disarming humanity. Thus, in Canadian waters and along the coast, U-boats spawned tales of wonder and terror, and triggered more claims of uncanny dash and bravado than perhaps any other weapon of war. It is easy to see how myths continued up to the present day: stories of German submariners landing to buy groceries and go for streetcar rides, to eavesdrop on conversations over a glass of beer, or even to attend a dance at the local town hall. German sailors, the stories go, were everywhere: they marched sixteen abreast down the main highway into St John's, steamed into harbour by daylight to pick up suspicious men carrying sinister black suitcases, and – if we can believe an operations report of the Flag Officer, Newfoundland Force – one local resident even sighted a U-boat flying through the air. Alas, these are merely tales. History has another, but equally fascinating story to tell.

The threat of German U-boats in Canadian waters presented a major challenge to coastal and convoy defence in the Second World War. After the intrusion of U-boats into the western Atlantic in the First World War, Canadian minesweepers, escorts, harbour defences, and convoy routes were all predicated on the concern that major staging points for coastal and transatlantic convoys – Halifax, St John's, and even ports in the St Lawrence itself – might be blockaded or even attacked by one of the "most sinister" weapons of technological and psychological warfare that maritime forces had yet encountered. Significantly, Canadian naval authorities had warned the ill-prepared government as early as August 1939 that the major threat to Canada's seaborne trade would be from raiders and submarines in the approaches to Halifax, St John's, and the St Lawrence. But not one of the handful of ships available for naval service at the time was equipped to wage antisubmarine warfare. Fortunately for Canada, however, German Naval Staff was first to withhold its inshore operational sorties until Operation Paukenschlag (Drumbeat) in January 1942. But then with slight exception it pressed hard to the end.

Beginning with U-111's tentative exploration of the entrance to the Strait of Belle Isle in June 1941, which led to the positioning in the area of a patrol line of twelve U-boats in October that year, the German patrols peaked in January and February 1942, when up to twenty-four U-boats stalked the seas from the Newfoundland Banks westward. They soon penetrated the St Lawrence River to within 172 miles of Quebec City and explored deep into the Bay of Fundy and the approaches to Halifax harbour. With the exception of operations in the fall of 1941, when U-boat packs approached Canadian shores, the inshore war was characterized by the solo sortie. From 1942 onwards, Canada's shores held for them few mysteries and few surprises. These at first highly trained members of an élite command in the German navy, with the highest mortality rate of any armed service, carried off their missions with dash, daring, and often amazingly good luck. By war's end, with resources and experienced men nearing depletion, their less-trained and frequently inexperienced successors doggedly pursued their tactical goals when the war had turned irrevocably against any German hope for victory and when, it could be argued, their strength was more urgently needed in waters closer to home.

While cordoning off the sea lines of communication, U-boats sent valuable reports on weather and shipping, and explored deep into Canadian shores. They reconnoitred traffic patterns and checked for soft spots in defence. They landed spies, laid mines, built an automatic weather station, and attempted to rescue escaped German prisoners of war. They attacked merchantmen and warships alike until forced to withdraw. Sometimes they attacked with deck guns after all torpedoes were spent. Seeking this elusive enemy over thousands of square miles of ocean taxed the Canadian Navy to the limit of its stamina, ingenuity, and imagination. Large numbers of the Royal Canadian Navy Volunteer Reserve (RCNVR), the "Wavy Navy" of volunteers who with a small component of experienced mariners in the Royal Canadian Navy Reserve (RCNR) swelled the small regular force from some 1900 personnel with thirteen ships in the year 1939 to 90,000 with 400 ships by 1945, defended the inshore routes.

These waters were in fact as harsh and dangerous as the mid-Atlantic convoys ever experienced. The common enemy of Germans and Canadians alike was the sea. The Atlantic, with its fog and often violent seas, swirling mists, and freezing rain, obscured attackers and targets alike. Ambiguous temperature gradients and saline layers linked with strong currents and irregular coastal seabeds to provide the worst conditions for the detection of submerged submarines the defenders could meet. A castaway in these seas could not last long. Days when nerves and energies were often stretched beyond endurance shifted with seemingly endless days of routine and boredom when virtually nothing seemed likely to happen at all. Then suddenly the convoys (or U-boats) would appear, attack would follow counter-attack, and some sailors would live to recall the conflict.

Those judging the effectiveness of Canada's antisubmarine forces in the broad reaches of the western Atlantic, the Gulf of St Lawrence, and the St Lawrence River in the years 1939–45 would do well to reflect not only on the primitive experimental "asdic" detection units available, but on the special oceanographic obstacles to locating submerged submarines that prevail in Canadian waters. These problems, as will be seen, were crucial. The Swedish experience almost forty years later in 1981–4 is perhaps salutary. Despite sophisticated equipment and combined operations deployed in the geographically constrained waters of their western archipelago, the Swedes have repeatedly failed to flush out known submarine intruders. Equally important in 1939–45, however, is the complex organization of coastal and deep-sea convoys, and the great number of ships in convoy that actually managed to get through the U-boat cordon. Convoy routes criss-crossed inshore waters between Quebec City and Sydney and Halifax, Nova Scotia; between river ports in Canada and the ports of Labrador and Newfoundland; they ran from Halifax to Boston and New York. Deep-sea convoys with their "leavers" and "joiners" branching from

Sydney, St John's, Halifax, Boston, and New York crossed the dangerous Atlantic between North America and Great Britain. Allied ships convoyed 527 merchant ships across the Atlantic in 1939; 4053 in 1940; 6974 in 1941; 7423 in 1942; 9095 in 1943; 9794 in 1944; and 4816 by the end of the war in May 1945. All in all this constituted 42,682 merchant ships, of which 438 were sunk. The story of Canada's Naval Control Service Officers (NCSOs) who managed the convoys has yet to be told.

The reconstruction of Canadian coastal operations in their full complexity lies beyond the scope of this study. It is an enormous task that official historians are endeavouring to complete by long-term research that may not bear fruit for another decade. By recourse to detailed U-boat records, however, a single researcher can focus on a somewhat more compact historical source that not only tells a complete story, but also provides vital information to other historians about the view (to borrow an army metaphor) from "the other side of the hill." It none the less proved to be a task requiring an equally thorough grasp of Canadian, American, and British sources.

How the forays of Admiral Karl Dönitz's "grey wolves" grappled with Canadian naval forces is a previously unwritten history that is eminently worth recounting. With the exception of generalized historical accounts and occasional journalistic flourishes, the details of U-boat operations in Canadian waters have remained until now largely unanalysed in official files, or else linger in the memories of aging seafarers. Over a generation has passed since the Battle of the Atlantic drew to a close. Former opponents have now gained a certain critical distance from those wartime events that conditioned their lives. They can now recount their experiences, even the harrowing ones of sinking ships and dying men, with some objectivity. Such is the passage of time that former combatants, like the commanding officers of U-806 and HMCS *Clayoquot*, have now shared their experiences with one another as between friends.

I am indebted to many German and Canadian veterans, without whose encouragement and support this account would not have been written. Their frank discussions and warm hospitality during my frequent research visits in Canada and Germany have contributed more to my understanding of the Battle of the Atlantic than can be reflected in this volume. I particularly acknowledge Commander Craig Campbell, RCNVR (HMCS *Clayoquot*), and Captain Klaus Hornbostel (U-806), whose story of their encounter in the murky seas off Halifax on Christmas Eve 1944 first set me in search of U-boats in Canadian waters. From these gentlemen I began my journey through the U-boat fraternity. While many others have equally helped in many ways, I acknowledge the special assistance given by Captain Klaus Hänert (U-550) who first introduced me to a type VIIC *Atlantikboot* in Kiel; Captain Klaus G. Ehrhardt, formerly flotilla engineer at St Nazaire, and Mr Karl Böhm, technical adviser to Bavaria Studios film production of *Das Boot*, for detailed technical discussions on German submarines; Captain Kurt Dobratz (U-1232) for offering me the only extant copy of his War Diary covering his Canadian operations, and for much advice during my many congenial visits. Many others, as well, provided me with memoirs, memorabilia, and perceptive recollections and advice: captains Kurt Petersen (U-541), Hans-Edwin Reith (U-190), Hermann Lessing (U-1231), Heinz Franke (U-262), Hans Hilbig (U-1230), Volker Simmermacher and Harold Gelhaus (U-107), Helmut Schmoeckel (U-802), Admiral (formerly lieutenant) Paul Hartwig (U-517), former first officer W. von Eickstedt (U-553), and former watch officer Professor Günther Freudenberg (U-536). Kapitänleutnant Joachim Timm, director of the Federal Republic's Naval Signal School Museum in Flensburg-Mürwik, introduced me to Second World War communications and cipher systems. The former chief of staff U-boat Operations, Admiral Eberhard Godt, who succeeded Karl Dönitz as Commander U-boats (BdU) on the latter's promotion to Grand Admiral in 1943, reviewed with me my reconstructions of U-boat patrol tracks and discussed points of strategy and tactics. For discussions and hospitality I acknowledge the U-Boot-Kameradschaft Kiel e.V. (particularly Captain Addi Schnee) and the Salzburger Marine-Kameradschaft (Mr Emmi Metz).

I wish to thank former Lieutenant-Commander L.C. Audette (HMCS *Coaticook*) for kind access to his unpublished memoirs, and for recounting the search of Escort Group 27 for Dobratz's U-1232; Mr R.S. Williams for recollections of LCdr E.M. More and HMCS *Ettrick*; Mr Bill Bender, for recollections of the Gulf Fairmile patrols; Captain A.B. German, who served in HMCS *Weyburn*, for recollections of action against U-517; Mr Jake Warren, former navigator of HMCS *Valleyfield*, and Mr Ian Tate, the ship's senior surviving officer; Mr Roland Taylor, former watch-keeping officer, and Mr Gorde Hunter, former engine room artificer, who survived the attack against their ship HMCS *Magog*. Many German and Canadian survivors read and commented upon my early drafts of their experiences. The grid map was drawn by Ken Josephson, Technical Services Section, Department of Geography, University of Victoria.

For their encouragement and readiness to consult on thorny problems I thank my professional colleagues: Dr Alec Douglas, Dr Roger Sarty, Dr Marc Milner, and Mr Dave Kealy (Directorate of History, Department of National Defence); Dr Jürgen Rohwer, director, Bibliothek für Zeitgeschichte, Stuttgart, who among other things granted access to his unpublished key to U-boat deployments and placed the facilities of his research institute at my disposal; the staff of the Bundes- und Militärarchiv in Freiburg, Germany, for assistance in tracing uncatalogued materials, providing all available records on U-boat operations, and research space during frequent visits. I have been assisted by Mr Malcom Wake, director, RCMP Museum, Depot Division, Regina, who granted me access to the museum's espionage collection, and arranged for RCMP photographs; Staff Sergeant R.J. Henderson, RCMP, made available his private collection of wartime memorabilia; Chief Superintendent P.E.J. Banning, RCMP, departmental privacy and access to information coordinator, and his staff, kindly provided information on the espionage activities of the former German spies Langbein and von Janowski. Mr Richard Niven, director, Base Hydrographic Office, HMC Dockyard, Esquimalt, supported me in the reconstruction of U-boat patrol routes by providing hydrographic charts and navigational publications. Rear-Admiral Robert Yanow and Vice-Admiral James Wood enabled me to research a large part of this book while I was on naval duty.

For critical reading of the original manuscript and helpful advice I wish again to thank Dr Rohwer and Dr Douglas and also Dr James Boutilier of the Department of History, Royal Roads Military College, Victoria.

Research has been supported by grants from the University of Victoria, and from the Social Sciences and Humanities Research Council of Canada.

Notation and Abbreviations

The term "Canadian waters" in this volume refers to the Canadian war zone broadly depicted in "RCN Operational Plotting Sheet – East Coast of Canada" (Department of Mines and Technical Surveys, Ottawa 1942), which spanned longitudes 50° to 69° west. Contemporary Canadian hydrographic chart L/C 4001 "Gulf of Maine to Strait of Belle Isle" reflects the actual area under Canadian jurisdiction from the latitude of New York to Labrador, and eastward to 41° west. On these two charts and on a variety of large-scale small-area ones, I have plotted the tracks of U-boats against Canada. My account none the less takes cognizance of the shifting control zones, and follows the significant exploits or the pursuit of U-boats that depart the zone after operations off Canadian shores. There are, of course, cogent historical reasons for including New-foundland as wartime Canadian territory. Not the least of these are its well-known significance for the RCN in the Battle of the Atlantic, Prime Minister Mackenzie King's early policy statement that "the defence of Newfoundland would always be a primary Canadian interest," and the fact that it joined Confederation in 1949. This seemed a practical ap-proach towards defining the area for descriptive purposes, and for dis-tinguishing those U-boat operations whose principal focus was specifi-cally the western Atlantic inshore zone, which became the direct responsi-bility of Canadian authorities in Halifax and Newfoundland. I have adopted a similar convention by referring to the authority of Rear-Admiral L.W. Murray in Halifax as Commander-in-Chief Canadian Northwest Atlantic (C-in-C CNA) even though it was known as Com-manding Officer Atlantic Coast (COAC) until 1943.

The key to my analysis of U-boat operations, and to my reconstruction of U-boat patrol tracks, was the formerly top-secret German grid system. German Naval Operations had divided the oceans of the world into major squares of approximately 360 nautical square miles in area. The actual lengths of their perimeters on Mercator charts varied according to latitude and longitude, such that no single formula accounted for the size and location of all squares in the world's oceans. Though photographic reproductions of these grid charts have been available for a number of years, the mathematical method for deducing their harmonics was not published until 1983. As the photographic impressions proved inadequate for navigational purposes before the formulae became available, I deduced the grid system for Canadian waters by recourse to German navigational data. Once I had positioned the major squares in the area of my interest, the development of the grid pattern was simple. The German navy described each major square according to a two-letter and two-number sequence. Thus, for example, the area covering the mouth of the St Lawrence River was BA ("Bruno Anton") 36; that immediately off Halifax BB ("Bruno Bruno") 75; that off St John's, Newfoundland, BC ("Bruno Caesar") 41. Each of these major squares or grids can be further subdivided into nine smaller squares, which are numbered from 1 to 9 according to the pattern on a touch-tone telephone dial. And each of these smaller squares can in turn be further subdivided into nine and numbered according to the same system. This permits fairly precise description of geographical position without recourse to latitudes and longitudes – for example, BB75278 where HMCS *Clayoquot* sank. Because of its cryptic character, the grid designator could be radioed "in the clear," that is, in plain language. Later in the war, when the Germans feared their codes were vulnerable, it too was transmitted in encrypted form. German War Diaries utilized the grid-system designators almost without exception. It was the occasional exception to the practice that enabled me to derive the coordinates for the grid system in Canadian waters. I then superimposed the system on current Canadian hydrographic charts, and plotted routes for each U-boat on the basis of detailed navigational data contained in the official U-boat War Diaries (Kriegstagebücher), KTB for short. Only then could I begin to write the present narrative. I have reconstructed actions and encounters by comparison with all available German records, as well as analysis of War Diaries and reports of proceedings of various Canadian commands and subcommands, be they RCN or RCAF. In order to capture the immediacy of submariners' observations as logged in their War Diaries, and at the same time to reduce the number of notes to the text, I have interpolated the abbreviation KTB after the quotations. Unless otherwise specified, all translations from the German are mine. Distances at sea are given in nautical miles. Except as specifically mentioned, they are approximate, based on the large-area small-scale charts. Ranges, depths, and altitudes are expressed either in imperial or metric units, depending upon the source of information. Spellings of place-names conform to *Sailing Directions* published by the Department of Fisheries and Oceans, Ottawa.

U-boat Command underwent various reorganizations, the description of which exceeds the scope of this book. Its founder and mentor, Admiral Karl Dönitz, though succeeded to this post of BdU (Befehlshaber der Unterseeboote) or Commander U-boats by his chief of operations, Admiral Eberhard Godt, on his own promotion to Grand Admiral in 1943, continued to exert his personal influence over the U-Boat Arm. I therefore follow the convention of referring to the senior U-boat authority as BdU, in order to remind the reader of the charismatic leader behind the grand strategy. Specialists will recognize nuances: U-boat groups designated by visceral names such as Raubgraf (Robber Baron) and Schlagetod (Bludgeon) reveal the hand of Dönitz, and less strident names like Violett that of Godt.

ABBREVIATIONS

AB	Able Seaman
ACIs	Atlantic Convoy Instructions
ADC	Aircraft Detection Corps
A/S	Antisubmarine
asdic	Underwater sound ranging device (acronym for Allied Submarine Detection and Investigation Committee)
B-Dienst	Beobachtungsdienst (German radio monitoring and cryptographic service)
BdU	Befehlshaber der Unterseeboote (Commander U-boats)
CAT	Canadian anti-acoustic torpedo gear
Cdr	Commander
C-in-C CNA	Commander-in-Chief, Canadian Northwest Atlantic
Capt.	Captain
COAC	Commanding Officer, Atlantic Coast
CPO	Chief Petty Officer
DEMS	Defensively equipped merchant ships
D/F	Direction finding
DR	Dead (i.e. deduced) reckoning position
EG	Escort Group
ERA	Engine Room Artificer
FONF	Flag Officer, Newfoundland Force
FuMB	Funkmessbeobachtungsgerät (German: search radar)
GHG	Gruppenhorchgerät (German: multiple hydrophone array)
GMT	Greenwich Mean Time
GSR	German search radar (see FuMB)
HF	High frequency

HF/DF	("Huff-Duff") high frequency direction finding
HMCS	His Majesty's Canadian Ship
HMS	His Majesty's Ship (i.e. British)
HMS/M	His Majesty's Submarine
KTB	Kriegstagebuch (German: War Diary, official records)
LCdr	Lieutenant-Commander
LS	Leading Seaman
Lt	Lieutenant
MAD	Magnetic anomaly detector
MLs	Motor launches (i.e. Fairmiles)
NCSO	Naval Control Service Organization (also, naval control service officer)
NOIC	Naval Officer in Charge
NRMA	National Resources Mobilisation Act
NSDAP	Nationalsozialistische Deutsche Arbeiterpartei (German: "Nazi" Party)
NSHQ	Naval Service Headquarters
PO	Petty Officer
QPP	Quebec Provincial Police
RADM	Rear-Admiral
RCAF	Royal Canadian Air Force
RCMP	Royal Canadian Mounted Police
RCN	Royal Canadian Navy
RCNR	Royal Canadian Navy Reserve
RCNVR	Royal Canadian Navy Volunteer Reserve (the "Wavy Navy")
RN	Royal Navy
RNCVR	Royal Navy Canadian Volunteer Reserve (designation of the naval reserve in Canada in the First World War)
SBA	Sick Bay Attendant
SBT	Submarine bubble target
Skl.	Seekriegsleitung (German: Naval Staff)
Slt	Sub-lieutenant
sonar	Sound Navigation and Ranging (American abbreviation for asdic, q.v.)
SS	Steamship
USCG	United States Coast Guard
USS	United States Ship
VHF	Very high frequency
WACIs	Western Approaches Convoy Instructions

For the full gravity of the German submarine warfare to strike us, we have to regard it more as the Germans see it than as we may think of it.

Editorial, *Winnipeg Free Press*, 22 April 1943

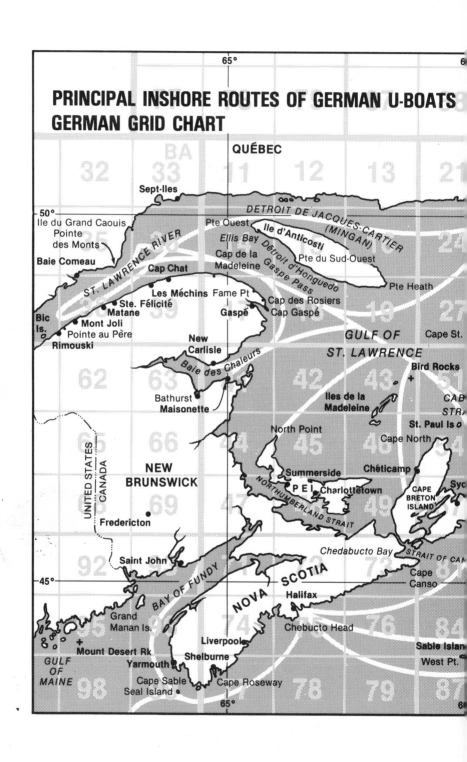

PRINCIPAL INSHORE ROUTES OF GERMAN U-BOATS
GERMAN GRID CHART

U-Boats against Canada

Introduction

Germany's U-boats projected an aura of mystery and power disproportionate to their finite strength. Emerging in the First World War as a
wide-ranging instrument of maritime combat, they suggested to many
that German technology had perverted the traditionally accepted morality
of war. When unrestricted submarine warfare resulted in the sinking of
large numbers of merchant ships, including some spectacular incidents
like the sinking of the unarmed passenger liner *Lusitania* in 1915, the
U-boat came to be regarded as an agent of that typically German "frightfulness" (*Schrecklichkeit*) of which Allied newspapers so frequently spoke.
Thus when shipping losses threatened to force Britain out of the war, the
U-boats appeared to many as the ultimate weapon: surreptitious, ubiquitous machines that could attack with precision and impunity. Though
they failed in their ultimate strategic purpose in the Second World War,
they became, in the hands of Admiral Karl Dönitz, tools of psychological
warfare.

Potential victims regarded them as at best ungallant devices, at worst
profoundly evil. Rejecting the ethos of squaring off openly ship to ship,
and man to man, U-boats now "lurked," "prowled," "stalked their prey,"
"hit and ran." Such was the rhetoric of Allied journalism of the 1940s that
nourished folklore and myth wherever these "underseas marauders" and
"rattlesnakes of the deep" dared to strike. Their seeming invisibility and
invulnerability addressed the private fears of surface sailors who as yet
knew no real defence. Bitter reproaches vitiated official debate on the
legitimacy of underwater warfare. An early critic of 1902 had condemned
the use of U-boats as "underhanded, unfair, and damned un-English"; for
some in the First World War, their use verged on sheer "infamy." By 1941
they had revealed themselves to others as "inhuman and barbarous."[1] By
this time images of clandestine warfare had stirred the generally sober
judgments of Canada's first naval historian, Gilbert Tucker, for whom the

mine and the submarine were now "the two most furtive and elusive products of the Industrial Revolution."[2] Sinister by design, as he commented with uncharacteristic bathos, "they walk in darkness and destroy in the noonday." They were indeed "so menacing" as to signal the demise of surface sea power itself.

If we are to believe an official German summary published in 1939 – and Dönitz's memoirs suggest that we should – Germany drew specific conclusions from its First World War submarine experience.[3] So did other countries, notably Britain, but they underestimated the capabilities of U-boats. The Canadian naval staff, although it based some of its planning in 1940 on the possibility of U-boats attacking shipping in the Gulf of St Lawrence, at first seemed, like the British Admiralty, to have forgotten the visit of U-53 and the mercantile submarine *Deutschland* to U.S. ports in 1916. The operations of German U-boats U-155, U-156 and U-117 off Nova Scotia and Newfoundland during the late summer of 1918 should have provided Canadian and British military authorities with ample evidence of the extent of German submarine technology. But where two isolated articles in Canadian newspapers of 1941 only went so far as to describe the First World War U-boat deployments to Canada as nothing more than "spotting" reconnaissance missions, no Canadian strategic assessments on the eve of the Second World War showed any recollection of these early exploits at all.[4] Yet U-boat attacks in 1918 had constituted a manifest German advance into Canadian waters.[5]

The *Deutschland*, the first cargo-carrying U-boat, whose 1700-ton displacement was huge even by the standards of the Second World War, clearly demonstrated Germany's advanced submarine technology. While in Baltimore in July 1916 it had loaded important industrial materials for its beleaguered military forces at home: 402 tons of bulk crude rubber, 375 tons of nickel, and 95 tons of tin. The mission foreshadowed the transport by U-boat of vital raw material from the Far East in the 1940s. The *Deutschland*-class submarine was powerful for its day, and even by later standards had an astonishing range. Carrying eight officers and sixty-five men, it had a surface endurance of 17,000 miles at 6 knots. Despite a limited submerged range of 50 miles at 7 knots, its underwater speed was scarcely exceeded in the next twenty years. The *Deutschland*'s normal cruising speed of 12–14 knots gave it a comfortable speed margin to operate as a raider. Limited underwater endurance prevented such vessels from operating as true submersibles or *Unterseeboote*. They were "diving boats" (*Tauchboote*) that submerged only briefly as the tactical situation warranted. Functioning essentially as surface raiders, they felt bound by maritime convention and international law to give fair warning of impending attack. During one of its early cruises, for example, U-156 covered over 11,000 nautical miles on the surface, but only 55 actually submerged.[6]

The ratio between submerged and surface range would change little as technology developed into the 1940s until the refinement of the schnorkel in 1943–4 radically altered the character of U-boat warfare. The schnorkel, quite simply, was a tube projecting upward from a submerged U-boat and reaching just above the surface of the water. Fitted with non-return valves, it permitted the intake of air and the simultaneous emission of exhaust for submerged diesel operations. In the event the U-boat dived deeper while schnorkelling, or if passing waves smothered the schnorkel's head valve, the atmosphere in the U-boat itself provided the diesels with an air buffer on which they could draw for 60 seconds. This caused the diesels to exhaust into the boat. At such times the inboard suction caused excruciating ear pains, and the air turned foul. Despite sometimes severe discomfort, the system allowed greater submerged speeds, conserved batteries for silent submerged running on electric motors, and even permitted recharging of batteries without bringing the U-boat to the surface. Before introduction of the schnorkel, the U-boats submerged only for immediate tactical reasons. Thus the 11,000-mile Canadian mission of U-111 from May to July 1941, and the 8000-mile cruise of U-123 the following January 1942 ran only 3.7 and 3 per cent submerged respectively. The 10,000-mile mission of U-69 between September and October 1942 ran 10 per cent submerged. From this point onwards, with the telling combination of the German schnorkel and the increasing pressure exerted by Allied air supremacy, cruises became shorter while submerged time increased. The 4800-mile cruise to Canada by U-548 from May to June 1944 ran 65 per cent submerged. U-boats were approaching the time when they would, all too late for any possible German victory, become true submersibles.

For the moment, however, the so-called *U-Kreuzer* of the First World War operated as diving cruisers. *Deutschland*'s sister ship, U-151, was converted for war with two 15-cm (5.9 inch) guns, two 22 pounders, one machine-gun, twelve torpedoes and six tubes, and 400 rounds of ammunition for each gun. The guns on this class of U-boat were larger than any of the fixed emplacements around Canada's fortified ports. After two more round trips to the United States, the *Deutschland* itself was converted for war, and patrolled as U-155. Fitted with torpedo tubes and two 15-cm guns, it departed Kiel in early August 1918 under the command of Kapitänleutnant Erich Eckelmann to lay mines off Halifax and the Nova Scotia coast. It completed its task, although the mines eventually broke loose and destroyed no ships. Like all the U-boats operating off the North American coast at this time, it worked virtually unopposed.

The Canadian Navy, as an arm of the much touted Pax Britannica, was ill equipped and ill organized to deal with this U-boat emergency. The reason for this lay in Canada's dependence upon Britain's Royal Navy, for the waters of the eastern seaboard formed part of the Royal Navy's North American and West Indies Station. This consisted mainly of cruisers based in Bermuda, Jamaica, and Halifax. Halifax had but one, HMCS *Niobe*. Launched in 1897, the 11,000-ton RN cruiser had arrived ceremoniously in Halifax on 21 October 1910. The date had been chosen to mark the 105th anniversary of Nelson's victory over the French fleet at the Battle of Trafalgar.[7] Intended to operate "under the direction of the Ministry of the Naval Service of Canada," as the Admiralty expressed it, she was obsolete on arrival. The *Halifax Herald* was enraged at Canadian taxpayers having to support "that obsolete, non-fighting junk heap." Other newspapers harangued pro and con depending upon their political bias. Though it may be argued (with Tucker) that this vessel and the "east coast patrols [of small boats and old yachts] were a successful venture in imperial cooperation," whereby the British Admiralty prescribed the general policy while "the Canadian service cheerfully accepted its subordinate role," the colonial perspective led to long-term problems that really only emerged in the Second World War.[8]

Predatory U-boats off the American coast since 1916 had caused grave and growing concerns in Canada that German "U-cruisers" might assault her ports and shipping lanes. Yet the Borden government had yielded to pressures from the British government and the Admiralty not to undertake its own shipbuilding program; this despite the Admiralty's conviction that Canada really ought to have provided herself with thirty-six steam-driven vessels to patrol her own waters instead of the dozen indifferent ones she actually possessed. Borden indeed protested to the British government early in 1917 that "Canada, upon British advice, had done nothing about [its own] naval defence." The Dominion, he stated angrily, could not now mobilize itself because "recruiting for overseas forces in Canada has denuded this country of most of the suitable men for such purpose, and every available gun has been sent to the British government."[9] The Admiralty in London could do little more for the moment than offer sympathy.[10]

Alarming reports in the *Halifax Herald* and others throughout the summer of 1918 warned the populace in the most strident tones of "Hun Submarines" off Nova Scotia and of the "devilish work [of] the Kaiser's Pirates" in sinking vessels on innocent passage. In June the *Herald* reported the twenty ships already lost to submarine action on the Atlantic coast, and continued updating the tally until action ceased in September. It reported victims landing along Nova Scotian shores, published eye witness accounts of the "Sub Monster off Halifax," and ultimately claimed that "Poison Gas Is the Huns' Latest Diabolic U-Boat Murder Method on This Side of the Atlantic." It proclaimed the German submarine "the direct and most ruthless menace of the war – the sea's hidden and undiscoverable grim reaper."

While the *Halifax Chronicle* (and indeed Naval Intelligence itself) faced the threat with moderation, the *Herald*'s increasing hysteria attributed the U-boats' success to "Hun Spies in Halifax." These "Enemy Aliens," its spurious commentaries urged, had been feeding vital information to the U-boats lurking nearby, and were ultimately "Responsible for the Murder" committed by German raiders offshore. Arguing vehemently that the "Imperial City [of] Halifax Must Be Purged of Treachery," it concocted its own plan: a $5000 reward for information leading to the discovery of "a Hun Submarine Base on the Nova Scotia or Bay of Fundy Shores," and a further $500 for the "First Arrest of a Hun Spy." In almost paranoic desperation it published on 10 August 1918 "The Herald's Drastic Program for Dealing with Spies and Alien Enemies"; this included the immediate arrest without cause of all suspicious persons, and the removal of all non-British persons to inland labour camps. In support of its inflammatory "Drastic Program," the *Herald*'s front page displayed the names of 500 "Alien Enemies Running Loose" in Nova Scotia; 150 additional names followed a couple of days later. These lists, purportedly exposing "The Enemy in Our Midst," pilloried Nova Scotian citizens of German and Eastern European origin. Oblivious to its slander, and insensitive to the centuries-old tradition of German settlement in such areas as Lunenburg, the *Herald*'s tirades harangued the public to "Keep a Watchful Eye on Alien, Naturalized or Un-Naturalized, or the Native, Who is 'Doing the Kaiser's Dirty Work' in Nova Scotia." If we can trust the *Herald*'s histrionic judgment – and the front-page results of its own opinion polls suggest that we should – the Halifax populace remained "Utterly Oblivious and Callously Indifferent to Danger." Yet there remains little doubt that the successful operations of enemy submarines had at the time made an extraordinary impact on the Maritimes that subsequent Canadian planners disregarded.

Meanwhile U-156, which had departed Kiel for North America on 15 June 1918 under Kapitänleutnant von Oldenburg, sank ships from Newport to Boston before commencing Canadian inshore attacks by battering the British motor schooner *Dornfontein* into a useless hulk on 2 August some 7 miles south of Grand Manan Island in the Bay of Fundy. She had been carrying lumber from Saint John, New Brunswick. Intelligence gathered from harassed and anxious fishermen by Americans and Canadians suggested that the submariners had expert knowledge of dangerous shoal waters from Woods Hole, Mass., to Nova Scotia. Survivors of U-151's attack off the U.S. coast in June had identified its skipper, one Captain Neufeldt, as having served for five years as a gunner's mate in the U.S. Navy. In any event, on 5 August 1918 a front-page account in the *Halifax Herald* reported "Six Vessels Torpedoed by Latest Type of Hun Sea Wolf: Crews Landed at Nova Scotia Ports." Von Oldenburg's U-cruiser was then observed to "lay off Seal Island all night with her deck awash, and displaying a brilliant light which was distinctly seen from the shore, and [by] morning she was still there." That day he attacked the 4808-ton Canadian tanker *Luz Blanca*, outbound from Halifax some 35 miles southwest of Sambro lightship off Halifax. This would be the scene of many sinkings in the 1940s. Yet in 1918 Halifax naval authorities could not respond to the *Luz Blanca*'s emergency signals while she fled back to within 17 miles of the lightship before sinking. A Canadian patrol vessel picked up eighteen crew.

The front page of the *Halifax Herald* for 6 August 1918 announced the news in terms that would be familiar to Haligonians twenty-four years later in 1942: "Hun Sub Torpedoes Oil Tanker off Halifax Harbour." For the Halifax reporter the incident provided a "Thrilling Story of the Fight between the Hun Sea Wolf" and its desperate victim. Next day, Admiral C.E. Kingsmill, Director of Naval Service in Ottawa, forwarded a secret memorandum on the U-boat menace to the Captain of Patrols, Walter Hose, in Sydney, Cape Breton. Warning of the "heavily armed" enemy submarines "operating in Canadian waters . . . either with 5.9 inch or 4.1 inch guns which are usually of high velocity and long range," he proposed both defensive and offensive tactics.[11] These included hydrophones, depth charges, firing at the pressure hull and, when all else failed, zigzagging in order "to throw the enemy off his aim." Though he had to concede that Canadian patrol vessels were no match for the German submarine, he urged his sailors to make every effort to at least cause damage.

Kingsmill's directive may have been cited during the only Canadian naval court martial of the First World War for failure to engage the enemy. U-156 had stopped the schooner *Gladys M. Hollett* of Le Have, Nova Scotia, on 6 August 1918 after having destroyed the Yarmouth schooners *Nelson A. Holland* and *Agnes B. Holland* off Lockeport, Nova Scotia. In a manner typical of U-boat warfare at the time, it had evicted the crew with its personal possessions and then sent a boarding party to remove all valuable material such as provisions and stores before setting lethal scuttling charges. The schooner's crew had departed the scene in dories with understandable haste. The Canadian patrol vessel HMCS *Hochelaga* (Lt Robert D. Legate, RNCVR) had meanwhile approached the scene, followed at some distance by the senior officer in HMCS *Cartier*, and the trawlers TR-32 and TR-22. At the last, *Hochelaga* sheered away in order to consult with the senior ship astern while U-156 submerged. Barely avoiding the charge of cowardice, Lt Legate was dismissed from the naval service for not having tried to "inflict damage or destroy the enemy."[12] A patrol vessel found the schooner on her beam ends with sails set and towed her to port with her crew. Ill disposed towards the Canadian Navy, the *Halifax Herald* of 12 August blared, not unjustly: "What's the Good of a Fleet of Patrols that Can Not Catch Submarines?"

U-156 executed a particularly successful ruse de guerre on 20 August 1918 by capturing the 239-ton Canadian steam trawler *Triumph* 60 miles southwest of Cape Canso and arming her as a raider under the German naval ensign. For the *Halifax Herald*, this was an "Irony of Fate"; she would "Make a Good Decoy to Lure Former Sister Fishing Vessels to Quick Destruction." This became a self-fulfilling prophecy. Known by sight to almost the whole fishing fleet, she easily stopped and destroyed six schooners, leaving their crews to row home in dories. While flying the Danish flag on 23 August "the Pirate Triumph," as the *Herald* now called her, sank the 4700-ton steamer *Diomed* and the Gloucester fishing schooner *Sylvania*. On 25 August she sank the 610-ton British steamship *Eric* out of St John's, Newfoundland, and delivered its crew safely to a nearby schooner. By this time fishermen and their families had become greatly alarmed and were demanding increased protection from their governments. Survivors of attacks by U-156, the *Herald*'s headlines claimed, now knew that the "Captain of the Hun Sea Wolf, Armed with Powerful Guns, and Capable of Coping with a Light Cruiser, Pledges Himself to Annihilate Our Fishing Fleet." The German plan of breaking North American morale by sinking tonnage close to home elicited different responses from Canada and the United States: the Americans recalled their destroyers from the Pacific, while the Canadians called for help from the U.S. and Britain. In both cases, the German attacks had given a foretaste of one of the later Dönitz doctrines of pinning down the enemy at home by submarine threat.

Kapitänleutnant Otto Dröscher's U-117 executed the final First World War U-boat operation in Canadian waters, after having laid three minefields in American waters, sunk nine American fishing vessels (for a total of 265 tons) in rapid succession, and then picked off larger prey: the 3875-ton Norwegian SS *Somerstad*, the 7127-ton American SS *Frederick R. Kellog*, and the 6978-ton Dutch vessel SS *Mirlo*.[13] Typically, German Naval Staff in February 1941 reviewed Dröscher's War Diary when preparing the first major assault by U-boats against North American waters in Operation Drumbeat. Now, however, U-117 moved northeastward unchallenged on to the Banks of Newfoundland. Such are the ironies of migration and war that on 30 August 1918, U-117 sank two Canadian schooners manned by German-speaking crews. Edward Eisenhaur's 136-ton *Elsie Porter* was returning to Le Have, Nova Scotia, after fishing on the Newfoundland Banks when Otto Dröscher stopped her with three rifle shots across the bow some 145 miles southeast of Cape Spear, Newfoundland.[14] In sea state 4, with heavy swells under overcast skies, Dröscher allowed the schooner's crew to escape in their dories before sinking the vessel with scuttling charges and inviting Eisenhaur aboard the U-boat for a drink. Three hours later, U-117 stopped Frederick Gerhardt's 136-ton schooner *Potentate* some 150 miles southeast of Cape

Broyle, and took Gerhardt, his son, and another crew member aboard for interrogation.

Dröscher's log notes nothing of this meeting, though survivors insisted that he was particularly interested in steamer routes "from Newfoundland to Canada."[15] Gerhardt apparently divulged nothing, though he was allegedly threatened either with removal to Germany or pressed service as a local pilot. Neither extremity occurred. In the next war, however, Dönitz explicitly ordered the capture of merchant skippers for intelligence purposes. Asked why he was sinking schooners, the captain of U-117 purportedly replied: "You are helping to feed America." One of the next war's excuses would be that they were helping to feed Britain. Having offered Gerhardt some refreshments in the officers' mess, Dröscher set the three men free in their 19-foot, flat-bottomed dory to row the 140 miles to shore. Three days and nights later they met the fishing fleet. Dröscher had meanwhile removed all newspapers for intelligence purposes, confiscated such stores as he wished, and sunk the vessel with scuttling charges. As we have seen, the summer's run of the *Halifax Herald* alone, had the schooners carried it, would have given Dröscher ample demonstration of the tactical and psychological impact of German "frightfulness" (*Schrecklichkeit*) off Canadian shores.

The St John's *Evening Telegram* of 2 September 1918 estimated in a sober back page account "that upwards of seventy Bank fishermen whose vessels have been sunk by the Hun raider within the past few days [were] making for land in their dories." That day's edition of the *Halifax Herald* quoted "the marine department" in Ottawa that "eighteen submarine victims" had landed in St John's, Newfoundland, by dory; indeed, "recently sixty-four sailors [had] reached North Sydney," Cape Breton Island, after rowing as much as 300 miles. But the crew of the *Elsie Porter*, the *Telegram* explained as a case in point, had none the less received "the very best and kindest" treatment at German hands. Next day it rendered a glib account of what the harrowing experience meant to *Elsie Porter's* skipper: "[he] had suffered a loss of four or five thousand dollars [and] can easily begin again. The captain is a splendid specimen of physical perfection ... He is the type of man who has built up the British Empire and made it what it is today." His ethnic resilience apparently compensated for the government's failure to provide war risk insurance, of which more later.

In the course of time, the innovation of submarine warfare eventually brought about the change in naval thinking that countenanced and indeed accepted the "surreptitious" unlimited warfare Tucker had still found repugnant in 1941. This is but further confirmation of the principle that technology dictates morality. Submarine technology and tactics forced a re-evaluation, albeit exceedingly slow and myopic, of warfare at sea; it marked the declining importance of battle-fleet confrontations on which naval doctrine of the late 1930s and early 1940s was largely predicated. Surprisingly, however, until well into the Second World War, official Allied circles still regarded the U-boat more as a nuisance than as a major threat. The Allies were not alone in their failure to grasp its potential. For even in Germany a conservative and traditionalist insistence on the value of a capital-ship blue-water navy restrained the visionary strategies of Dönitz's charismatic leadership. Canada's pre-war analysis reflected an essentially British (and erroneous) view.

Writing in 1937, Chief of Naval Staff Commodore Percy W. Nelles, RCN, reasoned that "if international law is complied with, submarine attacks [on merchant shipping] should not prove serious." And in the event of "unrestricted warfare ... the means of combating submarines are considered to have so advanced" that the telling system of convoys and combined air/sea operations would wreak a heavy toll of U-boats and likely "compel the enemy to give up this form of attack."[16] Canadian naval doctrine, like that of its British model, did not alter from 1937 to 1940.[17] While Nelles's prediction came true in the very long and almost disastrous six-year run, his short-term appreciation was flawed on at least two serious counts: failure to know his enemy, and inadequate grasp of the actual capabilities of state-of-the-art naval technology. He assumed that Dönitz would wage war in the style of the First World War. This was a dangerous over-simplification. Moreover, like so many of his RN counterparts, he put too much faith in the new underwater detection device called asdic.

Asdic is an acronym for the Allied Submarine Detection Investigation Committee, established in 1918 to solve the problem of locating submerged submarines. It was a system for underwater sound detection. The U.S. Navy called it Sonar (Sound Navigation and Ranging), a term now exclusively used in all NATO navies. Asdic detection, with its hand-operated wheels and clumsy cranks, was not an exact science. Expressed quite simply, an oscillator/transducer fitted in the water beneath a ship's keel would, when connected to a transmitter/receiver for about 1/10 second, emit a loud high-frequency "ping" along the direction to which the hand-operated wheel of later models had turned the transducer. Early models were rigid, thus making it necessary to turn the whole ship back and forth in order to "sweep" across the area forward of the beam. An "echo" might be heard if the transmitted sound struck a reflecting surface such as a submerged submarine – or even a rock, a school of fish, or a lonely whale. Identifying the precise source of the echo was, of course, vital; it demanded not only reliable asdic, but an uncommon degree of aptitude and experience on the part of the operator. Knowing the approximate speed of sound in water (4820 ft/sec) that, of course, varies with temperature and salinity, one could deduce the "target's" range. Even under ideal conditions, maximum detection range lay between 1200 and 1500 yards. The echo of a stationary target produced a steady pitch. A target moving either toward or away from the asdic vessel caused the echo's pitch to increase or decrease respectively. This Doppler effect is familiar to all who have listened to the sound of a passing railway train; it became an important tool for gauging a target's manoeuvres as an attack progressed. Not until 1944 did the introduction of asdic type 144Q enable the attacker to calculate the target's depth. Thus, up until that time, attackers could only guess the correct depth setting at which to prime their charges. This was a serious disadvantage, for such bombs would only cause serious damage if they exploded within 20 feet of their victim. The odds against hitting – even under ideal conditions – were high.

In its passive mode, asdic could operate as a hydrophone by "listening" for extraneous sounds in the water, such as engine noise and propeller wash. But whether in active or passive mode, asdic operations were prone to serious distortion and obstruction by the natural elements. Thermal and saline layers, for example, or even opposing tidal flows and currents (such as the St Lawrence River and Gulf) could "bend" or "deflect" the asdic waves; this could give an operator the impression that the target was far removed from where it actually was. In addition, cavitation around the asdic dome caused by the attacker's own speed and hull shape could create a barrier to sound waves, thus virtually blanketing all means of target detection. Then, too, the pitching and rolling of a ship in rough weather could cause momentary asdic blackouts. In theory, of course, some of these difficulties could be calibrated in order to provide general operating guidelines. But the parameters of one particular latitude, sea state, weather condition, water depth, and density might not hold true in constantly shifting, regionally influenced conditions elsewhere.

If Nelles's trust was misplaced in purely technical terms, it was equally so in tactics. For, besides using the already obsolescent, if not even obsolete type 123A asdic designed in the 1920s (thus starting the all-too-familiar Canadian practice of going to sea with equipment no longer preferred in the navies of more powerful allies), Canadian ships used the equipment according to a British tactical doctrine that by 1940 proved ineffective against surfaced U-boats at night.[18] In fact, despite British theory, the night surface attack became a master-stroke of German tactics, while escaping asdic was commonplace.

The attitudes typified by Admiral Nelles account in significant measure for the lack of preparation for an antisubmarine war. The threat was deemed not to exist. Surface gunnery and the protection of coastal zones remained the navy's primary role. Destroyers with their 4.7-inch guns and eight torpedo tubes reflected the needs of "fleet" operations, of battleship and cruiser task forces with destroyer screens. In the eyes of the naval staff they were the best warship for Canadian purposes that their money could buy. Later, when aircraft carrier task forces seemed to be the wave of the future in naval warfare, the RCN again urged the need of strongly armed surface ships. But in the Battle of the Atlantic it was cheaper, smaller, slower and often more manoeuvrable corvettes, Bangor minesweepers, and frigates that became the real work-horses of the Canadian Navy. It was these unglamorous little ships that represented the most profitable investment ever made by the naval staff, reluctant though professional Canadian naval officers were to admit the fact.

Canadians at the beginning of the Second World War enjoyed the luxury of distance from the scenes of U-boat warfare until the press evoked and exploited certain key events. Thus the sinking of the 13,581-ton liner SS *Athenia* on 3 September 1939 edged them a major step forward towards the almost total commitment that would characterize their naval contribution to the Battle of the Atlantic. Torpedoed without warning with the loss of 112 lives, among them a dozen Canadians, the *Athenia*'s loss lent impetus to Canada's dormant will to defend a political principle. The implicit declaration of a callous unlimited U-boat war, which the sinking of the lone, unarmed liner revealed to British eyes, had special significance for a geographically isolated Canadian population. It seemed to demonstrate that ordinary Canadian people had become U-boat targets.[19]

Politicians and press exploited all the latent pathos human interest stories provided.[20] The Gillespie children from the small farming community of Russell, Manitoba, had narrowly survived the harrowing ordeal. Little Margaret Hayworth of Hamilton, Ontario, had not. Recognizing her as the first victim of the war to be buried on Canadian soil, newspapers proclaimed "Ten-Year-Old Victim of Torpedo" as "Canadians Rallying Point." The U-boat killer revealed itself as no longer simply "German" but "Nazi." The epithet would henceforth attach to all German sailors, whether actually of the national-socialist party (NSDAP) persuasion or not. The funeral seems to have been the very national focal point the press described, or indeed which the media made of it. Attended by personal representatives of the prime minister, by the Ontario provincial cabinet, and dignitaries from all levels of government, Hamilton's St Andrew's Presbyterian Church filled to overflowing as "hundreds" followed the service on loudspeakers outside. George Drew, leader of the Ontario Conservative Party, addressed a special meeting of Hamilton City Council that had been convened for the sole purpose of passing a resolution expressing horror at the "tyranny, deceit and inhumanity of the German government." In Drew's words, the dead child was a symbol that should "go from the bounds of this Dominion as a challenge to all democratic nations." The event was a propagandist's coup. It had linked the First World War with the Second, had evoked a

German "tradition" of crimes against humanity, and proclaimed that no Canadian would now be safe.

Once awakened to the threat, the press did not need long to follow every possible story about U-boat intrusions and suspected attacks. This led as often as not to ill-informed and pointless speculation on Germany's capacity and intent, and to exaggeration of Canada's ability to respond. If the profusion of accounts baffled Canadian readers as to what kind of a war was being waged at sea, loss of the 29,150-ton battleship HMS *Royal Oak* left no doubt as to Germany's finely honed naval expertise. Günther Prien, in a "remarkable exploit of professional skill and daring" in U-47, as Winston Churchill described the operation, penetrated the heavily defended fleet anchorage of Scapa Flow on the surface during the night of 14 October 1939. He sank the capital ship with the loss of 830 lives, and escaped unscathed. British authorities released the story immediately. The Canadian press exploited the occasion to galvanize public opinion by linking the story with news of the anticipated departure of Canada's first overseas division. By splicing news of disparate and only marginally related events, the press gave the impression that Canada was responding in both timely fashion and in force.[21] The *Ottawa Journal*'s headline story "British Warship *Royal Oak* Sunk by Sub – Canadian Troops Go 'over' within 60 Days" is one of the early examples of the manipulation of news that marked the war years. Prien's raid served German propaganda well. The Canadian press joined others in quickly publishing reports from Berlin.

On the very day on which Prien's U-47 was insinuating its way into Scapa Flow, Canadian forces were bracing themselves for unprecedented combined operations against a U-boat threat deep inside the St Lawrence River. The official, though doubtless apocryphal, account illustrates the cheerful zeal of the armed forces in the face of Canada's deplorable lack of preparation for war.[22] At the outbreak of hostilities, Naval Service Headquarters (NSHQ) had designated Quebec City as one of the many naval control centres to operate under a Naval Officer in Charge (NOIC). Quite typically, a miniscule staff of former RN or RCNVR officers established its headquarters in the Customs House and set about organizing the port defences, inspection services, communications, and the myriad details of an operational control port. Their immediate defences consisted of two 1908-vintage, 7.5-inch guns in Fort la Martinière on the south shore, and an extended defence station some 15 miles below the city at St Jean d'Orléans. This provided coverage of the river with two 18-pounder guns that could only fire by day. NOIC Quebec's seagoing forces boasted the 73-foot ex-RCMP cutters HMCS *Chaleur* and *Madawaska*, each manned by ten men and armed with a Colt Marline machine gun and an assortment of rifles and pistols. The unarmed harbour patrol craft *Fernand Rinfret*, with its crew of three, rounded out the naval task force which would counter the threat. The wireless service of the Department of Transport provided NOIC Quebec with an impromptu early-warning system by means of a series of stations along the river, Gulf and Gaspé coast. They were all connected to Quebec by party-line telephone or landline telegraph.

On 14 October 1939 an alarming wireless report reached NOIC Quebec from Cape Salmon, some miles below Murray Bay, that two surfaced U-boats were proceeding upriver in line ahead. Naval authorities responded with imagination and vigour despite their incredulity. It was, of course, technically feasible for enemy submarines to navigate the river as far as Quebec City. Canada's virtually non-existent defences removed the need to submerge. In a rapid sequence of decisions, the military closed the Port of Quebec, advised the civil authorities of the threat, recalled army units from leave, and declared the Customs House and wharf a restricted area.

The next stage proved more complex, for the navy required arms more lethal than a First World War vintage .303 machine-gun. It appealed to the Department of Transport for two ships with a gun. During these rapid stages of early mobilization a local "submarine diviner" offered his services to the NOIC through army headquarters. Claiming certain undefined supernatural powers, and armed only with a plumb-bob, which he suspended over a chart of the St Lawrence, he fell into a trance while the lead weight pendulated and then quivered over a suspicious spot. He confirmed the presence of two U-boats some miles below St Jean.

Within four hours of the sighting, the lighthouse tender *Druid* and the fire tug *Lanoraie* arrived alongside the customs wharf to ship the promised guns. These arrived two hours later after several mishaps: two Vickers machine-guns pulled by a platoon of the Canadian army's "Van Doos" (Royal 22ième Régiment) in full battle gear complete with entrenching tools. Hourly reports from the "submarine diviner" hastened the loading. Only the *Druid* could be fitted with the guns as the *Lanoraie*'s deck arrangement left no room. The tug therefore assumed the role of "ramming vessel." As a last resort it could try to drown "the Huns" with its water cannon. The "Van Doos" hoisted their guns aboard the *Druid* and used sandbags to set up a kind of zareba on the boat deck.

Shortly after midnight the ships with their mix of civilian crew, sailors, fifteen army gunners and some twenty infantrymen set off at full speed in perhaps the strangest flotilla in Canadian naval lore. An unexplained red, very light flare, which gunners construed to mean "enemy in sight," caused all of them to let loose a barrage of gunnery, including a blind shot at a river buoy from the darkened St Jean battery. Two days later a terse press release from defence headquarters revealed that, while a lone submarine had indeed been "sighted in the St. Lawrence below Quebec City," neither the navy nor the RCAF had found a thing. U-boats would not, in fact, appear in the Gulf until May 1942. As will be seen, Canada needed all the respite she could get.

The early days of U-boat warfare provided Allied news reports with occasional examples of German gallantry and humanity at sea, despite the *Athenia*'s horror. But by 1940 the ambivalent mood of regarding U-boats with a mixture of fascination and respect, and only occasionally condemning the "evil Hun," had passed. Press reports and political cartoons now sharpened their features into lurid grimaces and contemptuous sneers. Total war had literally forced the U-boats under, and except in rare instances had prevented them from offering any solace to victims in their plight. It transformed perceived chivalry into apprehended banditry, and left little room in the victims' perceptions and imagination for a human opponent with merely a military task to perform. Honest sentiment, private fears, and personal loathing would be easily mobilized by a propaganda bureau that could shape the national will. Even without such official direction, Canadians were in no doubt that German naval forces were fighting for Nazi policies.

No longer would Canadians countenance "the amiable theory," in the words of one editorial, which distinguished "between the Nazi rulers of Germany and the masses of the German people."[23] All Germans were now "barbaric" and "brutal." The fact is, so assertions ran, that "Germany has made murder her national trade ... it is a nation dedicated to iniquity and evil." War against the "Hun" was therefore more than just a struggle for self-preservation. Higher principles were deemed at stake. U-boats, it was said, had revealed their "true" nature in the "heinous" sinking of the *Athenia*; they had confirmed their intentions by sinking the refugee ship the *City of Benares* with the loss of eighty-one British children who were being evacuated to Canada; they had forced the Allies to "Suspend Plan[s] to Evacuate Children from England."[24] Newspapers published a large photograph of a U-boat in harbour that "proved" that yet "Another U-Boat Prepares for Child Murder."

It was but a small step from such inflated assertions to the intriguing misinformation that the "Germans, in their devilish drive for world domination," had even abolished the Bible.[25] The complete destruction of Germany was seen as the only means for convincing "the Hun" that "war does not pay."[26] Indeed "every bomb dropped on Germany" was "a step in the regeneration of German character." Prime Minister Mackenzie King's CBC radio broadcasts to the nation on 27 and 31 October 1939 set the tone for press rhetoric in the months to come. War against the Nazis was now a "crusade to save Christian civilization."[27] Asserting the identity of his own convictions with "the mind of Canada itself," he proclaimed the "young men who are enlisting in our forces today [as] first and foremost defenders of the faith."

Newspaper feature articles on Canada's preparation for the naval war at sea strike the modern reader as quaint and naive in the extreme. Quaintness is, of course, a function of cultural perspective and taste;

naiveté in this case a failure of political acumen. One gains the impression that the sheer goodness of Canadians, and the plentifulness of their resources, could sustain them against all assaults of the enemy. In the first instance, reporters perceived the navy as a largely passive force. In this assessment they were undoubtedly correct. An article in October 1939 entitled "Watchdogs of Navy Guard Approaches to Canada's Ports" singled out the supposedly high-profile defences provided by the navy's harbour inspection service. As far as the press was concerned, the navy could speak with authority simply because "coast defence batteries [were] the real authority behind the orders of the inspection vessel." (The public had read no details of the navy's ragtag-and-bobtail combined operations off St Jean d'Orléans, Quebec, the previous week.) This wrong-headed view reflected an outdated tactical stance that many naval authorities shared: the predication of naval warfare on the surface gunnery of 1918.

Readers in the autumn of 1939 may have found little comfort in the breathless flimflam that flourished in announcing the "Big Role" that Canada supposedly even now played in the Atlantic convoy system: "Night and day, in mist, fog, rain and snow, the watchdogs [stand on guard while the] vigilance of Canada's sea fighters [plays] a big role in smoothing the way for ... ships steaming eastward across the Atlantic with the sinews of war for Great Britain."[28] Nor indeed would it have assuaged many fears to learn that "look-outs comb every foot of the heaving green through powerful glasses [while] on the bridge sleepless officers keep watch." The *Winnipeg Free Press* even assured its readers that "weather or no weather, that gate to the world of sea commerce [is] being guarded against all comers, grimly, efficiently naval guarded." The watch – without gyro, radar, or asdic – would have been grim indeed. The platitudes of the *Victoria Daily Times* for 18 November 1939 all but outdid Germany's myth of the dashing, disciplined Teuton. Canada's real front-line defence, the paper proclaimed, was her "jolly, well-behaved sailor boys, ... Canada's splendid young blue jackets [whose] hard working mothers and fathers have taught [them] to live well and honestly and face the world and its troubles with a grin." As the reporter intoned after his familiarization cruise: "It's quite a sight to see a sailor lad, with fresh cheeks and clear eyes, in oilskins and cap at a jaunty angle, standing on the plunging bow of a destroyer, holding fast with his toughened bare hands to a steel cable."

How far such frequent descriptions lay from the reality of the war at sea, only those who survived could really tell.[29] A storm-tossed, gut-wrenching destroyer or corvette was not the school outing the press sometimes portrayed. Nor indeed did the ill-clad gloveless "sailor boy" signify anything more than untrained youth sacrificed to the inadequate weather gear and equipment that plagued the Canadian Navy until well into 1943.[30] Yet by 31 January 1940, the *Winnipeg Free Press* reported with pride that

"Canada's Navy Stands Ready for Nazi Subs." The information derived from a press visit to naval ships and facilities in Halifax. The *Ottawa Journal* shelved the material until 15 April 1940 when it announced in a back-page story that "Coast Defence Units [are] Ready for Action against Enemy." The two stories, published three months apart, reflect divergent perspectives on a single theme. According to the earlier Winnipeg version, the navy had "spent thousands of hours patrolling the coast since war [had] begun" without really expecting any "enemy action on this side of the Atlantic until spring." In the later Ottawa version, spring had now come and the bold fight could begin. The first version accorded with the well-publicized opinions of touring Commander E. Ellsberg, USN, who ridiculed the possibility of significant U-boat attacks along the Atlantic coast. Though he expected Germany to "send one or two over" by 1941 "in an effort to scare the Canadian people," he explained that U-boats would never exert any influence on the outcome of the war.[31] Understandably, perhaps, the American "submarine authority," as he was described, had little appreciation of Admiral Dönitz's methods.

Dönitz had published his general views on U-boat warfare early in 1939 in the German naval journal *Nauticus*. Significantly, perhaps, it was not republished in English translation in Canadian naval circles until April 1943.[32] Dönitz described the U-boat's capacity for surprise attack, for laying mines, for reconnaissance, and of course for waging war on merchant shipping. He even described the Achilles heel of Allied defence and anticipated the psychological impact his U-boats would make. "Sea powers whose strength depends on keeping sea lanes open," he wrote, "regard the U-boat as a dangerous enemy." He followed this seemingly gratuitous comment with a vital pre-war policy statement that ought to have left no one in doubt as to his intentions: "Powers which can not *otherwise* hope to cut their opponents' lines of communication value the submarine highly and regard it as an essential part of their naval armament." Germany's surface fleet could not compete with that of the British. For this reason, the U-boat would form its major striking power. By September 1942 Canadian naval authorities were forced to admit privately that the "most potent naval weapon of the enemy has been the U-Boat."[33]

The Dönitz doctrine as later formulated and expanded prescribed large-scale anti-convoy attacks coupled with long-range solo sorties to distant enemy territory in the major oceans. As in the case of Canadian ports, the express purpose of these solo missions was to pin down Allied forces that might otherwise be deployed to greater offensive advantage. By operating close to the enemy's shores, U-boats forced the opponent to commit large elements of his resources to defence. The second version of the Halifax press tour suggested that perhaps one Canadian naval officer had grasped what this strategy might mean. In picking up the theme of a spring campaign that "Fritz is almost certain to attempt" in 1941, he gave a prophetic account of subsequent events. Though he erred in the timing of the attack and in expecting heavy U-boat losses to deter German campaigns, he anticipated accurately this effect of U-boat activities in Canadian waters: "If we don't get the first [U-boat] before he does some damage ... people will start seeing subs from Labrador to Cape Horn. Our lives won't be worth living, for every report has to be investigated."

Every submarine report had indeed to be investigated, or at least monitored, throughout the whole operational zone from $40°$ W (over 500 miles to the east of Newfoundland) to the meridian of Quebec City, and from New York in the south to Labrador in the north. This meant not only providing ships, sailors, and aircraft to patrol, hunt, and kill in the thousands of square miles of Atlantic Ocean, Gulf and river of St Lawrence; it also meant the establishment of shore-based direction-finding stations and wireless links. Military resources would never be adequate. As will be seen, training of civilian shore watchers and of local fishermen in the recognition of enemy ships and aircraft, and the development of a network of civilian reporting stations, became a vital adjunct to Canadian naval operations.

A complex variety of interrelated national problems reduced the effectiveness of search and attack during the early years of the war. Difficulties were increased not only by the inadequacy of industrial mobilization and the recalcitrance of many trade unions, but by the fact that war actually brought prosperity to a generation that had survived the Great Depression. Assessments of Canada's naval contribution to the Battle of the Atlantic have in the past tended to focus almost entirely on the colossal buildup of warships that industrial mobilization eventually spawned. It is now becoming clearer, however, that rapid expansion, inadequate training, and outdated equipment led to an unstable mix, and often resulted in necessarily poor performance.[34] Thus the development of a practicable maritime doctrine was vitiated by the very fleet expansion which was supposed to support it.

The wartime demands of duty, steadfastness, and self-sacrifice that military tradition imposed upon the front-line men stand out against the background of the consumer society living at standards of wealth it had not known before and still grasping for more. Strikes were commonplace in almost all trades and industries: at the National Steel Car Company in Malton, Canadian Electric in Toronto, Canadian Cotton in Hamilton, at the vital shipyards of Lauzon, Quebec, and at Midland and Kingston, Ontario, at the mines in the Yukon or Cape Breton, and with stevedores in St John's and Halifax. To be sure, the president of the Trades and Labour Congress of Canada had publicly announced that unions supported the Dominion's war effort. But his reasoning, that simply because the Nazis had abolished trade unions wherever they had gone, and that therefore "this war is our war," now strikes one as hollow in the extreme.[35] Whatever the root cause, disruptions and conflicts arising from strikes raised a long-unheeded call for responsible unions and anti-strike legislation. In other cases, private firms enjoying a boom economy indulged in labour poaching by enticing workers away from war production industries that paid less. In the conflict between money and duty, the former sometimes won.

Nor indeed was the concept of duty monolithic. U-boats penetrating deeply into the St Lawrence in 1942, for example, confirmed many a Quebecer's sense of duty to stay home and defend his native soil against the invader, rather than to leave it ostensibly unguarded while pursuing an unknown enemy on distant shores. It was a sense of duty that ran contrary to national policy. That policy, based on playing the most influential possible role in alliance warfare, demanded contributions in major theatres of war, overseas as well as in mid Atlantic. The overseas contributions led to conscription, so strongly opposed in Quebec. Whether conscription for overseas service was necessary or not – and it is true that very few conscripts found their way into action against the enemy – it certainly was a difficult concept to explain to people who were seeing ships sunk before their eyes with little apparent reaction from home defence forces.

The publicly acknowledged fact remained that as late as June 1941, in the words of the *Ottawa Journal*, "the war is still remote to many Canadians." As its editorial correctly explained, there was "great abundance not only of the necessary goods, but of luxuries." Apart from these obvious advantages, "vast numbers of Canadians have been affected little if at all by almost two years of war." Little wonder, then, that maritimers too attempted to catch the bandwagon of disposable income in the spring of 1941 by launching an annual campaign to attract tourists "to the ocean-pinched peninsula of Nova Scotia."[36] More appealing than contemporary recruiting posters for the navy, the ads offered escape: "If you love the Sea you'll love Nova Scotia ... come down, down by the sea ... and soothe those jaded nerves of yours – rebuild that tired, overworked body." The "free folders and maps" the provincial Information Bureau offered by mail would undoubtedly have pleased the spies and saboteurs of the "fifth column" of which newspapers repeatedly warned.

Weakened by such disparities, Canada sent her sailors to sea.

CHAPTER ONE

Portents and Preparations

On 31 August 1939, one day before Germany's invasion of Poland triggered the Second World War, the Chief of the Naval Staff in Ottawa provided the Minister of National Defence with a terse "Most Secret" situation report: "In the current international tension it appears that the major threat to Canadian seaborne trade will be from Raiders and Submarines in the approaches to the St. Lawrence, Halifax and Saint John, N.B., and we are unfortunate in having no ships yet available on the Atlantic Coast fitted with the Submarine Detection device."[1] Two destroyers (HMCS *Saguenay* and *Skeena*) lay alongside in Halifax to cope with Germany, while four destroyers in Esquimalt were to deal with the supposedly greater threat from Japan.[2] None had asdic. The navy would have to make last-minute arrangements to have this equipment fitted once antisubmarine operations had become its primary role. It would be a slow and frustrating process fraught with technical difficulties and lengthy delays extending on into 1944. But as far as public opinion was concerned in 1939, the Canadian coast constituted a hazardous zone that no enemy would dare assail. As back-page news stories ingenuously explained, it was "a death trap," a "virtual pest-hole [sic] for lurking Nazi submarines or sea raiders."[3] Such assertions were hopelessly far from the truth. The Canadian Navy was not only ill equipped for the immediate threat, but ill prepared for the necessary expansion that many professional officers with First World War experience, like Walter Hose and L.W. Murray, knew would simply have to occur. As Captain Murray had reported to his superiors six months earlier, "We have not even the necessary technical officers to set up the instructional Staffs required at [the] outbreak of war." And yet, he continued with self-assured understatement, "I have no doubt we could give some such inexpert assistance as is available." The navy, he felt, would at least be "much better off than the RCN was in commencing the St. Lawrence Patrol" of tugs, yachts and coasting vessels "at Sydney in June–September 1915."[4]

Germany's U-boat campaign escalated rapidly once war had begun. Early positioning of submarine forces facilitated decisive attacks. Yet even where Dönitz's moves were known to the Allies, censorship shielded most of them from public view. He had deployed the first U-boat wave of 14 U-boats as early as 19 August in anticipation of Hitler's intention to invade Poland on 25 August. These U-boats were deployed to form a cordon against British intervention. By the time of the postponed invasion date of 1 September, four more U-boats had augmented the wave. Though Hitler ordered temporary restrictions on his own submarine warfare after the sinking of the *Athenia* on 3 September, German U-boat attacks elicited a calculated response. Their earliest attacks provoked the planned defensive/offensive system that Nelles had contemplated in 1937, and that would characterize the Battle of the Atlantic: the convoy. Britain instituted her first Atlantic convoy from Liverpool to Gibraltar on 7 September. On 15–16 September, the first transatlantic convoys departed Kingston, Jamaica (convoy KJF-1), and Halifax (convoy HX-1). At the same time the German Naval Staff expanded not only its operational sea frontiers, but the range of authorized targets. On 2 October it cleared its ships and submarines for full-scale attacks against all darkened vessels in the limited zones around England and in the Biscay. The next day it included all armed merchant vessels. On 17 October 1939, three days after Prien's successful raid in Scapa Flow, the German Naval Staff authorized full-scale attacks on all enemy merchant ships with the exception of passenger liners. Twelve days later, even passenger ships in convoys became fair game. By definition, a convoy could be as small as a single ship under single escort. Not until 17 August 1940 would Germany's total blockade of England expose all ships in the zone to attack without warning, whether in convoy or alone. Significantly, this German operational zone was almost entirely congruent with the war zone prohibited to American ships and citizens by the terms of the U.S. Neutrality Act of 1939.

Continued German pressure increased the necessity of closely guarded convoy routes. Yet such movements in 'mass, such concentrations of merchant ships of similar speed under the protection of warships, attracted U-boats in concentrations of their own. These the British dubbed "wolf packs." But experience confirmed the more important tactical theory that the convoy forced U-boats to seek out the very warships that had the capacity to sink them. Escorts and support ships would not need to range the oceans in order to ferret out the U-boat. They would wait on station for the wolf pack to lunge at the bait, and then hunt and kill around and within the convoy itself. In the course of time, this forced a confrontation – dominated from 1943 by the absolutely vital air cover that turned the tide in the Battle of the Atlantic – and exacted serious U-boat losses, which drove the Germans to seek easier targets. As it turned out, the easiest targets were to be found where Allied defences were weakest. This might have affected Canadian coastal waters much earlier than it did, in 1942, had Hitler not forbidden U-boat attacks in the western Atlantic until late 1941.

Press accounts of the Battle of the Atlantic were confused, and did little to enlighten the Canadian public about the strategic situation at sea during the earlier months of the war. From excellent intelligence, however, it was clear to the Chiefs of Staff and Cabinet War Committee that the Germans' capacity to strike in Canadian coastal waters was very limited. At the highest strategic levels, therefore, Canadian coastal defences – sea, land, and air – were considered adequate to the threat. True, Canada was short of long-range patrol aircraft, and of destroyers to beef up convoy escorts. But until such times as the concentration of U-boats shifted from the eastern Atlantic, one simply had to cope. The real problem lay in controlling the most effective deployment of limited resources: in order to follow a consistent policy of securing the sea lines of communication to Great Britain and escorting convoys on the high seas, Canada had to deplete forces available for coastal defence. This was bound to create a problem in public morale if it became evident – as it would off the Gaspé coast in 1942 – that the result was more losses of shipping close to home than would otherwise have been the case. Editorials supported government policy.[5] As the *Ottawa Journal* for 24 March 1941 urged, should the Royal Navy and Air Force lose the battle, German battleships "could sail up the St. Lawrence." Canadians therefore faced "the stark, terrible truth," the editor trumpeted, "that our first line of defence – our vital line – is in Britain." Almost two years later, an editorial in the *Halifax Mail* for 11 March 1943 reiterated the view. It was attacking Quebec provincial MLA Onesime Gagnon (Union Nationale, Matane) on the issue of conscription and the diversion of naval forces from the endangered Gulf to the Atlantic. In the process, the editor pilloried the apparently fatuous "attitude of [Quebec] politicians, who in one breath complain of U-Boat activities and in the next inveigh against sending Canadian forces overseas in this war." His argument rested on the conventional wisdom that "the defence frontiers of Canada lie not in the St. Lawrence or within the geographical boundaries of the dominion, but far from home, an ocean's width and more away. The estuary of the St. Lawrence in this local conflict doesn't end with the Gaspé peninsula."

Nothing remotely threatening to national security on the high seas caught the imagination of the Canadian press until November 1941. Front-page stories now revealed that U-boats were operating "within sight of land." Minister for the Navy Angus Macdonald had confided to newsmen that the "Enemy [was] Seen from Shore [as] Two U-Boats

[were] Battled off Newfoundland."[6] Censorship prevented the public from learning that Dönitz's attack group Mordbrenner (Incendiary) had been hunting convoy SC-52 many miles off the entrance to the Strait of Belle Isle between Labrador and Newfoundland.

Actual events were radically different from those reported in the Canadian press, although the four U-boats of Gruppe Mordbrenner had indeed effected the deepest penetration of the western Atlantic of which Canadian authorities had become aware. Yet it was not the first such intrusion. Some five months earlier, in June 1941, U-111 (Kleinschmidt) had in fact undertaken the first sortie into Canadian waters since the First World War. U-111 had been in the Atlantic for a month when BdU radioed unexpected instructions for it to explore the "eastern exit of Belle Isle Strait" and then to explore Cape Race.[7] It was to remain in the assigned areas until it had clarified the tactical situation. Unless it sighted any traffic it was to maintain radio silence until its return voyage had left the zone west of 50° W safely behind.

The tenuous neutrality that the United States was enjoying, and by now exploiting, had made the area sacrosanct to German U-boats. The truce would not last much longer. BdU explicitly instructed U-111 to attack nothing in this area except "especially valuable ships, for example cruisers, troop transports [and] very large vessels." On receipt of his new orders, Kleinschmidt observed that "chart folios for large submarines contain[ed] not a single nautical chart, List of Light Signals, or Sailing Directions for Canadian and American coasts" (KTB). Indeed, German naval authorities had not even "prepared charts in enlarged scale for the operational zone" to which he had just been ordered. He depended entirely on the large-area small-scale German chart G 1870 (scale 1:8 million) and the route chart of the Atlantic Ocean (scale 1:6.25 million). German naval authorities did not publish their own detailed *Handbuch* and *Atlas* of the east coast of Canada until July 1942. Characteristically, even when landing a secret agent in the Baie des Chaleurs in November 1942, the boat U-518 would have to resort to the same chart G 1870. During nine weeks at sea, U-111 now reconnoitered the entrance to Belle Isle Strait and patrolled within striking distance of St John's and Cape Race. Heavy ice packs prevented its penetration of Belle Isle Strait on 10 June 1941. Elsewhere, pack ice, bergs, growlers, and fog prevented inshore operations.

Throughout the summer of 1941 Admiral Dönitz faced one of his most baffling and frustrating tactical problems: his inability to detect convoys. Even individual ship traffic seemed to have ceased, and the seas seemed empty. The Allies, he reasoned, must therefore have developed a special kind of long-range antisubmarine detection device that enabled their ships to elude his U-boat patrols. He was mistaken. In actual fact, Britain's top secret decryption centre in Bletchley Park was beginning to crack the German naval Enigma signals.[8] By October 1941 the Allies would be able to read most of the U-boat cyphered wireless traffic, and Bletchley Park was keeping NSHQ in Ottawa fully informed. Dönitz did not twig to this for the duration of the war. Now, however, in his attempt to block off the convoy routes from North America to the UK by a phalanx of U-boat "rakes," Dönitz established the series of patrol lines that eventually led on to convoy SC-52 and provoked Macdonald's announcement.[9]

On 19 October 1941, Admiral Dönitz organized all U-boats then on patrol in the Atlantic into three major groups that would form extended patrol lines from Newfoundland to Greenland. Gruppe Mordbrenner (Incendiary), consisting of four U-boats, headed directly for the Strait of Belle Isle in order to apprehend Allied shipping emerging into the Atlantic at the earliest opportunity. Eastwards stretched the nine U-boats of Gruppe Schlagetod (Bludgeon) and the seven of Gruppe Reisswolf (Ravenous Wolf). Dönitz eventually ordered U-123 of Schlagetod to guard the Strait while he shifted Gruppe Mordbrenner southward well to the east of St John's and Cape Race. The aggressive Hardegen of U-123, who would play a dominant role during Operation Paukenschlag (Drumbeat) in Canadian and U.S. waters in January 1942, was elated at the prospects of attacking the enemy so close to home. Contemplating his new patrol station, he wrote in his war diary: "We now had the possibility of advancing deep into Belle Isle Strait. That was a task just according to my taste. I therefore intend to thrust from the east between Belle Isle and Newfoundland. Once inside the foxes' lair, nobody will escape us unseen" (KTB). U-374 (von Fischel) picked up the Belle Isle Light on 20 October and in time gained the impression that "U-boats [were] not expected close inshore" (KTB), although U-208 (Schlieper) encountered a surprise attack by a "Martin Bomber B26 [coming] suddenly out of low cloud cover."[10] U-573 (Heinsohn) sighted the "continent and island of Belle Isle" and was forced under by aircraft, a fate suffered by U-109 (Bleichrodt) on the Newfoundland Banks.[11] When U-374 eventually sighted convoy SC-52 east of Newfoundland on 1 November, BdU re-formed twelve U-boats in the vicinity of the contact. He vectored them to U-374's signal, and designated them anew as Gruppe Raubritter (Robber Baron).[12] Hardegen in U-123 responded with relish: "Both engines full speed ahead. Up and at 'em with a roar! Cheerio, old lighthouse keeper of Belle Isle" (KTB). He and others had good reason to rejoice, for on that day the Atlantic U-boats claimed to have contacted five different convoys. As Hardegen wrote: the Allies "can see that the grey wolves have increased" (KTB). But while these events were occurring, hundreds of Allied merchant ships with thousands of tons of cargo were moving safely across the seas. The total number of ships convoyed eastward across the Atlantic rose dramatically from 527 in 1939 to 4053 in 1940, and 5050 in 1941. Of these, only 151 were lost to enemy action.

The battle for convoy SC-52 began on 2 November 1941 when the attempt of von Fischel (U-374) to penetrate the escort screen from astern was repulsed by HMCS *Buctouche*. Unable to evade the corvette's counter-attack on the surface, U-374 dived to 40 m as the explosions of six depth charges caused minor technical failures. U-374 touched bottom at 93.5 m, and while two vessels criss-crossed overhead with searching asdic, it carried out what would become the classical evasive technique of lying dead with all unnecessary equipment switched off. This is the first recorded instance of the bottoming tactic in Canadian waters. U-boat commanders would resort to it throughout the war in the coastal shallows, and invariably escaped detection. Hardegen's War Diary (U-123) recorded the sounds of battle throughout the entries for 1 to 3 November. He was elated by how well the pack system had worked: "Co-operation – you've won the day!" (KTB). Hirsch's U-569 sank one ship for 3349 tons; Linder's U-202 sank three ships for 8440 tons; and Mützelburg's U-203 sank two ships for 10,456 tons. Fog and radio disruptions brought an end to the conflict.

For reasons that can only have been politically motivated, Navy Minister Macdonald announced the "Battle" almost immediately when launching the corvette HMCS *Oakville* at Oakville, Ontario. There were now many U-boats between Belle Isle and Iceland, he explained; two had been attacked and one possibly sunk. His assertions about supposed Canadian successes some 300 miles off the coast had, of course, no factual basis. He doubtless felt it necessary to strengthen the national commitment for war by clarifying the immediacy of the threat. Rear-Admiral Percy Nelles also exploited the launching to warn the press that "Nazi" submarines would be operating off Nova Scotia in the very near future.[13] A Boston trawler later seemed to confirm the prophecy by claiming to have sighted a U-boat 40 miles southwest of Halifax.[14] Later, back-page articles embellished the story of the U-boat that "stalked" convoy SC-52 some "30 miles off Canada." They echoed supposed official sources about "U-Boats Lurking Unbelievably Close to [the] Canadian Shore."[15]

Significantly, such U-boat scares only made back-page news. Not even the news of a Canadian success gained higher priority. Yet the sinking of U-501 (Förster) in the North Atlantic and capture of forty-seven survivors by HMCS *Moose Jaw* and *Chambly* signalled to some observers that Canada's Navy had finally come of age.[16] The *Ottawa Journal*'s editorial on 20 November 1941 commented that up to now the Canadian Navy's story of recalcitrance and neglect had "not been a proud one." With the success of these corvettes, however, "we are now making atonement for the past and living up to the traditions of the British fleet." The sinking symbolized for the press a turning point in Canadian naval history that will "not allow us to go back to our naval folly, since so much of our future is on the seas."

This prophecy would not be fulfilled in the long term. For although the navy eventually went on to better things, and never relapsed into its terrible peacetime doldrums of the 1920s, it would suffer predictable and unacceptable cut-backs as soon as the war was over, and when the obvious danger had passed. But in the meantime, specific war plans had to be drawn up for the defence of the littoral. Geography and limited resources dictated the terms. While defence of Atlantic waters derived in large measure from the needs of transocean convoys, and more especially depended upon the higher direction of the war and upon international agreements in which Canada had no effective share,[17] defence of the St Lawrence River and Gulf formed a special case.

Prior to hostilities, various government departments and naval authorities had of course issued plans and memoranda of an informational or executive nature in order to develop or mobilize the resources under their command. The presence of German surveyors on Anticosti Island in 1937 focused public attention on the strategic value of the vital land mass in the controlling centre of the Gulf of St Lawrence. Once in the hands of the enemy, some Canadians feared, it would provide German air and naval forces with a crucial staging point from which to control the Belle Isle Strait, Cabot Strait, and indeed inland industrial centres throughout the Maritimes, Ontario, and Quebec. Some Canadians feared that the island would become a German colony or "German administered territory." Although the head of a party of German engineers visiting the island had explained that the group was merely seeking information "with no obligation to purchase," the incident constituted one of two scares that an editorial in the *Globe and Mail* identified. The other scare arose from the British Columbia rumour that "Japanese [-Canadian] fishermen were actually spies for the Nippon Government." J.S. Woodsworth and R.B. Bennett raised the Anticosti question in Parliament on 26 May 1938, and were assured by Mackenzie King that his government would not relinquish control of the island to any foreign power.[18]

Concerns for Gulf security triggered a defence plan by the Joint Staff Committee. The "JSC Plan For the Defence of Canada" of 27 June 1938, although quickly superseded by the "JSC Emergency Plan For the Defence of the Eastern Coast of Canada" of 16 September 1938, enunciated a basic policy.[19] It anticipated potential air attacks against Canadian inland targets, as well as sea-borne attacks against merchant shipping and even against the Port of Quebec. The planners feared the enemy's battleships and cruisers, as well as mines layed by armed merchant ships carrying motor torpedo boats; they expected, equally in error, as it turned out, aircraft and dirigible airships. The greatest threat seemed to come from three sources: from massive bombardment of the shores, from raiding parties, and from possible gas attack by air. But planners seem not yet to have appreciated the strength of the German submarine.

Where the first "JSC Plan" envisaged Canada's responding with a naval strike force based on Halifax and Sydney without the need for stationing ships in the Gulf, the second version outlined the formation of Eastern Air Command. Based in Halifax, it would control four operational zones covering not only the Atlantic provinces, but the St Lawrence Gulf and river as far west as the Saguenay. The Gulf squadron, based in Sydney, would consist of six Fairchilds, four Stranraer flying boats, and nine Wapitis – all obsolete aircraft unequipped for military tasks. Two equally inadequate Fairchilds and three Bellancas were to cope with the Gaspé and Anticosti patrols. Neither of these early plans, it should be noted, mentioned the use of Newfoundland as a base, but that does not mean that its importance was overlooked.

An Atlantic strategy subsequently known as "Plan Black," because of its having adopted a worst-case scenario of British collapse under German military forces, emerged on 10 October 1940.[20] Entitled "Joint Canadian-United States Basic Defence Plan – 1940," it set forth the defence requirements of the northeastern United States, eastern Canada, and Newfoundland that would arise if these areas should become "subject to attack due to the inability of the British Navy to exercise effective control of the North Atlantic." The strategy of this basic plan hinged on the concept of a German victory in Europe, and of German troops establishing a foothold in North America for future expansion. Such assault and expansion, according to the "Black" scenario, would be "preceded, accompanied and followed by intensive submarine, surface raider and aircraft attack on shipping in the western Atlantic, and by occasional hit-and-run attacks." While Plan Black addressed the principles of meeting such a threat, and although it described the Canadian-U.S. forces that "will" respond, it never commented upon or reflected the inadequacies and limitations of the resources at hand. Nor need it have done so, for the neutral United States disposed of such overwhelming battle fleets that Canada could, and did, rest comfortably secure under its protective shadow. The stance is familiar. With fifty American destroyers in Argentia, Newfoundland, alone, and fleet aircraft carriers at sea, U.S. Task Force 24 seemed to provide all the strength the Canadian Atlantic seaboard would need for some time.

The Japanese surprise attack on Pearl Harbor in December 1941 forced a U.S. deployment on broader fronts than the basic plan had anticipated. It not only initiated the Pacific War, but consequently altered the role of the RCN in the Atlantic. In May 1941 the Newfoundland Escort Force (NEF), created as a stopgap until the USN entered fully into convoy operations, thrust the RCN for the first time from a minor role in coastal defence into a major one of ocean operations. Pearl Harbor and the Pacific War, by drawing so many U.S. ships away, ensured that the major RCN role in ocean escort would be a permanent arrangement. This was a radical shift. For, as Milner has observed, even as late as the autumn of 1940 the Canadian Navy had prepared no plans for employing its "burgeoning corvette fleet as ocean escorts."[21] Indeed, the first Canadian corvettes that put to sea at the urging of British Admiralty, so Canadian Naval Staff observed in December 1942, were quite simply untrained.[22] What many would describe as a parochial approach towards maritime defence delayed Canada's ultimate commitment of strength as a major escort force in the Battle of the Atlantic. The priority given by planners to local defences also explains why minesweepers like the Bangors rarely swept for mines but were thrust into the breach of rapidly changing policy to carry out the work of convoy escorts on the high seas. As will be seen, Pearl Harbor radically changed Dönitz's modified advance on North American shores as well.

For the moment, however, the "Canadian-United States Basic Defence Plan" remained a theory with little grasp of the practical factors involved. It none the less reflected a growing concern in some sectors of Canadian society that a German invasion of the North American continent was a distinct possibility. Like the Ottawa Journal of 6 June 1941, newspapers speculated on significant battle signs: an Allied bomber had recently flown from England to Canada in fourteen hours; British ships were being sunk within 700 miles of the North American coast; the 45,000-ton battleship Bismarck, that had been sunk on 27 May 1941, had actually been intercepted off Greenland, "not more than forty-eight hours from Halifax." This means, the editorial urged, that Canadians, untouched as yet by the hard facts of war, were living "in a fool's paradise." But even more important in the light of the basic plan, all these "facts" now meant that "this war is coming closer [and] that the Atlantic, instead of being a barrier against Hitler, may become in the end a bridge ... to war against America – and Canada." Increasing clarification of the threat necessitated a refinement of Canadian countermeasures. "Plan G" (Defence of Shipping – Gulf of St Lawrence) constitutes the first comprehensive directive on the defence and control of vital shipping areas in the face of the U-boat threat.[23] It reflects the circumspection of its author, Commodore L.W. Murray.

Plan G distinguishes itself by its shrewd, if tentative assessment of the ramifications of Gulf defence, and by its forthright though anxious acknowledgement of the meagre resources at hand. Promulgated by the naval secretary, Captain J.O. Cossette, on 29 April 1940, four months before the first meeting of the Permanent Joint Board of Defence, and six months before Plan Black, it advised senior naval authorities of the seven phases through which maritime defence would if necessary be escalated. Direct responsibility would lie with the Commanding Officer Atlantic Coast in Halifax. According to the doctrine of Plan G, German submarines could be expected in the river and Gulf during the ice-free season from 1 May until 15 November. No more than three submarines were to be expected simultaneously. The plan was astute on this point, for that number was, in fact, never exceeded. Cossette's preamble enunciated what was to become the Canadian cachet of "defence by offensive measures" that Commander J.D. "Chummy" Prentice would evolve for the Atlantic escorts. It would lead to a conflict with British escort principles.

Canadians had first been exposed to British doctrine in the form of Western Approaches Convoy Instructions (WACIs) as early as 1940. Atlantic Convoy Instructions (ACIs) derived from them. Article 101 of ACIs described the escort's first priority as "the safe and timely arrival of the convoy at its destination."[24] The primary means for attaining that goal was "evasion." Clearly, this approach held little appeal for personalities intent on sinking U-boats, for ACIs insisted that escorts hold back unless offensive action could be undertaken "without undue prejudice to the safety of the convoy." Much of the unjust blame for the Canadians' apparent ineffectiveness in sinking U-boats may be traced to the fact that their role often precluded initiatives in aggressive action. And in any event, Britain's ability to decipher U-boat message traffic from May 1941 onwards made it possible to divert many convoys around the "wolf packs." By contrast, the U.S. "Escort of Convoy Instructions," to which Canadians were exposed operationally since the autumn of 1941, reversed the British priorities. For the Americans, the first duty was striking the enemy, and only then "conduct of the convoy clear" of him.[25] As noted earlier, this reflected the tactical approach of Plan Black, which the Canadian-U.S. Permanent Joint Board of Defence evolved in 1940. It is also implicit in Gulf defence plans "G" and "GL". This may in some way explain why Canadians often irritated the British by wanting to dash off to chase a U-boat. As Milner has explained, the Canadian approach struck the Royal Navy more as "cowboy" "roughrider" tactics than as professional naval discipline.

There may have been more than one element of truth in the RN's jaundiced perception of Canadian tactics if, for example, one considers ship's badges and gun shield crests as a reflection of personality: HMCS *Calgary* boasted a U-boat begging for mercy from a gun-toting cowboy astride a bucking destroyer; HMCS *Rimouski* a mounted cowboy lassoing a U-boat; HMCS *Dauphin* a "Mountie" astride a U-boat; HMCS *Sorel* a sorrel horse with a naval crown biting a U-boat in half; HMCS *Buctouche* a comical Adolf Hitler being thrown off the back of a bucking donkey; HMCS *Agassiz* a grizzly bear gripping a U-boat it is about to devour; and HMCS *Moosejaw* a startled Hitler on the run from a fierce-eyed, fire-breathing moose, which has just bitten a piece out of the seat of his pants. Such designs, Canadian Naval Staff observed, differed "markedly in character" from the types that had received official approval in the RN. Whereas an Admiralty committee approved RN badges according to established standards of heraldry, propriety, and decorum, the Canadian badges simply came into being.[26]

The U.S.-UK doctrinal conflict found independent resolution of sorts in the temperamentally more Canadian "Hints on Escort Work" issued by Acting Captain "Chummy" Prentice, Captain (D) Halifax, between March and July 1943. Lucid, personal, and sometimes rakish, the "hints" consisted of detailed recommendations on key aspects of convoy theory and practice.[27] Prentice insisted that Atlantic Convoy Instructions (ACIs) still formed the basis of Canadian doctrine, but argued that "our tactics must be flexible." Thus, while asserting the British tenet of the "safe and timely arrival of our convoys" as the prime object of all escorts, he allowed his historical view to bend the rules: "History has shown that the only sure way of achieving this object [of timely arrival] is to ensure the destruction of any enemy forces which approach ... Put into plain words ... 'get two escorts on to one submarine' and 'when you've got your teeth into the enemy don't leave him until he is sunk'" (part IV). As will be seen, this method led to the destruction of U-536 and U-845.

Had the heretical views of this in some respects misguided compromise reached Admiralty two years earlier, it would at the very least have aroused indignant surprise. But in 1943, when the Battle of the Atlantic had turned decisively against the U-boats, RN circles greeted Prentice's disquisition as both "interesting and refreshing."[28] Admiralty recognized with approval that the "Canadians have adjusted many of the instructions in ACIs to suit their own mixed escort groups." This constituted sympathetic recognition of the serious shortages in operational equipment for which the Canadians had to compensate by resorting to imaginative screens. Admiralty recognized, for example, that many of these mixed escort groups of Bangor minesweepers, corvettes, and destroyers "may have only one ship with [the latest] 271 radar." This was the only radar that swept automatically through $360°$ – though it took two minutes to complete a single revolution. This was none the less a clear advance over the British type 286, which did not rotate at all. The type SW1C (Surface Warning 1st Canadian) could at least be rotated manually. But, as Milner has explained, while all the Canadian destroyers carried type 286 in 1941, only fifteen Canadian corvettes were fitted with SW1C. Indeed, he points out, "from August 1940 to February 1942 only four U-Boats are known to have been detected on the surface with the aid of radar, and of this number only one was attacked."[29]

Seen against this background of developing technology and tactical doctrine, it is more readily apparent that Gulf defence Plan G of 29 April 1940 had struck an early compromise. It envisaged meeting the German threat "by means of adequate hunting and striking forces" as units entirely separate from convoy escorts that were tied down to particular convoys. This anticipated the formation of Support Groups, which in theory lent strength wherever needed. Yet at the same time, Plan G was realistic in preparing to "institute a modified plan using available material [in light of] the severe limitations imposed by the present shortage of anti-submarine vessels." By way of recompense, the plan reminded the navy that U-boats operating a long way from home would be labouring under severe time constraints dictated by problems of logistics and fuel. As it turned out, Dönitz himself reckoned an average time on patrol station of four to five weeks. Finally, Plan G cautioned that as all submarines could carry "at least twenty mines ... this form of enemy action must be legislated for." Although U-boats of the First World War had carried twice that many mines, and the large type XB minelayers of the Second World War as many as 66, the Canadian estimate was not as incorrect as it at first seems. The type VII *Atlantikboot* could carry only 16 mines; type IX, 22 mines; and larger IXC/40 that patrolled off Halifax in 1944, 21 mines. Type VIID carried 31 mines (15 in vertical cases, and 16 torpedo mines). Significantly, Germany built only eight of the huge type XB minelayers, the first of which entered service in 1942. They were mainly used as supply Boats, and very rarely laid mines.

Merely legislating for mine countermeasures indicates how tentative the Canadian defence plan really was despite its detail. Authorities at the time were considering equipping the Quebec City-based tug *Macsin* with a Mark V sweep, and expressed the hope that, while all available minesweepers must remain in Halifax, "one or more coil skids should be available for the destruction of magnetic mines in the near future." Despite the susceptibility of Gulf ports to mining, this assessment was strategically correct. As will be seen, German U-boats did not lay mines in Canadian waters until June 1943.

The strategic assessment behind Plan G spilled over onto Atlantic defences. Yet the allocation of forces reflected greater concerns about the potential threat from Japan.[30] The four asdic-fitted destroyers were still stationed on the West Coast, and the other two (*Skeena* and *Saguenay*) on the East. An antisubmarine tactical trainer had been purchased from the United Kingdom, but was sitting unused at Esquimalt. Four trawler-type 123A asdic sets had been purchased from the UK for the four recently built minesweepers (*Fundy*, *Comox*, *Nootka*, and *Gaspé*), but had not yet been fitted. These units were in any event considered obsolete by 1939.[31] The situation would not improve markedly even by June 1943. As then LCdr Desmond Piers observed at the time: "It is a blunt statement of fact that RCN ships are outdated in the matter of A/S equipment by twelve to eighteen months, compared to RN ... Canadian personnel are not getting the chance they deserve, due to lack of modern equipment."[32] The hunt for U-806 off the Sambro lightship in December 1944 would graphically illustrate the problem: only one of the twenty-four Canadian ships involved in the hunt had a Q-fitted asdic to calculate the target's depth.

By June 1940 the East Coast had adopted a series of defensive measures: (*a*) provided eastbound convoys with destroyer escort and aircraft support to the edge of the western Atlantic (where U-boats were not yet operating); (*b*) constructed an antisubmarine boom defence across the entrance to Halifax harbour off Maugher's Beach Lighthouse; (*c*) established an A/S boom inner patrol consisting of a 17 knot motor boat armed with depth charges (but of course no means for detecting a U-boat). The director of antisubmarine and booms complained at the time of the difficulty encountered in obtaining suitable naval reservists to meet the requirements for A/S-trained personnel: "RCNR ratings [professional mariners] lacked the necessary intelligence and VRs [civilian voluntary reserves] lacked sea time." In order to meet the situation, he reported having sent a group of sixty VRs to sea prior to their taking the course. Initial steps towards activating Plan G had already begun as well. The RCAF was about to build a base at Gaspé, Quebec, in which to house a combined operations room for both air force and navy personnel. The St Lawrence Signal Service System, linked by landline via Cap des Rosiers, and by telephone to Ottawa, Halifax, and Sydney, would be phased in with other commercial and military systems in order to establish a broad communications net. The lines, however, would not be secure for passing classified information.

Phase I of Plan G would commence on first indication of a U-boat threat in the Gulf. Naval Officers in Charge (NOICs) and Naval Control Service Officers (NCSOs) would route all inbound and outbound traffic individually along routes already designated on the St Lawrence Route Chart. Known as SLRC, this special issue of Admiralty Chart no. 2516 provided a wide selection of routes linking predetermined coordinates throughout the St Lawrence River and Gulf system. On receipt of the executive "QJA Message" from the Commanding Officer, Atlantic Coast, ships would be assigned routes identified by letters and numbers keyed to a list of coordinates through which these passed. Plan G did not envisage convoys at this stage. Because of the dire "shortage of hunting vessels," those few on hand would be stationed at as yet unidentified strategic points along the shipping routes. Consequently, phase II would rely solely on air patrols as far west as the Saguenay River. As the alarm escalated to phase III, "one and, if possible, two destroyers" would be based at Sydney with all available antisubmarine vessels deployed either to Sydney or Gaspé, or to both. Significantly, the ships would refrain from escort duties in order to "act as Hunting and/or Striking Forces as requisite." In order to reduce the area these vessels would have to search, and thus maximize the coverage by patrol aircraft, phase IV would reduce the area of military responsibility. This would be accomplished by warning all shipping by means of marine broadcasts and published Notices to Mariners that they use the Strait of Belle Isle, the Gut of Canso, and the Mingan Passage north of Anticosti Island entirely at their own risk. In other words, the armed forces were eliminating those particularly narrow choke points that easily lent themselves to control by U-boats. At phase V "at least four A/S vessels" would be stationed at Sydney and "four on Gaspé" in anticipation of phase VI: the Escorted Group System.

The Escorted Group System was a forerunner of the convoy doctrine later developed in Western Approaches Convoy Instructions (WACIs), Atlantic Convoy Instructions (ACIs), and the U.S. Escort and Convoy Instructions. Adjusting current wisdom to the exigencies of local conditions and available resources, it required vessels with a speed in excess of 12 knots to proceed alone, while requiring slower ones to cluster together for mutual comfort for passage from one check-point to another along the route. By strict definition, therefore, these "clusters" or "gaggles" of ships were not convoys. They would travel under cover of darkness alone, and be escorted during daylight between clearly defined points: Point P (on a line joining Cap Chat and Pointe des Monts) and Point Q (on a line joining Cap des Rosiers, Quebec, and Cap des Monts – possibly Southwest Point – Anticosti). Only as a last resort would phase VII be executed: the complete closure of the Gulf and river to all shipping. Plan G was suspended on 10 March 1941 and superseded on 25 April 1941 by Plan GL.

The new plan reduced the previous seven response phases to four, and assigned specific classes of warships to specific bases and patrol areas. Defined as "essentially a defensive measure," it none the less foresaw deploying "adequate hunting and striking A/S forces" at strategic locations. Six armed antisubmarine yachts were to be stationed in Gaspé and would operate from approximately 64° W longitude to the mouth of the Saguenay River; they would have a subsidiary base at Rimouski. A force of four or five corvettes and four motor torpedo boats (Fairmiles, perhaps) based on Gaspé would patrol the Gulf proper. RCAF aircraft would be based at Gaspé and Sydney in support of the Gulf surface forces. A further departure from the previous plan lay in the distribution of minesweepers. Even though magnetic minesweeping gear was still unavailable by spring 1941, NSHQ foresaw deploying one minesweeper at Rimouski, two at Gaspé, and five at Sydney.

The phases of the new plan differed from the earlier version in significant ways. Whereas the former Plan G initiated phase I on the executive signal announcing a U-boat threat, Plan GL assumed the threat as a matter of course. Thus the new phase I automatically came into effect on the opening of the navigation season. NCSOs still routed all traffic individually according to the St Lawrence Route Chart, but advised masters not to adhere too closely to designated tracks. Phase II would commence on receipt of an enemy report, and would as far as possible cause the diversion of all ships from the area of hostilities. COAC would order the nearest hunting group to search and attack, supported by the RCAF. The navy espoused the general principle of "avoid[ing] dislocation of the normal shipping" unless enemy operations became "of a serious and concerted nature." At that time, phase III would initiate convoys between Sydney on Cape Breton Island at the Atlantic entrance to the Gulf and Pointe au Père (Father Point) deep inside the St Lawrence River. Based on a speed of advance (SOA) of 8 knots, escorted convoys would require two and a half days for the journey. Allowing for delays, this gave rise to a four-day convoy cycle in the Gulf that could be handled by two escort forces based in Sydney. As before, ships travelling in excess of 12 knots would be routed independently. Finally, by excluding from surveillance the unthreatened, though mineable, waters westward of the Saguenay, and by not legislating for the Belle Isle Force, which in any event could not lend immediate support in a Gulf emergency, it effectively limited its jurisdiction. While NSHQ felt assured that the first three phases "cover all likely possibilities," phase IV provided for a council of despair in closing the Gulf to shipping entirely.

The German U-boat advance off the Atlantic coast in January 1942, which forms the subject of the next chapter, caused a comprehensive re-evaluation of the maritime defence system. Promulgated on 1 April 1942 as Plan GL2, it concluded from the winter operations of U-boats off Canada and the USA that further attacks could be expected against the St Lawrence River and Gulf shipping in the summer of 1942. While not excluding minelayers from German tactics, the plan assumed that torpedo attacks would be more likely. The plan was astute, for the obvious weakness and inexperience of U.S.-Canadian defences off the Atlantic coast would indeed encourage Admiral Dönitz to send his U-boats into the Gulf in a series of highly effective raids. As will be seen, only a serious shortage of mines prevented Dönitz from mining Canadian and American waters forthwith. None the less, Canadians even now faced serious problems of defence. For, as the preamble to Plan GL2 observed, "all available anti-submarine forces are [already] fully employed in the Mid Ocean or Western Local Escort Forces, in addition to providing Escort for coastal convoys and other essential duties."[33] The only solution under the circumstances lay in the utilization of newly constructed vessels to accompany shipping on passage from Quebec to Halifax.

This meant that recently built vessels fresh from the builders in the Great Lakes and Quebec, and with only housekeeper crews aboard for the transit down river, would play escort to merchant convoys facing a highly trained opponent. This accounts in large measure for German criticisms about the questionable professionalism of Canadians in the Gulf. Only after work-ups in Halifax would these new vessels be assigned to the various task and escort forces "as the situation at the time necessitates." Rapid expansion of the fleet made plans necessarily ad hoc, and sent untrained crews to sea with untested ships. At the time of promulgation, five corvettes (HMCS *Woodstock*, *Brantford*, *Port Arthur*, *Quebec*, and *La Malbaie*) were expected to be commissioned by 1 May 1942, with a sixth, HMCS *Kitchener*, following in July. Ten steam minesweepers were expected between June and late fall 1942. Two diesel minesweepers would be ready on 1 May, followed by seven more during June and July; the navy expected two wooden minesweepers without magnetic sweeping gear in May, followed by fifteen Fairmiles in June "subject to [the] arrival [of] electrical equipment," and the two depot ships HMCS *Provider* and *Preserver*. Ten more corvettes and three Algerine minesweepers were expected to be commissioned in the fall.

In all, this formed an enormous problem of co-ordination. The plan required the navy to arrange "for these ships to have all armament fitted, to carry out armament trials and to embark full outfits of ammunition" before they left Quebec City. Significantly, however, the crews would not yet have been trained to use the equipment. The procurement and testing of armament prior to playing escort would remain a problem well into 1943.[34] As a number of ships were being built in the Great Lakes for the U.S. Navy, it was also imperative to obtain U.S. permission to equip and use their new vessels for the escort mission as well.

The preamble of GL2 anticipated some of the difficulties that smaller vessels like armed yachts and Fairmiles would have in the frequently heavy weather encountered in the Gulf. If escorted convoys were to be organized at all, it was of utmost importance that some of the newly constructed vessels allocated be at least the size of a Bangor minesweeper. This, the plan insisted, would ensure "that at least part of the escort will be able to remain with the convoy in any [heavy] weather." As it turned out, when the Fairmiles' role was shifted under duress from general patrol to escort duties, they did not always function as Canadians had hoped. They were found to be of little use in bad weather, and their asdic domes tended to shake off in the steep Gulf seas. However, in the facetious judgement of an RN escort commander, they had by the autumn of 1942 "proved useful in picking up survivors from torpedoed ships and transferring them to the nearest port."[35]

Plan GL2 of 1 April 1942 consisted of three phases. Phase I commenced with unrestricted shipping throughout the Gulf and river for the duration of the normal shipping season. The terms differed from peacetime navigation in one respect only: inbound shipping was to be routed from Bird Rocks close around Gaspé at Fame Point, while outbound shipping under the direction of the NCSO would transit north of these tracks and have various diversionary routes on leaving the Gulf. Phase II would commence whenever newly constructed vessels arrived at Quebec. These would then escort "any available groups of merchant shipping from Quebec to Sydney." This too was an ad hoc arrangement, as no merchant vessels were to be delayed pending the arrival of what NSHQ called a "Man of War." Shipping would otherwise sail as unrestrictedly as before. The next phase depended entirely upon German initiative. Phase III, itself specifically designated Plan GL2, would "commence as soon as there is any confirmed attack by U-Boats against shipping in the Gulf or river St. Lawrence." In that event, all inbound traffic would be stopped at Sydney and all outward-bound merchant traffic at Quebec. In the latter case an assembly anchorage could be established to the south of Bic Island. Outbound convoys would then be sailed so as to connect with the appropriate transatlantic HX and SC convoys, which originated in Halifax, Sydney, and New York. Inbound traffic would be sailed from Sydney every three days.

Phase III required twenty warships for immediate duties with St Lawrence convoys: five Bangors, five armed yachts, and ten Fairmiles. Formed into five Escort Groups of one Bangor, one yacht and two Fairmiles, they would constitute a significantly lesser force than that envisaged in the earlier Plan GL. The Commanding Officer Atlantic Coast was directed to reallocate the strained forces under his command in order to meet this urgent commitment. In time, the navy would have the support of the RCAF. For the moment, however, the RCAF had only eight Catalina flying boats based at Sydney. These were totally committed to antisubmarine and convoy escort patrols with Atlantic convoys. Should U-boats actually activate GL2 in the St Lawrence, the plan proposed transferring three of these aircraft to Gaspé for St Lawrence patrols. It would base at Mont Joli any further aircraft that might become available. As it turned out during hostilities, the RCAF requested the navy to route convoys running between Quebec and Sydney south of the Magdalen Islands in order to take advantage of training aircraft operating out of Charlottetown and Summerside. This gave the Germans an impression of Canadian air superiority that in fact did not exist. By definition, training aircraft were inexpertly manned and were only rarely equipped to fight submarines.

The westward expansion of U-boat activity across the Atlantic in 1941 provoked a parallel development of escorted convoy routes moving westward from the UK. First using Iceland as a base, naval forces escorted convoys from the UK to 30° W. The use of St John's, Newfoundland, next facilitated protection as far as 45° W. The final link led to Halifax. Despite its serious shortcomings, the Canadian Navy played an increasing role.[36] The intrusion of German U-boats into the Gulf from the first sortie in May 1942 until their halcyon days that summer and fall when they sank twenty vessels, triggered Plan GL2. U-boat pressure on the Gulf had all but relaxed when the Admiralty in London requested as many escorts as possible to support the "Operation Torch" landings in North Africa in November 1942. Strapped for resources, Canada none the less allocated seventeen corvettes at the expense of her own Gulf and coastal convoys.[37] In the forthright words of the director of operations division, this allocation had "robbed coastal convoys of escorts."[38] There is no evidence that the Canadian contribution of ships was particularly vital to "Torch." It was an exercise in colonial deference to Britain.

Inadequate protection of coastal convoys led directly to the council of despair that Plan GL of 1941 had envisaged, but for which its successor, Plan GL2, had not provided: closure of the Gulf. A War Cabinet decision of 9 September 1942 closed the St Lawrence to ocean-going shipping by October 1942.

Practical considerations of logistics prevented the government from closing the Gulf as tightly as it might have wished, for 40 per cent of the vessels convoyed were engaged in the coastal trade.[39] Almost 24 per cent of this trade went to Sydney and Newfoundland, and the rest to ports in Gaspé and northern New Brunswick. Some vital materials, like coal from Sydney, iron ore from Wabana, not to mention bauxite and pulp wood, could not be stopped. Inter-island ferries had to operate, as indeed did shipping and newly constructed warships moving downriver from the Great Lakes. As the Chief of Naval Staff, Vice-Admiral Percy Nelles, advised the Minister of Defence on 7 October 1942, "it cannot be assumed that the ports of Montreal and Quebec, Sydney, Gaspé ... will by any means be closed down." Yet elimination of 60 per cent of Gulf shipping meant that the railheads of both Halifax and Saint John, New Brunswick, would have to be expanded and upgraded to provide "year-round service to capacity for the loading of Canadian products into ocean-going ships."[40]

Canadian authorities seem not to have examined the impact of closure upon the railway system. It is becoming clearer, however, that reshipment through American ports caused serious transport problems in Canada while diverting profits for goods and services to the United States. By 1943 over 26 per cent of all Canadian trade passed through the U.S., as did almost 22 per cent of Canadian trade with the UK. Canadian exports of flour through such distant ports as Tampa, Florida, and Wilmington, North Carolina, and of other shipments through equally distant ports, necessitated the rationing of box cars throughout the whole Canadian rail system.[41] Closure of the Gulf attracted strong constructive criticism within the naval service. A proposal by Commander R.B. Mitchell, RCNR, naval control service officer in Sydney, Nova Scotia, offered the Department of National Defence on 15 October 1942 a clear set of options, which it seemed to have not yet considered: the defensive mining of the Gulf and approaches.[42]

Then, as now, mines could serve either defensive or offensive purposes. By laying mines in precisely plotted positions in a "field" off one's own coasts and harbours, one denied the enemy free access while permitting the safe movement of one's own shipping through carefully charted channels. Conversely, by laying a similar "field" in enemy territory, one threatened the enemy's free movement in his own waters. Defensive fields were of two types: they were "uncontrolled" when the mines detonated according to their own internal mechanisms, and "controlled" when laid in an electrically linked loop and triggered from a remote station ashore or on board a patrol vessel. Offensive fields, as will be seen in a later chapter on U-boat minelaying, are uncontrolled. Some mines were anchored in deep waters and rose toward the surface at the end of long mooring cables. Others lay on the sea bottom in the shallows. A third type simply drifted about on the surface, driven by wind and current. It was the least effective, as not even the minelayer could be certain of its precise location.

By September 1939 British Admiralty had advised the Canadian Navy that defence loops, "though still in the process of development, [had] passed the purely experimental stage."[43] These came in two types: mine loops, as described above, and indicator loops, which merely indicated to a remote observation post when a surface vessel or submarine crossed it. The Admiralty considered fixed hydrophones of "doubtful utility as against skillfully handled submarines." The boom defences, indicator, and mine loops of Halifax approaches were the first to be built in the early months of the war. Though subject to updating throughout hostilities, they were largely completed by 1942. The boom defence stretched from York Redoubt (north of Sleepy Cove) directly across to the spit on McNabs Island. Southward, spanning the waters between Sandwich Point and the shallows of Lighthouse Bank, lay the six loops.[44] However, not until March 1942 did the RCN undertake the first attempt at laying an outer indicator loop at St John's, Newfoundland.[45] The difficulties were symptomatic of a variety of problems. Lack of equipment, tools, cables, and workboats delayed the project. In the words of the officer in charge of controlled mining, "we were forced to improvise practically everything."[46]

The Mitchell proposal for the defensive mining of the Gulf Approaches, alluded to earlier, reached the Chiefs of Staff Committee in December 1942 at a time of conflicting priorities. Though ultimately rejected on the grounds of impracticability and potential danger to friendly shipping, it remains a revealing document.[47] Mitchell had conceded that, in view of the desperate lack of escort vessels, closure of the Gulf and river constituted "the best possible decision to make under the circumstances." He none the less found closure "a severe moral and physical defeat to Canada's war effort" that could have been avoided by judicious mining. Mitchell was not alone in regretting closure, for in the spring and summer of 1943 the Ministry of War Transport urged NSHQ to permit even a few ships into Gulf ports; quite apart from the obvious advantage of transport routing, this "might have a good psychological effect on the labour" that was laid idle.[48] Quebec MPs were equally concerned. Mr Liguori Lacombe (Lib., Laval–Two Mountains) argued in the House of Commons in June 1943 that closure was ill advised, and that the resultant detour of goods by rail to Halifax was ruining Gulf ports while costing the taxpayer an extra million dollars per year.[49] Premier Duplessis would describe the event in the Quebec legislature in 1945 as a federal plot to ruin Quebec ports.

Mitchell addressed the problem of defensive mining directly. The fact that maritime surface and airborne patrols had "so far not prevented the access of enemy submarines to these waters" convinced him that the Gulf must be defended by controlling its three narrow entrances: Belle Isle Strait was 9.5 miles wide at its narrowest point with a maximum depth along the line of 40 fathoms; the Cabot Strait, some 51 miles wide at its narrowest point, could be "bridged" by a minefield running 13 miles from Cape North on Cape Breton Island to South Point Light on St Paul's Island, and thence 41.5 miles from North Point Light on St Paul's Island to Cape Ray, Newfoundland. The maximum depth along these lines was 260 fathoms. Finally, one could control the roughly 4-mile wide Gut of Canso. Mitchell's scheme argued for "eliminating the first [gateway], controlling the second and patrolling the third" by a constant Fairmile patrol. As soon as ice conditions permitted, Mitchell proposed laying a deep minefield in Cabot Strait by the "bridging" system and providing surface and air patrols close to seaward of the minefield. Finally, Mitchell proposed limiting the crossing of the minefield to daylight hours in order to lessen the risk of a merchantman coming into contact with a drifting mine.

Mitchell anticipated most of the reasons for which his proposal eventually failed. He knew, for example, of the Allied success in the First

World War in laying the deep Great Northern Barrage between Scotland and Norway in well over 200 fathoms. It was, therefore, technically possible to mine the Cabot Strait. The Chiefs of Staff Subcommittee, however, feared that the strong currents would effectively neutralize the mines by causing them to dip, and that ice floes could break them loose from their moorings. More importantly, he "recognized that the RCN at present possesses neither the experienced personnel, the material, nor the ships required for the operation." Under the circumstances, he offered his own services and those of two other RCNR officers who had also had "long years of cable work involving the mooring of buoys in depths of up to 250 fathoms." Such officers, he argued, "could be trained during the winter in the kindred subject of mine mooring." Mitchell proposed borrowing minelayers from the Royal Navy, or else adapting cablelayers then in Halifax. Mitchell's admirable scheme of "making do" with men and equipment reflects the way in which Canada went to war in other areas as well.

One such scheme was the Aircraft Detection Corps (ADC) on which the Canadian military came to rely. The Canadian maritime war zone was simply too vast for the limited military resources at hand. Organized and administered by Eastern Air Command for the express "purpose of reporting the presence and movements of all aircraft, U-Boats, raiding parties, suspicious persons, and ships in distress," it consisted of civilian volunteers.[50] Each volunteer regional director supervised an area of approximately 1200 square miles. Aided by other volunteers in their roles of chief observer and official observer, who operated in subdivisions of 48 square miles known as observation post areas, the ADC provided the Eastern Air Command with 24-hour ground surveillance. Even as late as 1942 the system was far from satisfactory, despite the training packages and identification kits that Eastern Air Command supplied. Communications presented a major difficulty, for the ADC had not yet reached its goal of having "at least one telephone in each Observation Post Area." Having sighted a suspicious occurrence, the observer might have to hike or row at least 6–8 miles in order to place a call. Communications proved to be the Achilles heel of St Lawrence antisubmarine operations. Early in 1943 Canadian authorities addressed the pressing need for updating the communications services by the addition of either telephone, teletype, landline, or radio, and urged the funding of a $1,020,000 program to enhance the fighting efficiency of army, navy, air force, and ADC units in the St Lawrence River and Gulf.[51] "An extremely efficient system of communications is essential if submarines are to be destroyed," one report observed. The actuality, even this far into the war, was desperate:

In general, the communications in the Gulf of St. Lawrence are very sparse and in many districts are non-existent. On the south shore of the St. Lawrence and on the Gaspé peninsula, only short privately owned lines are now available, and from Gaspé to Seven Islands on the north shore of the St. Lawrence, no communication exists other than radio. The north shore of the St. Lawrence has only a single wire telegraph line and this is very unreliable, being repaired by whatever passerby notices the need. Similarly Anticosti Island telephone is run on a very haphazard system and, although many sightings of submarines have been reported by the inhabitants of this Island, they have often been too late to be of value in locating and attacking U-boats.[52]

The development of communications systems advanced almost as slowly as the recruiting of ADC volunteers. A statistical review of actual manning levels for 1942 and the proposed levels for 1943 reveals both serious geographical gaps and the level of perceived augmentation (see table 1).

The organizers faced regional problems. On Anticosti Island, for example, itself as large as the Province of Prince Edward Island, Eastern Air Command could expand no further as it had already recruited "all available civilians" for the ADC. Recruitment of volunteers in Newfoundland proved difficult "due to shortage of persons with sufficient knowledge to act as ADC observers." Shortage of volunteers on the strategically situated Magdalen and St Paul islands prevented a twenty-four-hour watch. Elsewhere a hapless naiveté predetermined the failure to recruit, although RCAF authorities prided themselves on their largesse in providing as few as two bilingual ADC officers "to maintain intensive coverage in the area" of Gaspé. While the ADC could in theory provide the Canadian military with otherwise unobtainable information, it frequently became an irritating source of spurious "enemy" Intelligence, which diverted military patrols. Such well-intentioned misinformation lay in the very nature of amateurism.

U-boat attacks during 1942 on Allied shipping in the Gulf and river, as will be seen in subsequent chapters, had awakened Canadian military authorities to the inadequacy of their defences. Indeed, they revealed the advantages that local waters offered a submarine, which could lie safely on the bottom in shallow waters. Shallows, rocky bottoms, temperature and salinity gradients shielded them from shipborne asdic and air-dropped sonobuoys. The latter were passive submarine detectors first tested by the U.S. Navy in March 1942.[53] On hitting the water after the air drop, the cylindrical 14-pound buoy automatically released a 21-foot cable bearing a hydrophone equipped with an omnidirectional antenna. Simultaneously, it extended the aerial of its transmitter in order to communicate data to the aircraft. Launched in numbers in the vicinity of the submerged submarine, it in theory provided the searching aircraft with a set of coordinates for locating its target. For purely technical reasons – susceptibility to background noise and unserviceability in any weather approaching a

TABLE 1
Recruiting of ADC Volunteers

	Strength December 1942	Proposed strength December 1943
Newfoundland	369	921
Cape Breton	187	519
Magdalen and St Paul islands	10	120
Nova Scotia and Northumberland Strait	428	1153
Prince Edward Island	953	2069
New Brunswick	892	1680
Gaspé Peninsula	1017	2436
Anticosti Island	35	35
St Lawrence River (north shore)	77	1110

fresh breeze (17–21 knots) and moderate waves – early models were at best of only marginal utility in normal North Atlantic conditions. This, coupled with the fact that the batteries could not produce identical power, created severe difficulties in the vital process of comparing the signal strengths of the buoys dropped in a pattern. The battery-powered buoy could last as long as four hours, whereupon the sonobuoy self-scuttled and sank. In short, the sonobuoy proved to be an ineffective detection device. The Germans could, of course, not know this, despite the fact that they had been warned of the technical innovation. The link for industrial intelligence was the commercial travellers' route between the United States and Switzerland frequented by a "reliable" German agent code-named "Boston," and described by German records as an "American engineer with the New York Shipbuilding Corporation."[54] The War Diary of the German Naval Staff reveals that "Boston's" accomplice and courier, an "English engineer with the Austin Motor Company Ltd," delivered rudimentary data and drawings of the sonobuoy on arrival in Switzerland on 20 August 1943.

Despite continued closure of the Gulf from October 1942 through 1943 (of which the enemy could be expected to know nothing), the Chiefs of Staff Subcommittee anticipated "enemy activities along our Atlantic coast and in the Gulf and river ... on an increased scale." It warned that "the enemy will vary his tactics." These might include "mining operations and shelling (gunfire) of shore installations." Captain E.S. Brand, director trade division, advised the St Lawrence Operations Conference on 22–24 February 1943 of the shipping forecast: he anticipated 3,695,000 tons of freight moving in 1223 voyages at a rate of 79 voyages per week.[55] In addition, he anticipated between fifty and seventy-five small schooners, of 100–400-tons carrying capacity each, transporting pulpwood and pulp to Rimouski, Port Alfred, Quebec, and Trois Rivières. The timber trade would require an additional twenty-two ships a month.

The navy's acceptance of the commitment of escorts for these ships hinged on factors it seemed unable to control: deliveries on schedule of newly constructed warships; the return of fifteen corvettes that had sailed in support of the North African campaign; the return of six corvettes sailing in support of U.S. convoys; and the return of two flotillas of MLs operating in the Caribbean.[56] The return to Canada of such vessels permitted reallocation of patrol vessels between the Western Local Escort Force, the Halifax Force, the Halifax Local Defence Force, and those assigned to Sydney, Shelburne, Newfoundland, Botwood, and Quebec.

Fortunately for Canadians, only five German U-boats would challenge coastal inshore defences in 1943. Four of these conducted clandestine missions. Still, the naval disposition proposed by Canadians by May 1943 revealed the effectiveness of Dönitz's doctrine of pinning down enemy forces that might have been deployed elsewhere.[57] For example, the Chiefs of Staff Committee proposed six corvettes for Quebec for the protection of CN–NL convoys between St John's, Newfoundland, and Sydney, Cape Breton Island, as well as between Quebec City and Labrador; five corvettes and eight Bangors for Sydney to cover QS–SQ convoys between Sydney and Quebec City; eight Bangors for Sydney for the Sydney–Port aux Basques ferries and for the SSC and SB convoys between Sydney and Cornerbrook; and eight Bangors and six MLs in St John's for WB–NJ convoys; the latter ran the Wabana–Sydney route, and transited the waters between St John's and ports on the east coast of Newfoundland and Labrador. Ferries in the Gut of Canso and the Northumberland Strait would be covered by MLs. The Botwood patrol of six motor launches and one base-supply vessel would also cover the Strait of Belle Isle.

The St Lawrence Operations Conference made the NOIC Gaspé responsible for "all offensive operations against U-Boats in the Gulf of St. Lawrence, for detailing supporting forces for threatened convoys, and for rerouting of convoys in his own subcommand."[58] It charged the Army with responsibility "for local protection and resistance against enemy raiding parties" and in conjunction with the RCMP and other police forces, "the detection and apprehension of suspicious persons." The RCAF would continue the ruse of coverage in force by deploying training aircraft at strategic locations. Those at Mont Joli would be available "as a striking force against U-Boats in the vicinity," while training aircraft from Charlottetown, Summerside, Debert, Greenwood, and Chatham would overfly their sections of the Gulf. Only those from the latter-named three bases would carry antisubmarine depth charges.

German submarines reported throughout the war that Canadian navigational lights and beacons operated entirely under peacetime conditions. This apparent laxity astonished submariners accustomed to the tightly controlled navigational conditions that existed in the hazardous waters of the European war zone. Even as late as 1945, when Kurt Dobratz's U-1232 attacked shipping off Halifax, for example, Canadian maritime conditions elicited the incredulity and sometimes even scornful criticism of U-boat commanders. Not only did captains like Dobratz, Hornbostel (U-806), and Reith (U-190) find all pilotage aids available to them, but Canadian radio beacons provided precise navigational data for pinpoint fixes: Dobratz's log records receiving Sable Island at a range of 150 miles; the East Halifax and Sambro lightships, Western Head and Seal Island at a range of 300 miles. All beacons, it noted, operated under peacetime conditions according to "Notice to Mariners no. 3668" (KTB). Canadian and American government radio stations provided him with accurate weather forecasts on which he came to rely. These in effect told him when he could plan an attack, and when he might just as well lie low. The free accessibility of such plain-language broadcasts, he recalls, struck him at the time as somewhat ridiculous. The whole Canadian maritime posture seemed to him much like "little Johnny playing at war games."

In fact, however, the navy in co-operation with the Department of Transport had as early as 1939 introduced a rational system for controlling lights, fog signals, and radio beacons along the Atlantic coast.[59] However inadequate, these preparations offered a degree of control unprecedented on the coast. The order for the "Extinction and Control of Navigational Aids on the East Coast" was familiarly known by its key signal "A for Apples." Issued on 8 November 1939 as "Instructions to Lightkeepers, Fog Alarm Operators and Radio Operators," it outlined two simple "battle states" or operating conditions in its eight coastal areas. These areas were, in numerical sequence: the Bay of Fundy up to the U.S. border; the Nova Scotia south coast; Canso, from Country Island Light to Louisburg; Cabot Strait, including Bird Rocks and the Magdalen Islands; the Gulf area; Strait of Belle Isle, including the west coast of Newfoundland; the lower St Lawrence and Anticosti; and Quebec, covering both shores as far as Bic Island. By agreement with the governor of Newfoundland on 28 March 1940, Naval Service Headquarters added areas 9 and 10 on contiguous waters. Two weeks later, on 11 April 1940, it added area 11 covering the east coast of Newfoundland.

Once military authorities had assessed the level of threat either to the coast as a whole, or to any one of these areas, so the plan explained, the navy would cause Radio Station CBA in Sackville, New Brunswick, to broadcast the appropriate instructions. As a precautionary principle, naval and transport authorities had instructed all operators to listen to Station CBA on 1050 kc (285.7 m) every four hours on the half hour beginning at 0330 hours Atlantic Standard Time, and at such other times as Station CBA might advise. The cue "Carry Out Instruction A for Apples" indicated that no threat to the coast was deemed to exist, and that normal operating conditions for lights, fog signals, and radio beacons prevailed. "Instruction B for Butter" meant that a threat existed and that therefore stations must "extinguish navigation lights and cease operating fog signals and radio beacons until further orders." "Instruction C for Charlie" cancelled B and reverted to normal peacetime conditions. The navy could send blanket instructions for the whole coast, or else, depending upon localized threats, specify A, B, or C for any of its numbered areas.

The first set of lighthouse instructions went into operation on 12 November 1939. They were modified throughout the war in order to allow greater flexibility. From 1940 onwards the Canadian Broadcasting Corporation (CBC) amplified instructions on behalf of defence authorities by broadcasting to lightkeepers from previously promulgated lists of random code words. In time these code words became known to many maritimers. Thus words from one such random list might have given rise to the seemingly senseless announcement that "fishermen near Lurcher Light Vessel burn many a meal." Its meaning: the Lurcher Light Vessel must switch off the radio beacon (code word "burn"), extinguish lights ("many"), and cease fog signals ("meal"). The instructions seem to have been tentative, or at least little used, for once the "Battle of the St Lawrence" had startled Canadians in the summer of 1942, the Commanding Officer Atlantic Coast in Halifax, Rear-Admiral G.C. "Jetty" Jones, RCN, reissued the orders with copies of all supporting documentation. His orders reminded all military commands and civilian authorities (Department of Transport, CBC Radio, and Station CJBR at Rimouski) of the instructions to be followed "should it be necessary at any time to extinguish navigational lights and/or aids." By 15 May 1944, the instructions provided for five different operating modes instead of the original two. Now, instead of turning lights, fog signals, and radio beacons either on or off as a group, it was possible to order their use in virtually any combination. One could, for example, order the extinguishing of all lights, but continue to operate fog signals, and radio beacons – or whatever variant seemed prudent under the circumstances.

Convinced that extinguishing or dimming lights would endanger both coastal and ocean-going shipping in treacherous coastal waters, Canadian authorities rigidly resisted imposition of the instructions except in brief instances triggered by close inshore attacks. The high incidence of groundings and collisions of Allied vessels despite full navigational aids suggests that the decision to maintain normal operations may have been correct. And in any event, reflection on the total situation suggests that navigational aids provided the Germans with very little real advantage. U-boats ultimately attacked relatively few convoys and sank few ships. Indeed, it seems likely that not a single life would have been saved had Canadians diverged from, or disrupted "peacetime" procedures in 1944–5.

Lights aided the enemy tactically as well as navigationally. They provided a backdrop against which merchantmen loomed large. This emerged as a primary concern when a high-level subcommittee of the Chiefs of Staff Committee in Ottawa pondered the potential dangers to shipping caused by the constant illumination in the St Lawrence River and Gulf. But not until 23 February 1943 did Canadian authorities consider the possibility of changing their practice. The Chiefs of Staff Subcommittee now delineated four priorities governing the extinguishing or dimming of navigational aids: (1) to prevent the silhouetting of ships in the beam of light; (2) to comply with local black-out regulations; (3) to deny a navigational aid to enemy submarines or surface ships; (4) to deny a navigational aid to enemy aircraft.

After careful consideration, the subcommittee endorsed the wisdom of providing sufficient permanently available navigation lights, with the proviso, however, that the visibility of no light should exceed five miles. A glance at a nautical chart of the Gulf area reveals at least twenty-eight major lights whose brilliance necessarily exceeded that range: for example, the pilot station at Pointe au Père; Pointe des Monts at the mouth of the St Lawrence; Bird Rocks and St Paul Island in Cabot Strait; Heath Point and South West Point on Anticosti Island; Cape Ray and Port aux Basques, Newfoundland. The subcommittee proposed that such lights, though dimmed to five miles visibility, should be provided with some form of communications whereby at short notice they could exhibit their beams at full brilliance. With muted self-irony the "committee did not consider that it could usefully suggest the particular means of communication" for such lights. As we have seen, nothing was available. For purely tactical reasons the subcommittee preferred dimming of lights to a controlled black-out. By suddenly switching on darkened lights in order to assist shipping as it comes within range, it argued, one "automatically advertises the presence of such shipping." By contrast, the Germans seem to have encountered no difficulties in operating their own controlled black-out system in home waters. Known as the wartime illumination measure (*Kriegsbefeuerungsmassnahme*), it permitted the controlled illumination of navigation beacons on the pre-designated close approach of friendly forces. Canadian authorities promulgated their dim-out on 10 May 1943. It applied to the whole shipping season, and was reissued at the beginning of the shipping season in 1944.[60]

The 1944 dim-out affected not only navigation lights in the Gulf and river, but also "a strip of land 5 miles deep on both shores of the St. Lawrence river and Gulf, extending on the north shore from the mouth of the Saguenay river to the Labrador boundary, and on the south shore from Ile Verte (Temiscouata) to Douglastown (Gaspé)." Its success required wide public support. To this end Naval Service Headquarters mounted a broad publicity campaign by means of posters, press, and radio. It issued an official proclamation of the rules and areas affected, and distributed pamphlets to mayors and parish priests. Minister for the Navy Angus Macdonald launched the information program with a press release on 1 May 1944. As reported on the front page of the *Montreal Daily Star* and others for that day, Mr Macdonald reflected the priorities of the Chiefs of Staff Committee. The navy had not designed the measure in order to increase the navigational difficulties of any "unwelcome visitor," he asserted; it was intended to squelch sky glow from towns and villages, and to prevent the silhouetting of ships. He anticipated the objection that, as no ships had been lost in the area during 1943, the enemy must therefore have withdrawn: the apparent absence of enemy forces "should not be taken to mean that no attempts were made to penetrate our defences." It was therefore "prudent" to be forearmed.

The seeming ineptitude of the Royal Canadian Navy and Air Force in killing U-boats had long disturbed Quebecers along the St Lawrence River and Gulf. Adverse press irritated the military who, for reasons of national security, could reveal nothing of their serious problems with equipment, nor the natural characteristics of Gulf waters, which favoured the attacking submarine. Angus Macdonald therefore felt obliged to caution Quebecers that, while naval and air force countermeasures would not relax, "the difficulties of anti-submarine warfare are such that submarines will not reappear in the St. Lawrence this year." U-boats did indeed reappear in the summer of 1944. Civilian co-operation was therefore more vital to national defence than ever before. It would, he explained, "ease the burden which rests upon the shoulders of the men in the fighting ships patrolling the St. Lawrence." The populace did not always respond.

The RCAF had in the meantime commenced construction of six microwave early warning antisubmarine stations in the Gulf and river. Designed to detect surfaced or schnorkelling submarines by means of surface radar scans, the units had been located so as to provide blanket surveillance of principal convoy and suspected U-boat routes.[61] Information and plots from these six stations would be passed into operations rooms at Gaspé, Halifax, and St John's, Newfoundland.[62] Authorities expected the net to be completed by 15 September 1944. By 24 July 1944, Operational Research had completed its analysis of proposals to create "an anti–U-Boat barrier in Cabot Strait" consisting of radar and asdic patrols.[63] It rejected the idea of employing Fairmiles as the task required a large number of vessels: four for every hour that the barrier was maintained, each one sailing about 170 miles. Aircraft seemed the only solution. Based on the mathematical probability of sighting a U-boat as a function of its transit time on the surface, the researchers found Canso flying boats to be 40 per cent effective over one hour of patrol and Liberator bombers 75 per cent effective. Thus "the greatest efficiency is obtained by the use of Liberators," provided that half the aircraft were equipped for night flying. Only this way could the barrier function effectively. The RCAF commenced modified barrier patrols when U-541 sank SS *Livingstone* off Scatarie Island in September 1944, the month that the microwave net was completed.

The summer and fall of 1944, as will be seen in subsequent chapters, saw further U-boat intrusions into the Gulf, though indeed these did not constitute particularly serious threats. When the shipping season opened again in 1945 the Cabinet War Committee assessed the situation and formulated policy for the future use of St Lawrence ports.[64] The dark mood the minutes reflect had doubtless been deepened by such recent U-boat successes as U-806 (Hornbostel) sinking HMCS *Clayoquot* near the Sambro lightship on Christmas Eve 1944, and by U-1232 (Dobratz) sinking ships out of convoy BX-141 as they sailed single file past Chebucto Head in January 1945. Thus the Minister for the Navy conceded the necessity of using "the St. Lawrence River route for shipments overseas to a greater extent," a decision that "would entail additional strain on the Canadian Navy." He expected Dönitz to be consistent in concentrating "a considerable amount of his U-Boat activity in the Gulf and lower reaches of the river." This perceived threat forced C-in-C CNA to reallocate already thinly deployed vessels to Gulf defence. The Quebec Force would consist of two corvettes; the Gaspé Force of two corvettes, one Bangor minesweeper (for escort duties) and two M/L Fairmile flotillas; the Sydney Force of three corvettes, ten Bangors, three Western Isles Bangors, one Western Isles trawler, two M/L flotillas, and one depot ship; and the St Pierre Force of three French Fairmiles.[65]

German penetration of the virtually defenceless Belle Isle Strait in the summer of 1942 (see chapter two), had awakened Canadian authorities to their vulnerability here as well. As the staff officer (plans) in NSHQ recollected, "Germans are a methodical people and somewhat bound by precedent [and] there is good reason to suppose they will attempt to repeat the performance during 1943."[66] The Germans in fact never bothered with the unfruitful Strait again. None the less, not until 22 July 1943 did Canadian naval authorities issue the first Belle Isle Force operation order. Issued by FONF as "BIF 1," it allocated the supply ship HMCS *Preserver*, the Bangor HMCS *Trois Rivières*, and four Fairmiles to joint operations with thirteen Catalina aircraft of 116 Squadron at Botwood under the control of No. 1 Group RCAF at St John's, Newfoundland. The plan called for the naval force to undertake antisubmarine duties from Red Bay, Labrador. Towing a 20-ton water barge and escorted by Fairmiles, HMCS *Preserver* arrived at Red Bay on 2 August after a foggy passage enlivened by a near collision with an iceberg that the escort's radar did not detect.[67] *Preserver* was moored so as to permit her after 4.5-inch gun to command the bay's entrance. The escorts encountered further difficulties on 10 August when Fairmiles 054 and 055 suffered a head-on collision while carrying out a patrol.[68] Sixteen convoys and several independent vessels passed through the patrol zone during the four months of the BIF 1 operations. The Fairmiles were found "not suitable for patrol service in the Straits of Belle Isle" because the peculiar combination of wind and current in the area could make the sea sufficiently confused to prevent asdic reception on the small ships' primitive equipment.[69] The rigid asdic, which could only "sweep" when the whole ship turned back and forth through the arc to be searched, had to be lowered by hand using an old-fashioned block and tackle.

The "Belle Isle Force Operation Order" for 1944 showed little change. Issued on 10 June 1944 as "BIF 2," it anticipated U-boats entering or leaving the Gulf via the Strait and contemplated the possibility of their laying mines.[70] Otherwise the scenario and players remained much the same: HMCS *Preserver*, one Bangor, and this time six Fairmiles instead of the equally unsuitable four. Air support was tentative, for the air force could only rely upon such aircraft as might become available in the course of events. Although the navy could not assure the services of a minesweeper for constant sweeping, despite the perceived threat, BIF 2 expressed the fond hope that "at the first indication of minelaying, it is anticipated one will be sent immediately." Just where it would come from, no one knew. For, even at the opening of navigation in 1945, C-in-C CNA could allocate nothing more than a Fairmile patrol for the Strait.[71] Pressing naval commitments elsewhere thus forced maritime defences in coastal waters into an ad hoc and somewhat haphazard stance. Indeed, until the cessation of hostilities, the inshore operational perspective would remain much as described in January 1943 by the Chiefs of Staff Subcommittee: "the plans of the three Services for the defence of the Gulf and River St. Lawrence ... are the best that can be devised with the forces and facilities which are expected to be available and are contingent upon other commitments not being permitted to interfere." The operative phrase in this confession ("the best that can be devised") was of course crucial. The necessarily secondary priority of maritime defence in home waters cast naval officers back upon their own makeshift resources to invent and to contrive. Even as late as 1945 the allocation of additional vessels would depend on "the course of naval warfare against Germany" in distant waters, and as judged by foreign, though friendly, powers.[72] Then, as now, independent policies seemed impossible.

CHAPTER TWO

Operation Drumbeat

"War Comes to Nova Scotia." 94 Lives Believed Lost in Torpedoing off Coast." With these words the *Montreal Daily Star* for 13 January 1942 announced the first wave of German U-boats that pressed close to home waters. The East Coast of Canada had long been familiar with the Battle of the Atlantic, and Canadian newspapers had long been reporting incidents of enemy "treachery" on the high seas and in European battle zones. But the war had always seemed to be waged in distant waters and near distant shores. U-123, a type IXB U-boat under the command of Kapitänleutnant Hardegen, was thus the first of the twelve German submarines operating from the Newfoundland Bank to Nova Scotia in mid January 1942 to awaken the Canadian public to a growing maritime threat. It would have taken a drumbeat (*Paukenschlag*, the German code word for Admiral Dönitz's strategic advance off the North American coast) to alter Canadian perspective on what many Canadians had regarded up to now as a foreign war. Symptomatic of this attitude, opinions in both the public and the government were divided on a variety of national issues. In Parliament itself, in some respects as isolationist as the United States, acrimonious debate prevailed on whether or not to conscript for overseas service. U-123 off Canada's Atlantic coast crystallized an issue to which U-553 would attract attention with unexpected persuasive power a couple of months later in the St Lawrence River.

Admiral Dönitz had long anticipated open hostilities with the United States, but had wanted them on his own terms and with clear U-boat superiority. Prior to Paukenschlag, German forces had assiduously avoided maritime conflict with the U.S. Direct instructions from Hitler to this effect were strictly adhered to even though the Americans' posture of "belligerent neutrality" had often verged on open conflict. Dönitz was now caught in an internal struggle concerning the strategic priorities of deploying his U-boats. Hitler feared an Allied invasion of Norway and insisted on deploying the U-boats defensively off the Norwegian coast. Not fearing such an invasion at this time, the German Naval Staff argued for defensive deployment in the Mediterranean and off Gibraltar. Dönitz insisted in vain that U-boats were primarily offensive weapons that should now be in place off the North American coast. As it turned out, German persistence in keeping U-boats massed near Gibraltar would jeopardize the opening phases of war against North America.[1] In any event, Dönitz had requested of his superiors "timely warning" of any strategic shift in target areas in order, as he recalled, "to enable me to have my forces in position off the American coast before war was actually declared. It was only in this way, I pointed out, that full advantage could be taken of the element of surprise to strike a real blow in waters in which antisubmarine defences were still weak."[2] This time, however, it was Hitler and his staff who were caught completely off guard by a surprise attack; not by the Americans, but by the Japanese. Without prior consultation with their Axis partners, the Japanese attacked Pearl Harbor on 7 December 1941 – at which time not a single U-boat was in North American waters – thus precipitating America's declaration of war and forcing Hitler's hand before he was ready. On 9 December 1941 Hitler lifted all previous restrictions on U-boat warfare against American shipping and in the Pan American security zone.

If Germany had been caught by surprise and momentarily disadvantaged by the entrance of the United States into the Atlantic conflict, its Commander U-boats (BdU) saw at least certain short-term benefits on which he intended to capitalize despite his tactical unpreparedness to wage submarine warfare on the grand scale he would have wished. The activities of the U-boats had been increasingly constrained in the North Atlantic and European theatres by the two years of wartime experience during which "the English" as Dönitz noted in his War Diary of 2 January 1942, had developed techniques and technology. The opening of the North American coast to belligerent operations now "provided commanders with areas which are not hemmed in by defences and which offer better chances of success" (KTB). Dönitz was clearly counting not only on the relative inexperience of Canadian and American defence forces, but on the spirit of isolationism that had marked both countries despite their support of Britain's war against Germany. To Dönitz's mind, it was imperative to "take advantage of the situation before changes are made."[3]

Convinced of the strengths of the convoy system, of its ability to concentrate forces of escorts and "hunter-killer" support groups around a large body of merchant ships that under ideal conditions could literally roll over the opposing U-boats, Dönitz aimed at preventing convoys from ever forming. To this end, he designated as his principal targets "single ships so that no mass movements" would be possible. On 9 January 1942, he had distributed the first attack areas: U-66, U-123, and U-125 were assigned the east coast of the United States; U-109 and U-130 the east coast of Canada.[4] Travelling along great circle routes, however, all the U-boats would cut through Canadian war zones. With these first Boats, Dönitz's War Diary of 9 January 1942 records, Gruppe Paukenschlag was born. On 11 January, Dönitz noted his commitment of five boats to the area between Sydney, Nova Scotia, and Cape Hatteras. He deemed the VIIC Boat best suited for "the area south of Newfoundland where we can expect greatest traffic and least defence of enemy ships" (KTB). He committed the next four U-boats, the long-range IXC, to Trinidad-Aruba. He thus hoped to attack at their sources the principal Atlantic trade routes, and to pin down at these points escorts and defensive forces that might otherwise be used by the Allies in close support of the war in Europe. Dönitz's principal concern lay with diverting Allied strength from the possible invasion of Norway that Germany feared. "The greater our submarine successes in the Atlantic," he observed, "the less the enemy will even be able to think about preparing such operations."[5] Events were to prove to Dönitz that U-boats off the coasts of Canada and the United States could "be successful much longer than was expected."[6] Yet even by the end of January 1942, Dönitz's War Diary reveals a distinct sense of urgency despite his obvious elation about the voluminous tonnage sunk in the face of feeble defences. "This situation," he wrote, "must be taken advantage of with as many Boats as possible before defence measures are strengthened and convoy systems are taken up."[7]

How many U-boats were possible? On paper Dönitz's resources during Paukenschlag amounted to 259.[8] In fact, however, his resources were considerably less, for 99 of them were still undergoing trials. Of the remaining 160 U-boats, 59 were assigned to the training squadrons. This in itself reflects the very high priority given to training commitments, which always claimed a major proportion of all available U-boats throughout the war. This left 101 U-boats on "active service." Of these, 35 were in port for repairs, leaving only 66 at sea. Now, an operational commander's primary strength lies with those of his units on active duty in the designated operational or target areas. Of these 66 submarines "at sea," therefore, 18 were returning home either low on fuel, out of torpedoes, or damaged; 23 were outbound to operational areas for which fuel and weapons must be conserved; 1 was bound for the Mediterranean, the others for the Atlantic.

Thus Dönitz's fighting strength at sea on 1 January 1942 was a mere 25 U-boats: 3 on station in the Arctic, 6 in the Mediterranean, and 16 in the North Atlantic. And of these 16, no less than 7 were on "Norwegian operations" either off Sydesfjord, or Reykjavik, or northwest of the Hebrides; three were operating in the Atlantic west of Gibraltar, guarding the access to and from the Mediterranean. This left, his War Diary notes, "Six Boats operating off the Coast of America." Assessing his priorities for follow-up support of ongoing operations, Dönitz now designated 12 of the outbound Boats, consisting of one type IXB minelayer, one type IXC, and ten type VIIC "as second wave in the attack area St. John's, Halifax, or with the Type IX Boats as far as Cape Hatteras." The lowest number of Boats actually on duty in their operational areas occurred during the period 3–9 January: 3 Boats, all of them in the Mediterranean. The highest number occurred on 23–24 January: 22 Boats, of which 10 were operating off North America between St John's, Newfoundland, and Cape Hatteras.[9]

Operational figures for the period January–February 1942 show how little leeway was available to the German Naval Staff. Exigencies would always arise that demanded utmost flexibility. U-boats sometimes had to be diverted from assigned tasks in response to emergencies, as in searching for survivors of German vessels or downed aircraft. Dönitz's signed statement of priorities caused sharp differences of opinion in U-boat command, characteristic of the prevailing constraints and tensions: "Under present conditions every drop of fuel is vital for the Boats, if they are to maintain sufficient operational freedom in distant ... areas. It may well happen that a request for help will have to be refused for the sake of operational duties."[10] Not until the period between 16 and 25 December 1941 could the first U-boats slip out of their French bases in order to take up position at "the site of our first offensive, the area between the St. Lawrence and Cape Hatteras."[11] Dönitz set the date of "the first combined surprise attack" for 13 January 1942.[12]

Unknown to Dönitz, however, Britain's Government Code and Cipher School (better known as Bletchley Park) could decipher his Enigma signals to the German fleet.[13] This enabled the Operational Intelligence Centre under Commander Rodger Winn, RNVR, to maintain constant plots of U-boat deployment in order to vector convoys around the "packs." Vessels sailing independently – and this included most shipping along the North American coast – had to cope as best they could. Winn's Intelligence Summary for the week ending 12 January highlighted "the most striking feature" of the U-boat operations in the Atlantic: "a heavy concentration off the North American seaboard from New York to Cape Race," Newfoundland. Not only did he know the precise numbers of U-boats in each group; he also stipulated that "five U-Boats will reach their attacking areas by 13 January."[14] The attack would not be a surprise. Twelve boats would ultimately form a hunting line from the Grand Banks southwestward. Only two of them, U-552 and U-155, would survive the war.

Had Admiral Dönitz been permitted from the very beginning to develop his U-boat arm as the primary weapon of Germany's maritime strength, and had his torpedo experts come to grips with the prodigious number of torpedo failures, the striking power of German underseas warfare would have been overwhelming.[15] It might even have won the war. As it was, however, Dönitz still had reason to find the results of this first wave of Paukenschlag most "gratifying"[16] (see tables 2 and 3).

Technically speaking, Topp's U-552 did not belong to the Paukenschlag wave, but to Gruppe Ziethen, consisting of twelve VIIC Boats that operated from 8 January to 12 February to seaward of Paukenschlag.[17] But such were the dynamics and flow of Dönitz's tactical control that new groups formed, dissolved, and re-formed as quickly as circumstances required, and without administrative hindrance. Another group of IXC Boats operated further south off the U.S. coast. Two of them, U-106 and U-107, eventually moved northwards into Canadian waters.

The first of the Paukenschlag U-boats to reach Canadian waters was Kapitänleutnant Hardegen's U-123. It had left the security of the U-boat bunkers of Lorient, France, on 23 December 1941, and thus began its seventh operational mission. Only after departure did he open his sealed orders and learn his destination. This was standard procedure. By 24 December he was shaping his course over a great circle route towards Nantucket, a route that would take him through all six of the primary operational areas in the Atlantic. The most dangerous sector was passage through the Bay of Biscay. Allied air superiority had been pressing the German submarines with such consistency and severity that attacks always seemed imminent. It was a hazardous stretch of "no man's land" at the beginning and end of every cruise that had to be negotiated with utmost caution: submerged by day and surfaced at night. Many U-boats never survived. On this Christmas Eve, U-123 ran the Biscay gauntlet submerged. Hardegen, who frequently lent personal perspective to his War Diary, noted that day:

U-boat Christmas in the Biscay. Trees were set up in all compartments, decorated by the crew and covered with electric lights. Later the genuine firs were partly replaced by artificial trees. After a communal celebration and concluding meal, letters, packages and bags [of treats] were handed out. There were celebrations in individual spaces, and you could hear people singing the old Christmas carols. For a few hours this simple and impressive Christmas made us forget the war. (KTB)

By month's end, U-123 had covered 1245 nautical miles, only 41 of them submerged. At this stage of the war, German U-boats were technically speaking only "diving boats," and were not yet actual submarines capable of the underwater endurance that technological advances like the

TABLE 2

Paukenschlag: First Wave, 12–21 January 1942

U-boat	Type	Ships sunk	Torpedoed but not sunk	Sunk (tons)
U-123 (Hardegen)	IXB	9	1 (8206 tons)	53,173
U-130 (Kals)	IXC	6	1 (6986 tons)	36,992
U-66 (Zapp)	IXC	5	–	33,456
U-109 (Bleichrodt)	IXC	5	–	33,733
U-125 (Folkers)	IXC	1	–	5,666
U-552 (Topp)	VIIC	2	–	6,722
U-203 (Mützelburg)	VIIC	2	1 (888 tons)	1,977
U-86 (Schug)	VIIB	1	1 (8627 tons)	4,271

TABLE 3

Paukenschlag: First Wave Support, 8 January–12 February 1942

U-boat	Type	Ships sunk	Torpedoed but not sunk	Sunk (tons)
U-103 (Winter)	IXC	4	–	26,539
U-106 (Rasch)	IXC	5	–	42,139
U-107 (Gelhaus)	IXC	2	–	10,850
U-108 (Scholtz)	IXC	5	–	20,082
U-128 (Heyse)	IXC	3	–	27,312

schnorkel would help them achieve by 1944. It was 31 December 1941: "New Year in the North Atlantic. The Boat can look back to a successful year, and all of us move confidently into the new year, hoping for new successes which will contribute to the decision" (KTB). The decision (*die Entscheidung*) meant nothing less than the decisive victory of German forces which they expected that year.

Four days after Hardegen (U-123) had departed his French base, Bleichrodt's U-109 left the Isere docks in Lorient in company with Kals' U-130. BdU had marked U-109 for Atlantic combat, while U-130 had, at first, other duties. Its task as weathership in the North Atlantic augured little likelihood of tactical success. Yet a sequence of operational changes in the Atlantic Boats was to move it and others, like valuable chess pieces, into positions that had not yet been tried. On 2 January 1942, Kals received a message from the Commander U-boats directing Hardegen (U-123) and Zapp (U-66) to move into naval quadrant CB 60, 500 miles south of Nova Scotia, and for Bleichrodt (U-109), Lüth (U-43), and himself to advance to the meridian of naval quadrant BC 5889 (45° 15′ W). The Commander U-boats plotted the dead reckoning positions of his Boats, signalled them on successive days, and on 8 January 1942 assigned specific operational areas off the North American coast. He melded his U-boats into a new tactical unit: Group Drumbeat.

A low-pressure trough had been settling over the Atlantic during the final days of December 1941, causing shifting hurricane force winds and violent, confused seas. Pounded, wracked, and twisted by the increasing fury of the storm, surfaced U-boats felt paradoxically secure as a cork in a tempest. Heavy stern seas would roll right over conning towers, surge along the pressure hull, loft the whole Boat, and toss the "iron coffin" from the crests. Under such conditions, the officer of the watch and his look-outs withstood the debilitating rage of the elements alone. Fastened by safety harnesses in the open conning tower with the watertight hatch battened down securely beneath their feet, they rode their storm-tossed "bath tub," as they affectionately called the U-boat's bridge, for four bone-chilling hours until relieved. Bigalk, in U-751, following close behind in the second wave, recorded powerful breakers crashing over the conning tower, tearing his bridge watchmen against their harnesses. Engines ran slow ahead to conserve fuel, while the bridge watch up top rode the wildly tossing U-boat. In the stale, twisting, and yawing spaces below decks, half the crew worked while the other half tried to rest. And so the days without combat passed: watch on, watch off. Only the bridge watch left the confines of the "narrow tube," as submariners sometimes called their boat. Heavy headseas now drastically reduced the U-boats' advance over the ground. On 5 January 1942, U-109's War Diary noted: "Barometer falling markedly and fast." Foam-streaked towering waves twisting in spume from the direction of the wind toppled wave crests and tumbled violently into contorted troughs.

This same storm was mauling the final SC convoy of the season, the twenty-nine-ship SC-34, which had departed Sydney for the United Kingdom on 9 January 1942. Heavy weather damage forced seven of the ships into St John's, Newfoundland.[18] The destroyers HMCS *Skeena*, *Saguenay*, and *Ottawa* of the Newfoundland Escort Force (NEF) were so severely damaged that they had to be withdrawn for extensive repairs. This left the NEF with only four operational destroyers. In the words of the operations officer, FONF, the NEF had "never been in such low water" before.[19] The RCN would have few resources when instituting the first coastal convoy on 16 January: often as little as one Bangor minesweeper per convoy. Eastern Air Command flew 294 patrols in January, covering 686 ships in convoy "under the most trying and adverse weather conditions."[20] The command could none the less boast that both "RCAF and US aircraft were instrumental in the location and eventual rescue of several groups of survivors from vessels." In response to what Eastern Air Command correctly described as "an unprecedented rise in enemy submarine activity along the Eastern Atlantic Coast," the RCAF escalated its patrol commitments. These comprised not only patrols of the approaches to defended ports, but antisubmarine patrols and sweeps as well. The 294 patrols in January increased to 332 in February, 540 in March, and 665 in April 1942.

The first five U-boats to reach the eastern seaboard of Canada and the United States in "Drumbeat" attacked coastal shipping from mid January until the end of the first week in February with great success. After the intense combat conditions of the European theatre, submariners now met an unwary enemy, seemingly innocent of the conditions of war. Cities were fully illuminated, navigational aids such as buoys, beacons, lighthouses, and radio beacons were operating under peacetime conditions, ships ran frequently undarkened and alone, escorts were light and inexperienced. Coastal traffic tended to hug the shore under the misapprehension that U-boats feared the shallows. And the U-boats lurked in the shallows precisely because they knew they were not expected. Kapitänleutnant Hardegen of U-123 noted in his War Diary just how great his opportunities actually were:

The night of the long knives was over. A drumbeat (*Paukenschlag*) with eight ships, among them three tankers with 53,860 GRT. A real shame that in the night off New York there weren't besides me two large minelaying U-boats to plaster the place with mines; and tonight ten to twenty subs instead of just me. I'm sure they'd all have taken their fill. I have seen something like twenty steamers, some partially darkened, and a couple of tramps as well. All were hugging the shore. (KTB).

Again, he found the 600-m emergency band an invaluable tactical and navigational resource, for he could not only monitor shipping traffic, but also learn of such things as the withdrawal of lightships and the characteristics of the buoys that replaced them. The amount of shipping dropped drastically after the first sinkings and then – he added a line that the German Naval War Staff later elided – "All the private telegram traffic of Jews going to sea ceased."[21] Though Hardegen would be the first of the Paukenschlag commanders to brief Dönitz personally on operations in the unfamiliar North American zone, intelligence that the admiral's staff had extrapolated from cryptic signals anticipated the thrust of his remarks. As BdU observed: "The expectation of encountering many independently routed ships; clumsy handling of ships; feeble, inexperienced sea and air patrols and defences; was so truly fulfilled that conditions had to be described as almost completely of peacetime standard. *Independent* operations by submarines were therefore correct."[22] In this light, "wolf packs" would never be necessary in Canadian waters.

Ten days before the designated surprise attack, Hardegen grasped an opportunity for combat without betraying his position. Though he failed to engage on this occasion, it illustrates the manner in which U-boats exploited commercial and emergency radio frequencies. Standing some 450 miles east of Cape St Francis, Newfoundland, on 3 January he intercepted a Halifax broadcast advising the storm-battered, apparently rudderless *Dimitrios Inglessis* that a rescue vessel would be dispatched. She was one of two seriously weather-damaged vessels from convoy SC-63. BdU in Germany also intercepted the message, which he relayed to Hardegen with permission to attack. *Dimitrios*'s persistent plain-language emergency broadcasts gave approximate latitude and longitude, and provided a clear homing signal to both rescuer and enemy alike. In time, Hardegen monitored three-way transmissions between St John's radio, the rescue tug *Foundation Franklin*, and the anxious *Dimitrios*.[23] Then followed revealing broadcasts between *Franklin* and *Dimitrios* arranging the rendezvous and discussing details of recovery and towing procedure. All the while Hardegen fixed his own precise position by the radio beacons of Cape Race and St John's. Throughout the day U-123 was led by these signals; it noted "heavy [radio] traffic on the 600 m band," and overheard the victim's position report as "vicinity of Virgin Rocks" (KTB). This is the most dangerous topographical feature on the Grand Banks – a rocky ledge situated 95 miles east of Cape Race with a least depth of 14 feet over a small pinnacle rock.

Advancing on the surface that night through fog with its gun crew at action stations, U-123 heard the fog signals of two ships groping towards *Dimitrios*. He burst upon victim and rescuer passing lines while chattering on the intercom, only to find himself squared off against an unannounced "destroyer" at a range of a mere 100 m. As in other attacks, fog formed Canada's front-line defence. Undetected, he withdrew so as not to jeopardize his primary mission. Hardegen's later success would indeed justify his caution and restraint. He operated with daring and finesse close inshore with at times as little as 11 m under his keel, scarcely enough to cover his conning tower if he had needed to dive. "That would have been a sobering thought if I had attacked the destroyer with cannonfire," Hardegen recorded (KTB). His War Diary provides the sole record of what might have been the first U-boat attack in the Canadian operational zone.

Hardegen's U-123 sank the first victim of Paukenschlag in Canadian waters at 0148 GMT on 12 January 1942. This was his twenty-fifth victim of the war. Tentatively identified by means of photographs as a 10,000 tonner of the Blue Funnel Line (Holt Shipping), the 9076-ton SS *Cyclops* had left Panama with general cargo on 2 January en route to Halifax under the command of Captain Lesley Webber Kersley. Only the previous evening Kersley had intercepted the "SSS" (submarine sighting signal) of an anxious merchantman and had decided that danger was imminent. Following his sailing orders, issued by the Allied Naval Authority, he steered his darkened ship along evasive courses at full speed. Now zigzagging at 9 knots along the Boston–Halifax route, the *Cyclops* was completely unaware of the U-boat's presence. Having first sighted the vessel's smoke on the horizon, Hardegen moved into the classical frontal attack position in the twilight of a winter's evening.

Running in from ahead through darkness and mist, Hardegen made three attack approaches until a single torpedo smashed into the deep tank near the *Cyclops*'s starboard propeller from 1500 m. This was twice the range he would have liked. A dark, glowing blast column marked the hit as the ship settled deeply aft with flooded engine room. The explosion had also knocked one of the DEMS naval gunners overboard, commencing a dramatic sequence of events that his mates witnessed with horror as they watched him struggle in the water at the foot of the port ladder.

The vessel's senior radio officer, R.P. Morrison, had been on watch when the torpedo exploded, and directly executed the Master's Standing Orders by transmitting the "SSS" distress message. Hearing no repetition by any coastal station, he assumed technical failure and rebroadcast the alarm on the emergency transmitter on the boat deck. *Cyclops*'s signals had not gone unheeded, although the lines of communication were by no means direct. Radio Charleston (North Carolina) first passed her call via Boston to Dockyard Halifax, during which time both Radio Thomaston and the Canadian Naval Radio Station at Camperdown sought clarification and attempted to obtain bearings. Naval Operations Halifax diverted the Bangors HMCS *Burlington* and *Red Deer* to the scene, while Eastern Air Command scrambled a patrol. Despite his extreme range, Hardegen machine-gunned the vessel's deckhouse in order to stop the transmissions. The freighter's slanting decks prevented her from bringing her own gun to bear even though Hardegen watched her gunners clearing for action. Fearing "a gun duel," Hardegen fired the coup de grâce from 600 m at the port side, just forward of the bridge. Some of *Cyclops*'s crew had by this time climbed down the port ladder to reach the helpless gunner who had been toppled overboard. Scarcely had a look-out yelled from the mast that another torpedo was heading for the ship, than the would-be rescuers scambled up the ladder, leaving the gunner to take the full brunt of the torpedo, which ripped through him into the port side of the ship. A huge black and white blast column marked the point of impact as the deeply laden vessel broke in half. Her boilers and a quantity of ammunition then exploded with such intensity that the survivors feared they were being attacked by a raider.

Hardegen departed in haste for the U.S. coast. In a desolate scene repeated almost daily throughout the war, five lifeboats and eighteen rafts wallowed in the dark, filled with many wounded and dying men. Of the 181 persons aboard, only the medical officer and the ill-fated gunner had actually been lost with the ship. The other eighty-six casualties were to die from exposure in icy seas that crashed over the gunwhales and froze to their clothing during more than twenty hours adrift. Marine Gunner J.D.G. Green later reported drifting on a raft with eight crewmen: two died of exposure during the night, and two more in the morning. A Canadian survivor, 19-year-old Midshipman L.J. Hughes of Vancouver, described a similar ordeal: "Some of the dead men we pushed overboard. The others we kept to give us some shelter against the cold and the water which sprayed across the bows."24 So great was the relief of DEMS Gunner Green on being rescued that his affidavit recorded being "picked up by the cruiser that had been sent for rescue work." The "cruiser" – such ships were 8800-ton, heavily armed vessels, 585 feet in length – was actually the 672-ton, 180-foot-long Bangor minesweeper, HMCS *Red Deer*, which an RCAF Catalina flying boat had vectored to their aid. The minesweeper would perhaps never look so large again. After operations off the United States coast and a journey of 8277 nautical miles (only 256 of them submerged), Hardegen's U-123 arrived safely at its home base in Lorient, France, on 9 February 1942. In BdU's assessment, it was a "well-planned and executed mission with excellent results" (KTB).

Newspaper coverage of this first sinking reached the Canadian public almost immediately. It provided photographs of survivors, stylized maps, and substantive (though scant) operational details. Significantly, the more dramatic reports appeared in the Quebec anglophone press. Canadian authorities were at this point not so much concerned with withholding intelligence on "Drumbeat" from the enemy, as with rallying Canadian opinion (and perhaps even manpower). But if the sensationalism of this first U-boat attack "close to home" merited front-page prominence, the subsequent press commentary by the Hon. Angus L. Macdonald, Minister for the Navy, rated but a back-page column. The presence of U-boats from Cape Race to the U.S., he argued, signified not so much a strategic or tactical shift of German interest in Canada as such; America's declaration of war had merely removed the political obstacles before which Germany had previously balked. He then enunciated a principle of censorship and press restraint that was to be repeated throughout the war years: nothing would be published that could possibly provide the enemy with information about his attacks against Allied shipping; and nothing would be reported publicly about Allied attacks against enemy submarines. The principle was often observed in the breach.

By 13 Jauary 1942, Kapitänleutnant Topp (U-552) had reached a position of 55 miles south of Cape Race on the Avalon Peninsula. Kapitänleutnant Bleichrodt (U-109) had gained the most southerly tip of the Canadian zone some 210 miles south of the Grand Banks of Newfoundland. Kapitänleutnant Kals (U-130) was approaching his designated position in Cabot Strait. At about this time, BdU intercepted SOS signals from several ships south of Halifax to the effect that the SS *Evita*, *Dvinoles*, and *Tintagel* had collided while manoeuvring in convoy HX-169 outbound from Halifax.[25] Apparently not having realized how much the heavy weather had deflected his U-boats from the dead reckoning tracks of his plotting room, he directed them in successive messages to the easy prey. All declined the option as they wished to fulfil their immediate missions. In any event, the range was too great. Kals's U-130, for example, was by noon on 12 January patrolling 48 miles east of Scatarie Island in Cabot Strait where he wished to remain. It was a cautious plan in a quiet war zone, one indeed that must have lulled the crew into a false sense of security. When the first air attack occurred, Kals noted bitterly, the U-boat's "look-out wasn't paying attention." A low-flying Bolingbroke 9063 of 119 (BR) Squadron in Sydney – that Kals's observers could only describe as a "very fast twin-engined monoplane" (KTB) – spotted him 4 miles off, hull awash and conning tower clearly visible. Dropping from 700 feet to 200 feet, it dive-bombed Kals with two 250-pound charges.[26] The bombs exploded beyond lethal range as U-130 crash-dived and escaped. Five more aircraft (a couple of which Kals himself subsequently spotted) soon converged on the zone without raising any sign of enemy or wreckage.

Close after midnight GMT on 13 January, Kals's first target hove into view, just in time for him to "attack on the first drumbeat" (KTB). The tactical designator Paukenschlag had become for him a vivid symbol. At 0116 on a dark night with good visibility, some 44 miles northeast of Scatarie Island in Cabot Strait, U-130 approached its 12-knot target at a broad angle and fired from 1200 m. The torpedo ran for 72 seconds and struck the Norwegian steamer *Frisco* forward of the bridge. Only then did Kals "recognize a tanker of about 6000 tons whose deep-laden forepart could not be distinguished against the dark horizon" (KTB). At first the tanker seemed to show no effects whatever, except for its spontaneous wireless activity, which hastened its end. For because of their proximity to land and support forces, Kals could neither wait for her to sink nor suffer her radio transmissions. His coup de grâce ran for 28 seconds (430 m) and struck the vessel abaft the bridge. The after part of the ship burst into flames, which quickly spread to the midship tanks. The vessel was soon engulfed in "harsh flames" that remained visible over two hours later. U-130 had long since slipped off to the southeast to signal its success to BdU, but with a cautionary note: "Heavy air cover. I've been seen" (KTB). BdU confirmed receipt.

The early morning hours of the first day of Drumbeat offered ideal visual conditions for attack in the Cabot Strait. Just before dawn, Kals sighted the SS *Friar Rock* heading towards Sydney. She had sailed eight hours behind her Quebec–Sydney convoy in the hope of catching up. The next minutes placed Kals in the classical frontal attack position ahead of his lone 10-knot quarry. With a broad angle on the bow, Kals's first torpedo ran for 54 seconds (840 m) and struck below the forward cargo hatch. A second torpedo failed. Then, while his victim lay dead in the water, Kals rendered a calculated coup de grâce that ran for 37 seconds (370 m) and struck between bridge and funnel. It "stood on its head and thundered into the depths" (KTB) as a large layer of oil spread over the surface of the sea. Kals now moved off past illuminated fishing boats that formed a peaceful contrast to the destructive violence just past. Wisdom dictated that he withdraw temporarily from the Sydney–Cape Race route. Not until the afternoon of 17 January did HMS *Montgomery*, en route from St John's to Halifax, come upon seven survivors in a lifeboat, together with the bodies of twelve who had perished in the bitter cold.[27] Survivors reported that two lifeboats with nineteen men each had been launched, but one of them had capsized. They reported further incidents that do not coincide with Kals's War Diary. For instance, that "the U-boat had approached their [life]boat and fired either [a] torpedo or gun at them."

The German radio monitoring and cryptographic service (*B-Dienst*), the counterpart of the more successful Bletchley Park, had meanwhile informed BdU on the basis of Allied communications that several troop transports were gathering at St John's harbour. BdU relayed the information to both Topp (U-552) and Schug (U-86). On 14 January temperatures dropped dramatically to around 10° C below zero, causing heavy icing of periscopes and antennae as Topp advanced along the Avalon Peninsula of Newfoundland. Aircraft sightings marked his landfall. Numerous hydrophone echoes led past a disappointing series of fishing vessels until a prime target drew into its periscope sights. Just on the edge of visibility – that point where a low-lying surfaced submarine manages to discern the masts of ships without itself being seen – he picked out a sharp shadow looming larger. It was not the troop ship BdU had in mind, but the SS *Dayrose*. Delays in U-boat transmissions would cause German naval headquarters to count her as the first fatality of Paukenschlag. But Topp (U-552) now encountered serious problems, which eventually led German authorities to conduct a major inquiry and court martial at home. For in all sectors of the winter campaign, torpedo failures hinted at sabotage, incompetence, or both. Initially, however, BdU blamed his commanders. Thus, in responding to Bigalk's (U-751) radio reports of repeated torpedo failures, he insisted that such shortcomings merely demonstrated the importance of unremitting exercise on patrol, and that one could simply not practise enough when at sea. Dönitz was always extremely tough-minded on this point and proved a demanding and enervating taskmaster when personally supervising final "work-ups" and of course "perishers,'" the rigorous command courses that all submarine captains had to pass during the early years of the war. Yet the truth never seemed to occur to higher authority that the torpedoes were faulty. Commanders at sea were blamed for poor performance when in fact their weapons were sometimes inadequate for the task.

Topp now first approached *Dayrose* to within 800 m and fired a double salvo under conditions that guaranteed lethal hits. The first torpedo shot past the vessel well ahead of the bow, and the second expended itself in circles. The scenario would repeat itself throughout the campaign. Only the fourth torpedo struck the target and stopped her dead in her tracks. Wreathed in a pall of black smoke, the stricken vessel lowered her lifeboats and radioed for aid. Radio Camperdown passed the first warning of the torpedoing to Dockyard Halifax. Yarmouth Radio and Cape Race attempted to estimate her position and assess her plight until Topp's coup de grâce broke the vessel in two a half-hour later. U-552 immediately sent a necessarily laconic "short signal" (*Kurzsignal*) to BdU: "*Dayrose* sunk near Cape Race – much heavy weather – low temperatures – ten below today – Topp" (KTB).[28] As always, clinical brevity glossed over the human anguish of survivors in winter seas.

U-130 now stood off the southeast of the Halifax–Cape Race route some 65 miles southeast of Scatarie Island. Freshening winds in seven degrees of frost caused heavy icing of the Boat and forced him to submerge. Hydrophones were quiet, and periscope sights offered nothing but mist and rolling seas. With the exception of a brief destroyer sighting, traffic seemed to Kals to have stopped. In effect, the last SC convoy of the season had left, and the port of Sydney was closing down. Unaware, Kals once again moved into the area between Sydney and Newfoundland. Patrolling off Cape Breton Island, Kals monitored radio broadcasts including those from his headquarters in Berlin or Kerneval, France, though he himself maintained radio silence. He could take no chances of being discovered by radio ranging. Nor, as he observed in his War Diary, could he chance the low visibility by remaining long on the surface and thus expose himself to "similar surprises as yesterday or inescapable attacks from the air" (KTB).

A certain restlessness and will for battle must have gripped Kals and his crew as they ran for dreary and uneventful hours off an apparently lifeless and inhospitable coast. He decided on a thrust "into the 'Bay of Sydney' " (KTB) on the northeast coast of Cape Breton Island. The *Sailing Directions* of the day would have informed him of the port's importance: its steel manufacturing plants surrounded by rich coal fields, the exportation of steel products, pulpwood, and coal. North Sydney was also the terminus for ferries operating to Newfoundland. He would have known of the harbour's annual exposure to ice in winter. As Kals stood 20 miles off the harbour entrance and some 12 miles from the coast at 0600 hours GMT on 16 January 1942, he noted how unprepared for war this "brightly illuminated" industrial city seemed to be (KTB). Peacetime conditions prevailed everywhere. But as no targets emerged, he withdrew once again. His U-boat was heavily iced in the $-15°C$ weather, his watch on deck bitterly chilled. "The tremendous cold for which the crew is not equipped really causes us trouble," Kals observed (KTB).

Lack of suitable gear was not the only handicap German crews faced. Many had been provided with inadequate navigational data. Topp's U-552, for example, had meanwhile been patrolling on the surface in heavy seas off the entrance to St John's harbour. With both periscopes damaged by ice, he had on numerous occasions attempted a close approach in order to inspect the harbour defences. But "since I am equipped neither with *Sailing Directions* [Pilot Book] nor appropriate scale chart of this area I withdrew again" (KTB). He relied on his hydrophones, the range of which exceeded that of his periscope even during breaks in the fog. On 16 January he failed in his attack on "a four-stack destroyer" departing St John's in the early morning hours (KTB). Later that day, U-86 (Schug) torpedoed the lone 5000-ton SS *Toorak* about 10 miles from St John's. Operations of the Flag Officer, Newfoundland Force (FONF) detailed HMS *Lightning*, *Highlander*, and *Harvester*, who were inbound from the UK, to search the area and render aid. Two RCAF aircraft joined them as they escorted the crippled vessel back.[29] Topp was about to attack the four approaching vessels when one of the escorts forced him under. Cautious about attacking with only 50 m of water under his keel, Topp withdrew. That night he took up a waiting position in light swell off the fog-enshrouded south coast of St John's.

Just after midnight GMT on 17 January 1942, standing with only 30 m under his keel between a lee shore and a steamer escorted by two "destroyers," Topp attacked again from 880 m. His torpedo failure inexplicably launched one of the destroyers into hot pursuit with what Topp described as ack-ack fire. Equally inexplicably, the destroyer broke off the chase and left Topp to return to his prey. His next two torpedoes exploded at the end of their run without having touched their target. As a last frustrated resort, Topp now cleared his guns for action. But his upper deck was now so thoroughly encrusted with ice that the men could not even hack the guns free. Throughout the day, a series of aircraft sightings pressed him under. In any event, seas were now breaking over U-552 in subzero temperatures, and freezing on contact. Powerful waves repeatedly turned him away from targets. Unlike the modern nitrogen-filled periscopes, Topp's were filled with air and iced up severely under such extreme weather conditions.

Topp's U-552 sank the 4271-ton Greek SS *Dimitrios O. Thermiotis* at 0642 GMT on 18 January, 5 miles south of Cape Race, though indeed conflicting reports suggest that it was actually the 2609-ton American SS *Frances Salman* which had left St John's alone for Cornerbrook, Newfoundland on 17 January. According to these reports, the *Thermiotis* fell victim to U-86 (Schug) northeast of Cape St Francis. Be that as it may, Topp's attacks exemplified the problems that BdU faced in dealing with the torpedo experimental and testing authorities. Topp expended four torpedoes at textbook ranges and angles over a period of two hours before a single effective one found its mark. Repeated failures were, of course, psychologically unnerving. In preparation for his fifth shot, Topp analysed his failures by tracing the electrical and mechanical firing mechanisms, and reassessing his firing data. As he noted in his War Diary, "This fifth attack costs me a lot of conscious effort after the previous results." Thirty-four seconds (and 511 m) later the torpedo exploded against the ship's stern. Tall columns of smoke and water marked the hit as the vessel quickly settled stern first and sank. Topp watched lifeboats being lowered and heard her radio call "SSS de swgg" (submarine attack, from *Dimitrios O. Thermiotis*). Ten minutes later the ship's bow towered almost vertically 20–30 m in the air and paused. The hulk had gone down in merely 30 m of water. U-boats soon preferred the shallows to the depths, for they were most successful where least expected. In response to Topp's situation report about the "unexplained torpedo failures," the eventual sinking, and the fact that the "transfer of spare torpedoes from deck stowage [was] impossible due to icing and weather," BdU recalled him home.

Bleichrodt's U-109 had meanwhile reached his prescribed attack area 120 miles southeast of Halifax by 16 January. Temperatures dropped abruptly to $-10°$ C and ice formed in thick crusts as the U-boat cut its way through blowing snow. Bleichrodt had intercepted Kals's situation report to Berlin, and could observe with chagrin: "My neighbour Boat U-130 reports that it's been seen. Too bad, the Canadians are now informed about the appearance of German U-boats off their coast" (KTB). This was indeed correct. Soon Bleichrodt heard detonations at a great distance, and later suspected that Canadians were attacking his colleague. Germany's *B-Dienst* seemed to confirm his suspicions. It had informed BdU of a Canadian sub sight report, indicating that a U-boat had been seen some 13.5 miles east of Chebucto Head. BdU in turn relayed details to group Paukenschlag. As Bleichrodt commented in his War Diary: "Since I'm now 100 miles south it can't be me. Either Captain Kals has run into the area and has been seen, or it was merely wishful thinking on the part of the Canadians. In any event, the virginal character of this area is gone" (KTB).

At this time, however, Kals's U-130 was still operating off Scatarie Island, Cape Breton. He, too, was suffering from torpedo failures. On one occasion he himself almost became the victim when an escort, an "American Craven class destroyer" (KTB), turned to attack and forced him into radical evasive action. As the escort bore down upon him, Kals spun the U-boat on its axis by rapidly ordering "full speed ahead" on one engine and "full speed astern" on the other, so that the destroyer thrashed by his stern with barely 10 m to spare. Kals scrambled down the hatch during the ensuing crash dive and glimpsed a second destroyer off the stern of his intended victim. But the anxiety was not over, for the head valve of the diesel air intake had iced up, admitting 8 tons of water into the Boat. Out of balance, the U-boat descended too rapidly and struck bottom at a depth of "A-32" (48 m) on the 22-fathom patch 15 miles east of Scatarie Island. Kals observed in his War Diary: "At first I lie still with everything switched off even though the boat is working unpleasantly against the sea bed. The destroyers do nothing. I assume that their depth charge launchers are unserviceable due to icing." BdU later underlined the latter statement in red with a bold exclamation mark, for it might have offered an important insight into the problems of surface defences off Canada's Atlantic coast. An hour later, Kals freed his U-boat from the bottom and withdrew submerged. He would now operate for a few days on the Halifax–Cape Race line.

BdU now signalled Hardegen (U-123), Bleichrodt (U-109) and Schug (U-86) for situation reports, and gave Kals (U-130) permission to shift to a new combat zone if conditions at his current location were unfruitful. Kals left the Cabot Strait for four very sound reasons: (1) light commercial traffic, (2) air surveillance as intense as he had found in the English Channel, (3) strong "destroyer escorts," and (4) unfavourable weather conditions and frequent fog.

Bothered by the sighting of U-130 and by another that a radio report from *B-Dienst* reflected, Bleichrodt remained in the south. He would venture no further until "they'd quietened down up north" (KTB). Harsh weather conditions prevailed. The bridge watch secured themselves with safety harnesses "as the stern sea was rolling over the conning tower" (KTB). During the early moments of 19 January 1942, U-109 thrust into the coastal zone close to Cape Sable. At this southwest extremity, Bleichrodt expected an intersection of the NS-EW traffic routes. Rounding Seal Island at night in a stormy sea with long northwesterly swells, he encountered a deep-laden Yarmouth-bound freighter of 4000–5000 tons that had apparently lost her way. As the freighter lay dead in the water conversing with Yarmouth Radio in plain language about her position and route into harbour, Bleichrodt approached her under the same textbook conditions as Topp had experienced. Six faulty torpedoes fired over a period of two hours failed to sink her. Fearing transmission errors between his target indicator and the deflection angle calculator, Bleichrodt had in sheer desperation even resorted to aiming the last shot by eye, using the net guard as a cross hair. By this time an escort had arrived to lead the freighter into Yarmouth. Throughout the dark morning only the lights of fishing boats altered the desolate scene. Bleichrodt refrained from responding to his headquarters' request for a situation report, as he did not wish a lengthy broadcast to betray his presence, or to compromise his plans for the second attack inshore. Two days later, Bleichrodt received a direct order from BdU to report his "situation and success," but tenaciously maintained radio silence. BdU needed the information in order to plan his strategy; radio silence might suggest that U-109 had been lost. Yet BdU recognized the principle that the on-site commander was the best judge of his own circumstances.

During the afternoon of 19 January, Digby 756 of 10 (BR) Squadron, Gander, attacked an unidentified surfaced U-boat whose conning tower was fully exposed and pressure tanks awash some 58 miles off Baccalieu Island off the east coast of Newfoundland. Although the RCAF assessed the attack as "useless," re-examination of the attack diagram suggests that the impact of the three 250-pound depth charges that exploded over the bow of the submerging U-boat and in line with the conning tower exerted at least a severe dissuasive influence on its immediate tactics. While patrolling for convoy SC-65 three days later, Digby 740 of the same squadron sighted an unidentified U-boat 50 miles northeast of Cape St Francis. The aircraft dived at the fully surfaced 16-knot target, flared out at 20 feet with 25 feet of the diving U-boat's stern still visible, and fired three bombs. A jammed switch released only one, which exploded alongside the conning tower. Neither of two subsequent attacks produced any evidence of damage. U.S. aircraft bombed the periscopes of two submarines operating within 175–200 miles south of Cape Pine. Neither produced results.[30]

On 21 January 1942, the same day on which Bleichrodt's U-109 missed an unidentified, fully laden 6000-ton freighter 8 miles off Shelburne, Nova Scotia, with one of its dud torpedoes, Kals's U-130 sank the 8248-ton tanker *Alexandria Hoegh* 160 miles south of Cape Sable in heavy obscuring swells. His first torpedo struck the forepart of the vessel at 2221

GMT after a run of 54 seconds (880 m). The tanker's crew immediately took to two boats, as the vessel settled deeply by the bow. When a half-hour later, one of the lifeboats returned alongside the ship, Kals fired his coup de grâce from 400 m. As the War Diary records.

A strikingly broad, white, medium height blast column. The tanker breaks apart, both parts of the ship floating away independently of one another. The stern and screws tower ... out of the water. The after part of the forward half of the ship lies submerged. The inclination of the afterdeck has increased markedly. Both halves of the broken ship sag slowly and steadily deeper. No more help from me necessary. I'm off. (KTB)

Kals returned to his home port of Lorient, France, after further successful operations off New York. In all, his sixty-one day mission covered 8520 nautical miles. Typical for this pre-schnorkel period of U-boat warfare, he spent most of the tour surfaced. BdU praised his captain's "very well thought out and executed successful operation" (KTB).

Despite a wandering magnetic compass and an unreliable gyro, U-109 searched the waters from Yarmouth through Seal Island. Occasional distant targets, either too fast or under escort, eluded his approaches. One "destroyer" even passed directly overhead without attacking. Again, aircraft posed a constant threat. At 0812 GMT on 23 January 1942, U-109 fired a lethal torpedo at what it reported as the 6566-ton Yarmouth-bound Greek vessel *Andreas*. In the absence of Allied loss reports, this must in fact have been the 4887-ton British steamer *Thilby*. The torpedo crossed the 800 m of smooth sea in 28 seconds and struck abaft the funnel, sending a towering explosion cloud as the steamer sagged on an even keel and then gradually sank to the bottom, stern first. Bleichrodt meanwhile watched the crew getting into the lifeboats and easily distinguished the lights of boats on the water. The stricken vessel signalled its "SSS" on the 600 m band, which U-109 constantly monitored, and was told by Station Camperdown first to "wait." When Camperdown returned the call, it was too late; the ship had long since sunk over the sternposts, bows in the air. Her stern now rested at a depth of 40 m. Bleichrodt erroneously identified the vessel's call sign and departed to the southeast at high speed, in order to be out of the shallows by dawn. Flames and the white lights of fishing boats could be seen astern where the hulk lay.

U-109 had no further success in the Canadian zone. Bleichrodt's continued patrol from Seal Island to Shelburne, Liverpool, and Halifax was frustrated by air cover, surface patrols, and "the bright moonlit nights" (KTB). He observed by 26 January that the increasing Allied surveillance of recent days had been making it more and more difficult to carry out successful operations. By now convoy routes had shifted for the winter season, and in any event he was now low on fuel and torpedoes of doubtful efficacy. He refuelled from Kals's U-130 on 4 February north of the Bermudas as the two Boats worked their way home.

All U-boat commanders in the first wave of Paukenschlag had experienced torpedo failures. These diminished their striking power and threatened to undermine their morale. Undaunted by the bitter experience, Topp in U-552 compensated for his disappointment by an uncommon ruse. Perturbed by his inability to wage war on a grand scale with large vessels steaming by him east of the Newfoundland Banks, Topp adopted the style of his First World War predecessors in these waters. Acting one night as a surface raider, he ordered a 10,000-ton Greek freighter to heave to in a storm under the mere threat of being torpedoed if she did not comply. At this point Topp's only usable weapon consisted of the 2-cm machine-gun. His "Red Devil" insignia on the conning tower may have betrayed the theatrical, though deadly, flair with which he staged the ensuing scene. Topp broke surface 1000–1500 m astern his victim in near-gale conditions. Masses of tall waves were breaking along their extensive foaming crests as his signal lamp flashed in English: "Stop, send a boat." A couple of machine-gun rounds brought the unmarked vessel to a stop; further bursts from the machine-gun evinced replies from the freighter's hesitant signalman. Topp could scarcely read the response, "since the U-boat from time to time completely disappear[ed] behind the towering seas" (KTB). Finally the flashing light signalled in English: "Please, please, captain is coming." The master soon arrived in a boat with the ship's papers, and sheltered precariously in the U-boat's lee. Topp's crew had by now managed to clear the 8.8 cannon for action. Allowing the merchantman's crew to escape in lifeboats in the tumultuous seas, Topp's crew fired some 126 rounds of explosive and incendiary shells into the victim's hull. Almost three hours after the attack had begun, Topp noted in his War Diary: "the vessel sinks by the sternposts with a final blast of compressed flame from the forward hatch. In the darkness and with this sea running, no lifeboats can be seen. [We] continue homeward bound" (KTB). On 27 January 1942, having five days earlier chanced upon U-751 (Bigalk) and exchanged experiences in tumultuous mid-Atlantic seas, U-552 slipped quietly into the safety of St Nazaire.

The security service of the German Reich, which monitored the national mood both by close observation and by sampling public responses to newspaper and radio programs, observed on 26 and 29 January 1942 that special reports on U-boat successes off "the North American and Canadian coast" had "triggered great joy and surprise" throughout the country.[31] Particularly impressive was the U-boats' ability to carry the war across the Atlantic despite "the enormous distances." Following close on Pearl Harbor, the secret service advised, this signified to Germans a further "loss of prestige" for America. The German public, it concluded, now rather hankered for some news on the new U-boat types that would doubtless put an end to the battle.

Fragments of news of the Topp incident reached the Canadian public. The *Montreal Daily Star* reported on 11 February 1942, for example, that twenty-seven survivors of a Greek ship "that an Axis submarine pounded under the surface with a three and one half hour shelling" had reached "an eastern Canadian port." Once at Halifax, the "seamen [had] told of the merciless shelling of their ship and the gunning of its men in the lifeboats." Read between the lines, this account suggested murder on the high seas.[32] Canadian records provide no further clarification. But whether such stories were earnest assertion or journalistic flourish, they set the stage on which German U-boats loomed large as vicious predators, and created an image of the German U-boat captain that endured until well after the war.

Eight U-boats of the second wave, hunting from 21 January to 19 February 1942 in the operational zone stretching from the Newfoundland Banks to Nova Scotia, achieved less dramatic results[33] (see table 4).

This second wave focused on three points: the east coast of Newfoundland, the western side of Cabot Strait, and the Halifax Approaches. Only the heavy icing south of the Cabot Strait prevented penetration of the Gulf. In effect, then, the waters off Newfoundland and Nova Scotia remained the principal combat zones. Kapitänleutnant Oestermann's U-754, which had departed Kiel-Wik on 30 December 1941, attacked its first vessels on 22 January 1942 off Ferryland Head, Newfoundland. Canadian records do not unequivocally corroborate his claims of having sunk the two merchant vessels whose damage and destruction he clearly observed. One of them was possibly the 1344-ton Norwegian SS *Williman Hanson* in the three-ship convoy escorted by HMCS *Georgian*, *Wetaskiwin*, and *Camrose*;[34] the other was the 2153-ton Norwegian SS *Belize* on 24 January, 35 miles southeast of St John's, again triggering air/sea searches that revealed the bitter ravages of an ugly war. U.S. Navy aircraft sighted an overturned lifeboat and one man on a raft far out to sea. Neither were seen again. HMCS *Spikenard*, vectored by aircraft to a lifeboat with three survivors aboard, found only a swamped lifeboat containing four corpses. *Shawinigan*, too, came upon a derelict boat. Such sights would imprint themselves on the memories of many Canadian mariners. In the words of Alan Easton, commanding officer of HMCS *Baddeck* from 1941 to 1942: "During the war I saw many empty lifeboats, and never did they fail to give me an unhappy feeling, a conviction that the shadow of disaster floated close alongside or was hidden beneath, that its mysterious passengers had known fear, tragedy."[35]

During the early morning of 25 January, U-754 sighted the lone, deeply

TABLE 4
Paukenschlag: The Second Wave: 21 January–19 February 1942

U-boat	Type	Ships sunk	Torpedoed but not sunk	Sunk (tons)
U-754 (Oestermann)	VIIC	4	–	11,386
U-751 (Bigalk)	VIIC	2	1 (8096 tons)	11,487
U-82 (Rollmann)	VIIC	2	–	18,117
U-564 (Suhren)	VIIC	1	1 (6195 tons)	11,411
U-576 (Heinicke)	VIIC	1	–	6,946
U-85 (Greger)	VIIC	1	–	5,408
U-98 (Gysae)	VIIC	1	–	5,298
U-566 (Borchert)	VIIC	1	–	4,181

laden 3876-ton Greek vessel *Mount Kithern.* Contrary to regulations, she was burning her running lights.[36] Broken in half by two torpedoes, she sank in 15 minutes, a mere 2 miles off St John's. HMCS *Spikenard* picked up eighteen survivors.[37] U-754 sank the Greek SS *Icarion* 50 miles southeast of Cape Race on 27 January.[38] Mysteriously, Oestermann never saw any sign of life aboard: no movement, no boats lowered, no lights. After settling slowly with a broken back for three-quarters of an hour, the vessel "suddenly broke apart and immediately sank" (KTB). It was an eerie experience. In summarizing his mission on return to Brest on 9 February 1942, Oestermann modestly reported: "No special occurrences or experiences; steamers tend to set running lights, navigation beacons burning as in peacetime" (KTB). His work was routine. Admiral Dönitz observed, however, that it was a "well executed first mission of the Commanding Officer with a new Boat" (KTB). His subsequent Canadian missions, as we will see, were not so fortunate.

Bigalk's U-751 performed the second most important incursion of this wave that extant records describe. Having departed the Biscay port of St Nazaire on 14 January 1942, one day after the first wave had begun its "surprise" attack, U-751 crossed the Newfoundland Banks on 28 January, experiencing "heavy breakers over the [conning] tower [with] bridge watch harnessed in [and] Boat lurching and rolling violently" (KTB). Curving towards a Cabot Strait choked with fog and ice, it surfaced on 31 January 15 miles east of Green Island, Chedabucto Bay. On this day, Rollmann's U-82 sank the 1190-ton British escort HMS *Belmont* out of its convoy screen, 160 miles southeast of Cape Sable.[39] Poor weather conditions prevented operational flying until 2 February when the RCAF searched in vain for the *Belmont's* survivors.

On departing Chedabucto Bay, U-751 attacked the 8096-ton tanker

Corilla. Like the later account of the *Bayou Chico*, her action illustrates that much more than meets the eye lies behind the raw statistics of ships that have been "merely" torpedoed. Bigalk's fear that "the pitching foam-tossed U-boat can probably be seen at greater distances" (KTB) in the bright moonlight that he now encountered may well have been correct. For, just as he fired, *Corilla* turned sharply away and began broadcasting the alarm and her position on the 600 m band. Her stern-mounted gun opened fire, impressing Bigalk with its accuracy. The tanker's prudent zigzagging and the obscurity of the night prevented U-751 from choosing the most direct course to his new attack position, for he could never be certain of *Corilla*'s actual base course. Sometimes the vessel disappeared completely from view. He therefore tried to lull *Corilla* into a sense of security so that she would cease or reduce evasive action. U-751 trailed her unobtrusively for an hour and a half until the vicinity of Country Island Light, where it fired a triple salvo from 2500 m. The right-hand torpedo became a surface-runner, sprinting and skipping past the target over the high swells. The left-hand torpedo went astray without detonating. The centre torpedo, however, struck the vessel at the precise point of aim forward of the bridge after a run of 140 seconds (2100 m), exploding with a tall blast column at the ship's side. Within 4 minutes she again radioed her plight: "SSS *Corilla* torpedoed still afloat," while zigzagging toward shore and settling deeper by the bow. Again U-751 tried to run ahead to take up its advance firing position and bring the stern tubes to bear while rapidly reloading forward. At 0804 GMT *Corilla* again broadcast the alarm: "Send help immediately, we are sinking."

By constantly zigzagging, *Corilla* frustrated Bigalk's attempt to reach a favourable firing position. Bigalk soon observed the tanker's signal lamp flashing on the afterdeck at the shadow of "a destroyer or torpedo boat" (KTB). The escort was now heading at full speed in the immediate direction of U-751, but was "outmanoeuvred" (KTB). Preoccupied by the chase, the U-boat's bridge watch sighted a buoy 500 m distant to starboard in 60 m of water. U-751 veered off in order to avoid running on to "the Rocks" (KTB). The "Sunken Rock," otherwise known as "Split Rock," is situated 2.3 miles northeast of Country Island, and lies surrounded by dangerous shoal areas, ledges, and banks. Regretting now that *Corilla* could no longer be seen, Bigalk noted with some satisfaction that she too had perhaps "reached shallow water," or better still had "settled on a reef." In any case, he recorded, "*Corilla* won't be heading for England any more" (KTB). But the vessel had in fact made port on her own and sailed in convoys once again. The attack triggered heavy air surveillance, which forced U-751 to remain submerged.[40] Her hydrophones indicated no sea surveillance at all.

Working its way southward after midnight of 4 February 1942, U-751 picked up the flashing light of Little Hope Island, a boulder-strewn islet 2 miles east of Joli Point at the entrance to the small harbour of Port Joli. When two zigzagging shadows emerged from the darkness in the direction of shore, Bigalk construed an escort with a 3500-ton freighter. Firing submerged after a dud shot, he torpedoed the 4335-ton British tanker *Silveray*. She immediately broadcast the alarm. Forty-one minutes later, the third torpedo sunk her over the sternposts. Bigalk now chased the second shadow, an unidentified freighter Canadians at first thought was the *Silveray* headed for Liverpool harbour, some 60 miles southwest of Halifax. By the time U-751 had closed the gap to 1000 m, the freighter stood 1.5 miles off the harbour mouth. RCAF aircraft foiled Bigalk's attack. Two days later RCAF aircraft searching for *Silveray*'s survivors sighted a naval patrol craft retrieving an upturned lifeboat. Nothing else was found but wreckage and one more empty boat.[41]

U-751 had meanwhile withdrawn. Having experienced a torpedo failure off Chezzetcook Inlet, and having outmanoeuvred surface patrols, including a formation of "five trawler-like escorts" (KTB), U-751 in vain chased further targets. At one point escorts pursued the submarine into the coastal shallows. As the echo-sounder indicated "50 m of water and shelving," Bigalk altered away by tens of degrees, his pursuer assiduously following each course change, as they curved toward shore and then gradually arced back into open water. At 0335 GMT Bigalk ordered an emergency dive; he headed south for 5 minutes at dead slow, then shifted to slow. Hydrophone operators reported that the escort stopped several times: listening, searching, groping for a contact. Nine minutes after the emergency dive, the U-boat crew heard a single poorly placed depth charge. For the next hour, as the War Diary of U-751 records, the escort maintained its search pattern, while increasing its range. This was the technique of establishing an Observant around the perimeter of a submarine sighting, whereby the range circles were advanced along the suspected evasion course of the enemy submarine at its presumed speed of advance. In establishing an Observant, Canadian ships almost invariably assumed that a U-boat would move slowly into deeper water with greater sea room. As often happened, however, U-boats lay on the bottom in shallow water, or moved dead slow inshore. Thus U-751 escaped. No Canadian documents record the incident.

By 7 February, Bigalk had returned to the 100 m line about 8.5 miles off Little Hope Island Light, where he sighted the deep-laden 8000-ton *Empire Sun*. His first "G7a" straight-running torpedo inexplicably failed. Apparently unaware of the attack, the vessel continued its straight course without zigzagging while U-751 ran ahead to its forward firing position to allow the vessel to run into its sights. A shot with precisely the same data struck the *Empire Sun* at the point of aim by the funnel after a run of 51 seconds (620 m). She slowly settled on an even keel as the crew took to the boats. Her signal "SSS *Empire Sun* torpedoed 43.55 N, 64.22 W" was her last word. She sank within 20 minutes over the sternposts, her bow poised vertically in the air. Hours later the RCAF sighted a lifeboat under sail with three people aboard. Then a second lifeboat, crowded with survivors, entered Liverpool Bay. News of such incidents could not be suppressed by censorship; they quickly fostered the hearsay and folklore with which the Wartime Information Board would sooner or later have to come to grips.

Bigalk's final attack in the Canadian zone marks the second instance in which a U-boat with marginal tactical advantage played a bold and cunning game of deception. Like Topp (U-552) in his successful role as surface raider against an intimidated Greek freighter, Bigalk too had spent his torpedoes and pressed home an artillery attack. Under full moon and in moderate swell, some 36 miles south of Sambro Island Light, his gunners opened fire with 8.8-cm cannon at 2500 m. The *Atlantian* replied with what Bigalk described as "badly aimed 2 cm and cannon" (KTB). Broadcasting the "SSS" alert, the merchantman dashed off at full speed. Bigalk observed a hit on the freighter's afterdeck, but could neither maintain speed in the seaway without risk of washing his gun's crew overboard, nor aim accurately. All his shots were "lousy" (KTB), and he broke off further engagement.[42] Only when 60 miles southwest of Sable Island did Bigalk consider himself in sufficiently safe water to transmit his lengthy situation report to BdU. He had found all navigation aids functioning under peacetime conditions, and had experienced "moderate destroyer [sic] and escort activity." He was surprised to find air surveillance even at night, but only casual surface screening of coastal merchant traffic. The fact was, of course, that Canadians simply did not have an adequate number of ships to provide the necessary protection. To his list of successes, Bigalk appended with regret his six torpedo failures. This 50 per cent failure rate was about average for the fleet.

After a tortuous crossing of the Bay of Biscay, during which U-751 "bucked and twisted violently in heavy seas and took on lots of water," it entered St Nazaire locks on 23 February 1942 (KTB). Admiral Dönitz observed it was a "well executed operation, whose success was marred by failures of personnel and matériel" (KTB). Significantly, BdU blamed the shortcomings of armament production on the inexperience of operators at sea.

The third wave of U-boats assigned to Paukenschlag between 10 February and 20 March operated individually in the area between Newfoundland and Cape Hatteras. Six of them participated in the mid-Atlantic operation against convoy ONS-67 from 21 to 25 February[43] (see table 5).

TABLE 5

Paukenschlag: The Third Wave: 10 February–20 March 1942

U-boat	Type	Ships sunk	Torpedoed but not sunk	Sunk (tons)
U-504 (Poske)	IXC	4	–	26,561
U-96 (Lehmann-Willenbrock)	VIIC	5	–	25,464
U-432 (H.O. Schultze)	VIIC	5	–	24,987
U-404 (v. Bülow)	VIIC	4	–	22,653
U-158 (Rostin)	IXC	3	1 (7118 tons)	21,202
U-94 (Ites)	VIIC	4	–	14,442
U-578 (Rehwinkel)	VIIC	2	–	10,540
		1	(U.S. destroyer Jacob Jones)	
U-155 (Piening)	IXC	1	–	7,874
U-587 (Ul. Borcherdt)	VIIC	2	–	6,619
U-653 (Feiler)	VIIC	1	–	1,582
U-656 (Kröning)	VIIC	–	–	–
U-558 (Krech)	VIIC	3	–	21,925
U-69 (Zahn)	VIIC	–	–	–

Although their principal focus lay in the U.S. zones from Long Island southward, many of them initiated combat while passing through Canadian waters. U-96 (Lehmann-Willenbrock) stuck closest to Nova Scotia. On 19 February 1942 it sank the 7965-ton British motorship SS *Empire Seal* within 45 miles southeast of Cape Sable. Next day it sank the 2398-ton American SS *Lake Osweya*. On 22 February it sank two ships: at 0244 the 1948-ton Danish steamer SS *Torungen* by torpedo and gunfire within 30 miles southeast of Chebucto Head; and at 2257 the 8888-ton British motor tanker SS *Kars* some 14 miles southeast of Sambro Island Light. On 9 March it sank the 4265-ton Norwegian SS *Tyr* 40 miles southeast of Sable Island. Others fared less well. Kröning's U-656, for example, was destroyed with all hands on 1 March 1942 by American aircraft of the 88 Squadron some 25 miles SSE of Cape Race.[44] Ulrich Borcherdt's U-587, assisted by Rostin's U-158 during a surface attack against convoy ONS-67, patrolled close off the eastern coast of Newfoundland and fired three torpedoes into St John's harbour on 3 March. The harmless explosions triggered a fruitless hunt by HMCS *Minas*, *The Pas*, and *Lunenburg*.[45] U-587 sank the 900-ton Greenland escort *Hans Egeda* (variously reported as *Harose Guda*) on 6 March some 75 miles south of Tête de Gallantry, St Pierre-Miquelon, and reported having sunk two unidentified vessels in Canadian waters: an escort 120 miles southeast of

Louisburg, and a freighter 185 miles southeast of Cape Race.[46] Homeward bound, Borcherdt sank the 8032-ton derelict SS *Empire Celt* from convoy ONS-67. She had first been torpedoed by either U-162 (Wattenberg) or U-158 (Rostin). Borcherdt's repeated sighting broadcasts made him the first victim of a "Huff-Duff" (HF/DF) directed attack in the Atlantic war.[47]

Rostin's U-158 also fell victim to a "Huff-Duff" directed attack, though only after his second operational cruise to the Americas.[48] His reflections on Paukenschlag reveal serious defects in the German training that the extended Battle of the Atlantic would exacerbate. With the exception of his NCOs (non-commissioned officers), his crew had had no previous sea experience, and for the most part no previous submarine experience at all. They had none the less "worked into the new situation of a longer operational mission very quickly" (KTB). The lack of trained hydrophone operators on board was to his mind "very unpleasant" (KTB) in the extreme. This is perhaps one of the earliest admissions that, even as early as 1942, Germany was sending "green" classroom-trained crews to the front, though this would be commonplace by 1944. Rostin especially singled out for praise the "fighting spirit" of his men, "particularly [that] of the younger sailors" (KTB). When Rostin reached the U.S. coast after the action against convoy ONS-67, he found an altered situation from that which Hardegen, in U-123, had encountered not so much earlier. For now surveillance, especially the air cover, was much more attentive.

Von Bülow's U-404 undertook the closest approach to Halifax since the attacks of U-98 in February. Having sighted "ice fields" (KTB) in fog off Western Head, it patrolled close inshore between Halifax and Pennant Point. On 5 March 1942 it sank the 5112-ton American freighter SS *Collamer*, 10.6 miles east of the Sambro lightship after failed torpedoes. Thick fog and lack of targets impelled his departure for Long Island.

Oestermann's U-754 returned to join the last of the so-called third wave of Paukenschlag after a very brief turn-around in Brest. On 23 March he attacked his first ship in the Canadian zone. The 8700-ton tanker *British Prudence*, a straggler from convoy HX-181, sank within a half hour, 150 miles northeast of Sable Island. Oestermann now watched a second target – the *Bayou Chico* – lagging some 6–8 miles astern.[49] As the chase began, the SS *Bayou Chico* moved surprisingly close and bombarded U-754 with a deck gun, sending several rounds close aboard as the merchantman "zigzagged wildly" (KTB). The freighter's protracted evasive action prevented U-754 from getting into firing position, forcing it at best to remain at the edge of visibility in the mist, constantly matching courses with its intended target. The *Chico*'s SOS signals led FONF to construe a pack of U-boats trailing convoy HX-181. He deployed HMS *Witherington*, *Acanthus*, *Eglantine*, *Potentilla*, and *Rose* from St John's to provide additional convoy support. Oestermann's intention of attacking after nightfall failed, for the *Bayou Chico* outdistanced him in the fog and reached Halifax.

The *Bayou Chico*'s call had also summoned the RCAF support from Sydney's 119 Bomber Squadron. Bolingbroke 9066, commanded by the experienced 21-year-old Flight-Lieutenant C.S. Buchanan, surprised U-754 on the surface. Oestermann hastily dictated into his War Diary; the "three-engined bomber" (KTB) forced him to crash dive to 135 m as it dropped "two well placed bombs" in two separate attacks. The already standard technique of dropping "spaced sticks," comprising four 250-pound bombs each, had replaced the tactically inefficient single drop. Buchanan's flight log entry describes U-754 rising in excess of 45 degrees "in the air" after the first charge exploded 20 feet from the U-boat's bow. The air gunner described it with some exaggeration as standing "right up on her end as if the ocean was [sic] smoking a giant cigar." Buchanan then saw U-754 roll over on her side and "sink."[50]

The censor suppressed news of the supposed "kill" until five months later when intense U-boat attacks in the St Lawrence made it necessary for the government to demonstrate the effectiveness of its defences against foreign aggression. Air Minister Power's official announcement, embellished by human-interest stories written by the Armed Forces Information Services, received broad coverage. Publishing dramatic photographs taken by the navigator William Howes that revealed "the Nazi U-Boat" caught in its "death throes," the press credited Buchanan with having "sunk a U-Boat in the North Atlantic."[51] But U-754 had survived with minor damage, had subsequently attacked convoy ON-74, and in turn suffered a severe pounding by HMS *Witch* and HMCS *The Pas* 65 miles southeast of Sable Island. The vessels dropped forty-one "well-placed" charges (KTB), which sent the flooding U-boat reeling out of control well beyond tested limits to a depth of 220 m. For reasons unexplained and unrecorded, HMS *Witch* and HMCS *The Pas* suddenly broke off an engagement that with more tenacity would most certainly have led to a kill. They had sound reasons for doing so. In 1942 escorts could not afford to hunt to exhaustion because they would get too far away from their inadequately protected convoys. Oestermann returned to France for a much-needed eight week refit.[52] During this time, two U-boats, whose exploits are recounted in subsequent chapters, departed their Biscay bases on separate Canadian missions: U-553 to enter the St Lawrence, and U-213 on a clandestine journey into the Bay of Fundy.

Paukenschlag and associated submarine operations had, from January to March 1942, sunk forty-four ships in Canadian waters. This was a tonnage equivalent to one modern supertanker today. According to Germany's secret police, the German populace had greeted this achievement "with joy and satisfaction."[53] After the lull in December 1941, when no ships were lost, the first twenty-one losses in January 1942 disturbed Canadian naval authorities. Significantly, however, Canadians rallied their defences and, profiting from the Germans' repeated torpedo failures, reduced the loss rate: down to sixteen in February, seven in March, and four in April. Reports of these sinkings reached the Canadian public in delays ranging from three days to five months. They rarely contained much technical detail. Human-interest stories were stripped of any militarily useful information. Even today, with the availability of both Allied and Axis documents, it is virtually impossible to identify some incidents reported in the press. As in the typical case of the press handling of Buchanan's attack on U-754, incidents were manipulated according to defence needs. For reasons of security and national stability, the Wartime Information Board assured Canadians of Allied supremacy on the seas. It reminded them of the navy's dogged pursuit of a wily and unethical enemy, which had to resort to "sneaky fighting" and ganging up on its victims by "wolf pack tactics." It reported sinkings as having taken place in the "North Atlantic" or in "mid Atlantic." The close observer of newspaper coverage might soon have concluded, however, that "Western Atlantic" was actually a euphemism for an area just "off Canadian shores."

Government silence on submarine activity soon required official explanation, for it was all too obvious to those who worked on the East Coast that the Battle of the Atlantic was moving in. Unofficial stories of submarine encounters were current on the coasts of Newfoundland and Nova Scotia. Some fishermen even claimed that such meetings were all in a day's work. The crew of the Lunenburg schooner *Marilyn Clair* told of conversing with a passing U-boat while dressing fish one night at sea. Another U-boat was rumoured as having surfaced to ask fishermen for fresh food. The Lunenburg schooners *Robertson I* and *Robertson II* witnessed an attack at dusk, while the latter vessel claimed to have been tracked but left unharmed.[54] The Lockport schooner *Lucille M.* chanced upon a half-submerged, damaged lifeboat containing a dead body. This was reported as yet "another victim of Nazi warfare."[55] The find sparked speculation as to whether or not the lifeboat had been machine-gunned. The actual, or even suspected, presence of German U-boats was itself a type of psychological warfare that nourished the myth of a furtive and sovereign adversary. Fishermen, at least, would need some protection. Mr V.G. Poittier (Lib., Shelburne-Yarmouth-Clare) reminded the House in Ottawa during the debates on the War Risk Insurance Plan that in the previous war German submarines had "virtually destroyed the Atlantic fishing fleet." The House did not share Poittier's concern.[56] In July 1942 this tacit neutrality between U-boats and fishermen would end, and schooners would be shelled and sunk.

The navy took official action to calm the nation's doubts when then LCdr William Strange (RCNVR) of Plans and Operations in Naval Service Headquarters spoke to the Ottawa Canadian Club and the press on 5 March 1942: "It is obvious to everyone who reads the news that submarines now are operating not far from the North American coasts. This is no occasion for surprise, and certainly none for anything approaching dismay ... Such attacks may make the headlines, but they should not – in the public mind – be permitted to occupy unreasonable prominence."[57] The "trench warfare of the seas," as he rather theatrically described the Battle of the Atlantic, was essential to sustain Britain against Axis aggression; its success should not be measured by the frequency of U-boat attacks from whatever quarter, but from the volume of tonnage actually delivered to England. His point was valid. The government, he pointed out, had to keep silence about maritime operations in order to reveal nothing to "Adolf Hitler and that wretched little man Joe Goebbels." This, of course, implied that Canadians had to be kept in the dark as well. As will be seen later, the government faced the quandary of how to awaken the national will for conscription for overseas service and increased war production, while at the same time maintaining silence about the actual threat. As LCdr Strange exhorted:

It must be realized that only by observing the traditional silence of the Navy can we hope to place the enemy in that state of doubt, disturbance and mental distress which we conceive to be his proper state of mind.

Upon sealed lips depend not only our ships, not only the lives of fighting seamen in our warships, and merchant seamen engaged in holding the lifeline firm, but the success or failure of our arms.

Should we lose command of the sea, we cannot hope to win the war.

CHAPTER THREE

The First St Lawrence Sorties: 1942

The "Battle of the St Lawrence," to use the imaginative popular term coined by the *Ottawa Journal* in 1942, began as an independent spin-off from the sixth wave of German submarines to penetrate North American coastal waters in the early spring of that year.[1] It was not an actual battle, but a series of very effective U-boat sorties bearing grave tactical and political consequences for Canada's national defence. What began as tentative explorations by U-553 and U-132 in the spring culminated in autumn in the heaviest Canadian losses in the inshore zone: HMCS *Raccoon*, HMCS *Charlottetown*, and the passenger ferry SS *Caribou*. From 26 April to 23 May, BdU set thirteen U-boats against a variety of unescorted vessels, most of them outside the Gulf, which for one reason or another were not in convoy. The German patrols focused principally on the United States, though special missions like that of U-213, which landed a spy in Saint John, New Brunswick, revealed German interest in probing Canadian defences. Although May saw only six vessels actually sunk in Canadian and immediately contiguous waters (for a total of 23,542 tons), U-boat activity tied down Allied surface vessels. It also caused Eastern Air Command (EAC) to fly 560 operational patrols both inside the Gulf itself and off the eastern seaboard of Nova Scotia and Newfoundland. Operational training units and elementary training schools flew additional patrols.

The potential threat to the Gulf and St Lawrence River forced the RCAF to establish auxiliary detachments at Mont Joli and Gaspé, Quebec. It also moved the Royal Navy's Fleet Air Arm to lend Canada a Walrus flying boat that just happened to be available. Piloted by an RNVR Sub-Lieutenant and navigated (rather disastrously, as it turned out) by an RCAF sergeant, it was based on Sable Island, that desolate wreck-strewn outcrop of rock and sand 150 miles to seaward of Nova Scotia. The Walrus, a rather peculiar amphibious biplane of 1936 design, with a

TABLE 6
Sinkings in North American Waters, May 1942

U-boat	Ships sunk	Torpedoed but not sunk	Sunk (tons)
U-564 (Suhren)	4	2 (13,245 tons)	24,390
U-333 (Cremer)	3	1 (8,327 tons)	13,596
U-455 (Giessler)	1	–	6,994
U-593 (Kelbling)	1	1 (4,853 tons)	8,426
U-653 (Feiler)	1	–	6,225
U-135 (Praetorius)	1	–	7,127
U-432 (Schultze)	5	1 (7,073 tons)	6,110
U-553 (Thurmann)	3	–	16,995
U-588 (Vogel)	4	1 (7,460 tons)	13,927

single machine-gun and pusher engine, was supposed to have a range of 600 miles at a cruising speed of 135 mph. What with bad weather and unserviceability, the aircraft seldom flew; and when it did, it found no U-boats. Aircraft of Eastern Air Command did somewhat better despite unfavourable weather, and logged 3500 hours in the air for half a million miles in May alone. In addition to individual patrols, they escorted 114 coastal and feeder convoys consisting of 1576 ships.[2] U-boats off Canadian shores at first gained the impression that maritime traffic had been stopped. While this assumption served to explain to BdU the relatively modest amount of tonnage sunk, it failed to account for the switch in Allied convoy scheduling from winter to summer sailings.

Statistics covering all sinkings in North American waters during the month of May 1942 show that with the exception of U-98 (Eichmann), U-566 (Hornkohl), U-213 (von Varendorff), and U-352 (Rathke) – which for various reasons sank nothing – the remaining VIIC U-boats on station met with success (see table 6). Symptomatic of the course of antisubmarine combat, none of these U-boats survived beyond July 1944, though indeed all but one managed to survive the sixth-wave assault. The sole loss, U-352, failed in its torpedo attack on USCG *Icarus* on 9 May 1942 off Cape Lookout, North Carolina, and was in turn sunk with 24 hands by its intended victim. In all, four of the original thirteen submarines eventually fell victim to aircraft, one to a mine, and seven to surface vessels. U-553 disappeared without a trace in January 1943 after having left her Biscay port of La Pallice.[3]

The spring attack phase in Canadian waters began with the sinking of the 6994-ton *British Workman* on 3 May 1942 by U-455 (Giessler) some 170 miles SSW of Cape Race. U-588 (Vogel) contributed to the impression of a general advance by carrying out a brief series of submerged and surface attacks in Nova Scotia waters. It first sank the 4031-ton *Kitty's Brock* on 10 May, some 45 miles SSW of Cape Roseway, Nova Scotia, and ten days later sank the 2117-ton Norwegian *Skottland* 60 miles southwest of Yarmouth, Nova Scotia. That same day, 130 miles southeast of Cape Roseway, U-432 (Schultze) sank the 324-ton Boston fishing vessel *Foam* by gunfire.[4] The *Skottland*'s crew survived. Typical of many events that would follow, a Canso flying boat from Yarmouth sighted twenty-five of *Skottland*'s survivors in one lifeboat and on two rafts and attracted the attention of a fishing vessel to their plight by directing machine-gun fire across her bows during a low fly-past. The fishing vessel towed the survivors ashore. On 18 May, U-588 attacked the Free French freighter *Fort Binger* some 60 miles southwest of Yarmouth. One torpedo struck a glancing blow off her bow; a second missed the stern. Typically, neither one exploded. When U-588 surfaced for an artillery attack, the freighter turned in vain to ram and then continued a gun duel that lasted an hour. For reasons that are still unclear, the French eventually abandoned their ship, only to be returned to it by the RCAF rescue vessel *Arresteur*, despatched from Yarmouth in response to their call for aid. The incident triggered a full search for U-588, which was sighted on the surface next day by the SS *Ocean Honour*. U-588 would be destroyed with all hands on 31 July 1942 by HMCS *Wetaskiwin* and *Skeena*.[5] On that day in May, U-432 was hunting within 30 miles of Yarmouth, Nova Scotia. It torpedoed and sank the 1198-ton Canadian SS *Liverpool Packet*. In the same general area on 3 June, it sank by gunfire the 102-ton trawler *Ben and Josephine* and the 41-ton *Aeolus*.

While U-588 and U-432 stirred up the waters off Nova Scotia, and U-213 slipped an agent into the Bay of Fundy, U-553 was commencing its innovative sortie. Kapitänleutnant Karl Thurmann's U-553 had departed St Nazaire on 19 April 1942, and crossed the southern tip of the Newfoundland Banks on 3 May, where dense fog forced U-553 to proceed predominantly submerged as its course curved northward toward Cape Race. At 0400 on 5 May, Commander U-boats authorized Thurmann's free operations from the Gulf of Maine to a quadrant northwest of Sable Island. Admiral Dönitz quite typically accorded his commanders greater freedom in the operational zone than the Allies often realized. During the next couple of days, Thurmann spent maximum time submerged, exercising his crew in emergency procedures and preparing his torpedoes. The first target emerged from the fog at 1500 on 6 May, while U-553 was cruising submerged some 80 miles south of Burin Peninsula, Newfoundland: an eastbound steamer zigzagging about 30 degrees either side of her base course, accompanied by a "corvette or escort at 800–1000 m, with two guns and broad bridge structure" (KTB). The torpedo failed, probably having underrun its target. Three minutes later U-553 met its first Canadian defences: the escort turned bows-on at high speed, and dropped a "single depth charge at medium range," causing minor periscope damage and, after a second attack, the "normal technical failures" (KTB). The attack ceased as quickly as it had begun.

Next evening, while cruising submerged without hydrophone contacts 20 miles southwest of Cape Breton's Scatarie Island, U-553 suddenly felt the effect of three "accidental aerial bombs" (KTB), which again caused the "normal technical failures." Thurmann had intended approaching Halifax. Now, however, as repairs would likely take several days, he needed a quieter operational zone not too far removed from chances of combat. He therefore decided on thrusting into the Cabot Strait and Gulf of St Lawrence. According to his copy of the *Sailing Directions*, these waters would be ice free by the end of April. Outbound traffic for Atlantic convoy assembly points, he reasoned, could be expected through both the Cabot Strait and the Gut of Canso. Thus, later Canadian operational assessments notwithstanding, this first foray deep into Canadian territorial waters was not the direct decision of German Naval Headquarters, but an initiative left to the independent judgment of a submarine captain.

U-553 advanced throughout the sixth and seventh days of May along a broad westerly to northwesterly curve in order to close Cape Breton and Scatarie islands, thence bearing off to the northeast in order to enter the Gulf of St Lawrence. The entrance to the Gulf, a 56-mile stretch of deep water in the Cabot Strait between Cape North and Cape Ray, Newfoundland, holds but one principal danger: the wreck-scarred St Paul Island, situated in the Gulf 13 miles northeast of Cape North. Its deep soundings and absence of shoal waters give the mariner in reduced visibility no warning of navigational hazard. U-553 shaped course to the northwest to round St Paul Island within a 10 mile arc, then led on to the red sandstone Rochers aux Oiseaux (Bird Rocks), which it rounded during the night of 8–9 May, some 20 miles to starboard. It reached a point 10 miles southwest of South Point, Anticosti Island, by noon on 9 May 1942. Thurmann confirmed this position by means of the Heath Point radio beacon on the eastern tip of Anticosti. Despite the mists and occasional fog it experienced, U-553 faced no navigational difficulties, for "lighthouses and radio beacons were functioning under peacetime conditions: Scatteri [sic], Flint [Island, Cape Percé], Cap Ray, Sable Island" (KTB). His sighting of a "large steamer" escorted by "eight torpedo boat type vessels in broad search formation" when 10 miles southeast of Scatarie on 7 May had confirmed his suspicions of commercial traffic routes (KTB). From its noon position on 9 May, U-553 patrolled westward in fog into Gaspé

Passage to a position 15 miles southwest of Southwest Point, Anticosti Island, then southeast to Orphan Bank. At this point he retraced its route until 0400 on 11 May, when he turned toward Cap des Rosiers on the Gaspé Peninsula.

Throughout 11–12 May 1942, U-553 patrolled from 3 to 8 miles off Gaspé, concentrating its search until 15 May within the area Cap Chat to Pointe à la Frégate. Between his sighting of the patrol of 7 May and a small coaster on 10 May, Kärlchen ("Charlie") Thurmann, as intimates called him, found nothing encouraging. This led him to conclude that traffic must be moving intermittently toward Halifax or St John's just prior to the departure of principal convoys from those ports. In consideration of the prevailing peacetime mentality, Thurmann concluded that ships would generally depart Montreal and Quebec on a Saturday; he thus calculated their arrival time off Gaspé. The first vessel, he mused, would have to be "bumped off" as far from land as possible, so that U-553 could remain unnoticed (KTB).

Pieces of evidence, not always substantive as it turns out, had led Canadian naval authorities to suspect a U-boat in this area, though of course they could not know exactly where it could strike. A shore HF/DF station on 24 April had positioned the radio transmission of a German submarine at $46°05'$ W, a meridian running through Flemish Cap, the detached bank lying 90 miles east of the Newfoundland Banks. They therefore expected this U-boat to advance towards the Nova Scotian coast. But when a shore watcher reported an "unidentified submarine on a westerly course off Cape Ray, Newfoundland," a Gulf attack seemed more reasonable.[6] The only U-boat in the area was U-553. Ironically, however, it already stood at this time some 80 miles to the northwest in the Gulf of St Lawrence, and hence could not have been seen. None the less, seeds of doubt had been sown in the minds of Canadian defence officials, and while cruising on 10 May some 30 miles east of Percé in 12-mile visibility, U-553 was attacked by a U.S. Army "four-engined land-based aircraft" from an altitude of 700 m (KTB). The U-boat crash-dived, receiving by Thurmann's count "five bombs at medium range," which again seemed to have caused nothing more than the "normal technical failures" (KTB). The aircraft reported seeing "air bubbles and debris on the surface," although a search two days later by the Halifax-based mine-sweeper HMCS *Medicine Hat* failed to discover any traces.[7]

U-553 had not only been seen; it was suffering technical problems. Many of these could not be solved on board. Its periscope required welding, the motor for the bow-planes malfunctioned; repairs on the bow-planes themselves, which created "a horrendous noise in the hydrophones," might betray its position (KTB). Equally disturbing, the transmission of the target acquisition equipment was malfunctioning as well.

But "patience is the main thing," Thurmann noted in his War Diary. It soon paid off. The "St Lawrence Incident" began a few hours later.

Thurmann was watching a small coastal freighter move into his sights around 0500 GMT on 12 May when his eye caught a "fully laden, approx. 5000 ton" vessel with "four loading hatches and two heavy derricks" (KTB). It was the 5364-ton British *Nicoya* en route from Montreal to the UK. Thurmann gave chase. His first torpedo struck her stern an hour later, followed by a coup de grâce amidships that sank her 10 miles north of Pointe à la Frégate at 0615 GMT. Sixty survivors landed at Cloridorme and L'Anse à Valleau.[8] The *Nicoya* had survived almost a year longer than the Germans had intended, for on 20 May 1941 her captain's skilful and persistent evasive action had wrested her from the hot pursuit of U-111 on the high seas.[9] U-553 steered westward into the misty St Lawrence at 10 knots past Cap de la Madeleine until at 0800 GMT on 12 May 1942 a "very long, approx. 6000 ton deep-laden vessel with at least five loading hatches" hove into view (KTB). It was the 4712-ton Dutch ship *Leto*, en route from Montreal to the UK. Canadian assessments later attributed Thurmann's speed in locating the SS *Leto* either to "good intelligence of the St. Lawrence shipping" or to his knowledge that "the ships in the river would be ordered to port at once, and that he would have little time in which to make another kill." Additionally, so it was thought, he might have headed west in order to avoid possible "warships coming to intercept him" from the Gulf.[10] In fact, however, Thurmann was merely reconnoitering and had come upon the *Leto* by sheer chance. Thurmann's single torpedo struck her amidships from 1200 m. She sank 12 minutes later, 17 miles north of Cap de la Madeleine. Thirty-one survivors landed at Pointe au Père (Father Point), near Rimouski; twelve were missing. Within an hour of sinking the *Leto*, U-553 witnessed the explosion of its torpedo against a 3000-ton vessel that no records identify. Thurmann remained convinced that he had now attacked a total of three ships.

COAC's Staff Office Operations correctly surmised the reasons for Thurmann's method of attack: keep to mid-stream in order to avoid detection from shore and to allow sea room and depth for emergency dives. All his attacks were surface attacks – except for the third, which occurred scarcely one hour later. For at 0908 GMT, Thurmann sighted two more vessels emerging from almost due west and began his approach; this time against the dark backdrop of the Gaspé coast. The increasing brightness of the early morning forced him to dive, where he found it paradoxically too dark to pick up both ships in his periscope. Only "the second vessel" was visible; according to Thurmann, his single torpedo had struck aft from a distance of 2000 m (KTB). Mist prevented his observing whether the "3000-ton ship" he claimed to have hit had actually sunk. Naval Service Headquarters in Ottawa provided the press with no details, and none are mentioned in Canadian records.

These sinkings had immediate repercussions, both tactical as well as political. Plan GL for the defence of the St Lawrence was put into effect on 17 May, while political factions debated the significance of the threat.[11] At 3:30 PM EST on 12 May 1942, Naval Service Headquarters issued a lean announcement:

The Minister for Naval Services announces that the first enemy submarine attack upon shipping on the St. Lawrence River took place on 11 May, when a freighter was sunk. Forty-one survivors have been landed from this vessel. The situation regarding shipping in the river is being closely watched, and long prepared plans for its special protection under these circumstances are in operation. Any possible future sinkings in this area will not be made public, in order that information of value to the enemy may be withheld from him.

The announcement reached the front pages of that day's issue of the *Ottawa Evening Journal* and the postscript edition of the *Montreal Daily Star*, which proclaimed in banner headlines, "Freighter Sunk by Sub in St. Lawrence." The *Vancouver Sun* for 12 May headlined the occurrence, "Axis Sub Sinks Ship in St. Lawrence," but otherwise restricted its coverage to a précis of the official statement. Montreal's *Le Devoir* did little better in a back-page account on 13 May: "Premier torpillage dans le golfe Saint-Laurent." Maritime papers like the *Halifax Herald*, of course, could not publish the material until the evening edition of 13 May 1942. Headlines proclaimed the sinking while a stylized map showed a "Nazi" sea serpent curling around the Nova Scotia coast, winding through the Cabot Strait and biting into what was termed the "Ocean Steamer Route" west of Anticosti Island. Eastern newspapers were quick to inflate an almost non-existent plot with quotation, speculation, and paraphrase. This first Canadian response reached Berlin in advance of Thurmann's report. At 9:15 AM on 13 May the public radio broadcast of the German military (*Wehrmachtsbericht*) transmitted from Berlin its first of a series of largely fabricated news reports, which fleshed out the statement of the Canadian government and drew upon its own incomplete data. The broadcast, as monitored and translated by Naval Service Headquarters, explained that:

German U-Boats are now operating in the St. Lawrence River, the nearest approach to land. A German U-Boat sank an American 6000 ton freighter yesterday, carrying a cargo of jute from India for Montreal. The ship had made the long voyage from India safely, only to be sunk in the St. Lawrence. This is the first time that U-Boats operate so far from the sea. The news broke like a bombshell in

Canada and the United States. The United States [sic] Navy Department announced that no further report will be given in any future sinkings which may occur in this region.

The Nazi party newspaper *Völkischer Beobachter* would in time illustrate the German panache by publishing a front-page aerial photograph of "the St. Lawrence River in which the U-boats [were] now operating": it showed a meandering creek no more than 1500 m wide. The Canadian Naval Staff regarded the radio broadcast as propaganda fiction, a combination of haste and ignorance. Ignoring the facts, the Germans had even failed to distinguish in their broadcast between spokesmen for the RCN (in this case, Canada's Minister for Naval Services) and those of the USN. But in German eyes Canada had, in fact, no authentic image or identity distinct from that of a lackey of England or a pawn of America. Reporting on 14 September 1944 on the Quebec conferences, *Völkischer Beobachter* would endorse what it perceived as the British view that Canada was a "no man's land between Empire and USA." Even as late as January 1945, Canada presented no clear identity for the crew of U-Dobratz (U-1232). They regarded Halifax quite simply as *Amerika*, and spoke of "teaching the Yankees a lesson."

The Hon. Angus L. Macdonald announced the second sinking with a statement in the House of Commons on 13 May that eastern newspapers like *Le Soleil* or the *Halifax Herald* immediately picked up. This, he explained, was not a revocation of his earlier ban on news releases, because the two sinkings really formed a single incident, being so close together. The *Montreal Daily Star* (13 May 1942) now headlined "U-Boats Sink Another in St. Lawrence: Enemy Still Preying on Vessels in River," while the *Ottawa Journal* announced: "Second Ship Sunk in St. Lawrence: Two Vessels Lost about Same Time in Canadian River." Not until two days later did Montreal's *Le Devoir* report, "Le double torpillage" and reveal with perhaps some impatience that "A Ottawa, on n'a aucune nouvelle d'une attaque contre un troisième navire."[12] Newsmen were quick to ferret out stories by interviewing residents of Gaspé fishing villages, telephoning local authorities and witnesses, and contacting survivors wherever they might be found. They pieced together and (to the navy's chagrin) actually published a number of accounts that provided considerable detail on the operations of U-553.

The Director of Censorship responded on behalf of the Canadian Naval Staff by issuing to newsmen and broadcasters "Notes on the Publication of News Stories."[13] The "Notes" analysed press reports on the St Lawrence sinkings, and showed how seemingly innocent human interest stories and journalistic sleuthing could actually communicate substantive items of information to the enemy. The official government release, the censor argued, communicated virtually nothing vital except the fact that an attack had taken place and that long-standing countermeasures had been put into effect. The enemy already knew the first detail, he pointed out, and would have suspected the second. The newspapers, on the other hand, had permitted the enemy important inferences. They shed light on the number and size of ships sunk, the time and location of the action, the war readiness of DEMS (defensively equipped merchant ships), the prevailing weather conditions, escort procedures, and the logistics of the U-boat itself.

The German radio broadcast was not entirely off the mark in "reporting" the impact of these sinkings in Canada. If news of this U-boat action had not, in its phrase, "broke[n] like a bombshell," then it had, in the government's official paraphrase, caused considerable "consternation" and indeed political recoil. Both the *Montreal Daily Star* and the *Ottawa Journal* published a map of the Atlantic area from the Gulf of Maine to the Strait of Belle Isle, correctly positioning the attacks in "the broad stretch west of Anticosti."[14] *Le Soleil* published a similar map on 15 May revealing the startling news that "la guerre se rapproche du Canada." *Le Soleil* suspected U-boats very close to home on the south shore of the lower St Lawrence, even though "les autorités n'ont pas voulu révéler à quel endroit le ou les sousmarins nazis ont accompli leur oeuvre de mort."[15] Yet in the English-language press the Canadian Press caption "War Comes Nearer to Quebec with an Invasion of the St. Lawrence River" singled out Canada's francophone province as the "enfant terrible" in the debate on conscription for overseas service. The *Halifax Herald* (13 May 1942) regarded Mr Macdonald's announcement of the attacks as "a revelation that brings this war home directly to the people of the Province of Quebec." The *Montreal Daily Star* described how "veteran political observers" had commented on an irony in Quebec's stance. For, while "survivors from a ship torpedoed by a Nazi U-Boat in the St. Lawrence were being landed at a Quebec port, members whose ridings are close to the submarine area were scurrying around Parliament Buildings signing a paper protesting [that] they opposed Premier King," who at the time was "seeking freedom for greater war effort."[16]

The issue was in fact a struggle within the Liberal caucus itself: one faction having signed a resolution endorsing unlimited confidence in the prime minister; another faction, opposing any increase in his wartime powers, having been absent from the caucus meeting. By extension, however, the disenchanted faction was portrayed as representing Quebec's petulant expression of non-confidence in the government in which ten Quebec MPs – the same ten who had voted against the plebiscite legislation the previous winter – now rejected the resolution of Ernest Bertrand (Lib., Laurier) and its seconder G.A. McLean (Lib., Simcoe East). As newspapers reminded their readers, the ridings of three of the ten – Jean Francois Pouliot (Lib., Temiscouta), L.P. Lizotte (Lib., Kamouraska), and Emannuel D'Anjou (Lib., Rimouski) – bordered on the new St Lawrence war zone. The *Halifax Herald* prided itself on speaking for a constituency whose "citizens know that enemy submarines are operating just beyond the skyline." Maritime people, it explained, didn't need any chastening by such an "act of Hun piracy." Now, however, "for the first time, the undersea pirates have struck ... within sight and sound of Quebec habitations." Perhaps a change in attitude might be expected. Or, as its editorial pondered with inflated pathos: "Will these dread and heavy tidings serve now to change the minds of some who have contended that the armed forces of this country should not go beyond this country for its protection?"

The *Halifax Herald* might have spared its readers such self-righteous rhetoric, for the nation as a whole bristled with anomalies. Elements outside Quebec were no less loath to deny that Canada was in a state of war in which certain customary liberties of peacetime might have to be temporarily suspended. Vital shipbuilding yards in Midland and Kingston, Ontario, had in April 1942 illegally gone on strike because a worker had been demoted. This caused Labour Minister Mitchell in the Commons to compare the wilfulness of industry with the sense of duty projected by "the men who go down to the sea in ships, in corvettes."[17] In Nova Scotia, miners walked off the job in May 1942 despite the obvious and urgent need for coal, laying idle the Princess Colliery of the Nova Scotia Coal & Steel Company. Even the attempt at rationalizing the work of loading convoys by reorganizing the Port of Halifax and placing the longshoremen under a controller, Dalhousie Dean of Law Vincent C. Macdonald, met with heated opposition in the Commons. The Conservative House Leader, supported by Angus MacInnes (CCF, Vancouver East) and John Diefenbaker (Con., Lake Centre), attacked it, newspapers not incorrectly reported, as a "conscription of labour." The peacetime lighthouses, buoys, and radio beacons of Atlantic Canada, as the German submariners readily recognized, symbolized the country's approach to war.

The mounting toll of ships sunk (or believed sunk) in the St Lawrence punctuated the continuing conscription debate, both in the House of Commons and in the Quebec legislature. "Nazi" attacks close to Canada's heartland shed special light on the issue for those living along the river and Gulf. Triggered by the sights and sounds of sinkings, torpedoings, and wounded survivors, exaggerated rumours spread among the populace whose speculations on the actual scope of "the battle" were ironically nourished by the federal government's silence. As *Le Soleil* for 16 May 1942 tried to explain, "Les rumeurs les plus fantastiques circulent dans le

bas fleuve depuis qu'a été announcé officiellement que deux navires mar-
chands ont été torpillés ... On deduit que, d'autres torpillages ont été
effectués que la censure garde secret."

During this time, U-553 maintained constant radio "listening watch"
with BdU in conditions ranging from good reception to very poor. On 14
May 1942, while some 12 miles north of Rivière à Claude, Kapitänleutnant Thurmann broke radio silence and sent his first St Lawrence situation report: "In [naval quadrant BB] 1475 sunk two freighters 11,000 tons,
one 3000 tonner torpedoed. Light and radio beacons as peacetime, meagre
sea surveillance; very very attentive air cover" (KTB). He apparently was
not picked up by Canadian monitoring stations, which could have directed
searching forces on to him by HF/DF (high frequency direction finding),
as would happen a week later. Thurmann amplified these lean details in a
transmission of 16 May, again without being detected: "Intermittent heavy
feeder traffic without escort [via] Cape Gaspé, Gut of Canso, depending
upon [main] convoy departure. Have not hindered incoming traffic. Consider area promising. Submerged by day since 12th, unnoticed, high pressure [weather], 83 [m^3 of fuel remaining], 7 + 2 [torpedoes left]."

Six days later Naval Service Headquarters in Ottawa transcribed the
text of yet another public radio broadcast of the German military in
Berlin, proclaiming that a "German submarine penetrated through the
Gulf of St. Lawrence into the St. Lawrence River and sank, in defiance of
the guard of numerous naval and air formations, three ships totalling
14,000 tons."[18] The broadcast singled out three U-boat commanders,
Thurmann among them, as having "distinguished themselves, particularly
in American waters." This gave the Canadians a clue as to the identity of
the St Lawrence submarine. In fact, the German morale-building practice
of mentioning captains' names in public broadcasts, or using them in
place of U-boat pennant and hull numbers as addressee designators in
ciphers provided a personal dimension in Naval Intelligence to which the
Allies did not respond in kind. The crew of "U-Thurmann" heard this
particular *Wehrmachtsbericht* (military report) from Berlin while south-
bound in Cabot Strait off Cape Breton Island. The event caused "great
jubilation" on board (KTB). On 22 May, Thurmann and his crew received
a personal communiqué from Admiral Karl Dönitz for a job well done.
But as NSHQ had not intercepted Thurmann's situation report of May, it
concluded that Berlin's reference to a "third ship" had no more reliable
source "than a speculation made to the Canadian press by the captain of
the *Leto*." Date-lined Levis, Quebec, a front-page report in the *Ottawa
Journal* (14 May 1942) and others then claimed an interview with a
captain and a gunner of one of the two sunk vessels during a whistle-stop
en route by train to Montreal. These survivors speculated that the U-boat
"trailed one of its victims for 6 miles before loosing a fatal torpedo."

German records do not indicate whether these newspapers reports reached Berlin; as noted, Thurmann was likely the sole source of the information. NSHQ doubted this at the time, however, and based its opinion on the distorted fiction that "the drastic punishment meted out to German crews for deliberate exaggeration of their successes rendered it unlikely that the Commander had fabricated the story himself."[19] In this case, the Canadian stereotyped view of relations within the U-boat command obscured the facts.

Canadians had first reacted to the attacks of U-553 by instituting the convoy system. At 0330 on 21 May, 1942, Thurmann observed another of Canada's defensive responses: Cape Gaspé Light, including outer beacons, was now extinguished. It was one of those rare and transient occasions when navigational beacons were shut down in response to imminent threat, for higher authorities continued to assert the necessity of maintaining full navigational facilities at all times except in utmost and immediate danger to shipping. At 0400 GMT on 21 May, U-553 exited Cabot Strait about 5–10 miles east of Cap des Rosiers on the Gaspé Peninsula and transmitted a lengthy report to BdU. NSHQ in Ottawa D/F'd the transmission, placing the U-boat in effect 26 miles northeast of where it actually stood. NSHQ incorrectly concluded that Thurmann's two messages of 159 and 122 groups each were the "U-Boat's first communications with Germany by W/T [wireless telegraphy] and indicated that he was making his report just prior to returning to base." In fact, however, U-553 had only partially completed its mission, for "Boat A," as Canadian naval authorities had now designated it in their plot, intended to "circumnavigate Sable Island and then steer for Halifax" before rounding the southern tip of Nova Scotia to enter the Bay of Fundy (KTB). NSHQ anticipated that "the easy access of 'A' would prompt the German Admiralty to send further boats into the Gulf." A series of HF/DF fixes from 13 to 16 May indicating a "westbound U-Boat steering in a northwesterly direction at 10–12 knots," almost maximum surface speed, seemed to corroborate the hunch. It seemed probable to the Submarine Tracking Room in NSHQ, Ottawa, "that 'B' had been instructed to operate in the area southeast of Anticosti or in the Cabot Strait, and stayed in the Gulf only a short time after discovering that shipping was closely guarded." Whether B was U-455 (Giessler) or U-432 (H.O. Schultze) is not clear, though Thurmann's U-553 was the only U-boat to operate in the Gulf of St Lawrence in May 1942.

For the next three days thick fog from Cape Breton to Cape Sable hampered the operational cruise of U-553. Such conditions offered little prospects of success from the 20-fathom line to seaward, and the U-boat's low fuel reserves prevented reconnoitering further to the south of the fog boundary. Thurmann exercised his freedom by optimizing his tactical situation. Both his *Sailing Directions* and the monthly climate charts suggested a solution. As he wrote in his War Diary, he could expect "less fog in the Bay of Fundy" and might even find significant targets in the large harbour of Saint John, New Brunswick, with its "ten meters of water along the jetties and its drydock" (KTB). He therefore decided to enter the Gulf of Maine and then penetrate the bay as far as Saint John.

Thurmann began to round the southern tip of Nova Scotia in fog some 35 miles south of Cape Sable. No shipping emerged from the mists except for a three-masted gaff-rigged schooner on 25 May, approximately 45 miles southwest of Seal Island. The echo sounder had now broken down, leading Thurmann to patrol across the 30-mile-wide entrance to the Bay of Fundy in relative safety while effecting repairs. The bay's strong and uncertain tidal streams, the prevalence of fog, and the difficulty of obtaining safe anchorage in typically deep waters, as the *Sailing Directions* warn, demand that a seafarer navigate with "unremitting attention." A submarine could escape the tactical dangers of fog by submerging; it could not in the same way escape the strong currents, which here reach depths of 30 fathoms (50 m). As Thurmann worked his way around Lurcher Shoal, then steered on Southwest Head, Grand Manan Island, thence rounding to Saint John, he saw few targets: a motor sailer that passed ahead, a large neutral freighter with "Spanish colours illuminated on the ship's side" (KTB), fish cutters, and a single escort. At 0315 GMT on 27 May 1942 Thurmann surfaced off the entrance to the harbour, as U-213 had done two weeks earlier when landing its spy, and recorded in his War Diary: "Surfaced. Six miles off a brightly illuminated St. [sic] John. Radio and navigational beacons as in peacetime. Barrage at harbour entrance with a powerful searchlight which apparently is only tested a couple of times at the onset of darkness. Lay stopped on the surface." The scene offered an indifferent aspect as U-553 lay in a becalmed sea, in full moonlight, and brazenly signalled Berlin one more situation report. Throughout the next day Thurmann exercised action stations, and listened on hydrophones. Only occasionally did a ship exit or enter; only occasionally did an escort appear. Not until 4 June did an intercepted radio report from U-432 explain why the zone was empty: U-432 had been chasing a four-ship convoy in the vicinity, after having sunk the fishing vessel *Foam* south of Halifax a week earlier.[20] To Thurmann's mind it was "such a lousy piece of work" that his colleague had not let him in on the hunt (KTB). Each night U-553 lay quietly on the surface and radioed Berlin. On 29 May, from 0343 until 0705 GMT, Thurmann observed night exercises of aircraft flying at 500 feet over the water, and noticed groups of escorts moving to within 1000 m – all ran darkened except for a couple of unidentified vessels with navigation lights burning. He watched as one aircraft flew directly over the U-boat while escorts manoeuvred. His conclusion: "Apparently exercises in ship recognition by aircraft" (KTB). At 1015 GMT, U-553 again radioed Berlin. Gradually withdrawing southwestward, 60 miles down the Bay of Fundy, Thurmann began drawing his conclusions in the vicinity of Briar Island, 11 miles off the entrance to St Mary's Bay:

Six days and nights uninterrupted and unnoticed observation lead to the conclusion that St. John [sic], at least at the moment, is not used as a loading terminal for convoys. On the other hand, intense training activity with convoy protection, in connection with sub chasers and air cover. Further, a rather lively coming and going of corvettes, etc., suggest that St. John [sic] is used as a support base, equipment and resting place for screening and security forces in order to take the pressure off convoy assembly bases. (KTB)

Meanwhile, at midnight on 30 May, U-432 torpedoed and sank the 1188-ton *Sonia* off Seal Island, Nova Scotia. Nineteen survivors landed at Barington Passage, roughly midway between Yarmouth and Shelburne. As one of the survivors reported:

After the ship sank the U-Boat surfaced and whilst keeping her guns trained on the lifeboat an officer interrogated the Master with regard to her cargo, destination, etc. The Master in his turn asked the officer if he was [sic] a German, no doubt in surprise and happy wonder at not having been machine gunned, and was answered in the affirmative. The U-Boat picked up a lifebuoy with the ship's name on it, and also some other flotsam from the wreck.[21]

At 0400 GMT on 1 June 1942, Thurmann stood 25 miles west of Cape St Mary's and sent his final signal to Berlin on Canadian defences: numerous corvettes and escorts of all types, lively fishing activity, up to five "three-engined heavy land-based" aircraft in the air at one time. (Training activity over the Bay of Fundy had clearly impressed him.) He advised that he still had nine torpedoes and twenty-five days provisions, and intended to seek targets in U.S. waters. His fortunes changed on 2 June when after two torpedo failures he sank the 6919-ton freighter SS *Mattawin*. Seven lifeboats of survivors escaped. A Yarmouth-based Canso flying boat from 162 (BR) Squadron sighted the lifeboats fourteen hours later, dropped food and distress flares, and vectored the Norwegian freighter SS *Torvanger* to the rescue. Nine hours later the freighter picked up thirty-two survivors from two lifeboats and landed them at Halifax next day. A lifeboat with twenty survivors landed at Nauset, Cape Cod, on 4 June. Three days later the USS *General Green* rescued nineteen survivors and landed them at Nantucket.[22] One day after the attack, U-553 discovered an empty unmarked lifeboat, doubtless from the *Mattawin*. Thurmann's commentary on the find sheds light on living conditions aboard the U-boat, for the lifeboat contained delicacies that they themselves did not have: "Lots of well-preserved bread and chocolate for two complete meals; and condensed milk, too, and good-tasting vitamin tablets of enormously satiating effect, enough for fourteen days, all very welcome" (KTB).

Thurmann was beginning to count daily rations very closely as he now extended himself in the U.S. operational zone before returning home. On 5 June 1942, calculating that he had but seventeen days of supplies on board and that a fuel replenishment was impossible, he set course for his French base by skirting the fog boundary on a curve from the American coast and across the Newfoundland Banks. From 350 miles southeast of Halifax until clear of the Bank, Thurmann was bothered by air patrols. From his noon position on 10 June to the security of St Nazaire stretched 2200 nautical miles of inhospitable ocean, which at 180 miles per day would take thirteen days to transit. At this point Thurmann had barely fourteen days rations on board and was gravely concerned. He nevertheless returned to the vicinity of Virgin Rocks in response to radio reports of a UK–Halifax convoy, which he could attack with his three remaining torpedoes. At 2000 hours GMT on 11 June, U-553 was surprised on the surface by a still-unidentified flying boat approaching from 1500 m altitude 160 miles southeast of Cape Race. Thurmann dived to 40 m, but was bracketed by "two bombs starboard aft fairly close" (KTB). The "normal technical failures" (KTB) were reported and repaired. It soon became apparent, however, that the air attack had caused even greater damage, for the bombs had cracked the cylinder blocks of the port diesel, rendering the engine useless. His strained resources and the doggedness of "the same flying boat" (KTB) that kept him at bay soon turned U-553 away. For whenever Thurmann surfaced to hasten an approach to the convoy, this "stubborn fellow" would force the U-boat to crash dive and then circle around the point where the submarine had just disappeared (KTB). Under such circumstances, Thurmann had no hopes of success, and limped off to St Nazaire where he arrived at 1045 hours on 24 June 1942, one day after rations had given out. Admiral Karl Dönitz observed of the mission: "A well-executed and tough-minded operation. The captain's decision to penetrate into the St. Lawrence River is especially emphasized. It was rewarded with the success of three ships" (KTB).

The activity of U-boats off Canadian shores in June had caused Eastern Air Command to escalate its own operations to over 587,000 miles in 657 patrols. This meant almost 4500 hours aloft covering 147 convoys. During the month of July when, in the RCAF's phrase, "U-Boat activities reached a high pitch in Western Atlantic waters," Eastern Air Command would fly 891 operational patrols and cover over 700,000 miles.[23] The RCAF scented some success – for example, on 23 June some 35 miles SSW of

Sambro Island Light. Here, at 1000 hours GMT, Hudson 653 from 11 (BR) Squadron at Dartmouth, Nova Scotia, attacked a surfaced U-boat that might have been the homeward-bound U-432. The aircraft straddled the U-boat's hull with four depth charges while the conning tower was still visible. The U-boat resurfaced shortly thereafter, only to be strafed by 500 rounds from the Hudson's machine-guns. RCAF officials assessed this as an "excellent attack," which should have caused "crippling damage."[24]

Meanwhile, outbound from European waters, U-132 (Vogelsang) had begun its operational cruise to the St Lawrence in mid June 1942 with a fierce pounding by an unidentified corvette. The U-boat had departed its French base of La Pallice on 10 June for a journey that – despite its initial ordeal – would cover almost 10,000 nautical miles in sixty-eight days. Its route would run into the Gulf of St Lawrence via Cabot Strait and from there westwards through Gaspé Passage south of Anticosti Island to longitude 67° 37′ W, some 5 miles west of Matane, Quebec, on the southern shore of the Gaspé Peninsula. It would then patrol eastwards to Pointe Ouest, the westernmost tip of Anticosti Island, then return to Cap Chat before following Anticosti's southern coast through Gaspé Passage and onward to explore deep into the Strait of Belle Isle. Backtracking to the Gulf, U-132 would transit Jacques Cartier Passage (otherwise known as Mingan Passage) to the north of Anticosti and reconnoitre in now-familiar territory off Cap Chat and Ste-Anne-des-Monts. Its departure route would follow the southeasterly curve of Gaspé from Cap de la Madeleine to L'Anse à Valleau, and thence round the Magdalen Islands before exiting mid channel through Cabot Strait. It would be an unprecedented tour of Canadian inshore waters.

Now, however, on the evening of 13 June 1942, such prospects seemed less than likely. U-132 crash-dived under the onslaught of the corvette's well-aimed surface gunnery, sustaining periscope damage that forced it to remain between 18-m and 20-m depth if it wished to observe its pursuer. During the next two and one half hours, U-132 received 106 well-placed depth charges, which almost destroyed it as leaks and technical failures destabilized its buoyancy and trim. Despite engine room damage and tell-tale oil traces, U-132 escaped. Its captain, Kapitänleutnant Vogelsang, tenaciously steered deeper into the Atlantic in order to join six other U-boats in forming Gruppe Endrass. Admiral Dönitz had ordered the seven to "rake" along the course of Halifax–Greenland convoy HG-84.[25] This was the technique of forming line abreast about 20–30 miles apart at right angles to the convoy's suspected base course. The first U-boat to contact the convoy would shadow it, signal the others, and wait for the "pack" to assemble before attacking. But, on learning of the extent of U-132's damage, Commander U-boats ordered it home. The unshakeable Vogelsang replied that his Boat could "carry out the convoy task to the end" (KTB). Air cover prevented his reaching the convoy before the "wolf pack" search action was broken off by German U-boat headquarters on 16 June. U-89 (Lohmann) and U-132 were ordered to replenish from U-183 (Schäfer) before taking up new assignments in attack area CA off the eastern coast of the United States.

Vogelsang insisted on continuing his operations (KTB). He proceeded westward until 26 June when, at a position some 230 miles southeast of Cape Race, the Commander U-boats assigned him the Canadian combat area "Bruno Bruno." In so doing, Admiral Dönitz drew Vogelsang's attention to Thurmann's radio report, which had specified the zone BB 14 to the west of Anticosti as a "favourable attack area."[26] In a lengthy message, Dönitz then directed him to attack traffic at the narrowest part of "the pipe" (der Schlauch). This implied that he should advance as far into the St Lawrence River as a line joining Pointe des Monts on the northern shore with Ste Félicité in the south. Vogelsang in fact exceeded these suggested limits. Dönitz further advised that U-132 could expect intermittent traffic, "especially on Saturday, possibly on Sunday," and that defences probably consisted solely of air patrols. He specifically sought information on whether shipping also passed through the Strait of Belle Isle. If after "careful and dogged observation," the area should prove unfruitful, Vogelsang was at liberty to choose another attack zone. Thus, contrary to earlier assumptions about the operation of U-132 in the St Lawrence, Vogelsang did not in fact have "a detailed report of U-553's previous experience in the same area."[27] Thurmann could not brief Dönitz personally until at least two weeks after Vogelsang had left his French base.

While U-132 was skirting Newfoundland en route for Cabot Strait on 21 June 1942, the British submarine P-514 (LCdr R.M.E. Pain, RN) was travelling on the surface en route from Argentia to St John's, Newfoundland. It had been serving with Canadian warships in antisubmarine exercises. The passage of friendly submarines through one's operational area in waters likely to be frequented by the enemy had to be planned and protected. Disposition reports had to be signalled to all friendly commands, notifying them of the submarine's route, its identifying signals, and challenges. Submarine captains had to be briefed. They rarely transited such waters unescorted. Axis and Allies alike practised this basic principle of maritime warfare. On this occasion HMS/M P-514 was escorted by the Canadian corvettes HMCS Chambly and Bittersweet and two Royal Navy flower-class corvettes serving under RCN control, HMS Dianthus and HMS Primrose. Thick weather had closed in, separating P-514 from its escorts. It was now as alone as it had been when it ran aground in St Margaret's Bay on 8 April 1942.

Now, at 0530 GMT on 21 June, the Bangor minesweeper HMCS Geor-

gian (LCdr A.G. Stanley, RCNR) was escorting the St John's–Sydney convoy CL-43 south of Cape Pine on Newfoundland's Avalon Peninsula when she sighted a surfaced submarine. Convoy CL-43 was running one and a half hours late; this placed it 10 nautical miles behind the position promulgated in COAC's situation report to Allied warships in the local area. COAC had by this time altered the course of the submarine and its escorts in order to avoid contact with North Atlantic convoy SC-88 outbound from Sydney. But this convoy too was about 10 miles northward of its proper course. During his visit to the FONF operations room in St John's prior to his departure, *Georgian*'s captain had been shown the operations chart displaying the route of convoy SC-88. But as neither HMS/M P-514 nor its escorts had yet left harbour – as indeed had neither HMCS *Georgian* nor her convoy CL-43 – no routes had been drawn on this chart that might otherwise have hinted at a potentially dangerous convergence of tracks. In any event, Canadian authorities clearly understood it to be the submarine's responsibility either to avoid friendly ships altogether, particularly convoys under escort, or else be prepared for immediate and efficient identification.

Having received no disposition warning, HMCS *Georgian* took immediate, though cautious, offensive action by first challenging the unidentified submarine during the attack run. Admiral Dönitz would not have condoned this aspect of the Canadian captain's method, for he had always taught his own commanders that challenging an unidentified target betrayed one's position and effectively eliminated the element of surprise. Dönitz had reproved one of his own captains for having missed his chance of sinking an Allied vessel because he first tried to exchange recognition signals. By the same token, as deciphered Enigma signals showed, he was less than pleased when another U-boat captain, Ali Cremer (U-333), sank their own blockade runner *Spreewald* without having tried to establish her identity. It was a tense position for any attacker to be in. In all likelihood, LCdr Stanley had an uneasy hunch that his contact might be friendly. But, as the submarine failed to respond to successive challenges, HMCS *Georgian* rammed it, sustaining severe damage to her own bows. HMS/M P-514 sank with all hands off Cape Pine. Escorts searched the area when the mistake was discovered, but found neither survivors nor debris. Searches by trained antisubmarine personnel revealed no contact clearly identifiable as a bottomed submarine. Nor was it ever clarified why P-514 had failed to respond to the challenge.

A subsequent Board of Inquiry presided over by Captain E.R. Mainguy (who became Chief of the Naval Staff in 1951) correctly exonerated LCdr Stanley. In commenting on the proceedings of the board, Rear-Admiral L.W. Murray, at the time Flag Officer, Newfoundland Force, agreed that

Georgian's commanding officer had taken "the only action appropriate to the occasion and recommend[ed] that he should be commended for his prompt and efficient measures under difficult circumstances."[28] The sinking of the British submarine remained a well-kept secret until January 1946, when both the Canadian Press and Reuter's sought information on the "incident" of which they had somehow become aware. That HMCS *Georgian* had sunk HMS/M P-514 seems to have been the only fact the press possessed. In light of this, the Director of Naval Information, Cdr (Special Branch) William Strange, RCNVR, decided that failure to clarify the issue would invite the press to release a garbled version and expose the navy to criticism of having "covered up" an admittedly nasty and embarrassing issue. NSHQ in Ottawa and the Admiralty in London agreed to release a terse factual statement.[29]

This was not the only occasion when Allied forces sank one of their own submarines. In July 1944, for example, aircraft from a "MAC" ship (merchant aircraft carrier) in convoy ONM-243 sank the Free French submarine *La Perle*. The incident pointed to possible weaknesses either in communication procedures within the convoy itself, or else in procedures for transmitting friendly submarine intelligence from shore, or perhaps even both.[30] According to a spurious myth, *La Perle* had been sunk on purpose, "as no French ship was to be trusted." Such incidents were not confined to Allied operations. Germans sank their own kind as well, and under similar circumstances.

Admiral Murray's review of the inquiry into the loss of HMS/M P-514 raised searching questions about the navy's operational control of friendly submarines in passage near Allied convoys. Not the least of these difficulties, he noted in passing, was one that had bedevilled his organization for months: "the lack of any officer of experience [on his] operations staff" – with, of course, the notable exception of his own Chief of Staff. While Murray supported all reasonable measures to assure the security of friendly submarines – including the restriction of aircraft bombings along their promulgated route – he remained adamant on an important point of principle that had prevailed during *Georgian*'s attack: "I am not in favour of warning escorts of the possibility of meeting a friendly submarine as I do not wish A/S escorts, under my command, to be required to 'pull their punches' at any time when a submarine is sighted on the surface in vicinity of their convoy."

As U-132 approached the entrance to Cabot Strait on 30 June 1942, engine problems reminded Vogelsang that even minor depth-charge damage was gradually beginning to affect his Boat. The other concern was air surveillance, which began with a flying boat 58 miles northeast of Scatarie Island. By July 1942 many RCAF aircraft overflying the St Lawrence River and Gulf were equipped with what official records cryptically refer to as "special equipment." This was the ASV (air-to-surface vessel) radar with a theoretical range of 4.5 miles. At this time, however, ASV was useless for detecting U-boats in the Gulf, and even out to sea almost every sighting by aircraft was made visually. Not until late in the year did ASV detections begin to play a large part in mid-ocean operations, and not until mid 1943 did Eastern Air Command develop adequate ASV tactics. Ultimately, however, it did turn tactical advantage into Allied hands.[31]

U-132 faced no navigational problems, for besides the usual aids to coastal navigation, "radio beacons functioned under peacetime conditions according to the current List of Lights and Radio Signals" (KTB). Four days later, when 6 miles off Cap de la Madeleine, Vogelsang watched two 3500-ton vessels in ballast emerge from the mists well beyond range. Then, on 4 July, off Capucins 6 miles west of Cap Chat in the St Lawrence, he picked up three distant hydrophone echoes; fog enshrouded his targets. From shortly after midnight on 6 July until 0330 hours GMT Vogelsang observed ships gathering some 5 miles to the east of Baie Comeau until they had formed a twelve-ship convoy, too distant for him to attack. Surfacing, he glimpsed five inbound vessels in the area 5 miles distant off Cap Chat. Ship movements suggested a pattern; in this case, a change over of convoys and escorts. Here, at 0507 hours, on 6 July, Vogelsang began tracking Quebec–Sydney convoy QS-15 as it cut through a glistening phosphorescent sea in bright moonlight in a formation so tight as to give Vogelsang the impression of "overlapping vessels" (KTB).

What followed, according to Eastern Air Command, constituted "the greatest loss that was sustained in any one locality" in the western Atlantic that month.[32] Four independently targeted torpedoes fired from 1500 m struck both the 4312-ton Belgian SS *Hainault* and the 3382-ton Greek SS *Anastasios Pateras* 14 minutes later with two distinct explosions. This indicated two torpedo failures in the group. One of the steamers sank deeply by the stern. The sound of exploding torpedoes and bursting ships scattered the convoy "in all directions, the greater part inbound" (KTB), as U-132 edged to within five boat lengths of an escort. Still surfaced, U-132 fired at a 6000-ton vessel from 1000 m: torpedo failure. A further shot at another vessel under similar circumstances also failed.

At 0645 GMT, U-132 came to within 800 m of the 4312-ton British SS *Dinaric*. The lumber carrier flew the convoy Vice-Commodore's flag. Vogelsang torpedoed this "7000-ton vessel" amidships (KTB). Slipping around the *Dinaric*'s stern, he observed the vessel blow steam, list to starboard, and turn toward shore. German authorities credited U-132 with having sunk three ships for a total of 10,249 tons.[33] At the moment, however, Vogelsang was startled and distracted by the muzzle flash of guns firing star shell. He took U-132 into an immediate emergency dive as the Bangor minesweeper HMCS *Drummondville* (Lt J.P. Fraser, RCNR) attempted to ram; she then ran over the diving position and dropped depth charges. Vogelsang now encountered an uncomfortable anomaly of St Lawrence waters: the "shifting water layers" (KTB) of varying density prevented his submerging deeper than 20 m with the usual settings. U-132 hung at this level with a slight rising tendency as HMCS *Drummondville* bracketed it with "three well-placed depth charges" (KTB). As normal flooding procedures had failed to take the Boat down quickly enough, Vogelsang ordered the forward torpedo cells flooded. The Boat now "fell" to a depth of 40 m just as three more depth charges exploded within a range of 300 m. U-132 balanced at 80 m as three more depth charges exploded in the distance.

Drummondville's attacks exacerbated earlier defects that U-132 had suffered. Among other things, the main ballast pump damper was broken. This meant that Vogelsang could now only flood and pump by means of the fine-adjustment flooding valve. U-132 slipped inexorably to 185 m as Vogelsang tried to hold it level by blowing tanks. It rose briefly to 100 m as the last six depth charges exploded. Then quiet. Despite the U-boat's speed of slow ahead – the minimum speed capable of creating the necessary thrust and lift in a destabilized Boat without alerting the Canadian's hydrophone – U-132 sank to 180 m. With only 80 kg of compressed air remaining, Vogelsang finally blew all tanks and broke surface at 1746 GMT. All was quiet and dark; two escorts stood 2 miles off. U-132 dashed off at full speed, pursued by an escort that fired four star shells far from the mark. U-132 stood off in the enclosing darkness as the escort fired two groups of three-to-four depth charges into the illuminated zone.

Vogelsang was relieved that the Canadians had now quite clearly "lost" him (KTB); he followed the 100 m sounding into safe water where he would eventually lie on the bottom, rest, and wait. His pumping and flooding systems were damaged, one of the ballast tanks was no longer watertight, and he had lost 4 m^3 of oil, perhaps even leaving a trail on the surface.[34] *Drummondville's* captain later claimed to have sighted the enemy either "on its side, bottom up, or with the conning tower blown off."[35] Canadians claim to have seen much wreckage after it had dived. It is not clear from records on either side just when or how this occurred, unless U-132 had broken surface during one of her destabilized buoyant lifts. The British Assessment Committee, which exercised stringent adjudication criteria on behalf of both the RAF and the RCAF, concluded that there was "insufficient evidence of the presence of a U-Boat" at the spot where *Drummondville* had attacked, and quite rightly did not credit her with a kill.

The need to withdraw took Vogelsang to the westernmost tip of Anticosti, where he turned toward Fame Point on Gaspé Peninsula. Not until 16 July would his jury-rigged pumping and flooding system function satisfactorily. Heavy sea and air surveillance (KTB) in the St Lawrence River between Gaspé and Anticosti decided Vogelsang in favour of exploring the Strait of Belle Isle. In the early hours of 10 July 1942, just at the northeastern limit of the Gulf some 26 miles southeast of St Mary Island, Vogelsang transferred his forward torpedoes. At 1148 GMT, in German naval quadrant AH 9777, he met his first Canadian patrol: "two type 'Speedy' minesweepers and four patrol boats" (KTB). U-132 went to action stations at slow ahead, following "the six boats which pass through the narrows" (KTB) into Belle Isle Strait between Forteau Bay, Labrador, and Capstan Point, Newfoundland. After four hours of tracking, the crew stood down from action stations. Except for an occasional coastal sailing vessel off the Newfoundland coast on 10 July, sailboats and "four-engined land-based aircraft" on 11 July, and one steamer escorted by a destroyer on 12 July, Vogelsang declared the area operationally "unfavourable" (KTB). Commander U-boats confirmed at this time that Vogelsang could shift operational areas at his own discretion (KTB).

The beginning of the "Bataille du Saint-Laurent" aroused the latent suspicions of many Quebecers that the federal government had been neglecting to provide adequate defences. The government's steadfast silence about U-boat predations, which were painfully obvious to inhabitants along the St Lawrence River and Gulf, heightened a mood of anxious distrust. Petitioned by his constituents and provoked by the federal government's apparent insensitivity to the situation, Mr J.S. Roy (Gaspé) rose in the House on 10 July 1942 on an urgent question of privilege.[36] Having been informed by his constituency that "there have been some more ships sunk by enemy submarines since the time of the first attack on 11 May and 12 May last," and concerned that "three more ships forming part of a fourteen ship convoy [had been] torpedoed last Sunday night opposite Cap Chat in the St. Lawrence," Roy challenged the government. It should either clarify the situation forthwith or else convene a secret session in order "to inform the people's representatives as to the seriousness of the situation." Significantly, the prime minister himself responded by upbraiding Roy for his indiscretion by publicly broaching a subject, the details of which might benefit the enemy; and in any event, the PM continued, the release of any such information remained the prerogative of the Minister for Naval Services. This did little to assuage or reassure, and the Speaker of the House silenced Roy's further attempts at seeking clarification.

Roy returned to the subject three days later, on Monday 13 July. He felt compelled not only to press for concrete information but to defend himself against the serious innuendo that his previous question in the House had undermined national security. This time he could cite in his defence the views of the Saturday edition of *L'Action Catholique* to the effect that "half of the people in Quebec City" had known of the U-boat attacks before Roy had even mentioned them in the House. And besides, he insisted, he had allowed the endangered convoy a full day to reach safe haven before alluding to its plight. The reasons for government silence seemed obscure. Indeed, the weekend *Montreal Gazette* had attacked the government's obdurate censorship. In its view, "any effort to withhold information from the enemy" that was already an open secret in the "whole countryside and beyond," was frivolous at best. On the face of it, popular support seemed to have vindicated Roy's seemingly unpatriotic action. Yet the Speaker's constant interruptions prevented Roy from explaining his reasons for having introduced the question of the U-boat threat. In the absence of the Minister of National Defence for Naval Services, the Hon. J.L. Ralston himself now joined the fray.[37] Roy, he insisted, had done the U-boat commander a favour by reporting a successful mission to his superiors in Germany, without exposing him to the dangers of detection (Ralston clearly had "Huff-Duff" in mind). But by this time Roy's concern had gained ground. The Hon. R.B. Hanson, Leader of the Opposition, rose in his defence: "Reports were [now] widespread in the province of Quebec," and he himself had received many letters about it. Indeed, "at Matane and Cap Chat the situation was such that everybody knew it." At this point, Hanson focused on the crucial issue about which neither the House nor the people of Canada had yet been informed: "What is the [government's] position with respect to convoys in the St. Lawrence? Are there any? Should we not know the position at least in a general way? ... What is the position with respect to protection?"

Despite Hanson's conviction that precise statements "would have a reassuring effect," Ralston remained unmoved and declined comment. Irked by an obduracy that seemed out of character with parliamentary tradition and practice, CCF House Leader M.J. Coldwell (Rosetown-Biggar) called for a secret session of the House. This was a means to which not only the British Parliament but also "our sister dominions" were known to have resorted. While a secret session seemed a likely solution to this confrontation, the rancorous debate closed on a note that divided francophone and anglophone by pitting one myth against another. Navy Minister Macdonald arrived in time to portray the Quebec populace as a simpering pressure group, whereas "not once" had he heard any "complaints" from his own Maritimes. The slur was unfair, and the polarization had unfortunate consequences throughout the war. By now, however, newspapers like *Le Soleil* had revealed the heated debate under the rubric "Les torpillages dans le golfe Saint-Laurent" (14 July 1942). By now, as well, the German propaganda and press office in Berlin's Wilhelmstrasse had, from whatever source, gathered news of their U-boat's exploits in Canadian waters. On 21 July 1942, Berlin Radio announced the success of Vogelsang's mission. As transcribed by Associated Press and published in *Le Soleil*, the inflated account read: "seize navires alliés coulés en quatre jours."[38] Quebecers had cause for alarm.

Vogelsang in U-132 had meanwhile explored the western reaches of the Strait of Belle Isle and decided to return to Cap Chat where he had attacked Quebec–Sydney convoy QS-15. The most direct route lay to the north of Anticosti Island via the Détroit de Jacques Cartier, otherwise known as Mingan Passage. Yet, even as late as nine days after the attacks, patrol aircraft criss-crossed naval quadrant BA 36 from Les Méchins to Gros Mornes. These were predominantly flying boats, as Vogelsang recorded, but also four-engined land-based aircraft, as well as a variety of smaller vessels that sent U-132 routinely to action stations as it moved toward Matane. Hydrophone results in the area were "very bad and frequently deceptive," due to "water layering" in the river (KTB). U-132 sighted by periscope a "camouflaged 80–100 ton British sub chaser, pennant number 064" some 400 m distant and inspected its armament: "one 2-cm or 3.7-cm gun, 15–18 depth charges on the forecastle [sic]" (KTB). It was a Canadian Fairmile. On 18 July, U-132 patrolled on the surface in bright moonlight, and noted the tendency of coastal traffic to hug the south shore. Within twenty-four hours fog had blanketed the operational zone, preventing him from attacking a convoy. The fates seemed against him: fog by night, aircraft by day. As the RCAF reported, "large numbers of aircraft [were] sent out over the Gulf of St. Lawrence from Charlottetown on routine navigational training exercises in order to keep the Commanders of U-Boats operating in the area in a constant state of apprehension."[39]

Vogelsang's final attack in the St Lawrence began on the sunlit afternoon of 20 July 1942, when wisps of smoke off the promontory of Cap de la Madeleine betrayed the presence of Quebec–Sydney convoy QS-19. It had been an undisciplined gaggle. When HMCS *Weyburn* came upon it after having been detached from Sydney–Quebec convoy SQ-20 five hours earlier, convoy QS-19 lay sprawled over a 10-mile area. With no escorts in sight, *Weyburn* had rounded up the strays and eventually assumed the duties of Senior Officer from HMCS *Chedabucto*. The reorganized convoy resumed its course after four hours of shepherding: *Weyburn* in the van, HMCS *Chedabucto* and M/L Q-074 on the flanks, with M/Ls Q-059 and Q-064 astern. At 1315 local time, *Weyburn* had instructed *Chedabucto* to sweep down the port side and pass visual instructions to the Fairmiles astern.

Thus it was that from Vogelsang's perspective the convoy seemed escorted by "two motor vessels and one sub chaser" (KTB). U-132 held boldly to course at periscope depth in the glistening, placid river, despite the near approach of a Canadian Fairmile to within 700 m. The U-boat dived to 20 m to avoid her, and emerged in the centre of the convoy to fire a double salvo. One torpedo struck the engine room of the 4283-ton SS *Frederika Lensen* at 1339 local time, from 800 m, killing four men instantly. The second inexplicably failed. The explosion sent the remaining forty-three crew members to the lifeboats as the vessel swung out of line with thick clouds of steam and smoke bursting from her port side. On seeing the ship torpedoed, the lakers *John Pillsbury* and *Meaford* broke ranks at utmost speed and spurned the efforts of M/L Q-064 to round them up. HMCS *Chedabucto* immediately pulled alongside the *Lensen* but did not see the kind of gaping hole usually associated with a torpedo attack. Instead she saw a relatively narrow split with bulging plates, suggestive of an internal boiler explosion.[40] Records do not indicate the aggressive action of a merchantman that Vogelsang claims to have observed, though observers near the *Frederika Lensen* were convinced that an attacking Fairmile had "scored hits." Vogelsang heard the muffled sounds of nine depth charges during his rapid emergency dive.

U-132 returned to periscope depth at 1615 local time to find the *Frederika Lensen*, her lifeboats lowered, screened by a Fairmile and under tow by HMCS *Weyburn*. Well to the west now, convoy SQ-20 ran under the escort of HMCS *Charlottetown*. By midnight more escorts had gathered about the *Lensen*, supported by air patrols flying so low over the submarine as to force it to dive. Though aircraft had sighted U-132 elsewhere in the St Lawrence, she escaped on this occasion unseen. HMCS *Clayoquot* was meanwhile ordered to the scene to screen the damaged ship from further attack. The *Frederika Lensen* anchored the following day at Grande Vallée Bay. Here she broke amidships and became a total loss.[41] Two dull explosions, followed by sounds of cracking, wracking, and tearing of bulkheads brought U 132 to the surface to see its victim on the beach belching a tall column of smoke. Vogelsang summarized his observations in a lengthy situation report to BdU at 0750 GMT on 24 July 1942. He had encountered little of tactical interest on leaving Cabot Strait except innocent fishermen, whom he suspected of being submarine decoys.

Not until almost three months later did security restrictions permit publication of this "Daring Midday Sub Attack in the St. Lawrence." The syndicated account of Canadian Press staff writer Harold Freeman, who had been aboard one of the naval vessels, provided considerable detail on time and location of the attack, weather conditions, name of the torpedoed ship, and number of screening vessels. It also contained considerable wishful thinking in describing "the swift disposition into attack stations [that] made the water close to the convoy a veritable death trap for any submarine."[42] One of Freeman's tactical speculations, clearly attributable to his conversations with naval personnel, was that "the daylight raid had been the work of a single sub, for the express purpose of diverting some of the escorts, to leave the convoy more vulnerable to a concentrated 'wolf pack' attack that night." The concept of wolf-pack warfare had impressed itself on the popular imagination, and the idea put forward was not illogical. But, in fact, neither in the Gulf (where no packs operated), nor even in mid ocean, could anything have been further from the truth. Freeman's second speculation concerned the characteristics of German torpedoes. According to him, "naval men [had] explained that torpedoes, after they leave the tubes, do not travel in a straight horizontal line, but rise and fall in the water through a 4-foot span." The *Frederika Lensen*, by extension, had been struck on the bottom during an upward thrust of one of the torpedo's vertical undulations. This garbled rendition was not only logically inconsistent, but factually incorrect in contending that the torpedo's running depths were programmed to fluctuate along rhythmical lines. On the contrary, any vertical shifts were decidedly arhythmical and unplanned, and the German experimental unit (TVA) had for months been trying to prevent such unwanted variations in depth; until now, torpedoes had tended to underrun targets. But Freeman's article correctly anticipated the LUT and FAT target-seeking torpedoes that followed prescribed horizontal course patterns while remaining at set depths.

The last seven U-boats operating off the North American coast from 20 June to 28 July 1942 no longer found any valuable single targets. Few ships now travelled alone. Both sides regarded lone ships as an endangered species. Convoys concentrated both shipping and escorts in such a way as to invite the U-boats to come to the defenders. Thus, U-215 (Hoeckner) sank the 7191-ton American *Alexander McCombe* from convoy BA-2 southeast of Nova Scotia on 3 July, and was in turn destroyed by the escorts.[43] Twelve days later the successful U-756 (Heinicke), which had torpedoed an 11,147-ton tanker off the U.S. east coast, sank two ships in convoy. Counter-attacked by a patrol aircraft, U-756 was then rammed by the SS *Unicoi* and sank with all hands.[44] BdU recalled U-132 (Vogelsang), U-89 (Lohmann), U-458 (Diggins), and U-754 (Oestermann) to positions southeast of Halifax on 19 July. Between 30 July and 5 August successes were light: U-458 sank a 4870-ton merchantman; U-89 sank the 54-ton Canadian schooner *Lucille M.* 100 miles south of Cape Sable after having shelled her for 45 minutes; and U-754 destroyed the 260-ton American fishing vessel *Ebb* 120 miles south of Halifax. Eleven of the schooner's survivors landed in two dories in Clarke's Harbour next day. As one of them recalled, U-89 had come "within hailing distance, and in good English the commander [expressed regrets at having to] shell their ship, but he was under orders and had to obey." But, as far as the RCAF report was concerned, the "two small fishing vessels were ruthlessly attacked without warning ... by gunfire during the night."[45] U-754 had killed the *Ebb*'s master and wounded two of the crew; four men were lost. The RCAF, as will be seen, avenged them at the end of the month. Meanwhile, in a session of the House of Commons, which a front page account of *Le Soleil* (21 July 1942) dubbed "Une Séance Tumultueuse à Ottawa," the Gaspé MP Roy continued his demands for reliable information on U-boat activity. *Le Soleil* underscored his cause that day by announcing the sinking of the *Lucille M.* in a highly politicized context. The U-boats and the RCAF were, however, more active than the press could know.

On 30 July, Hudson 454K of 11 (BR) Squadron attacked a surfaced U-boat 60 miles southeast of Cape Roseway; it might have been U-89. The aircraft's four 240-pound depth charges exploded very close to the U-boats hull, producing debris and an oil slick 2.5 miles long. This convinced the RCAF that the "excellent attack" had caused "considerable damage."[46] Other sightings and attacks occurred in the Bay of Fundy, though we cannot be certain which U-boats, if any, were actually involved. The RCAF tracked the "damaged" U-boat next day and eventually sighted it "under water with large numbers of air bubbles ... coming from it as if it were trying to blow its tanks to rise." The RCAF considered the still-unidentified U-boat as "obviously in great difficulty." In all, RCAF aircraft reported more sightings in July 1942 than during any previous month.

Meanwhile, on 30 July, Vogelsang in U-132 sighted convoy ON-113, 25 miles southwest of West Point, Sable Island, a position that neither Diggins nor Oestermann was able to reach. Canadian authorities were concerned, for U-boats had for the past week been subjecting this convoy to "one of the most persistent" attacks so far experienced in the western Atlantic.[47] Vogelsang stood well ahead to starboard of the approaching Halifax-bound convoy: six ships broad and four ships deep. An A/S "sweep" patrolling down the starboard side of the convoy ran over him (KTB). Just as U-132 rose to periscope depth, the convoy executed a sharp zigzag and rolled over him in broad formation. Vogelsang fired a "double salvo at an 8000-ton freighter" (KTB) from 800 m, then quickly dived to avoid an oncoming vessel that ran directly over him. Turning submerged to parallel the convoy's base course almost due west, Vogelsang heard the detonation of his torpedo after a run of 28 seconds; then, "amidst the propeller noises of the ships, the audible cracking and breaking and wracking sounds" of a vessel disintegrating as it plunged into the depths (KTB). Vogelsang had sunk the 6734-ton British SS *Pacific Pioneer*. U-132 could not, for technical reasons, arrest its own descent until striking the bottom of Sable Island Bank in 80 m of water. Sounds of depth charges and asdic filled the U-boat. Vogelsang shut down all machinery including the gyro in order to escape the probing of three distinctly heard escorts searching intently overhead. During the noise and turbulence of each depth charge explosion, Vogelsang quickly switched on his pumps in an effort to raise U-132 from the bottom. At 0315 GMT, U-132 finally lifted free. The hydrophones revealed but a single "destroyer" that sometimes lay stopped as it cast its "scare charges" (KTB). With not a single torpedo left, U-132 rose to periscope depth to face a dark, quiet night.

Squadron Leader "Molly" Small's 113 Squadron of Hudsons was unique in the RCAF by keeping up to date with RAF tactical experience, and had for some time been reviewing its methods of antisubmarine warfare. It paid careful attention to new concepts. A new tactic now led to the destruction of Oestermann's U-754. Instead of persisting in the low-level patrols that submariners could readily spot and which they had doubtless come to expect, the squadron instituted the concept of patrolling at altitudes ranging from 3000 to 5000 feet.[48] This opened the possibility of effective aerial surprise attacks. The day chosen for the test offered ideal atmospheric conditions. Slight haze over the sea on 31 July restricted the upward vision of bridge lookouts, while providing aircraft at the planned altitude with a fairly clear view of objects beneath. It also provided a horizontal visibility of 5 miles. Hudson 625 of 113 (BR) Squadron out of Yarmouth, Nova Scotia, sighted U-754 at 1450 GMT. It was running fully surfaced 3 miles ahead at a speed of 8–10 knots. Attacking in a tight S-turn, "while the submarine's crew [could be] seen ... scrambling for the hatch," the aircraft released four bombs. "The entire deck of the U-Boat was visible" as the bombs exploded close aboard. Turning now sharply left, the Hudson machine-gunned the conning tower. A "heavy explosion" broke the surface 55 minutes later. While relieving aircraft patrolled the debris, Canadian surface vessels searched the target zone. HMS *Veteran* eventually discovered large quantities of oil, marking a U-boat on the bottom in 360 feet. The Canadian record correctly reveals a "kill."

BdU had meanwhile ordered Vogelsang's U-132 to take the most direct route home without, if possible, requesting any replenishment en route. He cruised on his port diesel until 5 August when repairs on the starboard permitted full power. The technical details of his voyage, recorded on 16 August 1942, the day he entered harbour, represent one of the few logistical summaries available from the period. During the sixty-eight day mission, U-132 had covered 8757.5 nautical miles surfaced, and 1143.9 nautical miles submerged. It had required 151.34 m³ of diesel fuel, 4692 litres of oil, 10,615 litres of drinking water, had fired all its twelve torpedoes, and sunk five ships for a total of 21,350 tons. In the words of the Chief of Operations to Admiral Karl Dönitz, Captain Eberhard (*der liebe Gott*) Godt, the mission had been "well executed." Indeed, "the Captain's decision to continue the mission after the depth charge damage [in European waters] and his toughness in the operational areas of the St. Lawrence River paid off and led to a fine success" (KTB). U-132 returned to Canada in the fall, but was lost with all hands off Newfoundland on 5 November 1942 in the explosion of an ammunition ship in Sydney–UK convoy SC-107.

August 1942 marked the most intense period of air operations in coastal waters that Eastern Air Command had experienced to date. Some 984 patrols covered over 816,000 miles during more than 6160 flight hours, and escorted 206 convoys comprising 3256 ships.[49] Dönitz's pressure tactic lay at the root of the unprecedented escalation of defence resources. Though only three antisubmarine attacks were carried out by aircraft (two by the RCAF and one by the USN), aircraft made an "unusual number" of sightings. The majority of these occurred in the Gulf of Maine and the Gulf of St Lawrence. Yet, as the RCAF observed, "no portion of our coast was entirely without attention" by enemy submarines. Canadian air power encountered but one major set-back. With the ditching of the Fleet Air Arm's "Walrus" based on Sable Island, Eastern Air Command lost what might have been an important command post. "Not sufficiently experienced in sea navigation" (as the COAC reported to British authorities), the navigator, Sergeant W.H. Finnie, RCAF, had failed to allow sufficient fuel in his calculations to return to base.[50] Piloted by Slt S.G. Cooke, RNVR, the biplane had only flown 20 hours of patrol that month. The corvette HMCS *Napenee* escorting Halifax–UK convoy HX-204 managed to pick up the two crew who had survived three days wallowing about at sea before the "Walrus" sank. COAC referred the "question of providing more experienced RCAF personnel, if required, for future patrols of this nature" to the Air Officer Commanding, Eastern Air Command. For undisclosed reasons, the question elicited no visible response. However, despite the upgrading of air resources elsewhere, the RCAF continued to rely heavily upon a proliferation of routine training flights over the convoy tracks in the Gulf of St Lawrence. The authorities remained convinced that "these aircraft must have an intimidating effect on submarine commanders," for by month's end not a single U-boat had attacked shipping in the zone that such training flights overflew. Training flights served similar purposes elsewhere as well.

Two attacks on what might have been U-458 (Diggins) are particularly noteworthy. The first began when Canadian shore stations D/F'd the radio transmission of a U-boat some 30 miles southeast of Cape Roseway, Nova Scotia, thus initiating an antisubmarine patrol by 113 (BR) Squadron in Yarmouth. Cruising at 3500 feet on the afternoon of 2 August, Hudson 645 sighted "a surfaced submarine, excellently camouflaged with grey paint" and travelling at a speed of 12 knots. The aircraft dived towards its target at 225 knots in order to close the 2-mile gap, levelled off at 50 feet, and dropped four 250-pound charges fused for a depth of 25 feet. It took 7 seconds for the U-boat to disappear beneath the surface, 1 second for the bombs to strike the water, and 1.5 seconds for them to sink to 25 feet. Calculating that a submarine diving at 8 knots will submerge 20 feet in 10 seconds, and advance 130 feet, the pilot had set his charge to explode astraddle the U-boat's pressure hull. The well-executed attack revealed some traces of oil and suggested minor target damage. According to the RCAF, "only the ability of the submarine crew in executing a crash dive so quickly ... saved it from serious damage."

The second attack occurred two days later some 85 miles to the east, when Hudson 620 on a navigation training flight from Debert sighted a fully surfaced U-boat while cruising at an altitude of 2000 feet. The U-boat lay 4–5 miles distant in 20-mile visibility when the Hudson nosed into a steep dive. Air crew fired 1140 machine-gun rounds just before pulling out at 50 feet to drop depth charges and claw quickly into a left-hand climbing turn. The air crew saw their tracers "ricocheting from [the] conning tower where the Germans were scrambling for the hatch," and gained the impression that the U-boat's gun crew had clung to their stations until the very last minute in an attempt to "fight back." The U-boat plunged steeply into the heavy sea as a depth charge exploded near its conning tower. Though the Hudson suspected a direct hit, the only hint of damage was a surface disturbance of large bubbles and a small oil slick. The aircraft reported having taken three "excellent photographs," and insisted on the unusual U-boat being strangely painted "grey-green and brown in colour, not unlike our aircraft camouflage." ASV-equipped aircraft, theoretically capable of detecting a U-boat at 4–5 miles, remained on the scene but discovered nothing other than red flares some 17 miles distant that they felt might possibly have been "signals from a helpless submarine." The Germans record no losses here that night.

By now, according to Canadian authorities, "an unusual lull" in submarine activity had set in. In the words of Eastern Air Command, "the absence of submarines, as evidenced by the lack of sightings and aggressive action on their part, was puzzling." A new wave was on its way. It would trigger what a war correspondent for the *Ottawa Journal* described as the "Battle of the St. Lawrence: a deadly no-trace-of-the-body business."[51]

CHAPTER FOUR

The Battle of the St Lawrence

Three U-boats departed Kiel-Wik independently early in August 1942 in order to investigate what Admiral Dönitz incorrectly suspected to be the principal egress for St Lawrence traffic into the North Atlantic: the Strait of Belle Isle. This 78-mile stretch of water between Labrador and New-foundland forms the northernmost exit for ships passing from the Gulf of St Lawrence to the Atlantic. It marks the beginning of the shortest route to Europe for Gulf and St Lawrence River traffic. U-boats had, of course, touched upon this zone in the fall of 1941, but had never focused upon it in any strength. What subsequently developed into the "Battle of the St Lawrence," though presaged by the solo sorties of the previous months, resulted principally from the initiatives of U-165 (Hoffmann) and U-517 (Hartwig) who after their eighteen-day Atlantic passage had found their assigned combat zones off Newfoundland unpromising. Not content simply to wait for targets to run into their sights, they sought them at their source. No other U-boats would approach the Gulf and river via the Strait of Belle Isle. "Pack" attacks against convoy ON-115 southeast of Flemish Cap from 2 to 4 August, and the sinking of the 4870-ton British tanker *Arletta* by U-458 (Diggins) east of Sable Island on 5 August alerted NSHQ in Ottawa to the possibility of further encroachments closer to home. Ultimately, "the Battle," as it is popularly called, involved five U-boats that penetrated the river during the summer and fall of 1942 as far westward as Pointe au Père, attacked five convoys, sank seventeen merchantmen, a loaded troop ship, and the two warships (HMCS *Raccoon* and *Charlottetown*), and finally outraged the populace by sinking the Sydney–Port aux Basques passenger ferry SS *Caribou*. Political responses and press reaction, as we shall see, were sharp and incisive, and led to the dubious decision on 9 September 1942 to close the Gulf to merchant traffic. This in itself was a major German coup, for it caused their enemies serious re-routing of war matériel, and equally serious political recriminations, which made themselves felt until well after the war. The grandiloquent flummery of a semi-official Canadian publication of 1944 underscored the navy's ability to make a virtue of necessity in the face of years of political obfuscation: the "Battle of the Gulf [was] a battle of ships and guns and men and shining courage on the broad waters of the St. Lawrence; a battle of words and politics in the nation's Parliament!"[1] It was not a Canadian victory; it was a Canadian defeat.

Rüggeberg's U-513, the first to arrive off the coast on 24 August 1942, and the only one of the three to remain outside the Strait of Belle Isle, encountered a desolation reminiscent of Norway at its bleakest. On one side of the entrance the steep, fog-threatened Labrador shore of granite and sandstone rising to flat-topped ridges and summits from 1000 to 1300 feet high; on the other, the almost featureless coast of Newfoundland from Cape Norman to Cape Bauld, reaching no more than 100–500 feet in height.[2] He could expect relatively ice-free navigation until the end of December.

Kapitänleutnant Paul Hartwig's tour in U-517 began with characteristic flair. The most popularized and adulated "enfant terrible" in the post-war Canadian press coverage of the St Lawrence campaigns, he became a Vice-Admiral in the German Federal Navy and Commander-in-Chief, Fleet. In the bright moonlit pre-dawn of 27 August, Hartwig attacked the 5649-ton American vessel SS *Chatham* escorted by the American Coast Guard cutter USCG *Mojave*. Forgoing convoy air cover, the two ships were running ahead of Sydney–Greenland convoy SG-6F consisting of five ships escorted by USCG *Algonquin* and *Mohawk*. From a retrospective American view, Greenland convoys "were given the slowest and worst equipped escorts, under Coast Guard officers and crews who had been given slight training in escort duty or anti-submarine work; and it was only by guess, by guts and by God that some of them were not completely wiped out by the U-Boats."[3] Hartwig's approach was a deft combination of that consciously understated image making and calculated tactics common to many naval leaders. It always remains important for a crew's esprit de corps that a captain demonstrate he can indeed perform, for that above all else inspires confidence. If he can carry it off with style, so much the better. Only after the explosion did activity on *Chatham*'s sloping decks and the "masses of lifeboats" (KTB) reveal that he had destroyed a troop ship. She carried 562 passengers and crew. *Chatham* sank within one hour with the loss of thirteen lives. She was the first American troop-ship lost in the war. No one saw U-517, despite clear weather and unlimited visibility. Hartwig passed around Belle Isle during the night, and then returned to find "sixteen fully loaded lifeboats." An aircraft now circled overhead while "a cutter flying a white flag" tended to the survivors. This was either the American patrol vessel USS *Bernadou*, or the corvette HMCS *Trail*, both of which undertook rescue operations. Canadian and American naval authorities attributed the small loss of life to each other's efficiency and resourcefulness.

Hoffmann's U-165 had meanwhile contacted the main body of convoy SG-6, advised BdU, and commenced attack. Two torpedoes struck the 3304-ton US cargo vessel SS *Arlyn*, a third missed, and the fourth damaged the 7253-ton U.S. tanker SS *Laramie*, which then tried to limp back to port. Five crew died. The *Arlyn* sank over an hour later with the loss of thirteen passengers and crew. Survivors landed at various points in Labrador, Newfoundland, and on Belle Isle itself. As in the previous attack, no one saw U-165. Hartwig eventually sank the "slow, unsteady vessel" *Laramie*, which had wandered into his sights after he had intercepted Hoffmann's report to BdU.

In the view of NOIC Sydney, the attacks had "greatly improved the liaison and relations between Sydney and the United States authorities in Argentia," Newfoundland. Until now the Americans had apparently remained aloof. BdU meanwhile had some reservations about Hartwig's request to shift his operations into the Gulf, but eventually authorized both him and Hoffman to enter the St Lawrence, while Rüggeberg patrolled off Belle Isle and if possible carried out a "surprise" attack "in the anchorage" of Conception Bay. By this time Hoffmann had already slipped off down the strait on his own. Hartwig followed.

Hartwig's first encounter with Canadians left him puzzled. Anticipating the chance for his own surprise attack in Forteau Bay, which the *Sailing Directions* described as a suitable anchorage for merchantmen at the western end of the strait, Hartwig entered surfaced during the dark hours of 1 September to within 20 m of the main jetty. On surface departure two hours later from the empty bay, he met an inbound high-speed patrol vessel approaching from ahead. It passed down the U-boat's side, then seemed to turn about, increase speed, and give chase. Hartwig accelerated in an attempt to escape, dived as soon as soundings permitted, and plummeted through unexpected density layers into the sandy bottom. Sounds of the escort's engines penetrated the U-boat, crossing eerily overhead. She circled repeatedly without dropping a single bomb, probing with asdic's threatening chirping and rasping tone that on close approach crescendoed to that of fine gravel cast along the U-boat's hull. Hartwig insists even now that "the Canadian could not have failed to recognize that he was holding a U-boat at bay." Such encounters convinced the German Naval Staff (Skl.) that Canadians lacked stamina. Germans would quickly appreciate the Gulf's special properties for distorting asdic.

Continuing inbound along the Labrador coast on 2 September, Hartwig sighted Quebec–Labrador convoy NL-6, the first of two convoys some 15 miles southeast of Luke Island, and escorted by HMCS *Weyburn* and

Clayoquot. The other was Labrador–Quebec convoy LN-7. Consisting of the SS *Donald Stewart*, *Ericus*, and *Canatco*, it was proceeding in the opposite direction into the strait, escorted well ahead off the port bow by HMCS *Shawinigan* and *Trail*. The confused circumstances of what followed gave rise to conflicting evidence in official reports. The two convoys were headed on practically reciprocal courses, and both groups of escorts had their full attention on the problem of keeping their convoys clear of one another. This enabled Hartwig to gain his advance position in the darkness for a surface attack on LN-7, even passing within 600 m of an escort. At the moment of firing, Hartwig saw "an escort turning hard about and running toward" him (KTB). It was *Weyburn* in the van of NL-6 that had turned to ram. Unable to overtake U-517, she opened fire with her 4-inch gun, "causing the U-boat to submerge."[4] Captain A.B. "Tony" German, the son of the NOIC, Gaspé, and at the time a junior officer, recalls being "on *Weyburn*'s bridge ... when we bumbled into [U-517] just as he fired his first salvo and sank [the 1781-ton laker] *Donald Stewart* ... It is a fact that *Weyburn* didn't get a sniff of him on asdic although we'd seen him twice, as large a life." All but three of the *Donald Stewart*'s crew were rescued by HMCS *Trail* and landed in Quebec. As in Forteau Bay, Hartwig was surprised that *Weyburn* refrained from a thorough A/S counter-attack.

The attack led to increased air patrols and to harassment by aerial bombs. The RCAF remained a more constant threat than the navy. In fact Hartwig recalls the stress that RCAF surveillance, scare charges, and attacks caused his watch officers. Planes would unexpectedly swoop down on them, buzz them, drop out of a cloud, or skim low over the water out of the sun and drop bombs which, even when inaccurate, made "one hell of a ruckus" ("*Mensch, das knackte lustig!*"). All his officers had been badly shaken by such attacks and advised him of their preference to stand their watch submerged. They no longer felt confident about the patrol situation on the surface. This confirms RCAF suspicions at the time that at least one "submarine should carry back to Germany a very flattering record of our aircraft's [sic] readiness off this coast."[5] Indeed, one aircraft had attacked U-517 twice in succession. On other occasions, patrol on the St Lawrence was so quiet that they cruised on the surface with the forward hatch open. This was, of course, a serious risk, but one worth taking considering the need for fresh air and the marvellous tranquillity of the scene. The crew, as Hartwig recalls, also experienced moments during the beautiful Gaspé autumn that remained with them over forty years. These were moments that dispelled anxiety and thoughts of war, moments of sheer poetry. Many still recall a very early morning off a Gaspé shore. Only one small building in the tiny settlement showed any signs of life as the light of dawn began to hint at a new day: a shack with lights on, and smoke curling invitingly from its chimney. Conversation on the U-boat's bridge – between captain, officer of the watch, engineer and look-outs – moved casually and even intimately between the ranks, slipping from one memory to another. For Europeans, particularly those from small towns in Germany whose thoughts turned to similar scenes at home, the single illumined hut in the village could only be that of the baker preparing his *Brötchen* for market: delicious freshly baked crusty rolls that form the traditional German breakfast. Thoughts of fresh-baked bread edged out the realities of the hard tack and tinned foods aboard. They intruded a note of nostalgia into the half-earnest, half-whimsical banter about launching the dinghy for a trip ashore. The desire remained a haunting dream.

U-165 had by this time penetrated the southern portion of the Gulf to the western shore of Cape Breton Island, where on 5 September it failed in its attack on the lone 1895-ton Canadian cargo ship SS *Meadcliffe Hall* off Chéticamp. The U-boat turned northwest into the Gaspé Passage in the hope of intercepting traffic in the narrows between Pointe des Monts and Ste Félicité. Rüggenberg's daring daylight exploit with U-513 that same day in Conception Bay, Newfoundland, had widespread repercussions. Having penetrated surfaced into the shallows of Wabana anchorage off Bell Island during the night, he submerged in the morning and sank two deep-laden vessels: the British 7335-ton SS *Lord Strathcona* and the 5454-ton SS *Saganaga*. Both sank in 3 minutes. Thirty-three crew of the *Saganaga* died. The explosions provoked sporadic gun-fire from the Bell Island shore batteries: a 200-foot ceiling prevented A/S operations by the RCAF Hudson and Digby that swiftly reached the scene. U-513 met no further success until its destruction of the 7174-ton freighter *Ocean Vagabond* off St John's, Newfoundland, on 29 September.

The sinkings in Wabana anchorage kindled the same flames of unrest in Newfoundland as those in the St Lawrence River and Gulf had done in Quebec. Newfoundland's obvious isolation and colonial status prevented complaints from being raised in Ottawa. One accepts the loss of escorts and merchantmen in convoy as the "fortunes of war," as the operations officer of FONF observed. But "the loss of ships at Wabana and close to St. John's, although also the fortunes of war, are harder to explain to a population who considers anything sunk on their doorstep is due to a dereliction of duty on the part of the Navy."[6] U-513's successful attacks, in the words of FONF's operations officer, had provoked "a clamour for protection from outlying ports out of all proportion to their value in the strategic plan as a whole." As in Quebec, news of U-boat attacks spread rapidly despite the firm grip of the official censor. The discrepancy between common knowledge and official silence struck the popular mind as a "cover-up." The cumulative effect of these sinkings and those of U-518 on 2 November led to the construction of antitorpedo nets, which, however, would not be completed until the end of December 1942.

Kapitänleutnant Hartwig had meanwhile scouted to within a 32-mile arc south of Heath Point, Anticosti, when he decided to cross the Gulf to the Gaspé Peninsula. At 1000 hours on 7 September he intercepted Hoffmann's signal regarding convoy movement within the broad naval quadrant BA 36, whose western and eastern perimeters enclosed territory from Les Méchins to Gros Mornes. This may have been the same signal to German Naval Headquarters claiming the sinking of two vessels west of Les Méchins.[7] Hartwig correctly assumed that the convoy would likely tuck in close to the Gaspé coast and that his best position would therefore be as close inshore as possible. By mid morning he waited off Pointe à la Frégate to join the battle for QS-33.

For many hours prior to this signal, Hoffmann's U-165 had been tracking the Quebec–Sydney convoy QS-33. Consisting of eight merchant ships in two columns, it passed Pointe au Père east of Rimouski at 1630 GMT, escorted by a Gulf Escort Force in the following screening positions: the Senior Officer in the corvette HMCS *Arrowhead*, and the Bangor minesweeper HMCS *Truro* maintained station to port and starboard respectively of the lead merchantmen; the Fairmile HMCML Q-083 sailed in the van, HMCML Q-065 stationed dead astern of the convoy with the Armed Yacht HMCS *Raccoon* one-half mile off her port quarter. U-165 attacked the convoy in reduced visibility off Cap Chat in the early hours of 7 September 1942 and sank the 2988-ton Greek vessel *Aeas* 5 miles northwest of Cap Chat at 0205 GMT.[8] HMCS *Arrowhead* illuminated with star shell, which cast a cone of light as far astern as *Raccoon*'s lonely station off the convoy's port quarter, where she was seen – by all accounts – for the last time. *Arrowhead* completed her A/S search, picked up twenty-nine survivors of the *Aeas*, and returned to her station. Survivors were landed at Gaspé, two crew were missing. Not completely convinced of a U-boat's presence, Canadian authorities attributed the loss of *Aeas* either to "a torpedo or to an internal explosive." Two explosions quite likely confused the issue: the first from Hoffmann's torpedo, and the second 15 minutes later by a severe boiler explosion that sent her to the bottom. The loss of HMCS *Raccoon* (ex *Halonia*) was both mysterious and macabre.[9]

According to the monthly report of the Staff Officer Operations in Halifax, then LCdr H.S. Rayner, RCN, HMCS *Raccoon* had reported at 0240 GMT on 3 September, just minutes after the sinking of the SS *Aeas*, that she was being attacked by torpedoes. One apparently passed 25 feet ahead of her and the other directly beneath, forward of the bridge. She then seems to have run up the track for 6000 yards dropping depth charges, but obtained no contact. Around 0500 GMT, almost three hours after the loss of *Aeas*, HMCS *Arrowhead* temporarily left station to sweep ahead of the convoy. At 0512 hours off Martin River Light, several ships heard two explosions in rapid succession followed by a short blast of a ship's whistle. Despite the darkness, witnesses claimed to have seen two columns of water off the convoy's port quarter. As this was *Raccoon*'s station, it was generally assumed that she had "contacted the night's prowler and was executing a depth charge attack."[10]

Arrowhead swept down the port side of the convoy to a point well astern of *Raccoon*'s assigned station, but reported neither sightings nor contacts. German records, based on receipted signals from U-165, indicated that Hoffmann had sunk the *Raccoon*.[11] But in the convoy and screening forces no one assumed that the yacht had been destroyed. Seven hours after her demise, NOIC Gaspé radioed *Raccoon* to report her position, course, and speed. She was presumed lost with all hands when no word was received. Gradually some details emerged. On 21 September a life-jacket marked with the yacht's pre-war name *Halonia*, together with small pieces of wreckage, was washed up on the west side of Anticosti Island near Ellis Bay. Four weeks after the sinking a patrol found the very badly decomposed body of Slt R.H. McConnell, the only body from *Raccoon* ever found. It was buried at sea with full honours. Five days later *Raccoon*'s motor boat was found at Thunder River, then more flotsam and part of the yacht's bridge. The Board of Inquiry concluded that she had sunk as a result of "direct hits by one or more torpedoes" while conducting a depth-charge attack. In the absence of Hoffmann's log, we will never know.

Convoy QS-33 meanwhile, reduced by sinkings and scattering to four ships and four escorts, was joined by HMCS *Vegreville*. As the morning of 7 September wore on, the convoy converged on U-517, which at 1306 GMT first picked out "three fat steamers, each at least 6000 tons, screened by four escorts and one aircraft" (KTB). As distance and firing angle remained unfavourable, Hartwig shadowed submerged for three hours, then surfaced to assume his advance firing position. Rain, mist, and fog reduced visibility markedly. At 1724 hours he signalled Hoffmann that the convoy now stood off Cloridorme, running two abreast in "box formation" with the escorts on the flanks. Forced under by air cover that seems not to have spotted him, he reached his firing position just as the formation zigzagged directly towards him, bracketing him between the first and second vessels. Hartwig spun 180° around and fired four single shots as one of the escorts approached to within 200 m from dead ahead and then sheered off to her screening position. At his periscope, Hartwig observed his salvo sink three ships at 2100 GMT some 18 miles east of Cape Gaspé: the Greek cargo vessels *Mount Pindus* (5729 tons) and *Mount Taygetos* (3826 tons), both with war cargoes including tanks, and the Canadian cargo-carrier SS *Oakton* (1727 tons).[12] Why the *Oakton* was carrying coal to Sydney is by no means clear. Torpedoed within 3 minutes of one another, the three ships sank in 15 minutes. The *Oakton* had no casualties, the *Taygetos* had five, and the *Mount Pindus* had two. Fairmile Q-083 landed seventy-eight survivors at Gaspé where they boarded a train for Montreal. The Gaspé–Montreal rail link provided reporters with direct access to unauthorized news throughout the U-boat campaign.

Radio Berlin's news broadcast that day on the Atlantic conflict, denigrating Canada's naval role, seems to have drawn on the earlier sinkings in the St Lawrence. But like all effective propaganda, it contained sufficient truth to sound authentic:

The loss of twelve merchant ships totalling 80,144 tons in the month of August [1942] led Britons and the English [sic] to take desperate defence measures. Now, for example, the Canadian Navy, which is nine-tenths composed of requisitioned fishing boats, coastal ships, and luxury yachts, is obliged to create an escort system ... with these third class ships. This service comprises a third of the threatened maritime route between Canada and the British Isles.[13]

About the same time, Hudson 403 of 113 (BR) Squadron, Chatham, New Brunswick, sighted Hartwig's U-517 from an altitude of 4500 feet.[14] The air crew reported that "the submarine was painted sea green with the conning tower painted white, so that at a distance the U-Boat could be mistaken for a sailboat." This was but one of the many claims about idiosyncratic camouflage that German records do not corroborate. Adopting the dive-bomb and low flare-out technique that had proven successful in sinking U-754 on 31 July south of Cape Sable, the Hudson launched its attack at the unsuspecting target. Unable to lose sufficient altitude, the aircraft overflew the still-surfaced U-517 at 800 feet, photographed it through the lower nose panel, and machine-gunned the conning tower. The Hudson released its bombs after Hartwig's conning tower had submerged. Analysis of the attack and a large oil slick some 4 miles square convinced the RCAF that the Hudson had "seriously damaged [and] probably sunk" its target in 150 fathoms. In fact, however, U-517 remained unscathed.

One week later, on 14 September, the Minister of National Defence for Naval Services, the Hon. Angus L. Macdonald, announced for the first time that HMCS *Raccoon* "had been presumed lost through enemy action while guarding a convoy of merchant ships, and that it must be presumed that all hands were lost with her." He appended a casualty list with the names of next of kin. Mr Macdonald now explained that there had been an increase in the tempo of enemy activity "on Canada's side of the Atlantic," but for security reasons divulged nothing about the exact loca-

tion. That four merchant ships had also been lost emerged almost paren-
thetically. This left readers wondering whether the ships had been sunk in
Raccoon's convoy or elsewhere. Canadian newspapers picked up the
story with varying degrees of emphasis. Quebec City's *Le Soleil* (13 September 1942) headlined "Cinq navires ont été coulés," and linked the
sinking with the loss of HMCS *Raccoon*. That day's late edition of the
Montreal Daily Star fleshed out the brief official announcement on its
lower front page and tried to reconstruct the situation from snippets of
information under the heading "East Coast Convoy Battle Claims All
Hands." Only the *Toronto Daily Star* drew attention to the Canadian
Press statement concerning the "eighty survivors" who had arrived in
Montreal by train. This of course could only have referred to a St Lawrence action. The *Halifax Herald*'s editorial page for 16 September followed up the previous day's announcement with a funereal sketch captioned "Their Flag Was Never Lowered" showing a half-submerged naval
ensign slipping beneath a dark and brooding sea.[15] Bearing *Raccoon*'s
name in stylized letters as though written in freshly drawn blood, its
bathos was meant to evoke feelings of revulsed patriotism in the face of
Nazi aggression. Reports placed *Raccoon*'s loss in the context of the
"Battle of the Atlantic in which Canadian warships are bearing one-third
of the burden." By 1944 they would bear almost one-half.

The Battle, in the words of an earlier announcement from naval headquarters, was "now of far greater scope than ever before experienced."
The *Ottawa Journal* for 15 September endorsed the view that the engagement that led to the destruction of *Raccoon* when "battling subs" was one
of "a number of fights involving the Canadian Navy as a result of a recent
northward thrust by the German undersea raiders." The Minister for the
Navy had provided the basis for this assertion during a speech in Hamilton
the previous week. However, while obviously massaging the same script,
both the *Ottawa Journal* and the *Toronto Daily Star* emphasized the
minister's more encouraging fiction that "the Navy had recently scored
successes against U-Boats," which he would announce as soon as security
permitted.

The *Ottawa Journal* was perhaps the most informative of all in remind-
ing its readers of the German submarine strategy consequent to the United
States entry into the war: "The German submarine fleet enjoyed 'good
hunting' along the United States coast and in Central and South American
waters." Here the U-boats had met "comparatively slight resistance in
sinking unescorted but valuable ships." Air defences had now "stiffened,"
the losses "fell off," and hence the U-boats had shifted northward "hoping
to catch the transatlantic traffic by surprise after its long period of com-
parative freedom from serious attack." Now, however, "escorts of the
North Atlantic convoys, largely Canadian ships, were ready for the Ger-

mans." Just how prepared the Canadians actually were might have been observed one week earlier by the decimation of St Lawrence convoy QS-33.

On completion of his attack against this convoy, Hartwig headed for Cap des Rosiers some 18 miles to the west, and then followed the Gaspé coast westward as far as Cap de la Madeleine. Three escorts abreast appeared by mid morning on 8 September, apparently carrying out a hydrophone search for the previous day's marauder. Hartwig's emergency dive was again hampered by the water layers of varying density that frustrated the smooth execution of this otherwise swift and calculated manoeuvre. The notation "Damn the layers" punctuated his War Diary during his St Lawrence operations. Allied surveillance for the next couple of days alternated between escorts and aircraft. At dawn on 10 September in German naval quadrant BA 3677 off Capucins, U-517 was executing a routine dive when it sighted a shadow off Cap Chat: "probably Hoffmann" in U-165 (KTB). This was his final glimpse of his colleague. The next shadow was equally doomed.

The Flower-class corvette HMCS *Charlottetown* (LCdr J.W. Bonner, RCNR) had been transferred on 12 July 1942 from the Western Local Escort Force to the Gulf Escort Force with which it subsequently escorted eleven convoys on the Quebec–Sydney route. The first two volumes of her deck log record the hourly details of her brief service since commissioning at Quebec City on 13 December 1941. The last entry of volume 2 had been signed off on 5 June 1942 by a whimsical connoisseur of the eighteenth-century English novel: "And now, dear reader, turn to Book III to see what happened next." Little could the writer know that Book III would go down with the ship and that any "dear reader" interested in the sequel would have to piece bits together from the most disparate and often conflicting sources. In company with HMCS *Clayoquot* (Lt H.E. Lake, RCNR) and HMCS *Weyburn* (LCdr T.M.W. Golby, RCNR), and reinforced by Fairmiles, HMCS *Charlottetown* had safely delivered her last convoy, SQ-35, to Red Islet off the mouth of the Saguenay River, some 30 miles southwest of Bic Island. It was generally considered safe to send ships up river from this point without escort because the shoaling waters were deemed too risky for submerged enemy submarines. As soon as the convoy had disappeared, HMCS *Charlottetown* and *Clayoquot* returned down river on 11 September 1942 without refuelling at Rimouski. This was perhaps a decisive error.

At 1055 GMT *Charlottetown*'s officer of the watch fixed the ship's position by a visual bearing on Cap Chat Church, and a radar range. As so frequently happened on journeys at this time of year, a steeple piercing through the fog banks ashore often provided an officer of the watch with the only visual contact for coastal pilotage. His dead reckoning position for 0800 local time – which he barely reached – placed him 6 miles off shore, with *Clayoquot* 1 mile on his port beam. The two ships had been making good a course of almost due east at 11.4 knots in light fog and swirling mists, but contrary to sound practice were neither zigzagging nor proceeding at greater speed. Senior authorities subsequently criticized them for this neglect of routine evasive action, and did not accept the excuse of *Clayoquot*'s presumed shortage of fuel. For, as it turned out, *Clayoquot* still had sufficient reserves to sustain extensive A/S searches. It might be said in their defence, however, that maintaining station in fog by means of their relatively primitive radar would have necessitated their steering a straight course. Asdic and radar were operating all morning, although asdic conditions remained relatively poor.

Neither *Charlottetown* nor *Clayoquot* had any indication of U-517's presence until Hartwig's double salvo struck *Charlottetown*'s quarter at 0803 local time, after a brief run of a mere 14 seconds. Hartwig was so close that he could see the depth charges stored on his victim's quarter-deck, which would contribute so heavily to loss of life.[16] *Charlottetown*'s Executive Officer, LCdr George Moors of Fort William, was on the bridge when his ship was hit; Able Seaman R. Pearson of Vancouver claimed to have glimpsed the first torpedo, which "struck aft and turned the ship completely around so that it headed in the opposite direction."[17] The engine room artificer was apparently the only person killed by the torpedo itself. All other casualties occurred in the water.

Immediately after the first torpedo had struck, as the Executive Officer later reported, the crew proceeded to abandon ship. No order to abandon was necessary because of the obviously severe damage to the ship's stern. *Charlottetown* was settling so rapidly aft that ship's company automatically followed ingrained, routine emergency measures. The starboard sea boat was "launched, but the port one could not be gotten away due to the list of the ship and the fact that it was inboard with davits swung out" and gripes off.[18] Anxiety, fear, and determination filled the ship's last minutes. But heroism and compassion overrode even the instinct of self-preservation. Telegrapher Fred Rush (Winnipeg) gave his life-jacket to Engine Room Artificer Miller who could not swim, before himself going over the side. Rush swam about in the choppy, oil coated sea until picked up by one of the rafts. He was one of those injured by exploding depth charges as *Charlottetown* sank. Tommy MacDonald of Peterborough lost his life while trying to retrieve a drifting Carley float for his floundering shipmates. Survivors extolled Sick Bay Attendant Cecil Bates of Brandon who attended the injured throughout their ordeal even though he himself was hurt.

All but three of the ship's company of sixty-four had apparently gotten clear before *Charlottetown* went down, some swimming, others on floats and in the boat. One was later picked up clinging precariously to a bully-beef box; another floating on one of the ship's fenders. One of the last survivors to leave was the ship's mascot Screech, who was flung into the sea at the last minute by Frank Dillon. The dog's master, Able Seaman Charles Garland of Gallagher, New Brunswick, was lost with the ship. He had, in the words of the First Lieutenant, "show[n] especial gallantry in standing by and passing out lifejackets from the locker, giving them all away when he himself could not swim." As *Charlottetown* sank inexorably by the stern, the commanding officer coolly assisted with rafts and the boat, made sure that everyone was safely off, and in the best traditions of the naval service, was the last to leave his ship.

At the periscope of U-517, 4 minutes after his first shot, Hartwig observed *Charlottetown*'s bow rise skyward as she slipped stern first to the river bottom 900 feet below. But just as she began to settle, the first of a series of depth charges on her quarterdeck exploded, followed by four or five more as *Charlottetown* reached greater depths, and the pressure-activated pistols discharged. Unsure whether these initial detonations were from an aircraft or an escort – lack of time and the thick fog prevented sweeping the horizon by periscope – Hartwig dived to 120 m. For some four hours after the attack, U-517 heard either "depth-charge detonations or the explosion of ammunition" in the sunken corvette (KTB). U-517's hydrophones picked up the sound of breaking bulkheads and the hulk dropping into the depths, yet its War Diary notes neither hydrophone contact with a searching escort nor its own detection by asdic. *Charlottetown* survivors in the water sustained severe internal injuries from these detonations. Some died almost instantly. Others, like the captain and Tommy MacDonald, survived the blasts, only to succumb later in extreme pain. Others fell victim to the cold and the oil. *Charlottetown*'s Executive Officer recounted details of the aftermath:

Before the ship sank completely, most of the crew were in the rafts or in the starboard boat. The boat at that time had seventeen men in it, but we managed to collect a few men in the water and transfer them to a float, and then [later] four more who were severely injured. This operation took up about one and one-half hours, and no dead bodies were seen except that of the Captain who[m] we finally picked up and lashed to the rudder, after filling the boat with living men ... After rowing for about an hour [towards] shore to fetch help the rudder was torn adrift by the weight of the Captain's body and he was left adrift because we could make better time [without him] and he might possibly be picked up by another ship when the fog cleared.

Immediately after observing the attack on HMCS *Charlottetown*, HMCS *Clayoquot* altered course to face the possible position of the submarine.

Sweeping with asdic 80° either side of her bows, she started the zigzag pattern that the two ships ought to have executed throughout the voyage. Her depth-charge attacks knocked out her wireless transformers, thus preventing her from reporting the enemy contact until over three hours after the torpedoing had taken place. Subsequent contacts were equally lost in the difficult asdic conditions of the St Lawrence. HMCS *Clayoquot* swept through the area in thick fog, eventually retracing the route on the basis of the excellent antisubmarine track maintained by Mate D. Roberts, RCNR. By 1130 local time she reached the very survivors who 90 minutes earlier had cheered her on her high-speed dash past them to attack a suspected U-boat contact. Only now could a terse "Most Secret – Immediate" message advise NOIC Quebec of the sinking. He despatched three screening Fairmiles an hour later. *Clayoquot* had now taken fifty-eight survivors aboard, "thirteen badly injured from depth charge explosion and shock." She arrived at Gaspé at 2230 hours.

According to the Executive Officer of HMCS *Charlottetown*, "fifty-seven survivors ... seven of which [sic] were suffering from severe internal injuries" were landed. Able Seaman Donald Bowser had died en route "from injuries sustained" and was buried by Surgeon-Lieutenant E.L.G. Alford, RCNVR, in Gaspé Protestant Cemetery, there being "no undertaker in Gaspé, PQ." ERA Thomas MacDonald died two days later on 13 September 1942 at Hôtel Dieu Hospital, Gaspé, of internal injuries, as did Leading Telegrapher Edmund Robinson. Almost a month later, on 10 October, the river delivered the last traces of the ship: a Carley float and minor wreckage washed along the shore of Ellis Bay, Anticosti, where debris of HMCS *Raccoon* had drifted.

Navies expect to lose ships and men in war. But in the case of HMCS *Charlottetown*, serious errors in judgment had increased the calculated risks involved. Following a review of the evidence submitted to the Board of Inquiry into the loss of HMCS *Charlottetown*, Rear-Admiral Murray, Commanding Officer Atlantic Coast, concluded that "neither of the ships were short of fuel and should have been zigzagging according to the common practice in waters known to be frequented by the enemy." Nor was there any evidence to show that depth charges stowed on the quarterdeck had in fact been put on safety settings. "Had this been done, several lives would probably have been saved." Since no general orders existed at the time enforcing the wearing of lifebelts while at sea, RADM Murray added that "such orders should be promulgated forthwith."[19]

HMCS *Charlottetown*'s destruction "By U-Boat in Atlantic Encounter," as one newspaper proclaimed, provided the press with a broad source of stories and photographs from 18 September (the day of the minister's lean announcement of the sinking) to 24 September.[20] As usual, the press inflated the official statement, patched in details provided by home-town survivors, photographed family reunions, and speculated on the war at sea. It quite rightly emphasized the "calm heroism," "cool efficiency," and the cheerful spirit of discipline, dedication, and self-sacrifice that marked relationships in the shipboard "family." Cdr P.B. German, RCN, NOIC Gaspé, officially reported that the "bravery of all officers and men of HMCS *Charlottetown* [was] in keeping with the traditions of the Navy."[21] Yet news stories focused on the salient dramatic feature of the sinking and subsequent casualties: that the ship and her men had virtually died on her own "depth bombs." Despite this irony, however, the press managed to project another more stirring, though patently less accurate, image: *Charlottetown* was "sunk in battle with subs in Atlantic [while] fighting off an enemy submarine attack on a convoy." On 13 September, the *Halifax Herald* linked the *Charlottetown* sinking with the loss of HMCS *Ottawa* (LCdr C.A. Rutherford) and 109 men.[22] The *Halifax Herald* for 19 September subordinated *Charlottetown*'s news to a subheading under the banner headline story of HMCS *Assiniboine*'s "Spectacular Victory over Huns" by ramming U-210 (Kapitänleutnant Lemcke) and taking prisoners 400 miles off Newfoundland.[23] Though *Assiniboine*'s encounter had actually occurred some six weeks earlier, on 6 August 1942, the *Herald*'s use of the delayed press release permitted the inference that *Assiniboine* and *Charlottetown* had actually been in simultaneous action – perhaps even in the same convoy screen, and perhaps even battling the same wolf pack.

Editorializing on the theme of the "Gallant Men" to whom "the nation pays deep tribute," the *Halifax Herald* explained that news of *Charlottetown* and *Assiniboine* had imparted "greater understanding of the nature of the struggle against the undersea enemy." Habitually fantasizing on behalf of the whole of Canada, the editor now mixed the two incidents and proclaimed: "That story of the hours-long combat on the surface of the Atlantic, of guns firing at point-blank range, of destruction of fire controls, of flames sweeping the bridge area – of men cheering as they rained explosives on the enemy – that story is one of the most dramatic in the annals of Canada's young and growing naval establishment."[24] The crew of *Charlottetown*, however, knew otherwise and kept silent.

Shortly after noon local time on 15 September, Hartwig correctly identified an amphibious aircraft as the advance reconnaissance of the awaited Sydney–Quebec convoy SQ-36, which he sighted two hours later. Having patrolled the St Lawrence the past four days in mists and fog from Cap Chat to Fame Point, and Bird Rocks to Cap des Rosiers, he felt confident. SQ-36 seemed to contain "twenty-one steamers and at least seven destroyers, corvettes and escorts." It was steaming in "seven columns of three ships; ahead three sweepers [and] on the sides two escorts each, two long-range screens, and one aircraft" (KTB). In fact, however, it was screened by a single destroyer (HMS *Salisbury*), the corvette HMCS *Arrowhead*, the Bangor HMCS *Vegreville*, and three Fairmiles.[25] The lines of command and communication in the screening force were not entirely clear. HMCS *Arrowhead* had been Senior Officer when the convoy had left Sydney, but had been relieved of her authority on the arrival of the British destroyer HMS *Salisbury*, which joined a full day later. Having joined temporarily from the Western Local Escort Force, *Salisbury* in all probability knew very little about the routines and patterns which had been established. Nor was she necessarily experienced. There was, therefore, some confusion as to what was to be done, and by whom, a fact that might account for the 16-minute delay before anything was done at all once the U-boat got into the middle of the convoy. All escorts were apparently sweeping ahead for mines, which *Arrowhead* had for some reason suspected.

Hartwig still recalls the technique of silently drifting back into an approaching convoy: at night the CO would stand below at the periscope, his favourite position for attack and control, while the officer of the watch and two look-outs manned the bridge; by day, he remained submerged. Mounting tension, fear of aircraft attack, the gnawing questions of whether one should continue with the tactic or pull out; all this pressured an already overburdened nervous system. But "one develops a sixth sense, like a tiger in the jungle," he recalls. One controls one's energies coolly, and runs the ever-present calculated risk. Now slipping back into firing position, Hartwig observed the formation alter course abruptly 30° to port, leaving him outside the convoy on the starboard side. Captivated by the destroyer's movements, which ran down 400 m to port and then zigzagged 150 m off his starboard, Hartwig let himself get too close to the convoy, about 120 m off. He fired a salvo of four torpedoes "at two overlapping steamers in the second column" (KTB), observing his "eel" strike before "depth charge explosions" forced him into an emergency dive where he could observe no further results.

U-517's torpedoes struck the 2741-ton Dutch vessel *Saturnus*, which was riding in ballast, and the 2166-ton Norwegian *Inger Elisabeth* on their starboard sides, sinking them in 15 minutes. Four men died. Survivors were landed north of Gaspé, from where they were taken by truck into Gaspé en route for Montreal.[26] The explosions that forced U-517 to dive derived from three defensively equipped merchant ships (DEMS), SS *Llangollen*, *Cragpool*, and *Janetta*; they claimed direct hits and near misses on more than one periscope, but in fact had fired independently on U-517. Counter-attacks by *Salisbury* and *Arrowhead* produced inconclusive oil on the surface. As *Salisbury* reflected, "since most of our ships have been sunk westward of Gaspé Passage, the extemely poor [asdic] conditions must be known to the enemy who have often fired their torpedoes during the day and made good their escape." ,The point was well taken.

Hartwig had wisely advised Hoffmann in U-165 that the convoy was advancing down the Gaspé coast. At 1010 GMT on 16 September, U-165 attacked SQ-36 in the clear daylight some 12 miles northwest of Cap Chat. Though ships sighted his periscope at the time of the attack, he managed to torpedo the 6624-ton British cargo ship SS *Essex Lance*. HMCS *Vegreville* took her in tow and then passed her to the salvage tug *Lord Strathcona* for the journey to Quebec, where she arrived on the evening of 22 September. The ship was eventually repaired and returned to service. The 3667-ton Greek freighter, SS *Joannis*, however, went down in 10 minutes. The escorts counter-attacked with no apparent results. Thirty-two survivors from *Joannis* and forty-eight from the *Essex Lance* were taken aboard Fairmile Q-082 and landed at Dalibaire.[27] Shortly thereafter, U-165 torpedoed its final ship from convoy SQ-36; the 4570-ton American SS *Pan York* survived. That same day, Hudson 634 of 113 (BR) Squadron at Chatham sighted the fully surfaced U-165 from an altitude of 4300 feet and nosed into the steep dive characteristic of the latest tactic. The bomber's white camouflage permitted an undetected close approach. Firing 361 machine-gun rounds, the Hudson flared out at 50 feet and bracketed the submerging U-boat with four 250-pound depth charges fused for 25 feet. An oil patch hinted at damage which, in the absence of the German's War Diary, cannot be corroborated.[28]

In the following days, Hartwig and Hoffmann encountered situations and potential targets too numerous to discuss here in any detail. Suffice it to say that a combination of Canadian air superiority and rapidly dwindling shipping drastically reduced the Germans' combat effectiveness. On 9 September the War Cabinet Committee in Ottawa had acceded to the British request to close the St Lawrence, a decision it more readily accepted in light of the exigencies imposed upon it by an earlier British request for seventeen escort vessels to support the Torch landings in North Africa planned for November 1942. Such ships could, of course, only be provided by reallocating the already over-committed coastal patrol force. As we have seen, the demands of purely coastal trade precluded the complete closure of the Gulf. Naval control of shipping (NCSO), could only cope with the new situation by introducing more flexible convoy routing. The swiftness of the War Cabinet's decision, despite prior consideration by naval authorities, caused the immediate diversion of inbound convoys to either Saint John, New Brunswick, Halifax, or Sydney; it left the navy virtually no time to phase out QS-SQ convoys running between Quebec City and Sydney, Nova Scotia. Closure angered

Quebec politicians by blatantly diverting transportation and trade over-land and led to the rapid development of ports and railheads outside the province. Hartwig recorded the radical shift in traffic by 25 September.

Two events during this period left Canadians the impression that they had destroyed at least two U-boats. Both involved Hartwig. While over-taking Sydney-Quebec convoy SQ-38, HMCS *Georgian* (Lt Falkner, A/CO) sighted U-517 on 21 September off Cape Gaspé "on the surface ... at a distance of 1000 yards, the periscope and part of the conning tower showing." In his startled attempt to "bust the escort," Hartwig caught sight of "men running aft to the depth-charge equipment" as he executed an emergency dive while *Georgian* tried to ram. *Georgian* crossed over the swirl with the first of a series of deliberate attacks that lasted two hours, and reported the U-boat suddenly surfacing astern. U-517 then "turned over on her side with definite wake astern and sank." The Staff Officer Operations in Halifax judged it "probable" that the U-boat had been destroyed. Though Hartwig again had reason to curse "these layer-ings" (KTB), no data in his War Diary is consistent with breaking surface or with rolling on its side.

Three concentrated air attacks from 25 to 29 September from Ellis Bay, Anticosti, to Cape Gaspé, demonstrated the effectiveness of RCAF antisubmarine tactics. They invariably struck U-517 close aboard. Hartwig recognized all of them as "well-placed bombs" and respected the machine-gun fire that regularly raked his conning tower. Government authorities withheld news of these attacks until they could exploit their full political advantage. On the final occasion, an aircraft of 113 (BR) Squadron re-turning to Chatham, New Brunswick, from patrol "skillfully attacked [U-517] with depth charges and machine gun" before the U-boat managed to submerge and escape.[29] Surfacing somewhat later after an extended journey at relatively shallow depth, U-517 found an unexploded bomb lodged on its foredeck by the gun. It had obviously been set to explode at a depth below which the U-boat had been cruising. Once the crew had rolled it over the side, it exploded at depth. Aircraft continued to harass U-517 and block its approaches to shipping until it left the Gulf of St Lawrence permanently on 2 October 1942. Limited targets and shortage of torpedoes and fuel forced the U-boat to leave.

Hartwig next day provided one of many proofs that U-boats refrained from attacking neutrals, despite what might have been interpreted as provocation. Approaching three escorted and fully illuminated vessels close enough to read their names by periscope and check their flags – the Swedish *Fenris* (1950 tons) and *Bardaland* (2595 tons), and the Greek *Mongabarra*, which had departed Montreal two days earlier – he identi-fied them as "genuine neutrals" that ought not to be "knocked off" (KTB). According to the rules of war, however, a non-belligerent travelling in convoy and accompanied by belligerent escorts was fair game. In retrospect, Hartwig sees Canada in error by having placed the Swedish ships in such a dangerous position. They would have been entirely safe travelling alone and fully illuminated. It would have been an easy matter for Hartwig to have sunk them, but thoughts of potential political repercussions held him back. Hartwig's hunch was indeed correct, for Dönitz later counselled his captains to "shoot anything, but don't touch a Swede."

The very obvious U-boat activity on the St Lawrence had increasingly alarmed the residents along the Gaspé coast who were constant witnesses to events about which both the government and the press remained silent. Action by Quebec parliamentarians, as we saw earlier, provoked federal/ provincial polarizations that were already at flash point. The urgent request for a secret session of the House of Commons submitted by Mr J.S. Roy (Independent, Gaspé) and supported by Conservative Leader of the Opposition R.B. Hanson and CCF House Leader M.J. Coldwell in the summer of 1942 met the vehement protestations of the Minister for the Navy. In response to Roy's pressing entreaty for assurances of protection, Angus Macdonald had refused "to change the disposition of one ship of the Canadian Navy for [Roy] or all the questions he may ask from now until doomsday."[30] Five days after this outburst, on 18 July 1942, the prime minister convened the secret session. The opposition parties considered the July sinkings to have been severe enough. But German intrusion in late summer and throughout the fall seemed more severe than ever. Mr Roy therefore wrote the prime minister in early October requesting that Parliament convene immediately in order to debate the shipping situation. On 13 October 1942, several days after the public announcements of the adventures of U-165 and U-517, and one day prior to the delayed release of the July sinking of the *Frederika Lensen* off Cap de la Madeleine, Mr Roy advised the press: "The people of my constituency want to be assured that the defences along the St. Lawrence are adequate and whether the air force's defences against the U-Boat menace are directed along the most effective lines."[31] The prime minister, however, saw no reason for convening Parliament before January 1943. Three days later, news of U-69's sinking in the Cabot Strait of the Sydney–Newfoundland ferry SS *Caribou* would puncture the government's silence.

German propaganda authorities followed these confrontations with considerable interest. Thus in a German front-page article describing the U-boat battle "From Cape Town to Canada," the Nazi party organ *Völkischer Beobachter* for 4 November 1942 pilloried the alleged prevarications of Ottawa: "In Churchill's best flimflam [politicans had] denied ... the numerous sinkings in the Gulf of St. Lawrence," which even the Germans knew was known by the populace "despite [Ottawa's] secrecy." On 18 December 1942 it trumpeted statements attributed to Transport

Minister C.D. Howe to the effect that U-boats were sinking twice as many ships as the Allies could build.[32]

Crassly manipulating news in a public-relations ploy to assuage the public's undoubted feelings of vulnerability, the Hon. C.G. Power, Minister of National Defence for Air, released news of the air attacks against U-517. He had been holding the details on ice for three months. Articles in the *Ottawa Journal* for 16 December, for example, billed the story "RCAF Sends Nazi Submarine to Bottom of St. Lawrence," and "U-Boats Get into St. Lawrence but Not All Get Out." The *Halifax Herald* announced "RCAF 'Gets' Another U-Boat," and published a photograph of the "devastating" attack. Newspapers insisted that this "probably meant death to the lurking undersea raider and his crew." The press massaged the usually brief official release, and in the process managed to interview the crew who divulged material for a flamboyant human-interest account of the war at sea. Flying Officer R.S. Keetley later suggested that a considerable amount of sheer luck played a part in these attacks: "We just stumbled upon them during our regular antisubmarine sweeps." The press did not accept his view. His success, trumpeted the *Halifax Herald*, was nothing less than the result of "eternal vigilance."

While Hoffmann and Hartwig enjoyed their success, Rüggeberg patrolled off Newfoundland in U-513 for seventeen tedious days of almost continuous fog. Forays along the eastern coast, except for the initial assault on the Wabana anchorage, drew nothing but the disconcerting encounter when Rüggeberg all but "pranged into a destroyer" (KTB) in thick fog off St John's harbour. Not until 29 September did he torpedo the 7174-ton SS *Ocean Vanguard* just 3.5 miles east of the Port War Signal Station of St John's. At the end of his disconsolate patrol, Rüggeberg summarized his observations on commercial traffic, noting particularly the single escort guarding the entrance to St John's each day, and the constant air surveillance. All lights burned under peacetime conditions, except for the restricted use of St John's and Cape St Francis. Bull Head and Fermeuse Head, he reported, were extinguished. It appears from this and other observations that of all the war zones in what was to become the Canadian Northwest Atlantic, Newfoundland alone exercised regular control over its navigation lights; U-69, however, was to find the lights of Gaspé dimmed after its attack off Métis Beach. This was the type of *Kriegsbefeuerungsmassnahme* to which German submariners had been accustomed in European waters. The illumination measure controlled navigation beacons within broad parameters of the expected arrival and departure of friendly units, but otherwise denied their use to the enemy. The system was never really exploited in Canada, although military authorities had considered the possibility when preparing successive issues of the Gulf Defence Plan. Hartwig departed the Cabot Strait on 8 October

1942, and crossed the Newfoundland Banks on 9 October one day before Rüggeberg left his coastal patrol zone. Both arrived in Lorient, France, on 19 October after a swift passage. Hoffmann's U-165 was destroyed in the Biscay on the final leg home.[33] U-517 was sunk on the outbound leg of its next mission. Carrier planes from HMS *Victorious* destroyed the U-boat in the Biscay on 21 November 1942. Fifty members of the crew were saved.

Just one day prior to U-517's sinking of HMCS *Charlottetown* on 11 September, U-69 under the command of Kapitänleutnant Gräf was laying mines in Chesapeake Bay. This was the first step of a mission that eventually culminated in one of the most (in)famous sinkings in Newfoundland maritime history. On completion of his special mining operation, Gräf received authorization from Dönitz's headquarters to choose further operation areas as he saw fit. His choice led him deep into the St Lawrence River and then to Port aux Basques. During the days that followed, from Cape Hatteras to the Newfoundland Bank, aircraft remained his principal threat. Rarely did Allied ships cause him any concern except on two occasions when he feared the presence of a "submarine decoy" (KTB) or Q-ship. There is no evidence on the Canadian side that such vessels were ever employed here, although the U.S. Navy had deployed them without success off the East Coast at the end of March 1942.[34] U-69 rounded St Paul Island in Cabot Strait on 30 September in exceptional visibility, which permitted a view of both sides of the strait from North Cape, on Cape Breton Island, to the Newfoundland coastline by Cape Ray. During the next couple of days, U-69 executed an elongated box search of the western side of Cabot Strait on the northwest-southeast axis off Cape Breton Island where SQ and QS convoys might have been found if the Gulf had not been closed. Impressed by the seeming impossibility of success in this area. Gräf boldly set course for German naval quadrant BA 3830, just 10 miles short of the zone reached by Vogelsang's U-132 during its July patrol off Matane. No U-boat had yet proceeded further up river. Vogelsang's record was about to be broken.

Gräf's patrol sweep through a constant blanket of radar waves that triggered his "GSR" (German search radar) warning device led him through the mouth of the river between Pointe des Monts and Ste Félicité–Cap à la Baleine on 6 October. It led past Baie Comeau where he explored off the tidal flats of Rivière Manicougan (Battures de Manicougan) before sweeping back to a westward mid-channel patrol off Matane. Here at 0138 GMT on 9 October, Gräf's U-69 commenced its attack on Labrador–Quebec convoy NL-9. This was one of the vital coastal convoys that closure of the Gulf could not preclude. Seven vessels escorted by two "destroyers" (actually the corvettes HMCS *Trail*, *Shawinigan*, and *Arrowhead*) were advancing at 7 knots. A steady maximum amplitude squeal on the GSR during the next three hours of manoeuvres left little doubt in Gräf's mind that Canadians had caught the critical phase of his attack run-in. The tone ceased on the final leg. The sudden break in what must have been a firm radar contact hints at technical inexperience in the screen, but in all likelihood was the fault of the notoriously unreliable SW1C or SW2C fitted in Canadian escorts. But as far as Gräf was concerned, the Canadian "radar operator was having a gorgeous snooze" (KTB). Gräf's bold persistence paid off.

At 0420 GMT on 9 October, Gräf's double salvo from 2000 m struck a 4000-ton freighter (KTB) – actually the 2245-ton ex-Finnish vessel SS *Carolus* – some 8.4 miles northeast of Pointe Mitis Light.[35] This attack 173 miles from Quebec City was the deepest approach to date. Gräf observed a tall dark blast column followed by almost immediate fire throughout the ship as she broke apart and sank to the river bottom in 2 minutes. The escorts responded with star shell in order to illuminate the scene with the glaring light of day. Watchers on shore witnessed the display from as far away as Pointe aux Outardes on the western tip of Péninsule de Mani-cougan on the northern shore of the river. Residents on the southern shore could actually hear the explosions of the attack and the ensuing hunt. One of Gräf's "destroyers," the corvette HMCS *Arrowhead*, rescued eighteen of the *Carolus*'s crew, some of whom had been clinging "desperately to empty gas drums, bits of wreckage and life rafts for three-quarters of an hour."[36] The sound of distant depth charges followed Gräf's withdrawal to his next patrol station off Cap Chat.

News reports of the attack reached the public within a week. On 15 October 1942, the Minister of National Defence for Naval Services issued his customarily terse statement to the effect that a United Nations' merchant ship had been sunk "by a torpedo from a German U-Boat a few days ago" in the St Lawrence near Métis. He explained little more than that the U-boat had not been seen, and that eighteen merchant sailors had been rescued; twelve were still missing. With typical inventiveness, the press ferreted out further details from watchers on shore and survivors and managed to publish stories that provided the enemy with crucial information on U-boat operations and Canadian defence. These stories doubtless created a stir in senior military circles, for they were in clear contravention of the "Notes on the Publication of News Stories," which the official censor had issued in May 1942 in consequence of the St Lawrence incident. Banner headlines of the Quebec City *Le Soleil* for 15 October, for example, announced "Fréteur torpillé à Métis Beach." Date-lined Métis Beach, its story revealed the extent of the U-boat advance: "C'est la première fois qu'un sous-marin ennemi est signalé aussi haut dans le Saint-Laurent." This added fuel to Quebec's political fires. The *Ottawa Evening Journal* (15 October 1942) headlined the occurrence

"U-Boat Sinks Ship below Rimouski." An interview with the unnamed quartermaster of the sunken vessel, and with others equally convinced of the effectiveness of the Canadian counter-attack, provided the stirring subheading "Canadian Escorts 'Got U-Boat' at Métis Beach." A front-page map whose perimeters embraced the area from Rimouski in the east to as far west as North Bay and Parry Sound, and from Kingston (plus a section of Maine in the south) to Abitibi in the north, illustrated that the "Submarine Menace Creeps Stealthily Up St. Lawrence." This brought the "U-Boat depredations to within 220 miles of Quebec City." Clearly, they were now attacking Canada's heartland. News stories, which for security reasons were usually date-lined "an East Coast Port" were now date-lined "Métis Beach."

Pieced together in the usual collage of fact, well-intended inaccuracy, surmise, and fiction, the stories communicated the correct date ("shortly after midnight last Thursday" – i.e. 8–9 October), the time ("12:15 a.m."), and the position of the attack to within 21 miles of Rimouski. They clarified the number of survivors, the unprecedented character of the U-boat foray ("further up river than any previous submarine attack"), the U-boat's modus operandi ("fired at close range from a point not more than 2.5 miles from the nearest shore"). They explained further that the "Navy's ships make patrols in the river and escort convoys," that the "Air Force maintains a 24-hour patrol" and that in this case "operational aircraft were sent to the scene at once." Publishing the observations of "Octave Gendron, lighthousekeeper, and his family [of thirteen children] who live on a point jutting out into the river," amply identified Pointe Mitis Light as the reference point for the attack. In addition, remarks attributed to rescued Montreal naval gunner Alex Dawson to the effect that "nearly thirty depth charges were dropped by the warships" which likely "trapped the sub in these confined waters and then administered the death blow" confirmed two facts: that merchant ships in the St Lawrence carried professional naval gunners (Dawson himself being identified as one of them), and that escorts faced special problems of counter-attack. Read in conjunction with U-69's attack report transmitted to Berlin within twenty hours of the event, gleanings from the garbled "human interest" account would have provided the Germans not only with confirmation of Gräf's success, but with intriguing insights into various aspects of Canadian defence. It would have afforded insights, as well, into the social temper in which the "Battle of the St Lawrence" was being waged. As the navy minister amplified, Canada had to prepare for even greater trials:

Although some abatement in the toll of merchant ships taken by submarines in the eastern Atlantic has been noticeable in August and September, the continuing attacks in the St. Lawrence have impressed the conclusion upon us that there can be no relaxation of our efforts. And there can be no abatement either in our efforts to increase our Navy so that we may cope with the dangers of the trying months that still lie ahead.

As though a reflection of that extra national effort, the Civil Service Commission, now three years into the war, was recommending extending its traditional working day from 6.5 to 7.5 hours, in part by accepting a modest reduction of the customary 1.5 hour lunch break. Men at sea could bargain for no such comforts.

One day after the attack, Montreal's *Le Devoir* featured a front-page report of the impact on federal politics of "Les torpillages dans le fleuve et le golfe Saint-Laurent." Quoting J.S. Roy that "la situation est encore plus grave que lors de la séance secrète de la Chambre des communes l'été dernier," it lauded the Gaspé MP's personal success in pressing for a secret session of Parliament. Not only was this vital in order to evaluate the threat, but to assess Canadian countermeasures. Indeed, it argued, Navy Minister Angus Macdonald had had to drop his "previous air of superiority" and adopt a completely different attitude. Reflecting sympathy for members of Parliament like Roy who had vital first-hand information that the government refused to discuss, the article focuses approvingly on Quebec's principal divergence from Ottawa's national defence posture – namely the defence of Canada *in* Canada: "La défense du Canada au Canada est sans contredit notre premier devoir et le plus oublié." Next month's illegal strike by welders and fitters in the shipyards of Lauzon, Quebec, would exacerbate an already tense situation.[37]

U-106 (Rasch) had meanwhile entered Cabot Strait after having traversed the Newfoundland Banks under constant air surveillance. Each time he surfaced, the radar-activated warning device forced him under again, pressing him into an irritating and unproductive "dolphin-like tour" (KTB) of the south coast of Newfoundland and the suspected convoy routes off Cape Breton and Gaspé. The pressure of air surveillance wore on his nerves and in time caused him to leave the zone completely. But during the afternoon of 11 October 1942, while running submerged 12 miles southeast of St Paul Island, Cabot Strait, he briefly gained the upper hand on sighting Cornerbrook–Sydney convoy BS-31. The short, rough sea prevented until quite late his spotting the two steamers escorted by a flying boat. Somewhere in the distance he heard the "fast propeller sounds of destroyers" (KTB). This was actually the armed yacht HMCS *Vison*, the sole escort vessel. The merchantmen approached in broad formation as U-106 gained optimum firing position. It only permitted a shot at the last vessel in line: "Fortunately it is the larger one, typical ore-carrier, bridge right forward behind a very short forecastle, then heavy-duty derricks and the funnel aft" (KTB). It was the 2140-ton British freighter *Waterton*. At 1347 GMT, Rasch fired two individually targeted torpedoes from 300 m that struck the vessel on the point of aim, one forward and one aft below the funnel. Observing the SS *Waterton* immediately settle aft over the sternposts, he veered off sharply in order to avoid passing underneath the hulk.

The flying boat's presence forced him to dive deeply. Canso R of 117 (BR) Squadron, patrolling one-half mile off the *Waterton* at a height of 750 feet had immediately dived at the stricken vessel at the moment of attack, and arrived over her at 150 feet at the very moment when the second torpedo struck. The explosion "envelop[ed] the aircraft in a cloud of smoke and debris." Despite constant operation of its "special equipment" (ASV), it could not find Rasch.[38] Unknown to Rasch, however, the 422-ton armed yacht HMCS *Vison* (Lt W.E. Nicholson, RCNR), which was escorting the convoy, obtained a firm contact and attacked with a single depth charge. Rasch had by this time reached a depth of 30 m and felt the jarring, sharp detonation of what he assumed was the flying boat's "aerial bomb" (KTB). HMCS *Vison* pressed home the attack with twelve further depth charges. Rasch recorded "fast propeller noises and two series of depth charges, the first of which are fairly well placed; to judge by propeller noises, two destroyers are at it" (KTB). Typical of the area, "hydrophone conditions were very bad" (KTB) and "the two destroyers" (actually only HMCS *Vison*) had little real hope of holding a firm contact. Equally typical was the shifting water density, which at one point rendered U-106 too heavy and suddenly plunged it to the bottom in 90 m of water. U-106 then descended to 185 m where it remained for eight hours unscathed.

HMCS *Vison* rescued the entire crew of the SS *Waterton*, which had gone down in 8 minutes, and landed them at Sydney. This was U-106's only success even though it penetrated the St Lawrence as far westward as to within 3 miles off Les Méchins on 16 October. Admiral Dönitz had on 12 October 1942, given both Rasch and Schwandtke (U-43) freedom to operate in this northwestern quadrant, which had seemed to promise success during the dark nights of the new moon period. Finding no traffic, Rasch withdrew "dolphin-like" into the Gulf and out through the Cabot Strait. Each time he surfaced, aircraft radar triggered his warning device and sent him into a crash dive. The RCAF had thus created conditions "exactly like those in the Biscay" (KTB). Though not entirely convinced that he had in every case been detected by aircraft radar, the constant bleating of his FuMB radar warning device left him little choice but to submerge to the relative safety beneath. Of crucial importance, the FuMB could only indicate the direction from which radar waves emanated, but not the range. "We need a device," he noted in his War Diary, "which indicates the distance as well" (KTB). Rasch had spent an inordinate amount of time submerged because of aircraft threat (an astonishing forty-two out of ninety-seven days of the mission). This was an unusually long time for pre-schnorkel submarines, and Rasch had to pull back clear of all possible air cover in order to give his crew a chance to get fresh air. As he observed: "too much running submerged ruins the fighting spirit" ("*Zuviel Unterwasserfahren verdirbt den Kampfgeist*," KTB). Yet even within 50 miles of Cape St Mary's, Newfoundland, on 30 October "constant air cover" (KTB) prevented his approaching a tempting fourteen-ship convoy.[39]

Kapitänleutnant Schwandtke's Canadian patrol in U-43 began before noon GMT on 10 October 1942, some 150 miles south of Cape Race and formed a tactical counterpoint to the largely ineffective mission executed by Rasch. It, too, suffered gravely from Allied air activity, which triggered the submarine's radar warning device and kept it at constant tactical disadvantage by holding it submerged and out of torpedo range longer than Schwandtke wished. Particularly unnerving was the concern that his warning device did not seem to respond on all occasions, even when surface escorts could not have failed to detect him. Either his equipment was unreliable under all circumstances, he mused in his War Diary, or the Canadians had begun to use radar of a different wavelength. The ensuing disquietude and frustration while in the Cabot Strait did not prevent him from thrusting deep into the St Lawrence once BdU had given him permission on 12 October to move as far westward into the river as he wished. The very "considerable water stratification" of the St Lawrence provided a sense of security against the threat of asdic detection even when his hydrophones picked up propeller noises and the "ping" of asdic (KTB). On receipt of his clearance for broader operations, Schwandtke transited Gaspé Passage to Pointe Ouest, Anticosti, where he picked up the 200-m sounding line. This he followed along the northern coast of Quebec, past Pointe des Monts, and into the so-called "slot" in the river mouth. From 16 to 18 October Schwandtke patrolled from Cap Chat westward to a point 10 miles south of Baie Comeau. Here, but a few miles from where U-69 had sunk the SS *Carolus* on 9 October, Schwandtke was alerted to an antisubmarine technique that virtually eliminated any chances of his success on the river. On several occasions he observed that within an hour of his having been ranged by aircraft radar, escorts "apparently under immediate notice for steam" appeared and carried out antisubmarine searches. Such "good co-operation between sea and air" struck him as "utterly disarming" (KTB).

On 19 October 1942, Schwandtke reached the westernmost position on the river of any U-boat to date: Pointe au Père, to the east of the Port of Rimouski. He patrolled the river mouth and Gulf of St Lawrence for seventeen days without carrying out a single attack. He signalled BdU on 24 October: "Advise against allocation of further U-boats – numerous unexercised patrol vessels, good co-operation with air" (KTB). As though to emphasize the point, aircraft surprised him once more on 25 October 1942, just as he was developing an attack off Cap Chat against a coastal convoy consisting of "approximately ten steamers and six destroyers or escorts" (KTB). "Four well-placed bombs" sent him into an emergency dive to 140 m (KTB).[40] Schwandtke doggedly patrolled between Cap Chat and Matane from 28 October until 4 November, finally signalling BdU that commercial traffic and surface patrol craft had ceased abruptly. The Gulf was now closed and the shipping season in any event almost over.

Persistence in the face of adversity may have certain military merits. Certainly Admiral Dönitz lauded Schwandtke's "tough-minded tenacity" in sticking to a fruitless mission even though circumstances had long since suggested that he seek his fortunes elsewhere. But Dönitz's assessment of the mission completed by his veteran skipper Rasch in U-106 should in all fairness have been inscribed in Schwandtke's War Diary as well. Dönitz credited Canadian air power with preventing Rasch from achieving more than his modest success of sinking the SS *Waterton*. Both Rasch and Schwandtke agreed that the Canadian Navy's close co-operation with air support more than compensated for the inexperience and minimal strength of its surface patrols. Indeed, as the Germans were soon to learn, this crucial air/sea combination would shift the balance against the U-boats in the Battle of the Atlantic.

Gräf's attempts at combat operations in U-69 were equally badgered by the regular bleating of his FuMB radar warning device. From 9 October through 11 October, aircraft radar pressed him under with such frequency that he had difficulty maintaining charged batteries and compressed air bottles. Considering further operations in this area "inadvisable" (KTB), Gräf headed for Cabot Strait. Here, on 13 October 1942, some 18 miles northeast of St Paul Island, he received BdU's warning of the inbound passage for Montreal of three grain ships: the SS *Formosa*, *Camelia*, and *Eros*. Thus it was that his sweeps between Cape North (Cape Breton Island) and Cape Egmont for vessels that ultimately proved to be neutral Swedes drew him by sheer chance across the path of the railway ferry SS *Caribou*. Its rigid wartime schedule seemed to have been inviting the disaster it now encountered. The attack against civilians in Canadian waters sharpened the political debate by evoking fears of an unprincipled enemy who attacked with impunity.

The 2222-ton Rotterdam-built SS *Caribou* had arrived in St John's, Newfoundland, on 22 October 1925 as the newest of the "Gulf Boats." Since the turn of the century, her predecessors – the SS *Bruce*, *Lintrose*, and *Kyle* – had provided the sole link between the railheads of their owners, the Newfoundland Railway in Port aux Basques and the Canadian National Railway in North Sydney, Nova Scotia. The 266-foot *Cari-*

bou underwent a brief refit on arrival in order to strengthen her hull for navigation in ice, and spent the subsequent seventeen years transporting passengers and freight across the 101-mile stretch of open water between these principal ports. She occasionally operated as a sealing vessel in the spring.

Family traditions characterized this "Gulf Service" whose crews lived in the communities near the Channel-Port aux Basques–Southwest Coast area. Whole families depended upon the company, and sons followed fathers to sea in its ships. Perhaps more than anything else, this aspect of coastal life brought the realities of war at sea home to the peaceful Gulf coast communities, which had up to now felt relatively secure from the threat of the German submarine fleet. Newfoundland seafaring families had for generations understood the risks of their profession, but with *Caribou*'s regularly scheduled runs as the SPAB-convoy (an acronym for its terminal ports, Sydney and Port aux Basques), crews no longer asked whether the U-boats might strike, but simply when. Despite allegations to the contrary, however, no evidence indicates that adherence to a regular ferry schedule played any part in the *Caribou*'s detection and ultimate destruction.

Suspected U-boat contacts were not uncommon, such as when Fairmile Q-062 escorted the *Caribou* to Port aux Basques and attacked after midnight on 11 October. The Fairmile may possibly have detected U-106, which nine hours later attacked Sydney–Cornerbrook convoy SB-31. But the confrontation with U-69 was more than merely tactically significant. This submarine's attack at the very heart of coastal communities transformed a purely tactical manoeuvre into what Canadian politicians and press called a hideous deed. For among the thirty-one victims of the forty-six man crew, death at sea caused multiple bereavement in six families: Captain Benjamin Tavernor, a veteran of forty years at sea, and his two sons, First Mate Stanley and Third Mate Harold; Elijah and Bert Coffin; George and Jerome Gale; Clarence and Harry Hann; Albert and Garfield Strickland (the latter all from Channel); and Arthur and George Thomas of Port aux Basques. The Strickland family had already lost another member, Able Seaman Stanley G. Strickland, when the Italian submarine *Argo* torpedoed the destroyer HMCS *Saguenay* some 300 miles west of Ireland on 1 December 1940.[41] Thus when the toll of *Caribou* passengers was counted (among them five Trappers, four Toppers, three Allens, three Tavernors, and three Skinners), the press could claim with little exaggeration that "Many Families [were] Wiped Out."[42]

The SS *Caribou* departed North Sydney on schedule at 1900 Atlantic Standard Time on 13 October 1942 after having exercised "Life Boat Stations." Of the 237 persons carried (among them 73 civilians including mothers and little children, and 118 military personnel), only 101 were to survive the crossing. Wartime conditions dictated that the darkened ship steer an evasive route. This evening it steamed northward from Sydney towards Cape North before curving toward Port aux Basques with her single escort. Shortly before midnight local time, U-69 sighted a shadow followed by a smaller one astern. With relatively calm sea, very good visibility, and weak aurora borealis, U-69 soon identified "an approx. 6500-ton passenger freighter belching thick black smoke" travelling at 10.5 knots and escorted by a "two-stack destroyer" (KTB). It ran forward on the surface to take up its advance firing position. Gräf's errors in accurately identifiying both the class and actual size of the vessel illustrates the difficulties experienced by submarine commanders in estimating their successes. Such misinformation exacerbated the problems of the German Naval Staff in evaluating its own tactical and strategic position. Gräf's "two-stack destroyer" – the single-stack minesweeper HMCS *Grandmère* (Lt J. Cuthbert, RCNR) – had been correctly screening the *Caribou* from astern in accordance with the WACIs (Western Approaches Convoy Instructions) screening diagram intended for use of a single ship escorting a convoy. Subsequent analysis of U-69's attack urged the more appropriate view on Canadian authorities that such a ship would afford more effective protection zigzagging 2000–3000 yards ahead, or else – subject, of course, to the relative speeds of convoy and escort – circling the merchant ship at 15 knots at a distance of 3000 yards.[43]

Every tactical advantage rested with U-69 whose low-lying hull lay obscured from view as it chose both the time and the place of attack ahead of its target. Escorting from astern, HMCS *Grandmère*'s hydrophones would not have distinguished the U-boat's propeller noise from that of the *Caribou*. Under ideal conditions, her maximum asdic range would be no more than 1200–1500 yards. Even more critical, HMCS *Grandmère* was without radar. Like all the other escorts of the Sydney-based force, she had no prospect of having one until the procurement priorities of the Western Local Escort Force in Halifax had been met. Both ships, *Caribou* and HMCS *Grandmère*, were running blind.

SS *Caribou* was just 40 miles southwest of her destination at 0221 Atlantic Standard Time with HMCS *Grandmère* off her starboard quarter, when Gräf fired a single torpedo from 650 m at her starboard side.[44] This was his most favourable position despite the possible interference of the escort. The torpedo struck the *Caribou* in position 47° 19′ N, 59° 29′ W, after a run of 43 seconds, raising a tall dark blast column at the point of impact, exploding the ship's boilers and sinking her in 4 minutes. During these first crucial moments an undetermined number of lifeboats and rafts were destroyed. The unexplained fact of having accommodated some family members in different cabins contributed to the tension and anxiety when U-69's torpedo struck, for they now sought each other under chaotic conditions before gaining access to the upper deck. Many became separated in the confusion. One woman and her three youngsters were doubtless lost this way.

Gräf watched the vessel lurch down to her guard-rails with a heavy port list, and saw HMCS *Grandmère* at 800–1000 m turn first towards the *Caribou* and then accelerate in a sharp turn and "dash off" to attack him (KTB). HMCS *Grandmère* had in fact "sighted the U-Boat on the surface ahead and to starboard [and] attempted to ram."[45] There are suggestions that Captain Tavernor of the *Caribou* had also sighted U-69 and was attempting to ram. But as his ship had lost steerage way within seconds of the attack, this seems unlikely. Realizing that the excellent visibility prevented him from escaping on the surface, Gräf executed a swift full-power emergency dive, spiralling downward in the direction of the *Caribou* where the escort, he reasoned, would "not fire his depth charges" (KTB). The dive foiled HMCS *Grandmère*'s ramming attempt when she was but 150 yards off. Passing ahead of the swirl left by the diving U-boat, she dropped "a pattern of six depth charges by eye" in her wake; U-69 felt but a single harmless explosion directly overhead. By this time the U-boat's crew had heard the loud wracking noise of *Caribou*'s bulkheads as she sank to the bottom. Then followed twelve distinct depth-charge explosions (four at 150 feet, and eight at 550 feet) and the ticking of *Grandmère*'s asdic. *Grandmère* carried out the attacks in total darkness without even picking up the *Nebelbold* anti-asdic bubble decoys that Gräf had released. This is their first recorded use in Canadian waters.

When the torpedo first struck SS *Caribou*, the violent explosions jolted passengers from their bunks, sending them scurrying insufficiently clad to the precariously sloping decks, or in search of family members in the cabins below. There was little time for reflection. Water was rushing into darkened cabins and passageways, passengers groped for lifebelts and fumbled anxiously to fasten them and hasten to safety. Some survivors reported the sheer terror, panic, and "indescribable chaos" before the ship went down. They told of passengers scrambling for lifeboats and rafts, many of which had been shattered by the explosion; of a woman "in a frenzy of terror [who] threw her baby overboard and then jumped after it" to her death; of 15-month-old Leonard Shiers of Halifax who was lost at sea three times, only to be saved each time by a different rescuer. He was the only one of fifteen children on board to survive.[46] In all, the situation was "confused and desperate."[47] The swift destruction of the *Caribou* left survivors to a night of quiet desperation, debilitating hypothermia, and sometimes a lonely death. One witness recalled hearing "a short distance away a sailor, clinging to a piece of the shattered lifeboat, praying aloud. They tried to save him but he clung to the wreckage and died before their eyes." Exhausted and terrified as many were, the spiritual heritage of generations of seafaring Newfoundlanders gave them strength; the Lord's Prayer and the singing of hymns could be heard throughout the night. Clutching debris, an upturned boat, or huddled in overcrowded rafts for up to five hours, many survivors bore witness to selfless courage. Nursing Sister Margaret Martha Brooke, RCNVR, of Ardath, Saskatchewan, exemplified this spirit in her night-long effort to save her companion, Nursing Sister Agnes Wilkie, RCNVR, of Carman and Winnipeg. Brooke recalled the exhausting night spent with twelve others on an upturned lifeboat, clinging to ropes as waves washed them off one by one. Eventually: "Agnes said she was getting cramped. She let go but I managed to catch hold of her as best I could and hold her until daybreak. Finally a wave took her. When I called to her she didn't answer. She must have been unconscious. The men [who were left] tried to reach her, but she floated away."[48] Brooke's "gallantry and courage" won her the Order of the British Empire in January 1943.[49]

Severe overloading caused at least two lifeboats to capsize, spilling their already chilled and weakened occupants into worsening seas. The traumatic experience remained vivid even twenty years later when Gerald Bastow recalled the horrors of women and children floundering among the wreckage, and the meagre room on the few scattered rafts: "The first glimmer of dawn was greeted with cheers and a renewed attempt to start some songs ... During the next three hours our spirits rose and fell as aircraft were seen but did not come close enough to spot us. Then the wind began to freshen and the swell increased." A Canso of 117 (BR) Squadron, North Sydney, had in fact arrived on the scene three hours after the sinking and well before dawn. It found "rafts, lifeboats and wreckage ... scattered over the sea [and] one lifeboat ... 6 miles from the scene of the torpedoing."[50]

Characteristically, the image projected by the media throughout the war of stalking and ruthless Nazi marauders suggested a reason for these disastrous capsizings. The U-boat, some witnesses claimed, had actually surfaced beneath the boats and rafts, and tipped them over. Newspaper reports later emphasized that this was a particularly German form of tactical harassment. So psychologically ingrained were the expectations of how Germans would treat the victims of their maritime warfare, that gunner A.R. Fielding of Toronto expressed his relief that he "didn't see or hear any machine-gun fire" when the U-boat supposedly set about its business. U-69, in fact, lay submerged all the time. It remained so until sixteen hours after the attack, rising on only one occasion to periscope depth to observe "one PC boat [Fairmile], a motor sailer, and very heavy air surveillance" around dusk (KTB). HMCS *Grandmère* broke off her search for U-69 at 0420 Atlantic Standard Time on 14 October, in order to commence rescue operations. She found 103 survivors, two of whom died on board. She then continued the search until 0820 AST when she was relieved by the armed yachts HMCS *Reindeer* and *Elk*, the Bangor minesweeper HMCS *Drummondville*, the Fairmile Q-055, and the RCAF crash boat B-109. Several fishing vessels proceeded from Port aux Basques to assist. The survivors of SS *Caribou* landed at Sydney at 1640 AST on 14 October.

Gräf's very last torpedo struck the 7803-ton SS *Rose Castle* in Wabana–Sydney convoy WB-9 on 20 October 16 miles southeast of Ferryland Head, Newfoundland, but failed to explode due to a faulty detonator. Gräf watched her "yaw markedly," give a prolonged blast on her siren, stop, broach to, and then set emergency lanterns (KTB). Adverse weather conditions prevented a gunnery attack. *Rose Castle* continued her journey 20 minutes later, having broadcast news of the attack on the emergency band. *B-Dienst* in Germany heard her call and associated the alarm with an attack by Gräf. Her reprieve ended on 2 November when U-518 sank her in Wabana Anchorage, Conception Bay, while the U-boat was en route to New Carlisle, Quebec, to deliver a spy.

News of *Caribou*'s fate reached the Canadian public three days after the event. *Le Devoir*'s headlines announced, "Perte du traversier 'Caribou' avec 137 personnes dont 68 Canadiens"; *Le Soleil* headlined "Le 'Caribou' est torpillé: 137 morts." The English-language press was even more graphic. A back-page account in the *Ottawa Journal* proclaimed "Caribou Sinking Proves Hideousness of Nazi Warfare"; the *Halifax Herald* headlined the fact that "Women, Children [were] among Victims as Torpedo Strikes – Loss Is Greatest Marine Disaster of War in Waters Fringing Canadian Coast."[51] Photographs and eye-witness accounts emphasized the viciousness of the attack; they highlighted the courage and stamina of those who survived, and the human dignity of those who succumbed. For the first time, Minister for the Navy Macdonald polemicized in a style he had eschewed until now:

The sinking of the SS *Caribou* brings the war to Canada with tragic emphasis. We deplore the loss of officers and men of our fighting forces … Yet those for whom our hearts bleed most are the … women and children … If there were any Canadians who did not realize that we were up against a ruthless and remorseless enemy, there can be no such Canadians now. If anything were needed to prove the hideousness of Nazi warfare, surely this is it. Canada can never forget the SS *Caribou*.

Significantly, perhaps, his pathos only made back-page news. Press coverage concluded the *Caribou* sequence with a front-page hospital interview with the Calgary bride of two weeks who had survived her husband, Pilot Officer J.H. Barrett, in the sinking: "If what happened would shake many Canadians out of their complacency," she reflected, "then it was not in vain."[52] Whatever the impact in 1942, the sinking of the *Caribou* had no long-term effect, for in matters of national defence, Canada has no memory. Almost forty years later, in April 1982, U.S. Ambassador to Canada Paul Robinson had to remind a Canadian naval conference in Vancouver that Canada still "can't even defend the St. Lawrence River."[53]

CHAPTER FIVE

The Intelligence Gatherers: Langbein, Janow, and Kurt

War spawns sophisticated organizations and techniques for intelligence gathering.[1] German methods of espionage and counter-espionage embraced the same inventive variety of schemes found in the Allied camp: from high technology and *B-Dienst* decryption of Allied radio transmissions to the recovery of classified material from embattled derelicts and wrecks, the interrogation of prisoners of war, or even the capture of civilian mariners. U-boats delivered automatic weather stations to foreign territory and landed secret agents behind enemy lines. German Intelligence targeted Canada with two of these schemes. Significantly, perhaps, technology proved in this case more trustworthy than the human recruits, for the two reluctant spies, "Langbein" and "Janow," performed dubious services, while weather station "Kurt" survived undetected until 1981. Evidence suggests that German Intelligence had marshalled a surprising amount of ineptitude in hastily preparing the spies for tasks for which they clearly had little taste. The spy masters should not have been startled by what transpired, for a German military analysis, though jaundiced in the extreme, had urged the view in 1931 that "spies are without exception people with serious moral defects," a factor that led one such analyst to sympathize with Dante who had relegated traitors to the last circle of Hell.[2] The *V-Mann* or confidence man rarely enjoyed his master's full trust. The German Naval Staff insisted in December 1942 that "agents can never be regarded as absolutely reliable";[3] fearing possible betrayal, it had refused to send a U-boat to recover an agent from Iceland. By contrast, it sent two U-boats to Canada in order to recover German prisoners of war.

Von Varendorff's U-213 undertook in May 1942 the first of a series of clandestine operations by German U-boats in Canadian waters.[4] The operation thus slipped into the third and final phase of Paukenschlag, and coincided with the mission of Karl Thurmann's U-553 whose individual sortie had signalled the beginning of the Battle of the St Lawrence (see chapter three). The background to U-213's mission remains mysterious. The absence of both German and Canadian Intelligence records, coupled with cryptic notations in the U-boat War Diary, heighten the sense of intrigue surrounding the landing of the agent in Saint John, New Brunswick.[5] Within two hours of his arrival in Lorient from Brest on 24 April, von Varendorff completed his "discussion with the representative of OKW [German High Command] regarding the Special Mission" (KTB). The War Diary offers no clue as to the substance of the discussions or the intent of the plan. Less than three hours before departure next day, von Varendorff recorded "Leutnant (M.A.) Langbein on board." This was likely the agent's cover name (the "M.A." standing for his alleged naval branch, Marine-Artillerie) in order to explain away his unfamiliarity with submarines. Only the commanding officer would be privy to his real mission.

RCMP files and reports by witnesses reveal Langbein to have been "a personable man who made friends easily, who had an encyclopaedic memory," and who had lived in Canada from 1928 to 1932.[6] He had surveyed in Alberta, railroaded in Winnipeg, and mined in Flin Flon. The country had grown on him. Though one witness recalled his speaking only "broken English," others had heard him speak well with "an English" or even "a nice Dutch accent." He apparently returned to Germany to visit his parents, may have married, then underwent espionage training after mobilization in the army, and completed one mission in Romania. Secretly disenchanted with national socialism and the war, he had accepted the relatively tame mission of reporting on the location of Canadian industries and the activities around principal ports like Halifax. He was forbidden to engage in sabotage. This offered the opportunist an unprecedented chance of escaping to Canada where he hoped to "submerge" and live a life of ease. Reporting aboard U-213 in the guise of a naval officer, he carried a portable transmitter-receiver, a suit of civilian clothes, an old road map of New Brunswick issued by an oil company, and a forged National Registration Certificate in the name of Alfred Haskins of 182 Younge [sic] Street, Toronto, dated 16 October 1940. There are suggestions that the real Haskins was either a captured RCAF flyer, or a person whom Langbein had met in Canada. Finally, he held $7000 in large American bills, and $12 or $13 in Canadian funds. Both currencies would cause him problems.

U-213 departed Lorient on schedule on 25 April 1942 just six days behind Thurmann's U-553, crossed the dangerous Biscay submerged under a bright moon that provided the Allies with "excellent flying weather" (KTB), and shaped course westward on a deepened variation of the great circle route. "Bloody miserable weather from dead ahead" (KTB) forced the U-boat to consume a normally unacceptable fuel level of 3.6 to 4 m³ per day. This von Varendorff would only "put up with in view of the task." This comment suggests that he was labouring under a firmer deadline and operational priority than would constrain the secret mission of U-518 in the Baie des Chaleurs the following November. Unstable weather near the Canadian coast that could shift within a space of ten minutes from a clear sky to "an impenetrable wall of fog" impressed upon him that "successful operations require a good share of luck" (KTB).

Von Varendorff decided to enter the Bay of Fundy during the night of 12 May 1942 because, as he noted, "I have to expect deterioration of the weather, and navigational difficulties in fog and in the prevailing current are too great." He again observed that execution of the mission was costing a lot of fuel. His comments suggest a degree of anxiety, and that weather alone was urging him close inshore at this time. It was a considerable undertaking. Once inside the Bay of Fundy, he recognized more clearly than ever that his folio of charts was inadequate for the task. He doubtless depended on the large-area small-scale British Admiralty Chart no. 352, which the German chart depot regularly supplied. He lacked other navigational resources that his successors could consult – in particular, the detailed German *U-Boat Atlas* covering the east coast of Canada, which was not published for another month; it contained thirteen detailed charts of the Bay of Fundy. The *U-Boat Pilot Book* for the Bay of Fundy did not appear until August. In all likelihood, therefore, von Varendorff would have found navigational details difficult to identify.

German High Command had specifically asked that the landing take place "east of Saint John." At this point, his plan was simple: "run in by night, lie on the bottom by day, carry out the landing by night and where possible knock off a steamer near Saint John before departure" (KTB). U-213 picked up the Lurcher Shoal lightship, and easily passed Manan and Long Island while slipping past a few fishing vessels. It held to the starboard side in order to take advantage of the navigation beacons. All were burning under peacetime conditions. Only the irregular sweeps of searchlights at Saint John revealed the likelihood of Canadian defences. No patrols appeared. At 0300 local time, U-213 lay abeam Saint John to the south of Quaco Ledge. Von Varendorff now intended to wait until dawn before lying on the bottom in 60 m of water off the northern Quaco lightbuoy. This would place him 2 miles from the coast. By daylight he would approach shore at periscope depth to reconnoitre. Weather obscured all navigational beacons except for the bright flashes of St Martin Light as he slipped to the bottom at 50 m at 0630 local time. Throughout the day he felt the current tugging at the U-boat. Not a single hydrophone contact emerged. At 1830 he again approached shore at periscope depth to within 1 mile, but could see nothing in the mist.

The final phase began at 2230 local time on 13 May when U-213 surfaced to air the boat, charge batteries, and advance to within 1200 m of shore. The crew prepared the inflatable boat for launching while the watch on deck strained to identify the misty shore. At 20 minutes past midnight "the inflatable, in charge of the Second Officer and with two seamen, push[ed] off" (KTB). Visibility deteriorated markedly once the boat had disappeared from view. Von Varendorff's War Diary offers no hint about the nature or procedure of the mysterious landing. His chart revealed only that he had chosen "Melvin's Beach." RCMP recollections assert that Langbein landed in full naval uniform so that if arrested on the shore he could claim status as a prisoner of war, and not face the death penalty awaiting any captured civilian agent. Apparently expecting the inflatable to make a relatively brief run to shore and back, von Varendorff held U-213 on station against the strong westerly current with silent electric power. Von Varendorff and his Second Officer had arranged a series of light signals in the event they became separated in the murk. When the officer had still not returned by 0300, von Varendorff began flashing his signals towards shore. At 0430 local time, "four hours and ten minutes" after having pushed off, as von Varendorff anxiously recorded, the inflatable hove into view. It had taken three hours to find a suitable landing place after first attempts had failed along the "steep coast" of Melvin's Beach. RCMP reports place the landing near the mouth of the Salmon River, some 30 miles southwest of Saint John and a few miles from the village of St Martins. We can only conjecture as to what precisely occurred ashore. The War Diary simply records the inflatable's movements: "0720 [German time] landing completed, pushed off from shore, 0830 back on board." As von Varendorff noted, "the Second Officer's action was clear and definite, and is responsible for the successful landing despite the difficulties which arose through [severely reduced] visibility, current and lack of knowledge of the landing place." It was a fine though characteristically sparing tribute. U-213 signalled the successful operation to BdU on 16 May once clear of the Bay of Fundy.

Adverse weather conditions during von Varendorff's departure from Canadian waters frustrated all hopes of attacking merchant targets, though he himself was attacked by what might have been the Norwegian HNMS *Lincoln*, which reported having sighted a surfaced submarine on 15 May some 80 miles SSW of Yarmouth.[7] For the rest, the situation was "desperate: overhead a blue sky, and all around me fog" (KTB). Thus the security of merchant vessels in this instance derived not from his having "been given orders to land his human cargo and get out of the way without exciting undue apprehension on the part of those in charge of that defence area," as was charged in the House of Commons in 1952 when the spy story first surfaced officially in public.[8] BdU blamed von

Varnedorff's poor tactical record on lack of aggressiveness. Still, the special mission had been well executed, and BdU hoped that the young U-boat captain had at least learned something from his mistakes.

Upon landing on Canadian soil Langbein-Haskins buried in water-proof coverings the naval uniform and transmitter that he would never use, and set off after daybreak on a two-and-a-half-hour hike to St Martins. Here he spent the first of the outdated Canadian $2 bills that his counterpart von Janowski would pass off in Quebec next November. The bills had been issued in 1917, were about one-third larger than the current ones, and had long since been taken out of circulation. The St Martins' merchants seem not to have twigged to a problem until too late. From St Martins, Langbein proceeded by a combination of hitch-hiking and rail to Saint John, Moncton, and eventually Montreal. The embarrassment of large American bills led him to establishments that would accept the cash and give Canadian change with no questions. In such straits, he purportedly squandered his money until arrested as a found-in at a brothel. Booked under a fictitious name, according to the conventions of the day for customers caught *in flagrante*, he paid his caution and was quickly released. This must have been disillusioning for one whose pro-clivities for the flesh pots of colonial Canada, a senior RCMP officer recalled, had in the 1930s led him to The Half Way speak-easy in Flin Flon, Manitoba, and the company of Blonde Annie and Suede Anne. After a month in Montreal, Langbein moved to Ottawa where he lived unobtrusively from 19 June 1942 until 1 November 1944. He first moved into the now long-since demolished Grand Hotel on Sussex Street at George. This was apparently "one of the most extensively patronized establishments" in town, and was "a favourite spot for members of the armed forces and civil servants employed in the Daly Building across the street."9

It is unclear how long he remained in the hotel. In August 1943 he withdrew to a boarding house, explaining that illness had forced his retirement from the civil service. The family with whom he lived denied that he had acted the playboy that postwar press accounts made of him. On 1 November 1944 the now penniless Langbein set off from his home ostensibly on a fishing trip – and gave himself up to the Naval Intelligence Directorate. NID passed him to the RCMP, where he tried to convince an understandably sceptical Superintendent (later Commissioner) C.E. Rivett-Carnac that he had indeed landed from a German submarine. Investigations by Sergeant (later Inspector) Cecil Bayfield corroborated all of Langbein's allegations, uncovered the still-undisturbed transmitter, and an infantry spade and blanket that the "spy" had discarded. He had never engaged in espionage, and had lived solely on the funds with which Berlin had provided him. Langbein spent the remainder of the war in internment camp, and was repatriated at the end of hostilities. The hapless journey of von Janowski took a radically different turn.

The maiden voyage of the type IXC U-boat U-518 in the autumn of 1942 with her new captain Oberleutnant zur See Friedrich Wissmann was charged with uncommon risk and adventure. On this his first command, one indeed that Dönitz would subsequently regard as a model operation, Wissmann or *Wissmännchen* (Smart Guy), as he was affectionately nicknamed, was ordered to transport an agent to Canada while simultaneously exploiting every opportunity of attacking Allied shipping at important choke points on the Canadian seaboard. Admiral Dönitz still remained convinced that the Strait of Belle Isle formed a major egress into the Atlantic for Gulf shipping. The success of U-165 and U-517 in that zone had apparently not yet enabled him to grasp the system of convoy feeder routes (Quebec–Sydney, Sydney–Halifax, and Halifax–Boston), which in effect bypassed Belle Isle. These not only shepherded coastal traffic, but fed into the great Atlantic convoys from Halifax and New York. Only those convoys bound between Gulf ports and Iceland, or Quebec and Labrador, used the Belle Isle Strait at this time. The scant records of U-518's Canadian mission provide no clear indication of Wissmann's priorities. It is not entirely certain, for example, whether the timing of the agent's landing was either at Wissmann's discretion or that of the agent, or whether U-518 was first to deal with assigned tactical tasks before inserting the *V-Mann* (*Vertrauensmann*) into a locale predetermined by higher authority.

Under normal circumstances, commanding officers received precise navigation instructions indicating the latitude and longitude of the primary landing site, together with details about one or two alternatives. This was the case in Hilbig's landing of spies in Maine via U-1230. There is nothing to suggest this kind of care with Wissmann. Given the fact that commanding officers customarily received their assignments in sealed orders that could only be opened at a specific moment after departure, or else on receipt of a radio signal, we may assume that Wissmann's *Sonderaufgabe* (special task) had been the subject of briefings and discussions. Whatever the priorities might have been in theory, it is clear from the record that the agent, later identified by Canadians as Werner Alfred Waldmar von Janowski, had to sit out a long submarine operation until other tactical goals had been attained. It is little wonder that after forty-four days submerged he exuded the tell-tale musty "submarine stink," which among other things alerted the hotel keeper of The Carlisle Hotel to a stranger in their midst.[10]

Speculation about spy activity in Canada became widespread throughout the spring and summer of 1942. It had been nourished by reports in both the English-language and French-language press concerning German spies captured in the United States. The sheer sensationalism of such stories made the St Lawrence River and Gulf sound much more vulnerable than it was in fact. Thus, for example, the *Halifax Herald* for 1 April 1942 announced "Sub Reported Landing Germans on Coast – Spies Come Ashore, Report Back to Boats." The eye-catching headline obscured the fact that "the coast" in question was the American seaboard where spies had indeed been apprehended. Uninformed opinion on the subject subsequently caused ripples throughout the press. Second-hand information sometimes gave the impression of being canonical, such as on 22 May when Frances R. Farnum, director of civil defence for the State of Maine, warned that "accurate information is in the possession of police and army authorities to show that foreign agents have recently been landed on the coast of Maine."[11] As reported in the *Montreal Star*, he later regarded it as "entirely possible that the enemy may attempt to land parachutists or other air-borne troops in Maine" in order to back those foreign agents who had entered from Canada. Speculation on Canada's susceptibility to bomber attack was commonplace, if not even alarmist, as witness the *Star Weekly*'s edition of 28 March 1942, which published a full-page colour map revealing "North American Towns and Cities Now Shadowed by Axis Bombers." Pearl Harbor had proved that "it can happen here," it explained, while promoting the scenario of carrier-based aircraft off Canada's Pacific and Atlantic shores. The Nazis were thus 15 minutes from Halifax, 75 minutes from Quebec City and Montreal, and 2 hours from Ottawa and Toronto. Spy landings were, therefore, "softening up" operations before a major assault.

Le Soleil of Quebec City picked up the cue on 23 May: "Débarquement possible d'agents ennemis le long du St. Laurent." It pointed out the vulnerability of the whole Gulf region. On 29 June *Le Soleil* featured an American account of captured saboteurs who had apparently planned to enter Canada from the U.S.: "Des saboteurs projetaient la destruction d'usines au Canada." An expanded account in the *Halifax Herald* for 30 June revealed that six of the eight captured Germans, all former immigrants to the United States, had landed by U-boat with sweeping orders for forming a fifth column and destroying industrial centres. Such disquieting accounts provoked an official response from the RCMP to the effect that "no Nazi spies had been landed from German submarines off the Canadian Atlantic coast." It assured the Canadian public "that a vigilant 24-hour-a-day watch was kept by coastal patrols on both the Atlantic and the Pacific."[12] By this time, of course, Leutnant Langbein had landed undetected in Saint John, New Brunswick, from U-213, but had not yet surrendered. Quebec's Liberal Premier Adelard Godbout warned Mackenzie King in mid July during the bitter debates on the St Lawrence shipping crisis that the people of his province were on edge, and that "two reliable sources" had reported an attack on the wireless station at Ste Flavie airport by two men who might have landed from a U-boat.[13] Only the *Halifax Herald* (29 July 1942) pointed out that one of Canada's principal security cordons consisted of ubiquitous "ghost patrols" that covered the beaches "along Canada's rugged Atlantic coastline." This was the militia; at best it provided in-depth coverage of but one man for every 6 miles of shore. In Janowski's case, however the *Herald*'s rhetoric proved ironically prophetic:

Can spies and saboteurs land on Canada's East Coast? That question has been said many times since the round-up by the Federal Bureau of Investigation ... The answer to the question is: yes they can ... A much more pertinent question is, if they do land, how far can they get? The answer to that one is easy ... by the shortest route to the nearest gaol.[14]

But the seeds of disquietude had been sown in Quebec and could suddenly flourish. By announcing speculations of the Quebec Provincial Police (QPP) on the Farnum scare as fact ("Des saboteurs debarqués au Canada"), *Le Soleil* for 20 July 1942 reminded its readers of the need for home defence. Widespread announcements of the executions of the six spies caught in the U.S. did not diminish this sense of threat.[15] Lead articles about U-boat activity in Canadian inshore waters throughout the spring and late summer of 1942 (and the actual ravages of combat that many Quebecers could readily see) reminded Quebecers that "Les Nazis sont actifs dans le St. Laurent."[16] Under such circumstances, conscription for overseas service made little sense at all.

U-518 departed Kiel, Tirpitzhaven, at 0700 hours on 26 September 1942. It stopped at the usual staging point of Christiansand, Norway, where it topped up with fuel and water on 28 September, and then negotiated the Iceland Passage north of the Faeroes on 3 October en route to the open North Atlantic. It would not reach a home port until 10:35 AM on 15 December in the Biscay base of Lorient, France. According to Wissmann's account, he entered his initial operation zone at midnight on 18 October, some 60 miles northeast of Belle Isle. This portion of the tour almost matched Rüggeberg's seventeen days of uneventful fog-bound patrol in U-513 the previous month. By now, however, both it and U-517 had reached Lorient, and U-165 was destroyed. During ten foggy days on station, Wissmann saw little more than two fishing boats and found a "completely dead area" such as Schäfer's U-183 had encountered during his recent ten days in the southern section of the Belle Isle Strait. BdU radioed U-518 and U-43 for their belated situation reports. Schwandtke's U-43 was by this time in the Gulf of St Lawrence. Anticipating instructions to shift his operation area, Wissmann headed southeast around Newfoundland, and when 100 miles northeast of Cape Freels received final authorization to "penetrate towards BA and BB 10-40 during new moon period for execution of special task."

Wissmann's sole constraint seems to have been that of delivering the agent von Janowski some time during the dark nights of the new moon period. Otherwise BdU seems to have left him latitude to decide both on routes and methods. The direct route from his present position to Percé on the Gaspé Peninsula entailed some 560 miles northwestward into the Strait of Belle Isle and down into the Gulf. For undisclosed reasons, he chose the alternative: 950 miles around Newfoundland and into the Cabot Strait. By taking the longer route, he doubtless hoped to encounter targets. Indeed he had intercepted BdU's signal to Bargsten (U-521) and Schwartzkopf (U-520) indicating special opportunities in Wabana anchorage off Bell Island, Conception Bay. Wissmann recorded his intention of "paying the anchorage a visit as the two others are otherwise engaged" (KTB). Four wrecks in Lance Cove bear witness to the attacks of Rüggeberg's U-513 in September 1942, and to Wissmann's almost two months later on 2 November. As Wissmann recorded, the ships' protective barrage effectively "spelled their doom" (KTB). Paradoxically, the regular defensive sweep of army searchlights illuminated U-518's targets at sufficiently reliable intervals to facilitate a definitive surface attack with little risk of detection and retaliation. The army defenders had disregarded their Standing Orders which explicitly called for irregular intervals. At 0602 GMT, U-518 sunk the anchored SS *Rose Castle* and the French ore carrier PLM-27 with considerable loss of life, and damaged the SS *Flyingdale* when a torpedo struck a wharf.[17] U-518 left the scene at full surfaced speed around the south end of Bell Island, then turned outbound toward Western Bay Head and the safety of deeper and less-constrained waters. The four-hour action in Conception Bay had taken place entirely on the surface.

The offshore antisubmarine patrols that these sinkings now triggered led to a serious bombing attack on U-518 some 40 miles east of Cape Race, while en route for Cabot Strait. Not forewarned by his FuMB search radar of the close approach of a Digby at 3.5 mile range, U-518 all but fell victim to a stick of four 250-pound charges fused for 23 feet that struck the swirl of the U-boat's emergency dive. Fog rolled in over moderate seas and foiled the aircraft's further pursuit.[18] The attacks of U-513 and U-518 forced the Canadians to abandon the Wabana anchorage completely and to undertake the construction of antitorpedo nets off the Wabana wharves. Although the nets were completed by the end of December despite adverse weather, the U-boats had caused a major disruption in shipping schedules and defence patrols.[19] Allied memories of the effective attacks would strain already overstressed resources and priorities.

Wissmann consulted with his *V-Mann* on the final points of detail during the approach to Cabot Strait and scheduled the operation for the night of 9 November. On 8 November his War Diary records the first hint of the actual site for the agent's landing: naval quadrant "Bruno Bruno 4141," the northern perimeter of which ran from Point Bonaventure to Pointe de New Carlisle in the Baie des Chaleurs. No other documentation is extant. In purely navigational terms he had chosen well. The Baie des Chaleurs is the deepest in the Gulf, is free of shoals, and enjoys the mildest climate in the whole region. Fogs, which are frequent outside the bay, seldom penetrate towards the head, though rain and mist may well accompany easterly gales. With any kind of luck, all circumstances would favour the operation. The choice, as will be seen, was a major tactical error. A stranger cannot remain obscure in a tiny village.

This was not the first time that the 41-year-old von Janowski had visited Canada. He had apparently emigrated to the province of Ontario in 1930 where he had first hired himself out as a day labourer in the village of Ailsa Craig, about 20 miles from London. Here the 5-foot-7-inch, 150-pound immigrant later obtained full-time employment as a farm worker. A newspaper interview with the town's police chief immediately after the war evoked the judgment that von Janowski "was a good worker, but very cocky, boasting that he came from a prominent German family."[20] He later described his father as a colonel in the "78th Infantry Battalion." His pro-German attitude purportedly led to a much-discussed tiff with a stalwart First World War veteran who, in the police chief's words, "didn't like the way Janowski shot off his face about Germany and the last [1914–18] war." The townspeople seem, none the less, to have accepted him because of his engaging personality and his skill on the cello. He is said to have married, in 1932, a Toronto woman who regularly vacationed in Ailsa Craig. Some accounts suggest that she was a financially independent widow with her own business. In any event, it is generally agreed that the marriage remained happy as long as she provided him money for tuition in unspecified courses. She gave him an expensive camera with which he repeatedly photographed public buildings and waterfront scenes during independent tours of the province. They separated after he had spent some $3000 of her money. By this time, according to one account, his wife was living in fear of him, for during frequent indulgence in alcohol he would threaten her life. About a year before the outbreak of war he apparently left for northern Ontario.

Under what circumstances he returned to Germany is not clear. Other German immigrants in late depression Canada had been lured into returning by the obvious economic growth of Nazi Germany. Letters from home invited them back to share the good times. It may be that von Janowski felt so attracted as well. The mysteriousness of the subsequent interlude has triggered the imagination of post-war commentators.[21]

Whether he actually joined the French Foreign Legion in Marseilles, served with the German army at Dieppe after some time in a French jail, and later recommended himself to Nazi espionage circles because of his experience in Canada, is all a matter of conjecture. His motivation for espionage remains equally vague. His apparently superficial preparation for the Canadian mission, and his obviously ingenuous and cavalier method of executing the task suggest that German authorities regarded him as eminently expendable. At any rate, post-war newspaper reports would have us believe that the "slim, mousy-looking" man was no match for the "sharp-eyed ... vigilant and quick thinking" citizens of New Carlisle.[22]

U-518 entered Baie des Chaleurs via the south shore on 9 November 1942. It passed close aboard North Miscou Point and the Miscou Flats until it surfaced at 1900 GMT in moderate visibility off the Shippegan Channel. Wissmann would have verified his position by the range lights of Pointe de Petite Lambèque. The *UBootshandbuch*, which would not be issued in Berlin until 1943, would describe the bay as presenting no navigational difficulties whatever, particularly as the echo sounder would give ample warning of any shallows.[23] In the absence of any recent German *Sailing Directions*, Wissmann would have had to rely on a British edition, or else upon German and British Admiralty charts based on surveys of 1913. By choosing the southern route, Wissmann avoided by 14 miles the northern shore on which the agent would eventually land. But he risked the erratic tidal streams near the Miscou Banks. The hazardous banks themselves reach westward off the point, and extend for 2 miles offshore. Yet U-518 faced little real difficulty because of the large number of navigational lights that dotted the area. As U-518 shaped course toward the northern shore at 2300 GMT on 8 November, Wissmann found the weather and illumination favourable to his purposes: light wind from SSW, moderate visibility, with a moderately bright sky.[24] He noted the heavy highway traffic on either side of the bay (routes 132 and 134) and was pleased to find the area devoid of vessels. As the settlements along the shore gradually switched off their lights, Wissmann stood fascinated by the seemingly constant stream of automobiles.

The U-boat now ran in towards shore on a rising tide in order to carry out the special mission in quadrant "BB 4141 upper edge centre" (KTB). At 0336 GMT on 9 November, the crew on deck prepared the inflatable dinghy for launching. Von Janowski and Wissmann had chosen for the landing the beach lying just east of Sawyer's Point. Hidden from the settlement of New Carlisle by the wooded knoll of Pointe de New Carlisle, the beach provided not only seclusion, but access both to highway 132 and to the Canadian National Railway line. This was important, for the agent planned to locate as quickly as possible in Montreal in his assumed role of a radio salesman representing a Toronto manufacturer.[25] Once there, he was to contact Hamburg for further instructions. German Intelligence had apparently provided him with but a single contact: the Canadian Fascist Party under Adrien Arcand of Montreal. This group, he was given to understand, was sufficiently well organized and loyal to the Nazi cause to provide him all possible assistance. Paradoxically, no one had troubled to inform him that Arcand and ten of his most active and trusted associates had been arrested in 1940 and were still behind bars. This crucial oversight is particularly surprising in light of the fact that the "Arcand arrests" were front-page news in Canadian newspapers of the time. There is no evidence to support the specious anglophile myth that other "people in Quebec fed information to Nazi agents."

Approaching shore under electric power at 0435 GMT on 9 November, Wissmann flooded his forward diving tank in order to beach U-518 on the gently sloping shoals. It was half-past midnight local time, he observed, and isolated houses stood along the shore, which rose ahead of him some 15 m above sea level. A highway skirted the beach to his left (KTB). Fifteen minutes after U-518's bow slipped onto the beach, automobile lights swung unexpectedly along a curve in the road just to the left and swept across the U-boat and surrounding waters before continuing on towards the east in the direction of New Carlisle. "Completely flummoxed" (KTB) by the suddenness of this perfidious intrusion into the operation, Wissmann involuntarily ordered all hands to duck. They felt totally exposed as the lights flashed by about 800 yards off the bow. They illuminated "houses standing separately on shore," and enabled the crew "to pick out all the details" along the beach. The houses made a distinctly "dreary impression" on the Germans (KTB). Von Janowski had by now loaded his three suitcases into the dinghy before being rowed ashore. One suitcase contained the civilian clothes into which he would change once safely ashore. Once packed with his full naval uniform (blue officer's jacket, green canvas submariner's pants, and an officer's cap of surprisingly inferior manufacture) and buried in the sand, it would provide his alibi. In the event of capture, he would, as Langbein had ostensibly planned, claim to have deserted from a U-boat, and demand recognition as a prisoner of war.

The other two cases contained the tools of his trade.[26] The first contained the very heavy and cumbersome 40 W Telefunken transmitter-receiver that he had to lug up the beach and along the highway into town. The second, a deep-grained leather briefcase, obviously of German manufacture, contained an array of ready-use equipment: $4994 in Canadian currency, both current and (unknown to him) outdated issues; $1000 in U.S. $20 gold pieces; coding material including microphotographic copies of instructions; secret writing mediums in the form of matches; a 25-calibre automatic pistol easily concealed in the palm of the hand and manufactured by the Ruby Arms Company, Spain; a set of viciously spiked knuckledusters; emergency rations in the form of chocolate and dextrose tablets (which he believed to be far more potent than was subsequently revealed by analysis); several small maps of Saint John, New Brunswick, Toronto, Montreal, Quebec, Halifax, and general areas of eastern Canada; a metal identity disc of German military origin; a German soldier's pay-book cover, stamped with the tell-tale eagle and swastika; a Canadian National Registration Certificate, the original name of which had been replaced by that of William Branton, 323 Danforth Avenue, Toronto; a 1940 Quebec driver's licence treated in a similar manner. These Canadian documents may have been taken from Canadian soldiers after the Dieppe raid. A number of seemingly innocuous items completed the kit: a cardboard alphabet slide rule, presumably for developing primitive codes, and two books in English that he might have intended as sources for code texts. One of these was a pulp collection of badly written detective stories, and the other a special edition of P.L. Travers's *Mary Poppins*, published in Leipzig in 1939 with the imprint on the cover "Not to be introduced into the British Empire or the USA."

At 0120 local time on 9 November 1942, one hour and thirteen minutes after the landing operation had begun, the inflatable dinghy returned, "the *V-Mann* and his baggage having been put ashore well and dry" (KTB). Von Janowski changed into his grey turtle neck sweater and grey tweed suit, buried his naval uniform, threw away his shovel, and waited until dawn. U-518's bows lifted off as Wissmann pumped the forward tanks and eased astern on electric motors. The task, he noted, had been "executed soundlessly and unobserved." Despite occasional flickers of anxiety, the general ease of the operation gave Wissmann cause for satisfied reflection: "Because of the peacetime conditions we found there, I'm fairly convinced that the agent has made it the rest of the way" (KTB). The conclusion could not have been farther from the truth, for within twenty-four hours Leutnant Werner von Janowski had been arrested and was on his way to being "turned around" to work as a double agent.

Janowski remained at the base of the cliffs until approximately 7:00 AM when it was sufficiently light for him to make his way to the top. In the absence of German documentation to the contrary, his plans and decisions on landing strike one as impetuous. Certainly, after forty-four days in the confines of U-518, followed by a night on a cold Quebec beach, he must have longed for a bath. This is the only reasonable explanation for his brief stop in the small town of New Carlisle. Carrying the transmitter and the briefcase, he started to walk along the highway into town about 8:30 AM. He was picked up by a passing vehicle driven by CNR conductor James E. Coull who was heading into New Carlisle from his home several miles to the west. According to the *Montreal Standard* for 20 May 1945, this was Canada's "first contact with the trespassing Teuton."[27] Despite Coull's naturally inquisitive banter, they seem to have conversed little. As a former resident of Toronto and environs, Janowski's role at this juncture should not have been difficult. He described himself as a salesman for the Northern Electric Company and, with what seemed like foreknowledge of the town to which they were now heading, mentioned the hotel. He checked into the Carlisle under the assumed name of William Branton of 323 Danforth Avenue, Toronto. Von Janowski had no intention of remaining at the hotel any longer than necessary. He informed the staff that he only wished to have a bath and some breakfast before moving on. It concerned no one that he spoke English with a "foreign" accent.[28] Yet the brevity of his stay, his hesitant manner and rather odd body odour hinted at something amiss. Inexplicably, he claimed to have arrived by bus when in fact the first bus of the day would not arrive until noon.

The hotel proprietor's son, 23-year-old Earle J. Annett Jr, became involved when "Janow," as he was nicknamed in Germany, discarded an empty matchbox marked "Fabriqué en Belgique" and paid his bill by cash using two outdated Canadian $1 banknotes. Janowski later blamed his controllers with having double-crossed him by planting such incriminating clues. But, as young Annett informed the press in 1945, neither he nor his father had any serious suspicions even at this time despite their expectation "that the Germans would try to land a spy on the bay shore" some time during the war.[29] On learning that a westbound train would depart at 11:10 AM, Janowski declined Earle Annett's offer of a lift to the station and set off on foot, still lugging his cumbersome radio transmitter. As soon as Janowski had left, Annett telephoned Constable Alphonse Duchesneau of the Quebec Provincial Police. By now he had second thoughts about having been bilked with counterfeit money. He may also have communicated at this time his curiosity about a rather musty-smelling traveller who arrived so early on a non-existent bus. Duchesneau's subsequent inspection of the hotel room revealed Janowski's carelessness: he had forgotten an almost-empty package of Belgian cigarettes. Having grown suspicious, Annett followed Janowski to the station. Here he offered the mysterious traveller a cigarette, whereupon Janowski produced a box of matches identical to the one he had discarded at the hotel. At the wicket he peeled a new-issue $20 banknote from a large roll of bills to pay for the $3.40 one-way fare to Matapedia. With self-congratulatory hindsight three years later, the CN ticket agent, Mr D.D. "Dewey" Smollett, recalled the furtively "suspicious" character who prompted him "to phone Gus Goulet, the deputy sheriff."

As an editorial in the *Ottawa Citizen* remarked immediately after the war, the story had by this time already become "a Laurel and Hardy scenario."[30] Believing his suspicion correct beyond doubt, Annett notified the naval shore patrol, which was known to ride the trains en route to and from the base at Gaspé. But as the naval policeman, J. (Johnny) Lozinsky, had no authority to deal with civilians, both he and Annett jumped from the waiting train and drove off to the Quebec Provincial Police, housed in the Maison Blanche Hotel. Constable Duchesneau returned with them to the station, climbed aboard the train and sat down beside the suspect, while a colleague drove down the highway to the next station. Turning casual conversation to carefully probing interrogation, Duchesneau soon requested the suspect's ID and then searched the incriminating luggage. At this point Janowski declared: "I am caught, I am a German officer." His gun was in his luggage, and he had made no attempt to use the brass knuckles he carried in his pocket. Janowski-Branton played his cover story and claimed status as a prisoner of war.

Constable Duchesneau and his prisoner alighted at Bonaventure, Quebec, 9 miles to the west, and drove back to New Carlisle by patrol car. Janowski claimed the right to don his naval uniform and police officers conducted him to the site where he had buried it. The police acted more quickly in other respects than the post-war press realized. They notified the Staff Officer (Operations) in Gaspé who ordered a special antisubmarine patrol of the two Bangors HMCS *Burlington* and *Red Deer* into the Baie des Chaleurs for a two-day search.[31] Post-war newspaper reports berated the QPP for having allowed Janowski to claim POW status so flagrantly. RCMP officers, they asserted, had chastised the QPP for their lax handling of the case. There is, however, no publicly accessible evidence for this assertion, though indeed Janowski later informed a townsman who visited his cell that he too was "surprised to be so well entertained." Once changed into his naval cap and jacket, though apparently still wearing his tweed trousers, he was conducted to the QPP office in the Maison Blanche Hotel. At about 10:00 PM that night, Duchesneau took Janowski to the county cell and placed him in the charge of the jailer and county sheriff, Gus Goulet. Gus seems to have enjoyed chatting with "Janow," whom he next morning provided with a nourishing breakfast of fresh eggs. Duchesneau had by now informed Chief of the QPP Léon Lambert in Quebec, who in turn brought the RCMP into the picture. Around midnight on 10 November 1942, then-inspector C.V. Harvison of RCMP Montreal Headquarters formally took custody of the spy. The RCMP quickly removed him to Montreal where they utilized him as a double agent.

As the story emerged, Janowski regaled the police with the fiction that he had arrived in one of the most powerful submarines in the German navy. By his distorted account it mounted anti-aircraft guns, no fewer than four torpedo tubes, and carried twenty-two torpedoes and a crew of seventy. It was a type IXC Boat. An early report by Canadian Naval Intelligence of 12 November 1942 noted that the RCMP at New Carlisle had "arrested a suspicious character on 9 November," later identified as "a German Naval Officer landed at Gaspé from a U-Boat on 6 November." The navy seems to have accepted his alibi. By leading Canadian authorities to believe that he had landed three days earlier than had in fact been the case, Janowski was clearly attempting to dissuade the Canadians from pursuit. Wissmann's U-518 needed time to make good its escape. Yet from first alarm on 9 November until running low on fuel on 13 November, Burlington and Red Deer criss-crossed the bay in order to intercept their quarry. Once refuelled at Gaspé, they continued the search with the assistance of RCAF aircraft until daylight on 14 November. Watchers on shore often diverted the vessels with well-intended though false alarms. These reports contributed to the "twenty submarines sighted" by coast watchers and fishermen during the month of November. The search had commenced too late, for by 1100 GMT on 9 November, five and a half hours after having departed the New Carlisle beach, U-518 had passed the small exposed port of Chandler, Quebec and was heading for a cursory patrol in "U-boat alley" off Gaspé Bay.

Inspector Harvison's personal account of his interrogations and subsequent management of Janowski-Branton as a double agent provides the only reliable public record of this key event in the Canadian experience of counter-espionage. Under the guidance of a high-level interservice and interdepartmental steering committee, the RCMP established a radio transmitter for Janowski in the Montreal home of an RCMP interpreter identified only as "Johnny." He had served in U-boats in the First World War and would form part of the boarding party in the attempt to capture U-536 off Pointe de Maisonette, New Brunswick, one year later in November 1943. The output and range of the new transmitter exceeded that of the suitcase model the spy had brought ashore, and had to be calibrated carefully so as not to reveal to Hamburg that its man was now being managed. Using this system, the RCMP had Janowski pass carefully selected information to Berlin via Hamburg control. By establishing his credibility they hoped to extract clues as to the methods of Germany's intelligence-gathering agencies. The RCMP contacted Janowski's radio control station in Hamburg in December 1942 and exchanged daily messages with Hamburg until November 1943.[32] However, the information flow seems to have been one way. Hamburg apparently never attempted to contact Montreal, but waited instead for Janowski to initiate any moves. When communications broke off some time after November 1943, Janowski could raise no response to requests for guidance or assistance, not even when feigning having run out of funds. Yet even twenty years later, on meeting his spy in Germany, Harvison remained convinced that the ruse had succeeded.

The RCMP's success in managing Janowski as a double agent depended in very large measure on the secrecy of his capture in New Carlisle. Inspector Harvison's memoirs reveal that reporters had in fact gotten wind of the arrest, and that many had even arrived in time to ferret out stories from among the local residents. They would have had little difficulty in gathering sufficient details to kindle their readers' imagination about the proven threat to national security. News coverage of Janowski's arrest would not only have blown the RCMP cover, but would have confirmed Quebec's worst fears about the imminent Nazi threat. Harvison was doubtless sensitive to the whole "spy scare" that hovered over the Gulf, and in his subsequent autobiography praised the press because "not one line appeared until the lifting of censorship at the end of the war."

In fact, however, there were many leaks. On 23 November 1942, just two weeks after Janowski's arrest, the American magazine *Newsweek* published the first clues under a caption entitled "Canadian Note." It invited its readers to "watch for an announcement revealing the capture of a German submarine commander near New Carlisle, Quebec."[33] No further notes followed. But the very next day, on 23 November, Navy Minister Angus Macdonald gave a press conference during which he deftly skirted the spy issue when confirming the sinking of twenty ships in the St Lawrence River and Gulf in 1942. Asked directly if any spies had ever landed in Canada from German submarines in the St Lawrence area, Mr Macdonald gratuitously remarked that while it might be technically possible to land men at remote points on the shores of the St Lawrence, they could perhaps only "get by provided they spoke French fluently and wore civilian clothes."[34] Presumably he himself was aware of Janowski's arrest, though he may not have heard of the *Newsweek* leak. The next breach of security occurred in the Quebec legislature on 4 March 1943 when Mr Onesime Gagnon interjected, during a lengthy speech touching on national security, that a German spy had been arrested at New Carlisle just as he was about to give out important information on the defence of the St Lawrence. A number of newspapers referred to this statement next day, among them *La Presse* and *La Patrie* (Montreal), *L'Action Catholique*, *L'Evenement-Journal*, *Telegraph*, and *Quebec Chronicle* (Quebec City), and *Le Droit* (Ottawa).

There is no record of these reports having filtered back to Berlin. On the contrary, German naval records suggest that, despite these leaks, Janowski may have gained a degree of credibility that Canadian authorities could not have appreciated, though indeed Berlin did not express its confidence by playing any information into their hands. Thus an entry in the War Diary of the German Naval Staff for 24 April 1943 records an agent having reported a Murmansk convoy departing Canada on 19 April.[35] On 31 May 1943, the same War Diary recorded the report of a "very reliable agent from Canada" that had been transmitted on 17 May signalling the departure of "the first large wheat shipment" from the St Lawrence Gulf. The convoy, purportedly escorted by the unlikely complement of "fourteen ships including two cruisers and one to two aircraft carriers," could be expected off St John's, Newfoundland, by 6 May. As Allied Operational Intelligence well knew, BdU had no U-boats in the area to corroborate these claims.

If Harvison is correct that the RCMP ran Janowski for eighteen months before delivering him to British Intelligence in England, then his cover may well have been blown. The Fredericton *Daily Gleaner* ran a human-interest story on 14 June 1943 datelined Rimouski, Quebec, that appears to have been syndicated through the *Toronto Star* News Service. It would have received wide distribution. The account, headlined "CPC Organized on St. Lawrence – German Officer Spotted in Hotel by Woman," described the work of the Quebec provincial "Comité Protection Civile," which "guarded" the district in conjunction with the federal ADC "shore watchers." The Dominion government, the report revealed, had just "outfitted the CPC watchers with blue overall[s] and tin hats." With ingenuous frankness the report observed: "Typical of the work [that Quebec provincial] civilian observers and members of the Reserve Army are able to do ... is the story [which Bruno Grandmont of Rimouski] told of how a hotelkeeper's wife in New Carlisle, on the Bay [sic] des Chaleurs, nabbed a German officer last year." The account then summarized the essential clues (Belgian cigarettes, large-sized dollar bills) and revealed that the officer had "led the police to his cache on the beach, where he showed them his German uniform, a radio and handcuffs." Whatever other talents the German might have had, so the CPC civilian observer Grandmont had informed the reporter, "he wasn't smart enough to outwit the people of this peninsula." The next security breach occurred on 29 July when Col. Léon Lambert, joint director of the Quebec Provincial Police, addressed the Eleventh Annual Convention of the Quebec Police and Fire Chiefs Association in Quebec City. In describing the added responsibility that war placed upon their members, he claimed that the vigilance of the QPP was responsible for the capture of "more than one spy."[36] RCMP at the time considered the allusion a breach of censorship even though Lambert had revealed virtually no details. The Germans, they felt, would easily have inferred that the "one spy" to whom he alluded was Janowski. The RCMP would not yet have known of Langbein. Finally, on 27 December 1943, *L'Action Catholique* reported an announcement in the *Canada Gazette* that Alphonse Duchesneau had been decorated by the king. *L'Action Catholique* correctly guessed the reasons: "On croit savoir que le detective Duchesneau a été decoré pour le courage et la présence d'esprit qu'il a manifestés en arrêtant un espion allemand."[37]

The lifting of censorship restrictions at the end of the war brought forth a rash of partly factual, partly speculative accounts of Janowski's landing and capture. All were based on a lean official press release; many derived from conflicting interviews with local witnesses; none reflected any knowledge of either German or RCMP sources.[38] The story constituted "hot" front-page news for some papers; stale back-page news for others.[39] The accounts created a number of confusing myths, not the least of which held that the spy Janowski had landed "near jagged shores" of Métis Beach on the St Lawrence River, had "clambered on to the Métis rocks," and then made his way southward across the Gaspé Peninsula to New Carlisle before attempting to reach Montreal. There is no publicly access-ible evidence in support of the *Ottawa Journal's* claim of 15 May 1945 that "the deceiving of the Nazi spymasters in Hamburg was so successful that other German espionage agents [were] lured into betraying them-selves to the RCMP."[40]

The spy story had rather volatile repercussions in Quebec politics. In the words of the *Montreal Gazette*, "Battles against German submarines off the Gaspé coast were re-fought in the Quebec Legislative Assembly" on 15 May 1945 during a debate of the estimates of the attorney-general's department.[41] Liberal MLA Léon Casgrain had triggered the heated ex-change by asking Premier Duplessis whether he intended to reward detec-tive Alphonse Duchesneau for having captured the German spy. Duplessis' response was unequivocal. Duchesneau, he asserted, had been a Union Nationale appointee; it was due to his vigilance alone, and not that of the federal government, that the spy had been caught at all. Exploiting the political moment, Duplessis then voiced a long-standing Quebec concern: the inadequate defence of the Gulf and river, of which the spy's activities seemed incontrovertible proof. He alluded to wartime speculation in the province to the effect that federal forces had actually allowed German U-boats to penetrate the Gulf virtually unopposed. The express purpose of this federal deceit, he explained, was to close down the Port of Quebec and force the diversion of lucrative trade elsewhere. (This had in fact been somewhat the case when the river and Gulf were closed to all but the coastal trade in 1942.) Casgrain inadvertently cast himself in the role of a lackey of Ottawa by explaining that he had known of the New Carlisle incident since 1942, but had kept silent at the request of a "British Intelli-gence" officer who had interviewed Janowski. (This was likely Lt W.S. Samuel, RNVR, of Canadian Naval Intelligence). Casgrain's silence struck Duplessis as almost beneath contempt; the Quebec citizen should have revealed the threat instead of hiding behind federal censorship regu-lations.

Wissmann's U-518 remained in the Gulf until 17 November 1942, too late in the shipping season and too long after closure to meet with any success. The U-boat's departure from Canadian waters led it into the track of inbound convoy ON-145, some 200 miles east of Sable Island, from which it sank the 6140-ton SS *Empire Sailor* with the loss of twenty-one lives. HMCS *Timmins* and *Minas* landed forty-one survivors at Halifax.[42] Later U-518 torpedoed the SS *British Renown* and *British Promise*, and itself survived a devastating counter-attack in mid Atlantic. It was sunk with all hands by the new Hedgehog ahead-throwing mortars on 22 April 1945.

Weather reporting formed a vital part of German military operations. Given that weather systems generally move from west to east across the Atlantic, it was imperative that U-boats at sea enhance the reporting net of surface ships and shore stations by radioing data to BdU as frequently as possible. Some missions consisted almost entirely of weather-station patrols, either at the beginning or at the end of tactical missions. BdU often ordered U-boats to provide immediate data when they least expected it, such as during sorties close in to the North American coast, or while operating deep inside the Gulf of St Lawrence. Radioing such data frequently meant breaking a long period of radio silence and exposing oneself to Allied direction-finding stations. In support of these wide-ranging and highly mobile patrols, Germany built twenty-one land-based automatic weather stations that would provide specific data at predetermined transmission times. Fourteen of these unmanned stations were established in Arctic or subarctic regions (Spitzbergen, Bear Island, Franz-Joseph-Land and Greenland); five were located around the Barents Sea above Norway, and two were destined for North America. Only the first of those bound for North America, and planned for delivery by U-537 (Kapitänleutnant Peter Schrewe) in the summer of 1943, was ever in operation. The second mission failed when Kapitän zur See Mühlendahl's U-867 was sunk NNW of Bergen on 19 September 1944 by a Liberator from RAF Squadron 221. The attack left a macabre reminder of the loneliness of war at sea when the captain's body eventually washed ashore in Norway.

BdU charged U-537, on its maiden operational voyage in the summer of 1943, with the installation of automatic station WFL-26 (*Wetterfunkgerät-Land*) on northern Labrador.[43] Technical details were the immediate responsibility of scientific adviser Dr Kurt Sommermeyer and his technical assistant Walter Hildebrandt, both of whom shipped aboard. Code-named station "Kurt," it consisted of a set of meteorological instruments, a 150 W short-wave transmitter and antenna mast, and an array of nickel-cadmium and dry-cell batteries. The station was packaged in ten cylinders approximately 1 × 1.5 m diameter, each weighing approximately 220 pounds. The cylinder with the instrument unit contained a 10-m-tall antenna mast with anemometer and wind vane. In order to avoid suspicion if discovered, the Germans had marked the cylinders with the rubric "Canadian Weather Service." As it happened, the fact that no such organization existed by that name did not compromise the plan, for WFL-26 was not discovered and identified as German until July 1981. Once installed as designed, the station would broadcast a coded weathergram at three-hour intervals. To accomplish this, a sophisticated contact drum or Graw's diaphragm (named after a certain Dr Graw, then of Berlin) would transcribe the observed values for temperature, humidity, air pressure, wind speed, and wind direction into Morse symbols. These were then keyed on 3940 kHz to receiving stations in northern Europe. Transmission time for the whole weathergram, including one minute for warming up, did not exceed 120 seconds.

Heavy RAF and USAAF bombing raids on Hamburg and Kiel on 24 and 25 July 1943 delayed the departure of Schrewe's new type IXC-40. Allies had for the first time decoyed German radar by dropping streams of metal foil ribbons known as "Window," which functioned much like the German equivalent *Düppel*. The delays caused the repaired U-537 to drive into the increasingly violent autumn seas of the North Atlantic. On 13 October, a large breaker generated by extremely high winds surging from 45 to 60 knots ripped the quadruple anti-aircraft cannon from its mount and washed it over the side. U-537 had now virtually no anti-aircraft defences, a serious deficiency in a pre-schnorkel boat. The missing quadruple *Vierling* permitted accurate identification of U-537 in 1981 from a photo showing a side view of a U-boat anchored off a Labrador shore. On 18 October 1943, one month after U-537 had left Kiel, BdU ordered Schrewe to commence special operations by advancing due west towards the northern tip of Labrador. Schrewe headed westward at the slowest economical speed.

The choice of site for WFL-26 seems to have been left largely to Schrewe's discretion in consultation with the technical advisers. In order to avoid all possible contact with people ashore, especially with "Eskimoes trekking south at this time of year" (KTB), Schrewe wanted to set up the station as far north in Labrador as possible. He knew that ice was not yet a threat, and that he could in any event withdraw to the south if needed. U-537 ran towards the coast by dead reckoning as overcast skies from 18 to 21 October prevented an accurate astronomical fix of its position. Schrewe had decided to proceed with the mission regardless of a leaking Boat, flooding through a faulty diesel intake. He counted on repair work once anchored in a Labrador fjord. A test dive to 140 m after makeshift en route repairs proved the U-boat safe to penetrate enemy territory.

After five days of snow storms and dead-reckoning navigation, Schrewe sighted "Kap Shidley" (actually Cape Chidley) at the northwest tip of Labrador at 1230 GMT on 22 October. Schrewe worked southward from this point by depth soundings, passing down the poorly charted coast, which even today abounds in uncharted reefs and shoals. By now Schrewe could clearly distinguish the skerry, shale coastline that charts had led him to expect. He eased his way by echo sounder southeastward between Home Island and what he called "Arayal" (actually Avayalik Islands), and finally rounded the southern tip of Hutton Peninsula. At 1845 DWZ on 22 October 1943, he anchored in "Attinaukjuke Bay" (now Martin Bay), some 300 m from shore in position $60°4.5'$ N, $64°23.6'$ W.

Within an hour, a reconnoitring party set ashore by inflatable craft to locate a transmitter site. They would leave empty American cigarette packages and match folders on the site in order to decoy any subsequent Allied intruders. By 2130 the crew began landing the gear in two large 6-m inflatables. Schrewe posted armed look-outs on a rise of land in order to guard against surprise from the sea. Engineering personnel turned to maintenance tasks and periscope repairs, while other crew and technical staff worked throughout the night ashore in $2°$ of frost. By 1800 DWZ on 23 October, less than 24 hours after having anchored, the work was done. The first transmission of WFL-26 occurred three minutes late, but was otherwise technically perfect. Once assured of the mission's success, U-537 weighed anchor at 2240 DWZ, just 28 hours after having arrived. Schrewe signalled completion of the operation when 300 miles from the transmitter, and was granted freedom of operations in the Canadian zone. With the exception of other clandestine missions, U-537 was the sole U-boat off Canadian shores in 1943 with a specific Canadian-oriented mission. BdU signalled Schrewe twice on 26 October: once to warn him of the minefield that U-220 had just laid off St John's, and again 10 hours later to offer the redundant advice that the new moon offered him the most favourable opportunities off that port. Throughout his Canadian patrol, Schrewe continued to monitor WFL-26 and on a number of occasions reported intense jamming by a station that turned out to be German. For reasons we can only surmise, Canadian stations heard nothing from "Kurt" in Labrador. They were doubtless preoccupied with monitoring broadcasts from sea.

Allied radar constantly triggered U-537's radar warning devices during her entire southward passage off Newfoundland, and later while patrolling the Banks. Whether activating his Naxos on the 10-cm band or Wanze frequency scanner on 140–170 cm (800 Hz), "direction finding possibly from aircraft or from blimps cover[ed] the extended coastal approaches" (KTB). Not knowing the extent to which he had been detected, he chose the wisdom of operating predominantly submerged, surfacing only to charge batteries and to air the U-boat. The Submarine Tracking Room at Naval Service Headquarters in Ottawa had correctly suspected a U-boat "in the St. John's area" on 29 October. Evidence from HF/DF stations soon corroborated intelligence received from decryption services. FONF ordered a special alert, in response to which Eastern Air Command doubled its air patrols.[44] Schrewe became the object of a widespread "Operation Salmon" until mid November consisting of thirteen ships and numerous aircraft. It searched both south and east toward the twenty-four U-boats of Gruppe Siegfried then attacking convoy HX-262. Counter-attacks by HMS *Vidette*, *Duncan*, and *Sunflower* destroyed U-274, as proven by "wreckage and other souvenirs of human origin." Schrewe himself suffered air attacks on the Banks of Newfoundland and, despite his severe handicap, resorted to the current doctrine of engaging enemy aircraft by remaining surfaced rather than diving and exposing himself to a bombing attack at his most vulnerable manoeuvre. Schrewe soon realized that the air attacks had "turned the whole sea frontier sour" for further operations (KTB).

BdU summarized three disturbing anomalies on 5 November that seemed to point to a failure of his own equipment: the high number of U-boat losses the previous month; the increasing number of reports indicating that aircraft had attacked U-boats without triggering radar-warning devices; and the fact, as revealed through subsequent analysis, that convoys had made large diversionary course changes well in advance of the U-boat patrol positions through which they would otherwise have passed.[45] This suggested to him that the Allies had "once again" implemented hitherto unknown methods of detecting U-boats. Against these methods the Germans now seemed defenceless. As October 1943 drew to a close, the Staff Officer Operations, FONF, observed that "following the heavy attacks on ONS-18 and ON-202" the Battle of the Atlantic had "degenerated into nothing much more than a continual threat by the U-Boats necessitating the maintenance of strong [escort and support] groups." The Battle had, in fact, turned against the Germans in 1943. In immediate terms, the Staff Officer Operations, FONF, noted a "reluctance on the part of U-Boats to press home the attack." This altogether "happy state of affairs" seemed epitomized by the fact that "the alleged acoustic homing torpedo which caused such havoc in September has found no further targets, and the U-Boats have not had anything like the success expected against aircraft."

Several key factors were at work here that turned the tide in the Battle of the Atlantic irrevocably against the Germans. The single most significant factor was the extended range of Allied aircraft. It enabled them to close over the "Black Pit." This was a dangerous zone in mid Atlantic previously beyond the range of air support based either in North America or in Great Britain. It was in this "pit" that U-boats had attacked convoys with considerable impunity. As well, Allied decryption of German Enigma signals through the process known as Ultra made it possible to guide convoys around the U-boat positions. Whenever attacks did occur, yet another factor came into play: the Allies' successful use of convoy escort tactical diagrams based on mathematical principles. This was enhanced by the vital co-operation between convoys and Support Groups. The latter, strategically deployed either with or without aircraft carriers, could speed to the defence of convoys under threat of attack. The effective use of both shipborne and airborne centimetric radar, depending largely upon intelligence from Ultra, was a crucial tactical complement to these developments.

U-537 slipped alongside the Skorff Bunker at Lorient at 10 AM on 8 December 1943. Though her combat achievements amounted to little more than trading shots with aircraft and tying down Allied defences, the weather station had been a success. The Germans had also gained considerable experience with the strengths and limitations of a IXC U-boat that led to modifications in others of its class. Although the crew of U-537 reached home for Christmas, it was to be their last. They departed on 28 February 1944 for a lengthy operational tour in Southeast Asia, and were destroyed in the Java Sea north of Bali on 9 November 1944 by a torpedo from the American submarine USS *Flounder*. Of those who had sailed with U-537 to Labrador, only one person survived the war: Werner von Bendler had been put ashore for an officer's course just prior to U-537's final cruise.

CHAPTER SIX

Clandestine Operations: Escape and Blockade

Covert U-boat operations in Canadian waters embraced not only the spy landings and weather station, but minelaying and the attempted recovery of German prisoners of war. Such deployments in distant combat zones entailed considerable outlay in plans, equipment, and matériel, which at first glance might seem disproportionate to their success. Achievement, however, must not be measured solely in terms of ships actually sunk by mines or in prisoners rescued, but by the capacity of clandestine operations to exert both psychological and tactical pressure on the opponent's resources. Mining operations in 1943 and 1944, for example, exerted a direct impact on war industries and fiscal priorities by launching Canadians on the last shipbuilding program of the war. The planned rescue of prisoners by the Germans had a ripple effect on Canadian Operational Intelligence, Destroyer Command, and the RCMP, proving an effective corollary of Dönitz's principle of tying down the opposition. Dönitz's ability to penetrate Canadian defences with impunity raised serious questions about Canadian preparedness and expertise.

Admiral Dönitz and his staff saw striking advantages in the venture of recovering German prisoners of war from Canadian camps: encouragement of his imprisoned men, disruption of the enemy, the extrication of valuable submariners at a time when losses were high, and not least of all – the propaganda effect. In anticipation of his men falling into enemy hands, he had devised various means of communication for the exchange of vital information. For his part he required reports on how his U-boats had been lost, and on what weapons and methods the Allies had used. This required a communications system immune to censors who could be expected to scrutinize all mail passing through the regular POW postal links of the Red Cross. Communicated orally to commanding officers prior to their first mission, the keys to such codes were never written down. *Code Irland* was one of the simplest. It was a system in which letters of the alphabet represented the dots and dashes of the Morse code; it permitted the terse communication of lean data in seemingly innocent correspondence.[1] BdU staff divided the twenty-six letters of the alphabet into two groups of nine letters and one group of eight. The first letter of every word in any piece of correspondence indicated either a dot or a dash according to the following scheme: Group 1 (letters A to I) signified a dot; Group 2 (letters J to R) signified a dash. The last letter in each of these groups provided the reliable mnemonic *Irland* of the alphabet's division. In order to separate the resultant series of dots and dashes into the appropriate Morse combinations, letters drawn from the third group (S to Z) signified a "break" (//). A censor would scarcely twig to the fact that a U-boat commander's lament "*Meine Kameraden und auch ich waren lange in Sorge, denn ...*" ("My comrades as well as I were worried for a long time, for ...") actually named the weapon that had sunk them. Transposed into Morse symbols, the first letter of each word spelled "mine" (Morse: --//··//--//·//). In this case, nine words of seemingly innocuous plain language provided but a single word of coded communication. Clearly, one could not write a lengthy military report by this procedure. But it allowed an inventive writer (or an identifiable group of writers) considerable flexibility and scope.

These letter codes set the process in motion that eventually led to Operations Elster and Kiebitz. Correspondents would have written either to actual dependants or to a fictitious home address, from which BdU would collect. BdU had taken care to advise the families of his U-boat crews that POW letters might well contain information useful to the pursuit of the naval war; this might be especially true of letters with awkward syntax or unusual allusions. Thus the recipients forwarded the letters to BdU for analysis. Their replies, under BdU instructions, closed the communications link. As it took up to three months for a letter from a Canadian camp to reach Germany via Switzerland, the prisoner could expect to wait six months for a reply. Two complete exchanges of *Irland*-coded correspondence between BdU and the prisoners, the very minimum required to arrange a pick-up, could take a whole year. In the meantime, prisoners would exploit the waiting period to develop escape plans in order to ensure that the break-out could occur once a reply from BdU was received. Even if ultimately unsuccessful, drawing up escape plans boosted prisoners' morale. BdU supported such morale-building programs wherever he could. His staff sent Red Cross parcels containing contraband materials such as letters, maps, and tiny radio parts hidden in false-bottomed tins of food. As will be seen, the RCMP's interception of a Red Cross shipment of German books would uncover the plot to escape from Bowmanville, Ontario. Authorities could at best only sample the thousands of pieces of mail and hundreds of packages passing each month via the Red Cross between Canadian POW camps and Germany. Detection of contraband was thus largely a matter of luck.

German naval officers in Camp 70 near Fredericton, New Brunswick, had been communicating with BdU over a long period of time in order to arrange their break-out and passage home. Code named Operation Elster (Magpie), it had been planned in every possible detail by Kapitänleutnant Ali Cremer, then on the staff of BdU in Berlin.[2] Cremer passed the plans personally to Oberleutnant Heinz Franke, commanding officer of U-262 in La Pallice, Biscay, on 6 April 1943 just prior to the U-boat's third mission. Unknown to Franke, U-262 was to serve as a back-up Boat on the mission. Should the lead Boat get through the dangerous Biscay, Franke would of course never know what the orders contained, for he was only to open them on receipt of a special executive signal from his headquarters. As it turned out, the anonymous lead U-boat did not survive, and Franke took over. He was competent and battle-wise, despite his youth. Service aboard the battleship *Gneisenau* when she assisted the *Scharnhorst* in destroying the 16,697-ton *Rawalpindi*, for example, had impressed him with the capacity of an outgunned weaker vessel to absorb severe punishment and postpone her inevitable demise by the skill and determination of her crew.[3] He himself survived punishing attacks and eventually commanded one of the new type XXI U-boats in March 1945.

Franke had just cleared the heavily patrolled waters of the Bay of Biscay on 15 April 1943 after a nine-day passage from La Pallice when BdU ordered him to "execute special task Magpie." U-262 was to position itself by 2 May 1943 close off the pick-up point, North Point, on the northern tip of Prince Edward Island. Once having escaped from Camp 70, the prisoners would have to transit the 198 km from Fredericton to Moncton, and then attempt either the 80-km coastal route via Cape Pelé to Cape Tormentine, or else via the longer 100-km route via Sackville and Baie Verte. They would then face the 14-km ferry crossing of the Northumberland Strait to Port Borden, PEI, before they could negotiate the final leg: the 130-km route to North Point via Summerside, Tignish, and Seacow Pond. Exactly how they planned to undertake this journey is no longer clear. However, handmade maps and charts confiscated from German prisoners at other camps attest to a high degree of competence in cartography and intelligence gathering. Drawn to scale on wax paper, such colour-coded maps indicated roads, highways and railways, and provided details on contours and habitations.[4] Prisoners were equally skilful in producing the necessary Canadian documents and disguises.[5]

As for Heinz Franke in U-252, BdU had left the details of route and tactics entirely to his own discretion. "I suddenly found myself faced with a task, the execution of which would most certainly entail a few risks for U-boat and crew. And there were so many unknowns to be considered in my planning, both on the outbound leg as well as in the target area."[6] Franke had never operated in Canadian waters before, nor had he ever undertaken an Atlantic crossing. This was, admittedly, no different from his predecessors in Operation Paukenschlag (Drumbeat) in January 1942, or from the early ventures into the St Lawrence during the following spring and summer. But conditions of war in coastal waters had changed radically since then, and Franke was doubtless uneasy about the lack of opportunity for a thorough briefing prior to his mission, and for adequate discussion of his options. To this day, for example, he still does not know exactly whom he was to pick up. This might have had serious consequences on the beach.

Franke's navigation pack may not have been complete. At the very least, the standard pack for Atlantic U-boats contained large-area small-scale German and British Admiralty charts based on surveys of 1913. It is possible that Franke lacked the latest German publications concerning the Canadian coast, in particular the invaluable *U-Boot Atlas* of Canada's Atlantic waters. As it turned out, Franke's NCO navigator, Obersteuermann Herbert Garotzki, worked magnificently. In short, Franke recalls the poignant feeling of being entirely on his own. Certainly, the current captain's manual, *Handbuch für U-Bootskommandanten*, insisted on the principle that each submarine was a loner even when operating in packs. But the loneliness during some moments of operations like this seemed more extreme than others. Though he took his navigator and watch officers into his confidence, he never informed the remainder of the crew of the destination or purpose of the mission. Ignorance was a heavy psychological burden for the crew to bear.

Secrecy was of primary importance. Yet the constant requirement to report and shadow convoys on the outbound route created a conflict by potentially revealing his presence and intentions. Within six hours after receipt of the Elster signal, Franke reported a large convoy, and requested clarification of his tactical constraints. BdU granted U-262 carte blanche to attack shipping "up to the meridian through Canadian zone BB 9996." This meant longitude 52° W, which passed to within 30 miles of St John's, Newfoundland. U-262 would of course give Newfoundland a wide berth, sailing some 220 miles to the southeast, thus leaving ample scope for its predations. BdU's message had cautioned that whatever else transpired, the "deadline as ordered must be maintained" (KTB).

Information on the probable ice conditions during the critical period of Franke's operational schedule was far from encouraging, for he was given to expect a fairly consistent ice-field both inside the Gulf itself as well as in its Atlantic approaches. The eastward flow out of the Gulf would be moving the ice seaward, squeezing it through his only access to the target zone: the relatively narrow 56-mile-wide Cabot Strait. This would form a tactical choke point such as he had never before encountered. Having crossed the Atlantic undisturbed since 25° W, almost entirely on the surface, U-262 arrived off Cabot Strait on 25 April 1943, one day ahead of schedule. Where Franke had expected some concentrations of shipping, he was astonished by the seemingly anomalous absence of traffic and air surveillance. Settled weather prevailed: steady temperatures around freezing, clear atmosphere with up to 15-mile visibility, even at night, a pronounced aurora borealis, and luminiscent seas. Had his Metox radar warning device not broken down, he would have felt secure.

U-262 was not alone off Canadian shores. U-174 (Grandefeld) and U-161 (Achilles) had slowly edged westward on weather patrol since mid March, until ordered into North American waters where BdU expected them to encounter Halifax–UK convoys on the great circle route. The two U-boats diverged off the Newfoundland Banks in heavy weather, and under the debilitating air cover provided to convoys by the RCAF and the fifteen Liberator bombers the U.S. Army had just acquired in Gander. *B-Dienst* decryption led U-174 into a convoy some 120 miles southeast of Sable Island where it was destroyed with all hands on 27 April by a Ventura from U.S. Navy Squadron 125, based on Argentia, Newfoundland.[7] D/F bearings placed U-161 at this time some 60 miles south of Cape Sable. It had little success except for the First World War-style sinking on 19 May 1943 of the 250-ton Canadian brig *Angelus* en route to Halifax from Barbados with molasses. After allowing the crew to disembark, U-161 sank her with gunfire. A U.S. flying boat destroyed U-161 on 27 September 1943 off the coast of Brazil.[8]

Rear-Admiral L.W. Murray's Intelligence staff in Halifax regarded both the sinking of U-174 and the HF/DF of U-161 as evidence of "reconnaissance U-Boats" whose presence had disturbed an otherwise "exceptionally quiet" month.[9] An inhospitable April saw preparations for the new shipping season and the impending opening of the Gulf. The navy was gathering together the various ships assigned to Gaspé and Sydney for the Gulf striking force and the St Lawrence Escort Force, and those assigned to St John's for the Wabana convoys. The M/L flotillas assigned to Gaspé commenced work-ups with submarines and aircraft in anticipation of new inroads by U-boat forces. They would move into place as soon as the Gulf was ice free. U-262 could not wait that long.

U-262's brisk advance into Cabot Strait during the night of 26–27 April had gradually encountered the forecast ice conditions. The first thin layers through which it passed at reduced speed and without much discomfort soon merged into larger fields of drift ice increasing in size and thickness beyond anything that reports had indicated. Large chunks of ice, some of them 10 m square, surrounded U-262 until it finally stuck tight. As Franke recorded: "I'm held firm in a vast field of drift ice [from which] I have to assume that the ice thickens into a solid layer further to the west." The only solution lay in penetrating the Gulf submerged after precise calculation of battery reserves to allow the U-boat to return to open water submerged if the Gulf should prove to be frozen solid. Despite flooding of forward torpedo tubes caused by ice damage to the forward ports, U-262 submerged at rest through a hole in the ice at 0512 local time, and commenced its sixteen-hour run down "U-boat alley." Its first attempt at surfacing, some 36 miles northeast of Bird Rocks, failed on striking a surface layer of impenetrable ice. Franke returned to 20-m depth for a further advance of five minutes before attempting a second breakthrough. Blowing all tanks in order to give a sudden surge of optimum buoyancy, U-262 thrust its conning tower into the night air, leaving its hatch pinned down under a huge chunk of ice that the bridge had scooped out of the sea. A feeling of relief came over the bridge watch once the hatch was forced open and they could again see the stars overhead.

The momentary release from anxiety diminished Franke's concerns for the rather considerable ice damage U-262 had experienced: the port aft net cutter had been torn off, the bridge combing twisted, both the 8.8-cm cannon and C-30 machine-gun rendered useless, and the ports of three forward torpedo tubes bent out of shape. U-262 was now virtually defenceless. Franke and his crew none the less felt a distinct sense of security. Clearer water lay 500 m ahead in the Gulf, and the ice cover excluded any possibility of surprise or even attack by surface vessels. Nobody would suspect a U-boat in the Gulf at this time of year. They had ample time for charging batteries and airing the Boat in complete safety. If necessary, they would have no difficulty retracing their route beneath the ice. Air patrols could be the only source of trouble, particularly as U-262's radar warning device still did not function. Still threatened by large fields of pack ice, U-262 worked its way to within 32 miles of Heath Point, Anticosti, on 30 April, when Franke's sighting of open water confirmed his resolve to complete the mission. By 1 May, U-262 lay 110 miles on a direct course from North Point, PEI. Before dawn next day it dived to negotiate the final approach at periscope depth towards the low red cliffs that are skirted by reefs and shallow water, and extend to 4.5 miles off shore both to the north and the east.

U-262 slipped on to the eastern edge of North Point Reef in 30 m of water at 0631 local time on 2 May 1943. It lay about 4 miles from the coast. As the western side of the reef is steep-to, Franke had chosen the graduated and therefore easier access to shallow water. Franke had now fulfilled the first part of his commitment, but was by no means certain just how he would have to play subsequent sequences in the operation. On reaching periscope depth for his first examination of the pick-up point, Franke was startled by observing in his air-target periscope three "Maryland Type" aircraft circling over his position. It was "suspicious," Franke noted, that after days of isolation he should find air surveillance right on his target point (KTB). Yet his pragmatic nature also suggested the less dangerous and ultimately correct explanation that he lay under the glide path of a training field. German *Sailing Directions* had provided no hint of the RCAF bases at North Sydney and Sydney.

The tortuous suspicion that the operation had been betrayed and that the Canadians were lying in wait, continued to haunt Franke. At nightfall on 2 May he surfaced off North Point Light. The weather was "extremely favourable for carrying out the operation, dead calm sea and good visibility" (KTB). U-262 pursued its series of S- and N-shaped inshore patrol patterns day and night for the next four days, waiting for some signs from the beach that would trigger the recovery phase. They expected some sort of light signal, a Morse message perhaps, or even a small boat pulling out from shore. These details had not been arranged by letter code between the POWs and BdU, a fact that exposed U-262 to capture or destruction if the plan had indeed been discovered. Search patterns from the tip of Prince Edward Island past the leading lights of the small fishing village of Tignish Harbour led U-262 so close to shore as to court danger of discovery. The flashes of North Point Light would illuminate his upper deck and send a chill of apprehension through the crew.

Franke stood off North Point Reef for the last time in the early morning of 6 May 1943 and discerned not the slightest hint of movement ashore. Breaking off the operation according to orders, he headed NNE around the Magdalen Islands into the Gulf and then southeast via "U-boat alley" into Cabot Strait. "Such a shame," he recorded, "that I have to return without success" (KTB). It is one of the finest failed operations on record. The few reported U-boat sightings in the Gulf region by aircraft and onshore watchers may, by a stretch of the imagination, have marked the outbound passage of U-262. The 78th M/L (Fairmile) Flotilla could, in any event, not respond until after it had reached Sydney from Halifax on 16 May. On that day, however, an Anson training aircraft based on Charlottetown, PEI, and armed with only two depth charges, attacked what the pilot described as a "stationary submarine at periscope depth" in the zone between East Point, PEI, and the Magdelen Islands. U-262 had by now already transited this sector. But the Anson report insisted that its two successive bombing runs at an altitude of 100 feet, while the "periscope was still showing," had produced "some wreckage and oil slicks." Photographs of the scene did not turn out; other aircraft claimed more sightings during the next few days. Five days later, on 21 May, a Catalina flying boat of 117 Squadron at Gaspé, Quebec, reported having "attacked a submerged U-Boat" northeast of the Magdalens – many days after

U-262 had gained the open sea and replenished from the U-tanker U-459.[10] German records shed no light on the very remote possibility of there having been any other U-boat in the area. Certainly nothing on record explains the bravado with which NOIC Gaspé logged the inflated battle action in his War Diary for the month of May: "Enemy submarines made several appearances in the Gulf area. The excellent co-operation of the RCAF gave these visitors a warm welcome and it is regrettable that in the one case when surface vessels were near enough to the scene of a sighting to join in the hunt, no contact could be obtained."[11] Only after the war did Franke learn from a comrade returning from Canada that the "Magpie" break-out had been scuttled by an earlier unsuccessful attempt, which had resulted in increased camp surveillance. Had the prisoners of Camp 70 co-ordinated their escapes like their counterparts in Camp 30 at Bowmanville, the daring cruise of U-262 might not only have rescued them, but also have provided provocative propaganda material for Radio Berlin. There is no evidence that Allied Intelligence knew of the plan.

BdU was developing plans for yet another rescue while Franke's U-262 was en route to Prince Edward Island in April 1943. The rendezvous this time was Pointe de Maisonette, New Brunswick, which forms the north-western shore of Caraquet Harbour on the southwestern side of Baie des Chaleurs. The object of the mission was to pick up members of the self-named "Lorient Espionage Unit," which was attempting to tunnel out of Camp 30 in Bowmanville, Ontario, some time during September and October 1943.[12] The group was led by Otto "the Silent" (*der Schweig-same*) Kretschmer who, as captain of "The Golden Horseshoe" (U-99), had shared his country's highest military honours with the other two "Tonnage Kings" of the day, Joachim Schepke (U-100) and Günther Prien (U-47).[13] All three were lost to Dönitz once the Allies had sunk their famous U-boats over two years earlier in March 1941; Schepke and Prien were killed, while Kretschmer was taken prisoner. Other members of the escape group were Kapitänleutnant Hans Ey (U-433) who had been sunk on 16 November 1941, Horst Elfe (U-93) who had been sunk on 15 January 1942, and Kretschmer's Executive Officer and former adjutant to Admiral Dönitz, von Knebel-Döberitz.

Thirty-year-old Kapitänleutnant Rolf Schauenburg, the commanding officer of type IXC-40 U-boat U-536, which eventually undertook the mission, had had a colourful career since joining the navy in 1934. He had trained in the ship of the line *Schlesien*, had visited Great Britain for the coronation of King George VI, and touched in at Canada. He served aboard the *Graf Spee* during the Battle of the River Plate and was subsequently interned in Argentina. He escaped, crossed South America in the guise of a cloth merchant, was twice recaptured, and later released through negotiations of a German consul. He arrived back in Germany in

January 1941 via Chile. He is said to have served in minesweepers prior to entering the U-boat arm. Schauenburg seems to have been somewhat of a martinet in insisting that big-ship discipline, dress, and hygiene be observed in the stifling, incommodious, and often grimy conditions of a U-boat. German submarine tradition held that crews returned from operations unshaven and in battle fatigues, a style that Schauenburg apparently never permitted. One can sympathize with his demands, though at the time they may have undercut morale. One of his crew described him to Allied rescuers as "a fanatical and idealistic Nazi."[14] Recent recollections reveal that while he was imposing, self-possessed, and sometimes hard, he was, like many other senior officers, of a nationalistic rather than a national-socialist turn of mind. His men respected his strong and determined character. The twenty-volume Duden encyclopaedia, for which he made room in the cramped U-boat, is evidence of his humanistic bent.

Schauenburg apparently first learned of the rescue plan during a routine visit in July 1943 to Naval Headquarters in Berlin, after his first operational cruise in U-536 based in Lorient. According to the sensational account which Schauenburg provided the magazine *Kristall* in 1956, U-boat ace Addi Schnee had first suggested he accept the mission.[15] A special courier then delivered the necessary orders to Lorient. It is likely that two other U-boats had been assigned to the task in succession, only to be lost well prior to their arrival in the Canadian zone. Schauenburg might, therefore, have been less thoroughly briefed than the self-aggrandizing and exaggerated account in *Kristall* would suggest. In any event, he departed Lorient on 29 August 1943 under orders to proceed to a patrol position north of the Azores. On 12 September, BdU flashed him the laconic signal "Execute Operation Kiebitz – No Amplification" (KTB). This is the first officially documented fact in the sequence of events, and suggests that BdU considered U-536 to have held sufficient information to comply in full. Its crew remained ignorant of the purposes of the mission until the U-boat had reached Canadian waters. It is perhaps an irony of history that *Kiebitz*, meaning "lapwing" or "peewit," has a secondary sense: an onlooker at a card game. Schauenburg would ultimately do nothing but wait and observe, while Canadian naval officers played cards in Maisonette Lighthouse waiting for him to make a slip.

The escapers had meanwhile received confirmation of the rendezvous from Admiral Dönitz, and had purportedly even received tinned goods in the false bottoms of which were hidden Canadian money and a radio cipher in order to monitor the radio frequency used by German blockade breakers. Some fifty diggers advanced the tunnel from a shaft entered through a closet until seepage caused the tunnel to collapse. They then joined a second group of tunnellers who planned to dig a 100-m shaft, passing beyond the barbed wire and the adjacent road into bushes where an exit hole could be cut at the last moment. Plans called for Kretschmer's group reaching Pointe de Maisonette by 27 or 28 September.

Canadian Naval Intelligence had meanwhile informed the commissioner, RCMP, during the summer of 1943 that it had managed to crack "certain codes," which indicated not only a mass break-out, but the arrival of a U-boat in Canadian waters. Clearly, a co-ordinated plan was necessary. With Commissioner Harvison, an RCMP team searched the perimeter of the POW camp at night by using a long probe bearing a microphone attachment. Sounds of digging confirmed the tunnel's progress. The tunnel, Harvison later recalled, was "a bit of a masterpiece in engineering ... a distance of 300 feet."[16] The navy and the RCMP then came upon vital corroborating evidence among a number of books that had been sent to the prisoners from Germany through the Red Cross. They sent the books for examination to the Crime Detection Laboratory in Regina where former Staff Sergeant Stephen Lett, one of the original six members of the laboratory, made the crucial discovery. On opening up the binding of a copy of the Arnold Ulitz novel *Die Braut des Berühmten* (Berlin: Propylaen, n.d.), he found that "the cover concealed a number of valuable escape documents in the form of a marine map of the eastern Canadian coast, a forged Canadian National Registration card and a quantity of Canadian and American currency."[17] The nautical chart, as then-corporal Cecil Bayfield of the RCMP Intelligence Branch discovered, revealed the U-boat's pick-up point. Lett had discovered, on opening up the previous volumes, that their poor quality paper and binding prevented his restoring books to their original condition. He had, therefore, evolved the scheme of painstakingly photographing each stage of the dismantling so that he could reconstruct the binding with similar materials. Thus, with utmost craftsmanship and masterful subterfuge, the RCMP Crime Detection Laboratory created a duplicate cover, rebound the book after having photographed and replaced the original documents, and then sent the volume on to its intended recipients.

Warnings of Operation Kiebitz caused Admiral L.W. Murray to form a group of four, consisting of himself, Captain W.L. Puxley, RN (then commanding the destroyer squadron as Captain (D) Halifax), Lt "Rocky" Hill, RNR (commanding officer of an RN submarine being used for local A/S training), and the training officer, LCdr Desmond Piers.[18] Murray apparently appointed Piers as the key officer, with specific orders to capture the U-boat. Piers and Hill visited the Baie des Chaleurs on the pretext of investigating areas where the water conditions were better suited for antisubmarine training. They planned to place two "mobile radar units each off the Miscou Light about 2 miles apart." These might be difficult to hide as they each consisted of a truck and trailer. They were also concerned that "at that time radar was not a very well advanced science." RCMP and navy authorities had briefly considered the idea of allowing the prisoners to escape and then shadowing them to the pick-up. This became unnecessary once they knew where the U-boat was expected to land. They then developed a more realistic plan consisting of three phases.[19]

They would first allow the escape to take place and then capture the escapees as they emerged one by one in the woods beyond the exit of the tunnel. Secondly, on the false assumption that the U-boats in the St Lawrence and off the Atlantic coast monitored Canadian public radio broadcasts, they would inform the media of the mass escape. But they would divulge nothing of any captures. Subsequent news releases would reveal the names of prisoners supposedly captured at different points along the intended route eastward. But they would not release the names of the seven men whom the U-boat was expecting. This, according to the plan, should delude the U-boat commander into believing that his passengers had been successful and were well on their way. The third phase, "the reason for the whole operation," as Harvison recalled later, was to "capture the submarine intact." U-536 was now patrolling in the Gulf of St Lawrence, with orders to arrive off Pointe de Maisonette no later than 26 September 1943.

Capturing an enemy submarine required a skilled boarding party, such as would eventually be trained in 1945 when U-boats were surrendering peacefully. Now, however, they could expect violence. The plan called for an escort bringing the U-boat to the surface, whereupon a lobster boat armed with "a picked crew" and bearing "grenades, revolvers, daggers, smoke grenades," as Captain Piers recently explained, would heave a chain down the open conning tower (to prevent the hatch from closing) and take over. The chain technique was actually used during the general capitulation in 1945. According to Commissioner Harvison's account, seven volunteers would impersonate the seven escapees. They included the RCMP's mysterious "Johnny" who had doubled for the captured spy von Janowski in Montreal. In retrospect, Harvison regarded the operation's chance of success as "infinitesimal." Indeed, the "volunteers were brave men training for an heroic endeavour, but the chances were that, had the plot come off, they would have been dead but unsuccessful heroes." A "fifth person" was brought into the "top secret quartette." This was LCdr Sorensen, later Professor of German and Norwegian at the University of Saskatchewan in Saskatoon, who was then attached to Canadian Naval Intelligence. He had a doctorate from the University of Breslau and spoke fluent German. Piers had thought of the idea of having Sorensen go aboard in the guise of an escaped army colonel "senior in rank to the captain of the Boat [and] assume some kind of control." This was perhaps the most naive part of the plan. As it turned out, the Admiralty in London seems to have persuaded the Canadian Navy not to capture the U-boat but to destroy it.[20] Piers therefore arranged for a shore party to capture the escaped prisoners, and planned to station "ships nearby around the corner and a few miles away" that he would summon to sink the U-boat at first hint of its presence.

Another Bowmanville submariner had meanwhile been developing an independent escape. The plan of Kapitänleutnant Wolfgang Heyda (U-434) called for his crossing over the top of the camp wire by working a bosun's chair along a power line which was suspended on wooden power poles running through the camp and standing propitiously on either side of the barbed wire perimeter. He had made himself a pair of linesman's climbing spurs, jury-rigged the chair and the ropes, and was in effect ready to exploit the arrival of U-536. With the mass escape quelled by discovery of the tunnel, prisoners apparently rallied around Heyda, providing him with, among other things, the Canadian money they themselves would have used, and a somewhat ill-fitting Canadian army sergeant's uniform. Had he used the National Registration Certificate bound in the Ulitz novel, he would have travelled as Mr Fred Thomlinson of 46 Coswell Street, Toronto.[21] German recollections suggest that Heyda carried a skilfully forged document with Murray's signature authorizing him to conduct geological surveys on Maisonette Point on behalf of the navy. Piers recalls instead that Heyda's document indicated "that he had been discharged from the Royal Canadian Engineers in order to join the Northern Electric Company to make antisubmarine equipment." Whatever the documents actually were, Piers insists that they were all "beautifully done, exactly like the Canadian model, but all done by hand."

Heyda escaped alone on 24 September 1943 and apparently travelled by train to Montreal and then via Bathurst, NB, to Pointe de Maisonette. Sources take no account of the fact that he would have had to trek over 50 km along a route serviced by highways 11 and 320 as far as Pointe de Maisonette itself, or by a Canadian National Railway line that turned south just short of Grand-Anse. This would have left him 10 km to cover on foot. In any event, he subsequently passed through the Canadian army cordon at the point with his bogus authorization, and camped unobtrusively on the expansive sandy beach awaiting Schauenburg's arrival. The "point" itself is very difficult to distinguish on the ground because the coast along the seaward side is a long arc that eventually ends in a long barren sandspit jutting towards Caraquet. The beach at the point itself is rocky and characterized by low bluffs. The military cordon would, in fact, have aided Heyda in identifying the pick-up spot. The modern visitor to this popular summer haven will find no trace of any military presence. A modern navigation beacon rests on the foundations of the old lighthouse.[22]

U-536 had arrived in the Gulf of St Lawrence about 16 September 1943, apparently with orders to tune in for radio communications with the escapees from 23 September, and to arrive in the Baie des Chaleurs on 26 September, one day prior to the expected arrival of Kretschmer's group. Top-secret orders from Admiral Murray, passed by hand to the destroyer HMS *Chelsea*, as well as three corvettes (HMCS *Agassiz, Shawinigan*, and *Lethbridge*) and five Bangor minesweepers (HMCS *Mahone, Swift Current, Chedabucto, Ungava*, and *Granby*) initiated patrols south of the Baie des Chaleurs on 25 September; they sealed off the bay on 28 September once U-536 was inside. Backed up by Fairmiles, the nine ships swept inside the entrance in line abreast as U-536 sought its bearings.

HMCS *Rimouski* (Lt R.J. Pickford, RCNVR) had been assigned a special role in the operation.[23] She was one of the first ships to experiment with diffused lighting, a concept which was designed to render the vessel virtually invisible at night. According to theory, a darkened ship is visible at night because it appears darker than its background. Diffused lighting washing over the superstructure, so the argument ran, should cause the ship to blend into the sky and sea. *Rimouski*, known jocularly as the "Polish corvette," was fitted with a system of lights and automatic controls during her refit at Liverpool, Nova Scotia, and was painted in complementary shades. As the former commanding officer of Fairmile ML 053 recently recalled when describing tests of the system at Pictou, Nova Scotia: "It was uncanny; you could see the black shape of the corvette against the night sky one minute, and then [when her diffused lighting went on] it just faded out."[24] As Admiral (Retired) R.J. Pickford recently recalled, the system proved successful. For those aboard, however, "the effect was really weird." It was actually light enough to read on the bridge by night and walk about the upper deck without the usual groping and stumbling. "After years of blackout it was uncomfortable, but it really worked." Thus the "invisible" *Rimouski* was supposed to detach from the patrol line and close the U-boat, in Pickford's words, "steaming slowly with navigational lights, and diffused lighting on, pretending to be a small coastal vessel."

Just how the escapees were to communicate – whether by transmitter-receiver that a German aviator had constructed in Bowmanville, or some other means – is not clear. Final communications were to be effected by flashing light from shore. Once U-536 had made contact with the escapees, a landing party consisting of 20-year-old Sub-Lieutenant Günther Freudenberg and a stoker would go ashore in an inflatable dinghy equipped with an outboard engine. Young Freudenberg, now a senior professor of philosophy at the University of Osnabrück, later struck Allied Intelligence as somewhat of a swashbuckling adventurer. Interrogators reported that he had intended to land after the manner of American gangster movies with a lead weight in his woollen cap with which to belt any interloper. Dr Freudenberg, now a reflective pacifist, finds the appreciation of his role fanciful in the extreme.

Piers and his staff had meanwhile set up their headquarters in the lighthouse, to which they withdrew on 27 September for "a little game of cards." They had earlier received a cryptic message indicating that the mass break-out from Bowmanville had failed, but that one man had escaped in an attempt to make the rendezvous. About 8 or 9 PM on 27 September, sentries on shore accosted Heyda and brought him into the lighthouse to confront Piers. Like the spy von Janowski, he had, Piers recalls, "a pocketful of old money – $20 bills that hadn't been used perhaps since the late twenties."[25] The circumstances of Heyda's arrest cannot be confirmed, although the exchanged German naval officer Dietrich Loewe had informed the German Naval Staff by January 1944 that the Canadians had captured Heyda a mere 1000 m from the rendezvous.[26] Piers recalls having summoned the RCMP to deal with the prisoner "in accordance with the prearranged plan" but doesn't enlighten us as to what this was. They returned him to Bowmanville, where prisoners undoubtedly passed the word to Germany. Only after the war could Piers inform his fellow NATO officer Kretschmer of the clues that had betrayed Heyda. Schauenburg's article published in *Kristall* in 1956 provides an account worthy of a Hollywood gangbuster's script, for here the hapless prisoner faced the pernicious cunning of a leering, overbearing officer in the naval service, which had "called up three battalions ... in order to get the sub [and had] reactivated this lighthouse and recalled its prewar keeper from the Navy." Indeed to Heyda's surprise, the chief interrogator turned out to be "not a Canadian – but a British naval officer."[27] This was, in all likelihood, Lt W.S. Samuel, RNVR, of Canadian Naval Intelligence.

An uneasy feeling had bothered Schauenburg aboard U-536 since having entered the bay on 24 September, for not only did he find his charts out of date and important landmarks missing, but a cordon of "destroyers" through which he passed cast a suspicious mood, anxiously heightened by a bay strangely devoid of vessels. He remained submerged by day, surfacing only at night to charge batteries with his decks awash in order to present a minimal profile. At times he advanced to within 200 m of shore. During the night of 26 September, Schauenburg and his officers gained the impression that warships were gathering: six of undetermined type were apparently patrolling further out in the bay; a "destroyer" had taken station well inside, while a "corvette" seemed to have taken up a position off the assigned rendezvous point. To the crew of U-536, isolated observations from the beginning of their inshore sojourn confirmed a trap. The sense of entrapment deepened when a curious radio signal broke the silence on a different frequency from the one assigned for communication with the escapees. It called the sub to shore by means of a code word different from anything they had planned. Equally disturbing, someone had signalled from the darkened shore by flashing the German phrase *Komm, Komm* in plain language in a manner contrary to the promulgated identifier.[28] At this time the mobile radar units reported a contact to Piers, who was still interrogating Heyda. Then, "quite out of the blue," according to a German version, depth charges exploded nearby. Schauenburg now regarded the rescue as hopeless and turned his mind to his own escape. Acting on the correct assumption that the warships would expect him to seek deep water, and would not attack in shallow water for fear of being damaged by their own depth charges, he sought the shallows along the Miscou Flats. Throughout 27 September 1943, the day on which Heyda was captured, U-536 lay on the bottom and waited.

Schauenburg's U-536 crept out of the Baie des Chaleurs on the night of 27–28 September 1943 at a depth of 20 m, her hydrophones detecting the sounds of searching surface vessels. One such vessel gave the impression of following her for some considerable time. The crew heard depth-charge explosions some distance off and wondered whether they were scare charges, exercise bombs, or the real thing. British Intelligence much later recorded that warships had attacked "a contact off Chaleur Bay" that night. U-536, Freudenberg recalls, pressed on as close to shore as possible, almost skidding along the bottom with just enough water overhead to cover the top of its conning tower and periscopes. At one point during the evasion, U-536 became entangled in a fishing trawler's nets and could hear her winches working against the strain of her extraordinary catch. The Germans later found pieces of the net on both bridge and cable guard. No other reliable details have come to light. Curiously, some sailors in the Canadian patrols felt that the German U-boat they were hunting knew the Baie des Chaleurs even better than they themselves, and was perhaps even operating in collusion with the fishermen – particularly the francophones – from Quebec and New Brunswick. This striking artefact of francophobia could not have been further from the truth.

The aborted mission of U-536, survivors recalled, was not without some mitigating panache. At least the German myth insists that when outbound in Cabot Strait U-536 fired three faulty torpedoes at an unwary destroyer, which did not react. Canadian War Diaries reveal no enemy activity in the area at all. Post-war German accounts inflated this event.[29] Revived in one of Canada's German-language newspapers, the *Vancouver Courier-Nordwesten*, as late as 1979, the U-boat's quiet retreat emerged as "the master stroke of not only escaping from the Bay and the St. Lawrence mouth [sic] with his severely damaged Boat, but of sinking two Canadian destroyers with a salvo of the latest *Zaunkönig* [Gnat] target-seeking torpedoes." On 5 October 1943, some 180 miles due south of Cape St Mary's, Newfoundland, Schauenburg's cryptic message "*Kiebitz verpfiffen*" ("Operation Magpie blown") advised BdU that the mission had been betrayed. The submariners suspected a leak in the command system.

Schauenburg's final encounter with Canadians occurred under uncompromising conditions while homeward-bound northeast of the Azores on 20 November. After three to four weeks patrolling off Halifax and along the Nova Scotia coast without even once being able to manoeuvre into an attack position, U-536 now fell in with the eight U-boats of Gruppe Schill 2. It was shadowing the sixty-six-ship convoy MKS-30/SL-139 en route from the UK to Gibraltar and Freetown when the search patterns of three Canadian escorts converged: the corvettes HMCS *Snowberry* (Lt J.A. "Hamish" Dunn, RCNVR), *Calgary* (LCdr H.K. "Hank" Hill, RCNVR), and the frigate HMS *Nene* (Cdr J.D. Birch, RNR).[30] The sharp "ping" of asdic against the pressure hull of U-536 startled the unsuspecting crew out of its sense of security at a cruising depth of 160–190 m (525–625 feet). U-536 was low on fuel and out of torpedoes. HF/DF reports had alerted the escort screen to the presence of the pack. *Snowberry* in the stern station was vectored by *Nene* until she herself picked up the asdic contact at 1000 yards and dropped ten Mark VII depth charges in pattern "G" (settings of 350 and 550 feet), followed twenty-five minutes later by her "better of the two attacks" with pattern "E" (150 and 300 feet). As her commanding officer observed, "If it did not damage the U-Boat it at least shook him up badly."[31]

The attack was in fact devastating. The U-boat suddenly became stern heavy while lights failed, the fuse box burst into flames, and yellow smoke billowed. In short order, U-536 was thrust perilously into the perpendicular, balancing on its screws, and hurtling to a depth of 240 m.[32] Despite the violence of the movement, the resourceful chief engineer, Wilhelm Kujas, managed to stabilize the hopelessly damaged Boat from which he himself would not escape. As the U-boat rose to the surface and chlorine gas formed in the bilges, the crew gathered in the control room to abandon ship. The turbulence of the depth charges had barely subsided when the conning tower of U-536 broke surface fine on *Snowberry*'s starboard bow. *Snowberry* passed close alongside in a manoeuvre that led Schauenburg to report that he had ultimately been sunk by ramming. Having finally come to grips with the enemy, it is little wonder that *Snowberry*'s captain recounted lively and lurid stories to the press:[33] "The first round from the 4-inch gun scored a direct hit on the conning tower [while] Able Seaman Don Vyse of Peterborough, Ontario, kept his Lewis gun trained on the U-Boat's decks and mowed down the Nazis whenever they attempted to reach their big gun." Or again: "The submarine crew came tumbling out of the hatch, trying to reach the deck guns to blast us, but we swept her decks with our Oerlikons and pompoms ... It looked like a movie – the Germans throwing up their arms as they were hit and falling into the sea one after another." By this time both HMS *Nene* and HMCS *Calgary* had closed the U-boat and opened fire. HMCS *Snowberry* illuminated with star shell and, when firing ceased, moved alongside U-536 to inspect the Boat and its top-secret radar antennae. U-536 lay down by the stern, its decks awash up to its shell-smashed conning tower, the pressure hull riddled with bullets, the engines still running. *Snowberry*'s scraping alongside in a running sea was the closest she came to the ramming incident that Schauenburg reported to BdU. Seventeen out of a crew of fifty-five survived. Most had escaped in their one-man dinghies. As Lt Dunn gratuitously remarked, "There was no evidence to make us believe that these were members of the 'Master Race.' They were a very docile and thankful collection of survivors."

German U-boat tactics and technology had been ruggedly innovative since the earliest days of submarine warfare. Moreover, German operational and historical analysts developed appreciations of the weaponry in a way their Canadian counterparts could not. The same held for mine warfare and mine countermeasures. German naval forces profited from their wide experience with mines in the First World War, in which they accounted for 10 per cent of all tonnage sunk, while Canadians were caught completely off guard.[34] Wise maritime authorities always expect a mine threat. From an enemy's point of view, these weapons are, to borrow Churchill's description of corvettes, both "cheap and nasty." Minelaying is the enemy's way of altering the opponent's coastal geography according to his own purposes, and then controlling access to it. He may of course lay the field by aircraft or surface vessel, but his submarine minelayer holds a distinct advantage: it can lay the field in secret after having taken ample time to observe the opponent's traffic patterns and routines. It therefore operates with the very latest intelligence. The mere suspicion of enemy mines commits the defender to mine countermeasures. In terms of men and matériel these can be costly, time consuming, and seemingly unproductive. Yet, only by maintaining and patrolling "swept" or "sanitized" channels between harbours and convoy marshalling-points can the defender assure himself of the safe and unhindered passage of shipping through his own waters.

Germany's first attempt at mining Halifax Approaches and the southeastern shore of Nova Scotia from Cape Breton to Cape Sable was undertaken by the former merchant submarine U-155 (ex *Deutschland*) in September 1918.[35] Although the mines broke loose from their moorings and were, in any event, too thinly placed to form an effective blockade, the action demonstrated that, with slight technical improvement, a European opponent could seal off North American harbours. U-boats of the Deutschland class carried forty-two mines; the minelayers of the Second World War carried sixty-six.[36] Harbour defences were therefore imperative. The wisdom of providing controlled loops to prevent the intrusion of enemy forces, and minesweepers to clear one's own waters of enemy mines frequently intruded itself upon Canada's fledgling naval service in the years 1918–38. Though the RCN exercised minesweeping sporadically off Halifax and Esquimalt from 1912 onwards, neither its East Coast Patrols of the First World War nor the first ill-equipped coastal minesweepers for home use that entered service in 1938 could cope with the threat. Typical of Canada's reactive defence policies, the minefields laid by U-119 and U-220 off Halifax and St John's in May and June 1943 forced the navy into the last wartime shipbuilding program that it ever undertook. In direct consequence of the minelaying, the Naval Staff and Board approved orders for twelve 126-foot wooden minesweepers for the East Coast, and four for the West.[37] The RCN did not actually place the orders for the vessels until December 1943, six months after the Germans had laid the mines. The reason for this delay lies in a conflict of priorities. Until as late as 1941, the navy's stated policies had of course focused primarily on coastal defences against surface raiders, submarines, and mines.[38] In practice, however, Canada's growing commitment to Atlantic convoys meant that minesweepers were being turned to ocean escort duties for which they had not been designed. Thus, even by January 1940, the navy boasted but eight trawler-type minesweepers in Halifax and three similar vessels in Esquimalt; five motor vessels were undergoing refit for minesweeping duties.[39] The prior claims of the Admiralty in London for Canadian minesweepers for the European theatre exacerbated the problem even further. Despite Canada's strapped resources for home defence, she acceded in July 1941 to Admiralty's request for two minesweeping flotillas of eight ships each for operations in UK waters.[40] Such Canadian vessels contributed significantly to mine countermeasures overseas, but at the expense of their own shores.[41]

As early as 30 November 1939, BdU had gained the support of the German Naval Staff to mine Halifax harbour.[42] Only three military reasons argued against the plan's immediate execution: Dönitz's fear of splintering his meagre submarine forces; the need for a supply vessel to station itself south of Greenland to support the minelayer on its lengthy trek; and the severe winter now gripping the Atlantic coast. The political ramifications of such an attack required Hitler's consideration. "Operation

Halifax" reached his desk by 2 February 1940, and was held in abeyance pending further study. Despite the fact that German Foreign Minister Ribbentrop had voiced no objections whatever to the plan in principle, Hitler quashed it by direct order on 6 February 1940. He was seriously concerned about its impact on a neutral United States, whom he wished to remain out of the conflict as long as possible.[43] The Germans seem to have delayed further consideration of the possible mining of North American waters until 1942, although of course they used submarines, aircraft, and especially destroyers to lay the state-of-the-art magnetic mines off British ports and estuaries during the "Phoney War" between September 1939 and May 1940.[44] There were several reasons for this delay, not the least of which included slow production of naval mines, insufficient numbers of minelaying submarines, inadequate supply of TBM ground mines that standard U-boats could launch through torpedo tubes, and a preoccupation with the development of reliable torpedoes. In May 1942, however, the German Naval Staff minuted the observation that U-boats could be assigned mining missions in those areas otherwise closed to operations by surface vessels and aircraft. With a carrying capacity of sixty-six mines, their great range permitted delivery in previously inaccessible areas.[45] The eastern seaboard of the United States and Central America were among the promising long-term targets. The Naval Staff authorized BdU to co-ordinate mining with his torpedo warfare, and to commence as soon as SMA (English type GO) moored magnetic mines were combat ready. BdU did not delay. By 19 May 1942 three type VIIB U-boats had departed for the U.S.: U-87 was to mine the entrance to New York, U-373 the entrance to Delaware Bay, and U-701 the entrance to the Chesapeake Bay.[46]

BdU's rationale for the timing of the venture applied equally to his subsequent selection of Canadian targets: weak mine countermeasures in North American waters and the opportunity for fragmenting the Allies' resources. German minelaying, he reasoned, would not obstruct his subsequent torpedo assaults, as his U-boats would lay the mines in shallow waters unsuited to torpedo warfare. The mines would in any event remain lethal for no longer than two months. In September 1942, BdU chose the Canadian targets for the SMA mine: the territory between Boston and Cape Sable, off Halifax and Sydney, and from Cape Race to St John's. Fields laid in these broad areas, he noted, would not hinder the U-boats' torpedo operations. BdU proposed reserving the Cabot Strait, St Lawrence, and Belle Isle Strait solely for torpedo operations "as long as possibilities still exist there."[47] Although the *U-Boat Atlas*, companion volume to the *U-Boat Pilot Book* for the east coast of Canada, both of which were published in June 1942, paid meticulous attention to the Bay of Fundy as a target for mines, U-boats made no attempts to lay mines in the Fundy region.

Canadian inshore experience with mines prior to the arrival of German minelaying submarines was confined to drifting mines of British provenance. One had to assume that they were enemy until proven otherwise, as they were in any event dangerous to handle. Fishermen, rangers and the ADC were often the first to detect mines, and occasionally treated them with an ingenuousness that baffled the few professionals who knew how to deal with them. On one such occasion in July 1941, a certain Llewellyn Curtis picked up a drifting mine while fishing northeast of Horse Island, a barren outcropping off the northeast coast of Newfoundland. Fascinated by the strange object bobbing in the water, and covetous of the lengthy mooring wires he intended to salvage in order to moor his motor boat, he towed it home to La Scie Harbour, Cape St John. In the words of the investigating ranger two weeks after the event, "with the help of several men [Curtis] hoisted it on a pier and then rolled it a considerable distance to his store."[48] Curtis showed the ranger the marvellous device he had found in the sea and nonchalantly opened it up to display its mysteries. As the ranger reported:

I immediately saw Curtis and asked him to show me what he had picked up. I looked at the object from a distance and immediately concluded it was a Mine. It somewhat resembled a Bell Buoy and was the size of a Bark Pot. On the outside there were 8 pointed steel projections about 6 inches in length and $\frac{1}{2}''$ in diameter. Curtis removed these. At both ends there were steel plates bolted to the body of the mine ... Curtis removed one of the bolts in the centre of this plate and with it a small trap door came off. Through this small opening I saw wires and batteries, all apparently in good condition.

Lack of tension on the mooring wire may have been all that saved them from an explosion. By October 1942 the Canadian government was offering a $10 reward for the recovery of any mines within 2 miles of Canadian shores.[49]

Horst Jessen von Kamecke's U-119 laid the first minefield of the Second World War in Canadian waters on 1 June 1943. Following Dönitz's earlier mine doctrine of avoiding neat geometric patterns (which can easily be swept), von Kamecke laid his sixty-six SMA mines in a loose arc in order to seal off Halifax harbour from the outermost extremity of the Approaches.[50] Later exploratory sweeps carried out by Canadians radially around the Sambro lightship disclosed a ring of some 6–7 miles radius, with a northeastward extension towards the East Halifax lightship.[51] In rectangular terms, the field bounded an area approximately 18 miles by 25 miles, extending roughly from Shutin Island to 15 miles south of the Sambro lightship.[52] In theory, it formed an effective cordon. Yet on the very day that U-119 laid the field, the escorts of combined convoy ONS-8/ XB-56 sighted three surfaced mines some 6–7 miles south and southeast of the Sambro lightship. Canadian authorities broadcast mine warnings as soon as they had identified the mines as German. Shortly after midnight GMT on 2 June, they closed the Port of Halifax as a precautionary measure. Bangors diverted from the Western Local Escort Force assisted local minesweeping forces in opening a very narrow 15-mile channel through the field and reopened the port twenty-two hours later, despite the continued threat.

Inadequate equipment, inexperience, and lack of preparation made clearance difficult. This was equally true of the six BYMS (British Y-class minesweepers) then in Halifax undergoing acceptance trials: they had stowed their gear in anticipation of their transit to the UK. Their crews had been inoperative since September 1942, none of the vessels had any "LL" magnetic sweeps aboard, and none had had any opportunity for work-ups either singly or as a squadron.[53] Defects in sweeping gear and machinery began to appear after eight days of constant sweeping. The crews were also "feeling the strain, and key men, of whom only one rate per vessel was carried, were falling asleep standing at their posts." The threat of further minelaying kept the BYMS in Halifax for a further year.[54] By 25 June, the navy had destroyed fifty of the mines, believed two others to have self-scuttled, and recovered three. The dangerous task of mine recovery fell to a few Canadians in the Mine Disposal Unit, which had only formed in 1942. Though a great many Canadians had been working in the trade with British forces in all theatres of war, a mere handful served in Halifax.[55] The Halifax mine disposal officer, Lt G.H.R. Rundle, RCNR, dismantled the first of these mines with Ordinary Seaman John Lancien after it had been towed to Ketch Harbour by Fairmile ML-052 (Slt G.M. Schuthe, RCNVR).[56] These were the first buoyant moored magnetic mines to be recovered in the war. Rundle and Lancien received the George Medal. By 10 July the swept channel extended 30 miles to seaward. A fifty-ship convoy would require eight hours in transit.

Mine-countermeasures vessels faced often vexing problems of mine detection even when they knew the exact location of the field. For example, on 4 January 1943, HMCS Brockville's unauthorized anchorage in the vicinity of the controlled loop off Halifax broke the firing circuit and set mines adrift. Though minesweepers recovered eleven of sixteen mines within a month, the search for the missing five units continued intermittently from 5 February to 9 April "as weather and availability of divers and boats would allow." In all, the search occupied twenty-two working days, and the mines were never found.[57] The task of locating the mines was exacerbated by the fact that detection equipment could not distinguish between mines and "the comparatively large amount of scrap metal ... strewn over this area" over a long period of years by vessels in transit.[58] Whenever trawls, drags, or sweeps snagged any object too heavy or too well anchored to lift, it became necessary to send divers down to investigate. Now a basic principle of mine countermeasures insists that harbours and approaches undergo a bottom survey in peacetime in order to locate and identify foreign material that, during wartime sweeps, could otherwise be construed as enemy. A completed survey also facilitates identification of any new material, like mines, which might subsequently be detected. The RCN had disregarded this principle, and now reaped the dubious reward. The principle remains largely unobserved even today.

The sole victim of U-119's mission to Halifax seems to have been the 2937-ton Panamanian SS *Halma*, which struck a mine on 1 June 1943 while romping ahead of her Boston–Halifax convoy BX-56. She was 4 miles inside an area the navy considered dangerous, and sank without loss of life 6 miles south of the Sambro lightship. The American freighter *John A. Poor* struck a drifting mine off Halifax that may have broken loose from U-119's field. Later, Germany's radio surveillance and decryption service (*B-Dienst*) intercepted signals from the British vessel SS *Alva* on 7 June, and from the SS *Highland Count* on 10 June concerning mine damage incurred off Halifax. Allied records shed no light on these ships. Despite having taken only one victim, the threat of mines affected the port's flow of traffic throughout the month. Even when departures and arrivals were restricted to daylight hours, the constricted waters of the swept channel hampered convoy movements and occasionally led to collisions. The SS *Reigh Count* sank on 6 June within 20 minutes after colliding in the swept channel while manoeuvring in slow convoy SC-133. The mining caused severe dislocation. Among other things, it added six extra hours of steaming to SH and HS convoys running between Sydney and Halifax, tied down escort vessels for twenty-seven days, forced the navy to revamp plans for the deployment of BYMS minesweepers to the UK, and further complicated and delayed the sailing and arrival of ocean-going convoys. The average daily rate of employment for mine countermeasures cost the Canadians 7.7 ships for channel clearance from 1 to 3 June, 18.1 ships and two danlayers (which laid the so-called dan buoys to mark the edge of dangerous water, or the channels that needed to be swept) for exploratory and clearance operations from 4 to 21 June, and 14.5 ships for the "mop up from 22 to 27 June."[59]

Barber's 1600-ton minelayer U-220 departed her home waters on 28 September 1943 bearing the top secret "Operation Order St John's" dated 11 May 1943 that had first been assigned to U-219. It seems, therefore, that BdU had initially envisaged co-ordinating the operation with that of U-119 off Halifax. Now, however, U-220 was to operate at first as a U-tanker (as U-219 would have done) before undertaking phase 2 of its dual mission, laying mines during the dark nights of the new moon. The order directed Barber to "execute widespread mining of the convoy routes off St. John's," Newfoundland.[60] BdU's Intelligence assessment drew on two sources: the German decryption service (*B-Dienst*) and the observations of patrolling U-boats, in particular Rüggeberg's U-513. These sources assured Barber of ample targets: regular coastal and deep-sea convoy traffic, and warships movements. They correctly described St John's as the home port for relieving escorts and auxiliary carriers of transatlantic convoys; such convoys could be expected to switch escorts at a meeting point some 200 miles southeast of the harbour (U-548 would sink HMCS *Valleyfield* near this meeting point in 1944). BdU's orders advised Barber to expect about four "joiner" and "leaver" convoy sections per month, as well as coastal traffic to and from Halifax.

U-220 carried the full capacity of sixty-six SMA moored magnetic mines. Fitted with a flooder that would neutralize the mines after eighty days, they were to be laid at intervals of 400 m in ocean depths ranging from 50 to 350 m. Although BdU specified the geographical limits of the field (47° 26′ N to 47° 40′ N, and 52° 21′ W to the coast), he none the less permitted Barber to depart from these guidelines if local conditions and traffic patterns should dictate otherwise. BdU's subsequent warning to Schrewe (U-537), who shortly thereafter, as we have seen, proceeded towards the Newfoundland coast after having established his weather station in Labrador, indicates that Barber departed from these guidelines scarcely at all.[61] Barber was also free to choose the actual time of the operation. On completion, he was to report the mission as soon as possible, but under no circumstances within 100 miles of the field. The broadcast of the four code letters AFKP indicating the mission's success would be too brief for D/F stations to fix its position. The orders reveal that BdU intended to redeploy U-220 for an undisclosed third phase once "Operation St. John's" was clear.

Barber's field was discovered on 11 October 1943 when the British Y-class minesweeper BYMS-50 sank a floating mine in the approaches to St John's.[62] Eight more were sunk next day off the port.[63] These occurrences caused immediate ramifications: closure of the port, transfer of minesweepers and mine-disposal personnel from Halifax, and re-routing of convoys ONS-20 and HX-260 already at sea, in order to bypass the suspected danger zone. The mines claimed their only victims when the 3721-ton British SS *Penolver* and 3478-ton American *Delisle* in the Wabana–Sydney ore convoy WB-65 sank on 19 October about 15 miles south of Cape Spear, and approximately 10 miles south of the declared danger area. *Penolver's* crew survived. Twenty-seven of the forty-one aboard *Delisle* were lost.[64] Although minesweepers had buoyed the St John's swept channel by 29 October, adverse weather prevented further precautionary sweeps for a number of days and delayed the St John's-to-Halifax convoy JH-75 until 1 November. By this time aircraft from USS *Block Island* had destroyed U-220 with all hands in mid Atlantic.[65] By the end of November the navy had swept only thirty-four mines. It would never find the rest, and simply ceased sweeping on 16 December 1943.

When two torpedoes from U-845 (Weber) struck the SS *Kelmscott* two months later on 9 February 1944, some 7.5 miles from Fort Amsherst, naval authorities understandably suspected a mine. The incident provoked closure of the Port of St John's, the diversion to Argentia of Halifax–St John's convoy JH-81, and the diversion of four British Castle-class frigates and the destroyer HMCS *Annapolis*.[66]

The Germans' final attempt at mining Canadian waters commenced when Kapitänleutnant Hans Steen departed Kiel on 27 May 1944 on the first patrol of his 1600-ton minelayer and supply boat U-233. Steen, who had been commissioned in 1937, was popular with his crew, who considered him an efficient officer. In the subsequent opinion of U.S. interrogators, however, Steen's crew was "a poor one." Most of them were "totally lacking in previous U-Boat experience." A large number of them had apparently never been to sea before joining the navy. This was not unusual in 1944 and 1945. "As a whole," the interrogation report summarized, "they gave the impression of being the dregs of the reserve [manning] pools in Germany and [from the] shore stations on the Baltic, with a very small sprinkling of experienced petty officers to stiffen" the unit.[67] Steen had expected to put into Bordeaux on completion of his Canadian mission. As will be seen later, the deployment of U-boats in distant waters but a few days before the Normandy Invasion deprived German forces of vital naval support that they might better have used closer to home. BdU none the less continued his policy of keeping pressure on critical points abroad in order to prevent the Allies from sending greater resources to Europe. This alone explains why Steen was to lay sixty-six SMA moored magnetic mines off Halifax. They were each fitted with 1300 feet of mooring cable, an 80-day self-scuttling "flooder," a 24-hour "arriving clock" or delay timer, and a "ship count" mechanism, which allowed the layers to pre-set the number of vessels that could pass safely before the mine became armed. This increased the hazard to the enemy and complicated mine clearance immensely. These new-type "pressure differential mines" were capable of maintaining a pre-set depth of 4–6 m below the surface regardless of tidal conditions. Changing tides caused a shift in water pressure, which in turn acted upon a regulator in the anchor; this caused the cable either to lengthen or shorten accordingly. Steen anticipated from one day to a day and a half laying mines off Halifax, for during exercises off Hela in the Baltic he had laid 132 similar mines within three days.

U-233 faced its final attack in a journey that had been harassed by aircraft when cruising submerged at 30–50 m, some 100 miles southeast of Sable Island on the morning of 5 July 1944. Without any warning, a loud whining noise, followed by high-speed screw noises, penetrated its hull. USS *Baker* of U.S. Task Group 22.10, at the time under Canadian operational control, dropped a full pattern of depth charges that sent the U-boat plummeting violently to a depth of 120 m. A second pattern forced Steen to blow all tanks in a last-ditch effort to escape the doomed U-boat. The crew began to abandon as soon as U-233 broke surface and the hatches were clear. Those who tried to escape via the conning tower were either killed outright by the guns of the U.S. destroyers *Baker* and *Thomas*, or else seriously wounded. Only those who slipped out of the forward hatch got clear. Nine minutes after the attack had begun, USS *Thomas* rammed U-233 abaft the conning tower, trapping all personnel working in the after torpedo compartment, and in the diesel and electric rooms. The U-boat sank beneath the American's keel. The destroyers picked up thirty survivors from the crew of sixty. Steen himself succumbed to serious wounds and was buried at sea.

BdU would send no more minelayers to Canada. Canadian naval authorities nevertheless continued to speculate on possible German naval intentions of laying more mines of an improved variety in Canadian waters. They pondered without result the "probability of a minelaying U-Boat being able to operate off any Canadian harbour at locations where the depths were 100 feet or less."[68] The Germans would indeed carry out such a feat on the surface in Chesapeake Bay by night. Meanwhile, Operational Research in Ottawa wisely advised the Chief of Naval Staff to countenance "no relaxation in keeping our minesweeping equipment (Oropesa and Influence) at the highest state of efficiency." The need to use it against actual mines would never again arise. Naval Staff declared the Canadian coast free from mines on 25 June 1945, some fifty days after the European war was over.

Censorship suppressed any news of minelaying until the torpedoing on 22 March 1944 of the coastal vessel SS *Watuka* in convoy SH-125 off Halifax by U-802 (Schmoeckel).[69] A Canadian Press release of mid July captioned "Sea War Was Near – Ships Sunk Off Halifax Headlands" described the *Watuka* attack as an "isolated incident notable [only] because in 1944 a U-Boat dared approach Canada's seaboard so closely." It went on to allay the public's fears by asserting that the only time when the U-boats "dared return anywhere near the coast after 1942 was when a submarine laid mines to choke off the entrance to Halifax Harbour." The mines, it observed, had been cleared without much inconvenience. The *Halifax Herald* for 15 July 1944 now revealed that "naval authorities ... confidently predict that never again would U-Boats stalk their prey within sight of shore dwellers in this city." This was wishful understatement. U-802 and U-541 were at this time already commencing their Gulf patrols, and HMCS *Clayoquot* and *Esquimalt* would be sunk in winter and spring 1944–5 by U-806 and U-190 within sight of Chebucto Head.

U-152 *Deutschland* class, August 1917. Note camouflage and the 15-cm guns fore and aft (photo: BfZ Archives).

Clearing ice off HMCS *Kamsack*, St John's Nfld, November 1941. L to R: ABS Jack Hunter, Harold Monk, and PO Bob Davies (PAC, PA 125852).

Kptlt Erich Topp at periscope of U-552 during "Paukenschlag," January 1942 (Karl Böhm collection).

Commissioning U-190, Bremen, 24 September 1942. Kptlt Max Wintermeyer on bridge. It surrendered to Canada May 1945 (photo: BfZ Archives).

Survivors of ss *Cyclops* alongside HMCS *Red Deer*, 12 January 1942 (PAC, C-54474).

Sydney–Porte Aux Basques ferry SS *Caribou*, sunk 14 October 1942 by U-69 (Maritime Museum of the Atlantic, Halifax: MP 18.180.2).

Front page of the *Halifax Herald*, 13 May 1942 (PAC, NL 12600).

Victory Bond advertisement, the *Montreal Daily Star*, 2 November 1942. Hull insignia, number, and design are propaganda fictions (PAC, NL 12595).

"Danke schön!" Poster of Wartime Information Board, Ottawa, produced by the National Film Board (R.J. Henderson collection).

Spy equipment of Lt von Janowski, landed at New Carlisle, Quebec, from U-518 on 9 November 1942 (courtesy RCMP Museum, Regina).

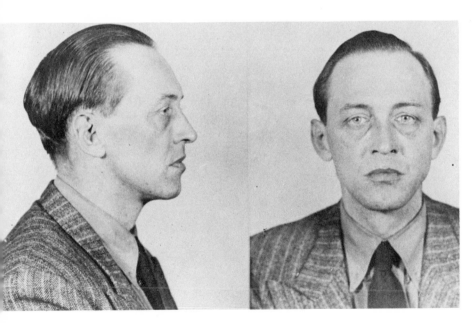

Lt Werner von Janowski as double agent (courtesy RCMP Museum, Regina).

Kptlt Peter Schrewe on bridge of U-537.
Note UZO (surface target optic) for transmitting
visual target data to tactical room
(courtesy Franz Selinger, PAC, PMR-81-430).

Automatic weather station WFL-26 ("Kurt") landed on Labrador from U-537 on 22 October
1943 (courtesy Franz Selinger, PAC, PMR-80-487).

Flotilla Cdr Günther Kuhnke (left) welcomes Kurt Petersen (right) with traditional bouquet on return from the St Lawrence, October 1944 (courtesy Kurt Petersen).

Crew of U-548, which sank HMCS *Valleyfield*. Capt. Eberhard Zimmermann (white cap), in centre (photo: BfZ Archives).

Crew of U-806 prior to departure for Halifax, November 1944. Note section of schnorkel arm, right forward (courtesy Klaus Hornbostel).

HMCS *Magog* on 14 October 1944 with 60 feet of stern blown off by acoustic torpedo from U-1223 (RCN photo; PAC, CN-4008).

Lt Roland Taylor on shattered stern of HMCS *Magog*. Black ball (upper right) indicates ship at anchor (courtesy Roland Taylor).

The COs who sank U-845. L. to R.: LCdr George H. Stephen (LCdr J.E. Harrington), Cdr C.A. King, LCdr J.A. Burnett (photo: John Daniel Mahoney, PAC, PA 137695).

Blindfolded survivor of U-845 disembarking from HMCS *St. Laurent* in Britain (photo: John Daniel Mahoney, PAC, PA-137693).

Kptlt Klaus Hornbostel, Commandant of U-806, on return home after sinking HMCS *Clayoquot* (courtesy Klaus Hornbostel).

HMCS *Clayoquot*. Note SWIC radar at topmast (photo: BfZ Archives).

HMCS *Clayoquot*, 24 December 1944, with stern blasted into the vertical by acoustic torpedo from U-806. Photographed from HMCS *Fennel* (RCN photo, Defence HQ).

Clayoquot survivors alongside HMCS *Fennel*. Lower left facing upward, LCdr Craig Campbell (RCN photo, Defence HQ).

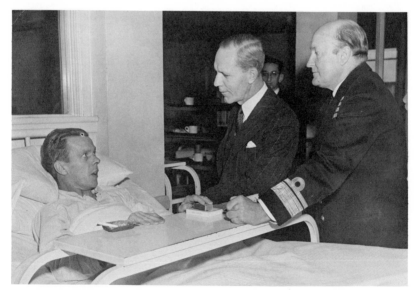

RCN Hospital, Halifax. L. to R.: *Clayoquot* survivor William Smith, with the Hon. Angus L. Macdonald, and Rear-Admiral L.W. Murray (RCN photo, PAC, A-1150).

Capt. Dobratz on bridge of U-1232 on return from Canada. Note Knight's Cross awarded for Halifax action, and fashioned on board by the Engineer (courtesy Kurt Dobratz).

A victorious U-1232 with "Halifax" on conning tower entering Kiel harbour, February 1945. Flag hoist indicates 5 sinkings (courtesy Kurt Dobratz).

HMCS *Ettrick* as might have been seen from periscope of U-1232 during attack off Halifax, January 1945 (PAC, S-2881).

HMCS *Esquimalt*. Note SW2C radar above topmast (RCN photo, PAC, S-426).

Scantily clad survivors of HMCS *Esquimalt* after torpedoing by U-190, 16 April 1945 (RCN photo, PAC, A-1379).

U-889 surrenders to Canadian forces, 10 May 1945. Note captain (white cap), section of schnorkel arm on right of tower, and recessed vertical intake stowed to right of foredeck (RCN photo, PAC, A-1423).

Extended configuration of captured U-190 in Sydney, NS. L. to R.: nav. periscope, attack periscope, schnorkel. Lower left fwd: retractable Hohentwiel radar antenna (D.J. Thorndick photo, PAC, PA-134173).

Tunis (FuMB 26) hand-turned, portable search radar in centimetric range, aboard U-889 (George Gaddes photo, PAC, PA-137700).

Bridge of U-889 facing aft. Note UZO (surface target optic) front right; far right, retractable Hohentwiel radar; aft, two twin 2-cm and 3.7-cm guns on afterdeck (George Gaddes photo, PAC, PA-134166).

Cartoon: "Their Constant Peril," *Halifax Herald*, 28 July 1942 (PAC, NL 12597).

Cartoon: "Spurlos Versenken" [sic], *Halifax Herald*, 19 April 1944 (PAC, NL 12598).

Cipher M ("Funkschlüssel-M") quadruple-cylinder naval coding machine (Photo courtesy German Naval Signal School Museum, Flensburg-Mürwik).

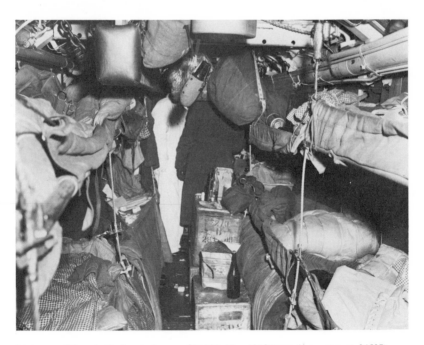

Living conditions in the forward mess of U-190, May 1945 (RCN photo, PAC, PL-36527).

"He Talked." Poster of Director of Public Information, Ottawa (R.J. Henderson collection).

CHAPTER SEVEN

Restless Interlude:
January–June 1944

The month of January 1944, as the Operations War Diary of Flag Officer, Newfoundland Force records, "was distinguished by an almost complete absence of enemy." Yet what was absent on the part of the violence of the enemy was, in the transmogrified phrases of the Naval Prayer, "quite adequately made up by the perils of the sea."[1] Heavy weather blanketed the western Atlantic, hampering the necessary close-quarters operations of escorts and convoys, and endangering converging and dispersing vessels at convoy joiner and leaver points. Severe westerly gales in mid ocean throughout the month and early spring caused the late arrival of west-bound convoys and revealed major flaws in many of the rapidly built Liberty ships, most of which developed cracked plates under stress. Convoying in heavy seas from Nova Scotia to. mid ocean led to frequent collisions, sinkings, and loss of life from which not even naval vessels were exempt.[2] This strained Allied resources as much as if the ships had been struck down by the enemy. Accidents and short maintenance layovers of Mid Ocean Escort groups at St John's placed "a very great burden on repair facilities as well as a strain on seagoing personnel." Redeployment weakened the defence of home waters even further. At the request of Admiralty in London, NSHQ in Ottawa had in December (1943) returned the six RN antisubmarine trawlers that had been operating from Sydney, NS. As a matter of course, it complied with a further Admiralty request for sixteen of the Bangor minesweepers that Canadians needed for escort and A/S assignments. These it allocated from the Western Escort, Halifax and Newfoundland Forces. By the end of February 1944, it sent two frigates and four corvettes of the Canadian 9th Escort Group to join ships of the C-in-C Western Approaches. Two of these vessels, HMCS *Swansea* and *Owen Sound*, would destroy U-845 south of Ireland on its return from Canadian waters.

In an effort to maintain some semblance of balance, C-in-C CNA exchanged three unmodernized corvettes in Halifax for two modernized ships from the West Coast. A similar type of trade-off occurred between the Royal Navy and the RCN. HMS *Ettrick*, the first of ten British-built RN frigates to be manned by the RCN, arrived in Halifax and was recommissioned on 29 January as HMCS *Ettrick*. She was a questionable gift. Halifax Naval Dockyard "found her to be in a filthy condition, showing a lack of upkeep prior to transfer."[3] She required three weeks of repairs to render her even seaworthy. NSHQ in Ottawa considered her dreadful condition sufficiently serious to advise both the Minister for the Navy and the Admiralty.[4] However, continuing the calm of December 1943, no ships in North Atlantic trade convoys were lost to enemy action in January and February 1944, a standard maintained in Canadian waters into the spring. Intelligence and action reports revealed that the Germans were by now virtually contained in the Western Approaches and the European theatre. But even here, as Rodger Winn had interpreted events from the Operational Intelligence Centre since November 1943, German naval strategy had consisted of "ill-coordinated and sullen responses to nervously abrupt changes of policy and diversions of effort"[5] by the German High Command.

BdU and Naval High Command East were meanwhile concerned about the heavy concentration of their submarines in home waters. In December 1943, for example, only sixty-seven U-boats of the Atlantic fleet were at sea. Of these, as few as thirty-one were actually on operational patrol. The others were either en route to station or returning home.[6] The beginning of 1944 saw little change in this ratio. Combat losses and damage due to the Allies' increasing tactical and technical superiority contributed in large measure to Dönitz's restricted movement.[7] Yet German forces suffered perhaps even more from the constraints imposed on the consumption of propulsion fuel, and from the heavy demands on training and front readiness. Only 168 of the 436 U-boats classified as "in service" on 1 January 1944 were actually combat ready or on patrol. Of the remainder, 181 were involved in work-ups and combat training, while 87 – or roughly 20 per cent of the submarine fleet – were designated as "school boats" or training vessels. BdU would later have to increase the proportion of training vessels. Having assigned 6 U-boats to the Black Sea, 13 to the Mediterranean, and 19 to the Arctic and Norway defence, Admiral Dönitz had in theory only 130 for Atlantic duty. This was 18 less than the theoretical level of the previous month. And less than half of those "in service" were at sea.

The high, though necessarily acceptable, losses of U-boats and experienced personnel had always been a critical factor in German war planning. Now, however, the cumulative effect had become crucial. If prospects of success were inordinately low, the prospects of a U-boat not even

TABLE 7
Attrition of Personnel

Period	Boats	Crew	Lost	Per cent lost	Captured or rescued	Per cent captured or rescued
			A. *Crew*			
I	148	6,356	4,665	73.4	1,691	26.6
II	112	5,534	4,956	89.6	578	10.4
III	85	4,376	3,659	83.6	717	16.4
Total	345	16,266	13,280	81.7	2,986	18.3
			B. *Commanding Officers*			
I	148		106	71.6	42	28.4
II	112		102	91.1	10	8.9
III	85		61	71.8	24	28.2
Total	345		269	78.0	76	22.0

returning from patrol were inordinately high. BdU assessed that during the previous months an average of "only 70 per cent of the U-boats" actually returned. The 30 per cent loss factor would increase. With a sense of impotence and frustration, BdU staff observed the Allies' seeming infallible grasp of the U-boat picture. Particularly crucial in this regard was the Allies' precise knowledge of the numbers and departure times of outbound U-boats leaving French bases. The British Government Code and Cipher School at Bletchley Park could now read Enigma signals in sufficient time to permit regular and precise air attacks in the Biscay. BdU persisted in blaming secret agents for the serious Intelligence leaks that ultimately victimized his submarines.[8] The Command's 1944 survey of losses of crew and commanding officers explains the pressing need both for recruits for the U-boat arm, as well as for the increased allocation of training boats. The context of Dönitz's mandate to wage unlimited submarine war explains why he now sent so many inexperienced crews to sea (see table 7).

Significantly, only 10 per cent of the survivors reached home to fight again. BdU attributed the increased crew losses (from 73.4 per cent in period I to 89.6 per cent in period II)[9] to the Allies' marked increase in both air offensive measures and their ability to detect U-boats. Equally important, prior to the fitting of U-boats with anti-aircraft defence (such as the upper-deck quadruple mounts), many U-boats were bombed while diving to escape Allied aircraft. This was their most vulnerable manoeuvre when attacked from the air. This fact, and the fitting out with anti-aircraft defences, in time led to the defensive tactic of anti-aircraft duels on the surface.

The survival rate increased in period III, which spanned the second half of 1943: in the case of crew, from 10.4 to 16.4 per cent, in the case of commanding officers from 8.9 to 22.2 per cent. BdU staff offered specific reasons for this shift. The foremost among them were that after introduction of strengthened anti-aircraft capability, fewer U-boats were sunk while diving or submerged than while engaging in surface combat with enemy aircraft. More sailors could, therefore, abandon ship in surface combat and could, it was explained, "under favourable circumstances be picked up by enemy surface craft." As commanding officers fought surface engagements from the bridge, their survival rate was generally higher than that of the crew. There were cases, of course, and U-845 was one of them, where personnel on the bridge became the very first casualties. Again, in contrast to the first half of 1943, carrier aircraft accounted for a larger number of sinkings. This meant that destroyers and other escorts were at hand to pick up survivors. Losses from depth-charge attack by escorts and hunter/killer groups, BdU staff pointed out, had eased markedly with the introduction in 1943 of the new T-5 Zaunkönig acoustic torpedo.

Despite the awesome odds against their survival, U-boat crews did not flag. With self-congratulatory pride, BdU recorded in June 1944 that the submariners remained "essentially unshaken in their inner bearing, in their will to be thrust against the enemy and in their thirst for battle." Convinced of the truth of such rhetoric, official circles regarded the submariners' doggedness as incontrovertible "proof of their military spirit." It bore witness to the "quality of human material" in the service, "the wages of thorough training, and the results of the close-ranked solidarity of the U-boat Arm." Such "gung-ho" and "can do" vocabulary ill accords with the more sober judgment of many front-line submariners. Vascillation in official circles between trumpeting rhetoric and cogent, persuasive analysis betrays the pervasive uneasiness that characterized not only BdU staff, but sailors at sea. The stridence of whipcrack sloganeering contrasts with the ominous warnings implicit between the lines of Naval Staff War Diaries. Self-sacrifice in the short run (one man, one death – one boat, one loss) could always be rationalized in terms of long-term gain. Thus one German diary entry argued that "holding the enemy at sword point" was not merely a slogan, but "a tactical, technical and above all a psychological necessity." Neither the German Naval Staff nor BdU could order a respite in the U-boat war, despite the urgent logic of doing so. If they eased off now, their argument ran, they would be unable to begin again once the new class of type XXI submarine had become battle ready. Yet BdU staff could not escape the terrible conclusion that little justified their present losses in the Battle of the Atlantic. Neither the number of personnel injected into the service, nor the commitment of material and industrial manpower, nor least of all the "blood tariff" (*Blutzoll*) seemed worth the paltry gains. Paradoxically, however, BdU insisted that "losses that bear no relationship to present successes must simply be accepted, however bitter they are to bear."[10]

Within this straitened context – weak Canadian defences and strained U-boat resources – Dönitz pursued his policy of thrusting his meagre reserves against the North American source of Europe's supply line. Six U-boats off Canadian shores would attempt to exploit the restless interlude before the Normandy Invasion that they knew must come soon.[11] Facing, by BdU's own assessment, overwhelming Allied superiority in virtually all sectors, the mere "struggle to survive in one's operational zone, let alone come onto viable targets" was severe.[12] Concerned about the physical and psychological stress that the crews of his VIIC Atlantic Boats suffered during lengthy and largely unsuccessful missions, BdU reduced their "on patrol" time to eight weeks. He could not credit his U-boats with much success in the North Atlantic: seven merchant vessels (13,000 tons), one patrol vessel and seven destroyers in April; one destroyer – actually the frigate HMCS *Valleyfield* off St John's – in May. The halcyon days of wolf-pack domination had passed.

The necessity for continued pressure on Allied supply lines meanwhile urged BdU to update more of his shrinking U-boat resources and despatch them to the North American coast. Withdrawing U-boats for lengthy refits of course reduced his effective striking power even more. Yet, in the absence of the proposed new high-speed submarine, his hope in the long run lay in compensating for the slowness of older types by equipping them to operate effectively in the very zones now dominated by Allied forces. Particularly important was outfitting with schnorkel. On the basis of his very first Canadian mission in June 1944, for example, Simmermacher in U-107 described the device as "a very useful means" not only for enhancing a U-boat's operations, but for enabling its utilization in many situations that would otherwise have been impossible.[13] He had in mind inshore operations under heavy air cover, and perhaps even clandestine operations. Curiously, BdU deployed the ill-fated minelayer U-233 to Halifax at the end of June 1944 without the device. It did not survive.[14]

Hellriegel's U-543, the first of the six U-boats to appear during the interlude, triggered extensive "Operation Salmon" combined air/sea searches after its D/F detection 300 miles east of St John's on 24 December 1943. Pursued by a weakened Escort Group W-10 out of St John's that was now reduced to the three ancient "four stacker" destroyers HMCS *Columbia*, *Niagara*, and *Annapolis*, it patrolled without success between Flemish Cap and Sable Island until 10 January 1944. So attenuated was the Mid Ocean Escort Force (previously called the Newfoundland Escort Force) that the detection of U-543 caused C-in-C CNA to send the four frigates HMCS *Swansea*, *Stormont*, *Matane*, and *Montreal* to the first A/S rendezvous 900 miles from their home base in Halifax. Throughout the mission, U-543's Naxos radar warning device betrayed the presence of airborne 10-cm radar and kept the U-boat submerged.[15] Weber's U-845 operated close off Newfoundland from 25 January to the end of February. Schmoeckel's U-802 patrolled unsuccessfully off Halifax during March and April and again in the autumn of 1944; Zimmermann's U-548 patrolled close inshore off Newfoundland and Nova Scotia from 25 April until the end of May, while Bielfeld's U-1222 and Simmermacher's U-107 concentrated on the Nova Scotia coast in June as near as Chebucto Head. U-845 and U-1222 were sunk while returning home.

U-107 achieved nothing more than a devastating artillery attack on the American fishing schooner *Lark* after two torpedoes against it had failed. The 3.7-cm cannon jammed permanently after fifteen rounds. Canadian naval authorities subsequently described the attack as a gratuitous act of frustration after the U-boat's "innocuous sojourn in our waters."[16] The schooner's crew eventually returned to their riddled vessel and negotiated the 300-mile passage home to Boston. The attack and subsequent D/F detections initiated lengthy and intense searches by U.S. Task Group 22.6, the carrier USS *Wake Island* and five destroyer escorts, the Halifax Escort Force, and the RCAF. Schmoeckel's tactically unimportant first Canadian patrol provides unexpected documentation of technical and surgical skill in combat medicine. Whenever possible, BdU had tried to post a medical officer to one submarine in any operational area so that U-boats in contiguous zones in serious medical emergencies could seek relatively swift assistance. Perhaps for reasons of distance, a doctor had shipped aboard U-802 for this first Canadian patrol. U-boats carried basic medical supplies but nothing for major operations. Thus it was, as Schmoeckel recalls, that U-802 became the scene of what was "certainly one of the most difficult surgical interventions in U-boat history,"[17] when the doctor undertook to remove a crew member's injured eye. With surgical instruments fashioned especially for the operation by technical personnel in the U-boat's tiny machine shop, the doctor successfully completed the task on the table of the miniscule wardroom as U-802 lay on the bottom in 100 m of water off Halifax.

In strategic terms, according to the Operational Intelligence Centre in March 1944, the fact that "a larger proportion of the U-Boat effort" than in previous months "is to be devoted to the Canadian area [was] consistent with [German] apprehension of the strength and skill of [Allied] hunting forces" in European and North Atlantic waters.[18] Indeed, many U-boats faced extended voyages with relatively green crews and faulty torpedoes.

Faulty workmanship was not uncommon during these days when Germany was hard pressed for expertise in the armament industries. As in the case of U-845 in Canadian waters, or U-550 (Hänert), which sank the 11,017-ton American tanker *Pan Pennsylvania* on 16 April southeast of Nantucket Island and was in turn sunk that same day by surface forces, such vital technical failures contributed to the destruction of U-boats. They encountered increasing difficulty in defending themselves. The interlude missions of U-845 and U-548 offer particularly telling examples of how human factors, tactics, and technology often influenced the war at sea.

The 35-year-old Korvettekapitän Werner Weber of U-845 would have been considered an old man at this stage of the war in which the average age of a U-boat commanding officer was 24 years. A member of the 1932 graduating class, he had served in surface ships for a time before holding a staff position in Lorient. As far as can be ascertained, his sea time was limited. His crew apparently considered him too temperamental and inexperienced to command a U-boat. Indeed, they ascribed their U-boat's ultimate loss to his negligence while charging batteries on the surface. The U-boat's badge, a giraffe with the subscription *Kopf Immer Über Wasser* (Head always above water), may have seemed a convincing talisman. None the less, his crew may have judged him too severely, though events off St John's indicated he was prone to over-react.[19] Most of his total crew of fifty-four joined at Kiel just prior to the mission. The eldest and most experienced submariner, the engineering officer, 37-year-old Oberleutnant (Ing.) Otto Strunk, had served in U-47 under Prien "of Scapa Flow," and had later served as an instructor at the submarine training school at Danzig (Gdynia). He had been commissioned from the ranks. A 31-year-old medical officer, a 30-year-old chief stoker, and a chief telegrapher constituted the experienced hands. The remainder was a relatively green crew, on an average 22 years old. The Executive Officer, and therefore second-in-command, was a 21-year-old Reserve Sub-Lieutenant. Significantly, Canadians faced similar staffing and training problems. Canadian naval authorities complained at this time that the "standard of officers recommended for the Command Course [was] falling," and that the Radar Training Centre in Halifax, which had just then become fully operative, could only now rectify the "ignorance" and "inefficiency" that prevailed among personnel at sea.[20]

U-845, a 740-ton type IXC U-boat, commenced operations off Newfoundland on 25 January 1944 after an unusual number of mechanical failures. The engineering officer considered that it ought to have remained in port another eight weeks for repairs. The crew suffered from the same heavy weather and tumultuous seas that were pounding Allied convoys at this season. They suffered too, from the extreme cold for which they had inadequate clothing. Ice formed on the inside of the pressure hull in the bow compartment. In the light of subsequently captured personal diaries, written in contravention of Standing Orders, morale was low. Weber wished to attack ships in St John's harbour. He could not hope to enter the harbour itself, as U-518 had done in Wabana, for St John's lay at the end of a long, narrow channel, cordoned by boom defences. When approaching it from the east, as Weber would have learned from the German edition of the *Sailing Directions*, the bottom is uneven. These irregular depths made submariners exercise caution. Cape Spear, on which the Port War Signal Station stood, rose steeply to an elevation of 264 feet and served as a salient landfall for vessels approaching from the south or southeast. But Weber was particularly wary of possible minefields, and decided to wait at periscope depth until he could follow an Allied vessel through the suspected dangers. On 1 February he attempted to follow the corvette HMS *Hadleigh Castle*, en route to St John's from Argentia, and, while still submerged, ignominiously grounded on Old Harry, a rock with a depth of 28 feet situated 0.6 mile northeast of Cape Spear. U-845 must have hit hard, for, with rudders jammed amidships, she could only get clear after considerable time and anxiety by going full speed astern. With one rudder useless, two ruptured diving tanks, the caps of two forward torpedo tubes jammed, and the jumping wires snapped, Weber considered the damage sufficiently serious to abandon ship and scuttle. He surfaced and, after a patriotic speech to his men, went to the bridge carrying a large German flag. The Engineering Officer dissuaded him from giving up the U-boat while crew jury-rigged the steering gear. Trailing an oil slick, U-845 withdrew from the coast on the surface in broad daylight. Weber's continued exercise of command must have been tense in the extreme. BdU's brief record of Weber's cruise notes laconically that Weber "touched bottom" and "withdrew to seaward to repair the damage." That must have been the sum and substance of Weber's situation report. He was promoted during the mission.

Interrogation reports reaching Canadian Naval Intelligence five months later in July 1944 (and four months after U-845 had been lost off Ireland) caused consternation and embarrassment. Old Harry rock, on which the grounding and "surrender" scenario had taken place, lay but 800–900 yards from Cape Spear Battery. It was therefore a matter of "operational importance," as Canadian army authorities observed, that the radar log be checked.[21] RCN Combined Headquarters requested the battery's radar plots for 1, 5, and 9 February, when U-boat activity was known to have taken place in the vicinity. The army intoned a litany of woe. A fire in the diesel shed had put radar out of action on 1 February. Despite restoration of power by 5 February, radar obtained but a single receding target at 20 miles. A further target was picked up at dawn on 9 February at a range of about 2.5 miles, but "radar made no further cuts, going off the air at this time." This can only have meant that the radar operator ingenuously followed the precise letter of established procedure: operate only during the hours of darkness, or on days when visibility fell below 5000 yards. The fact that he had picked up a contact seemed to have made little difference. There is no record of whether Cape Spear Radar had informed either the navy or the air force of its contacts. According to the RCAF Meteorological Section, visibility had remained unlimited while U-845 lay surfaced off Old Harry. Five months later, army personnel offered the gratuitous recollection of snow flurries and "quite limited" visibility. The peacetime mentality in Canadian waters, of which U-boat commanders frequently spoke, must have prevailed at Cape Spear. U-845 experienced all the tactical advantages the Canadian coast could offer.

On 9 February, in position 10 miles east of Cape Spear, U-845 fired a total of five torpedoes in two spreads at the 7039-ton freighter SS *Kelmscott*, which had sailed from St John's escorted by HMS *Gentian* to join convoy HX-278. Fired at one-hour intervals, one torpedo of the first spread struck Kelmscott at 1300 GMT, and one from the second at 1404. All others failed. In the mistaken belief that its victim had sunk, U-845 withdrew. The Bangor HMCS *Sarnia* was ordered to undertake an anti-submarine search with two M/Ls, while the tug *Samsonia* towed the damaged *Kelmscott* back to port. Since the possibility of German mines could not be precluded, the abortive attack triggered the immediate closing of the Port of St John's, and the commencement of exploratory minesweeping operations. These were not suspended until three days later, on 12 February, under orders from Naval Service Headquarters.

U-845 withdrew to the safer waters of Flemish Cap, while ten Canadian warships (including W4 Group and EG9) and five RCAF aircraft undertook a concentrated antisubmarine sweep. Here, at 2030 GMT on 14 February, U-845 was sighted on the surface by RCAF Liberator Q of 10 BR Squadron "Gander," which immediately pressed home an attack from a range of 4 miles. Following established anti-aircraft procedure, Weber opposed the aircraft with as heavy an anti-aircraft fire as he could muster; the aircraft reported the flak as intense. The Liberator replied with its nose and upper turret guns, killing one of the German gun crew and seriously wounding another. Six depth charges detonated outside effective range without damaging the U-boat. Weber must have cursed the Kiel dockyard for having removed his quadruple anti-aircraft mount and having replaced it with the lesser fire power of the single 3.7-cm gun. Dockyard had had its reasons. German authorities still regarded Canadian waters as relatively quiet, and in any event U-boats operating in the air-intensive English Channel and Biscay zones had a higher priority for the armament. Now, however, as the Liberator made its second approach, the 3.7-cm gun jammed, leaving U-845 virtually defenceless. The aircraft's last two depth charges detonated right beside the conning tower. U-845 left a large oil slick on the surface as it crash-dived out of control and reached what survivors later described as a "great depth" before regaining trim. The Liberator patrolled the area for an hour or more without further contact. During U-845's third close approach to the coast, Weber followed the 6090-ton SS *Pachesham*, which had left St John's alone on 15 February for Bay Bulls. He fired several torpedoes that detonated harmlessly against the rocks offshore. His quarry escaped. Weather now shifted targets out of Weber's zone. Abnormal ice conditions in St John's harbour and approaches had curtailed naval operations and shipping almost completely from 26 February, obliging all naval ships to resort to Argentia until the Port of St John's reopened. As Staff Officer Operations, FONF, somewhat whimsically reported: "These conditions also frustrated the Air Defence Corps [civilian onshore watchers] who lapsed into complete hibernation."[22] Clearly, it was now time for U-845 to return to home base in Lorient. Yet, as it shaped course towards the Biscay, BdU diverted it to intercept the forty-ship eastbound convoy SC-154. This would be the final task.

On the afternoon of 1 March 1944, HMS *Forester* led the main portion of Escort Group C-1 out of the secondary port of Argentia, in order to rendezvous with SC-154.[23] The group consisted of the destroyer HMCS *St. Laurent*, and the corvettes HMCS *Giffard*, *Regina*, and *Fredericton*. A day later they were joined by the Senior Officer (Cdr J. Byron, RNR) in the destroyer HMCS *Assiniboine*. Affectionately known as "Bones," the *Assiniboine* had gained a degree of renown by ramming and sinking U-210 on 6 August 1942 in the North Atlantic while escorting convoy SC-94.[24] Shepherding its charges through the rising gale of 3–4 March, which severely handicapped the escorts in their almost constant round-up of stragglers, EG C-1 was completed by the frigate HMCS *Valleyfield* and the corvette HMCS *Halifax*. Two of these warships would not survive the war. *Valleyfield* would fall victim to U-548 south of Cape Race on 6 May 1944 on her return from the UK, and *Regina* to U-667 on 8 August off Trevose Head, Cornwall.

Heavy weather buffeted the convoy along almost the entire route, threatening to scatter the ships. It also deprived the convoy of three escorts during a refuelling operation that disabled HMCS *Regina*. By a stroke of ill fortune, *Regina*'s steadying line fouled her screw in treacherous quartering seas and she was towed to Horta (Azores), first by the rescue ship *Dundee* and finally by the salvage tug *Salvonia*, escorted by *Valleyfield*.[25] On rejoining the convoy after recovery operations far astern, HMCS *St. Laurent* managed to pick up ill-defined skywave skips betraying the presence of U-boat transmissions from distant submarines. On the basis of intelligence gained by Bletchley Park's decryption of German Enigma signals, C-in-C Western Approaches had meanwhile diverted SC-154 to avoid suspected U-boat dispositions. The U-boat threat thus seemed sufficiently severe to warrant the diversion of the newly formed EG-9, which was on passage from Halifax to Londonderry with convoy HX-280. As fate would have it, an intense fire aboard the straggling 7700-ton Swedish motor ship SS *San Francisco* would draw HMCS *Halifax*, *St. Laurent*, and *Owen Sound* far astern of the convoy to assist. This later placed them in a favourable position to overtake U-845 as it shadowed the main body of the convoy. "Huff-Duff" would lead them to a kill.

U-845's search had brought it well astern of convoy SC-154 on the morning of 10 March 1944. Attempting to gain contact, it continued submerged for several hours at an exhausting four-fifths speed on electric power. Weber ought to have followed the more usual procedure of chasing the convoy on the surface under diesel power, but he doubtless feared the air cover to which German submarines were prone. At 1400 he informed his crew that the convoy lay ahead. By this time, HMCS *St. Laurent* (LCdr George H. Stephen, RCNR) and *Owen Sound* (LCdr J.M. Watson, RCNR) had regained much of the distance lost by having assisted SS *San Francisco*, and had closed to about 30 miles on the convoy's port quarter.[26] *St. Laurent*'s "Huff-Duff" interception of a U-boat transmission placed U-845 dead ahead. With HF/DF confirmed by both *Assiniboine* and *Swansea* in the convoy's van, the senior officer in *Assiniboine* initiated the routine hunting procedure of "cataracting" an escort down the bearing to a depth of 20 miles. The contact eluded detection.

The attempt of U-845 to close with the convoy in such haste severely jeopardized its tactical position. When the Engineering Officer reported that the batteries were 60 per cent discharged, Weber rose to periscope depth, saw nothing, and surfaced to charge his batteries. At 1624 hours, *St. Laurent*'s signalman, Walter Gallinger of Toronto, sighted an unidentified object about 8 miles ahead, just 2 miles from the "Huff-Duff" fix. *St. Laurent* made her sighting report at 1630. U-845 had only been on the surface about 15 minutes, too briefly to sustain further prolonged action submerged, when it, too, made a sighting: "destroyers" were overhauling it at high speed. Having been observed by the approaching ships for barely a minute, U-845 dived without having charged batteries. *St. Laurent*, her suspicions now aroused, thrust ahead at 23 knots. *Owen Sound* followed at an unaccountably slow speed of 12–15 knots. Neither ship streamed "Cat Gear" against the new acoustic torpedoes ("Gnats") that Weber might have fired if he had not been preoccupied with his escape. For this neglect the ships were criticized by Commodore (D) Western Approaches, who noted that *St. Laurent* was the only ship of the group to have been introduced to anti-Gnat tactics at the Tactical Table at Londonderry. This was one of the latest technological devices for teaching tactics. Whether the others had been given any instruction on how to use the new tactical equipment when it was put aboard at the Canadian base remains unclear. *St. Laurent* had, in fact, been exercising her anti-Gnat procedure daily throughout the voyage.

The Cat Gear was a Canadian-designed drogue similar to the Foxer used by the British to "out fox" the U-boats in the English Channel and the North Sea.[27] This new and disarmingly simple device constituted the Allied response to the German T-5 *Zaunkönig* acoustic torpedo. It consisted of a metal rig in the shape of a large crossbow towed by any escort fearing attack. Pulled through the water at speed it caused the two crossbars to vibrate or "chatter" violently. This produced a shrill tone that drowned out the lower-frequency noises of the ship's engines and screws, and thus decoyed the German torpedo. The Cat Gear could produce an unnerving effect on a U-boat's crew. Its principal disadvantage lay in creating so much noise as to obliterate the sounds emanating from the enemy as well. This, the German commanders soon construed, explained why the "squealing circular saw," as they frequently described it, was switched on and off during a search. The attacking ships themselves needed moments of silence for listening. Such silences made them vulnerable.

Asdic conditions during the hunt for U-845 were ideal, and the sea was calm. At 1647 hours, *St. Laurent* observed 300 yards away the tell-tale "swirl" marking the spot where the U-boat had dived and picked up an unequivocally clear asdic contact with both whistle and hydrophone effects. Standing too close for an attack herself, she now ran out 1000 yards to direct *Owen Sound* over the contact. At 1657 hours, *Owen Sound* dropped a pattern of ten depth charges. This was the first of a series of depth charge and Hedgehog attacks that would harass U-845 for the next five-and-one-half hours. The Hedgehog marked a crucial turning point in the development of antisubmarine warfare. It was an ahead-throwing weapon. Its multiple-spigot mortar could throw a ring of twenty-four torpex-filled antisubmarine contact bombs ahead of the ship, thus enabling her to engage a submerged submarine during the high-speed approach run without losing asdic contact. Though this particular attack brought nothing more to the surface than a stunned whale, later attacks drew debris and heavy diesel oil. U-845 had by this time reached a safe depth of some 180 m (540 feet). By 1730 the attackers assessed that the U-boat had reached an extreme depth of 700 feet. This was astute. Ever since the first pattern, subsequent attacks had fallen close to U-845, shaking it up considerably and on several occasions driving it to depths well below 200 m (600 feet). Several leaks developed, the most serious in the diesel room. All the while the crew could hear the eerie sounds of probing asdic. At one point, while attempting to shake off the pursuers, U-845 attempted to release SBT (submarine bubble target) anti-asdic decoys, which the Germans called Bold or Aphrodite. But the external-water pressure was so great that the decoy could not be ejected from the firing tube. U-845 released a large quantity of oil during its ordeal, to give the impression of having been badly damaged. "We kept up the depth charge diet," *St. Laurent*'s captain later observed, "and the Nazis in the U-Boat way down there must have had an uncomfortable time of it."[28] In fact, it must have been sheer horror.

After concluding that the U-boat lay deep, *St. Laurent* directed *Owen Sound* to commence Operation Observant. Taking the U-boat's last-known position as the centre or datum of a 2-mile square, the hunter undertook a clockwise search. *St. Laurent* now slipped into a stern position to direct a "creeping attack" as *Forester* (LCdr J.A. Burnett, RN) arrived at 1815 hours to relieve *Owen Sound*. A "creeping attack" was a slow attack against a deep target, and had the advantage of maintaining constant asdic contact with the U-boat without betraying the presence or position of the actual attacker. It was a type of "leap frog" or "hop-scotch" played by two attacking vessels. The directing ship would maintain contact with the target while the directed ship took up station astern with asdic switched off. This would deprive the U-boat of any opportunity of assessing either the number of opponents or the assailant's range. Once the directing ship had steadied up on the same course as the submarine, the attacking ship would pass close by her and take up a position between the two. The directing ship then conned the attacker right on top of the unwitting submarine and instructed it to drop its pattern of depth charges.

St. Laurent now assessed that if a creeping attack were to be used in this instance, it should begin quickly, as it would be dark by 2030. A night attack could be a risky business. As the convoy summary observed: "The ships would have to show lights [in order] to take ranges on each other, not to mention the fact that the U-Boat might well elude two hunters in the dark hours and escape on the surface." *Forester* carried out her "creep" at 1922 hours, followed in quick succession by *St. Laurent* dropping her twenty-two charges. A line of bubbles, and underwater explosions heard in *St. Laurent*'s engine room, suggested successful attacks. Ships lost contact soon after and commenced another Operation Observant.

No sooner had *St. Laurent* regained contact after a 20-minute search, than *Forester* reported her asdic defective. It was now up to *St. Laurent* alone to maintain contact. By 2130 a bright moon had risen above the clouds. Though another creeping attack would have been possible, the hunters deemed it wiser to "stooge around" to await the arrival of HMCS

Swansea. Under the command of Cdr Clarence A. King, RCNR, of Oliver, British Columbia, who as captain of HMCS *Oakville* had thrice rammed and then sunk U-94 on 27 August 1942 in the Caribbean, the *Swansea* joined Operation Observant at 2205, while *St. Laurent* held contact on the U-boat's tail, course 215°, at 2.5 knots. It was a significant feature of the relationship between Canada and Great Britain that a Royal Navy commanding officer, though junior in rank to his Canadian counterparts, would none the less be Senior Officer of the combined naval force. Thus, despite Commander King's arrival in *Swansea*, HMS *Forester* remained officially in tactical command.

A sudden shift in circumstances scuttled their deliberate plan to initiate yet another creeping attack. After twisting and turning to escape its pursuers for six harrowing hours, U-845 suddenly broke surface at 2234, just 1400 yards ahead of *St. Laurent*, and on *Forester*'s starboard bow.[29] *Swansea* at this time was 1 mile astern. The U-boat's batteries had suddenly gone dead, leaving it no alternative but to blow all tanks and attempt to escape on the surface. Racing off at "extreme emergency speed" (*3X Alle Kraft*) with superchargers on its two nine-cylinder MAN diesels engaged, it rapidly opened the range. U-845 managed close to 21 knots on sometimes violently evasive courses. *St. Laurent* opened fire with her 4.7-inch forward "A" turret gun and all oerlikons that would bear. Surprisingly, she did not stream her anti-Gnat gear until 17 minutes after the U-boat had surfaced. *Swansea* never did stream her gear. *Forester*, carrying no anti-acoustic gear whatever, held back from the chase for 15 minutes before surging ahead at a supposedly "safe" speed of 28 knots.

Once in position, all ships engaged the U-boat. In the seeming confusion of shells, it was next to impossible to judge the fall of shot. In the opinion of Commodore (D) Western Approaches, both *St. Laurent* and *Swansea* were ideal Gnat targets for 45 minutes of the chase; *Forester* had been overly cautious, and should have placed herself with all haste on the U-boat's beam. Weber in U-845 did in fact fire two torpedoes – but without result. A third failed even to leave the tube. The one 3.7-cm gun on the lower "Wintergarten", which had failed him in the air attack off Newfoundland, jammed again, leaving the gun crew to man the twin 20-mm guns for a brief 2 minutes. "I knew I had him cold," LCdr Stephen of Halifax commented, "and that this time he would not get away." Bearings and ranges were now passed from *St. Laurent*'s type 271P radar to the gun director with such precision that, during the opening five salvoes, she scored three direct hits, which killed the U-boat's Captain, First Lieutenant, and the entire bridge watch. Canadian radar personnel estimated ten to fourteen probable hits from the 4.7-inch "A" turret gun at ranges from 2000 to 3000 yards. In the words of gunner Fred Little of Victoria, British Columbia, in charge of one of *St. Laurent*'s 4.7-inch guns: "The first shot exploded right on the U-Boat's conning tower. Our gun's crew was dead on. Able Seaman Peter Scott of Toronto, the gun layer, was in HMCS *Ottawa* when she was torpedoed [and sunk by U-91 on 14 September 1942] and I guess he was looking for revenge. If he was, he certainly got it."

St. Laurent had meanwhile outstripped *Swansea* and was preparing to ram U-845, when the Senior Officer in *Forester* discouraged the idea, as the battle seemed about to be won by surface gunnery. *St. Laurent* now took another initiative by passing up the U-boat's port side at about 100 yards, with all guns bearing and dropping a shallow pattern of ten depth charges ahead of her. The U-boat appeared to be on fire at the base of the conning tower, and her 3.7-cm forward gun was hanging over the side. As Cdr Stephen commented thereafter: "We passed very close to him with all our guns blazing. Even the boys on the quarterdeck were firing revolvers, bren guns and sten guns, and tossing empty shell cases at the enemy. When opportunity came, I passed ahead of the U-Boat and let go a pattern of charges. He ran right into the explosions and was lifted clean out of the water. Then the Nazis began to abandon ship."

The U-boat crew, now under the virtual command of the Engineering Officer, had in fact been preparing to quit their vessel before the final explosion struck. For as soon as the diesels began to overheat the officer recognized the pointlessness of further combat. Having given the order to abandon ship, he himself remained below in order to scuttle his U-boat, and managed to escape through the galley hatch before she sank. *St. Laurent* had meanwhile opened the range to undertake a precautionary Observant as *Forester* and *Swansea* lowered whalers to rescue the survivors. Lt Ian Macdonald, First Lieutenant of *Swansea* and at the time in charge of one of the rescue whalers, described the desolation: "When we approached the submarine, we saw that half her conning tower had been shot away. It looked like a sieve. The captain and two others were lying dead there. No one in that conning tower during the battle could have lived. The survivors we picked up were all in good shape, but they did show considerable panic while floundering around in the sea." U-845 sank at 2338 hours in position 48° 47′ N, 21° 02′ W. Forty-five of her crew of fifty-four survived. *Swansea* had twenty-three, *Forester* had seventeen, and *St. Laurent* five. On regaining convoy SC-154 next day, *St. Laurent*'s Yeoman Ford flashed by aldis lamp a 250-word summary of the attack to Senior Officer of C-1. It concluded in part: "*St. Laurent* closed at 23 knots by orders from *Forester* to finish him, doing same as he passed down my starboard side firing all armament[,] bringing him to a dead stop and the battle was over. I have five prisoners. The A/S [asdic] worked tres bon [sic]." *St. Laurent* alone had expended 119 rounds of 4.7-inch shells, 1440 rounds of oerlikon, and 1410 rounds of small-arms ammunition. For the survivors of U-845, the tensions of submarine warfare and the anxieties of this abortive mission were now over. The task of killing the U-boat that had tried to keep its "head always above water" had been, in the words of *St. Laurent*'s First Lieutenant, "like an old-time sea pirates fight and we enjoyed it thoroughly." Despite his criticisms of the attack, Commodore (D) Western Approaches remarked that nothing could "detract from the offensive spirit shown by the Allied vessels and the weapon efficiency." Indeed, in "this first action for a very long time against a U-Boat by ships of a Group solely engaged in Close Support work, the careful handling of the hunt and the patient approach before the attacks on a deep target [were] most satisfactory." All parts of ship had reacted promptly, with consistency and precision. The Canadian victory would soon be avenged.

U-548 (Oblt. z. See Zimmermann) departed Germany's Norwegian base at Narvik under minesweeper escort on 23 March 1944 in company with U-1230 (Hans Hilbig) and U-244 (Ruprecht Fischer) on its captain's first operational mission. It had left Kiel-Wik two days earlier in a hailstorm for anti-aircraft exercises, and was now to operate as a weather station south of Iceland before seeking targets on the Newfoundland Banks. Zimmermann knew that U-845 (Weber) had been operating off Newfoundland from January through March, but had perhaps not yet learned of the U-boat's loss. Reports from U-539 (Lauterbach-Emden), which had entered the same area during the later weeks of the tour, and U-802 (Schmoeckel), which had been on station off Halifax throughout the month, had been encouraging. The three-month voyage of U-548 would cover a patrol track of 8004.6 nautical miles, and fetch but a single victim. Significantly, it spent 3167 miles, or 40 per cent, of the mission submerged; this bore witness not only to the improvements in U-boat technology since 1942, but to the perceived threat from air reconnaissance, surface vessels, and D/F stations. Air attacks punctuated Zimmermann's frequent weather broadcasts, and provided ample demonstration of the efficacy of the Allied D/F system. Zimmermann knew he had been caught in the enemy cross-bearings, and was doubtless relieved on intercepting BdU's signal ordering Hossenfelder in U-342 to assume his duties. Zimmermann's lengthy weather signals amounted to cumulative self-betrayal, for by the time he had sent his tenth, his zone was virtually criss-crossed by Allied D/F bearings. Aircraft from RCAF Squadron 10 sank Hossenfelder on Zimmermann's station on 17 April, one day after he had signalled what would have been Zimmermann's eleventh report.[30]

When U-548 reached the Canadian zone known by German code as "Bruno Bruno," BdU authorized it to undertake free manoeuvres subject only to the hazards of ice. Supported by earlier intelligence describing St John's importance as a turn-around base for both deep-sea escorts and coastal convoys, Zimmermann decided on 24 April 1944 to "at first steer on Cape St. Francis in order to run from there along the coast at periscope depth with the ice and current so as to stand off St. John's by day" (KTB). In severely limited visibility and heavy seas, U-548 depended upon the GHG hydrophone, which enabled it to "hear" farther than it could have seen, even in clear weather. Zimmermann's first reliable navigational fix – the cross-bearings of the lights of Cape St Francis and Baccalieu Head – placed him 8 miles off shore on 1 May 1944. From here he ranged in broad zigzag patterns from the northernmost reaches of Conception Bay to Ferryland Head, from 2 to 16 miles off the coast, his Naxos and Borkum radar detectors emitting sustained warning tones, and the sea occasionally filled with asdic pulses and hydrophone sounds. Reported U-boat sightings by aircraft, none of which actually referred to U-548 as it turns out, triggered the standard combined air/sea Operation Salmon search, which drew vessels from both the Newfoundland Escort Force and Escort Group C-5 then accompanying convoy ONS-233.[31] Gulf forces were now chasing false scents the RCAF had reported in the St Lawrence as well.

Aircraft reports constituted a vital source of operational intelligence that had to be checked out, however costly in terms of men, ships, and aircraft the searches might have been. Canadian forces could not permit themselves the false security of not having reacted at all. Yet in reacting to these alarms, they proved the correctness of Admiral Dönitz's doctrine that the presence of U-boats pinned down forces the Allies might otherwise have deployed elsewhere. Paradoxically, such intense surveillance effectively reduced the U-boat's chances of success, and in the case of U-548 thwarted the Boat as much as the heavy ice floes and bergs near the coast. Zimmermann's unsuccessful surfaced Gnat acoustic torpedo attack against the damaged SS *Baltrover* under "four stacker" destroyer escort on 3 May 1944 led to a sharp exchange of machine-gun fire with a Liberator, and a haunting A/S search as U-548 lay on the bottom off Cape Broyle, some 4 miles northeast of Ferryland Head Light.

The procedure for waiting out an attack on the bottom was fraught with tension. Only the minimum watch on deck remained closed up at their posts. All lighting, ancillary machinery, and equipment were switched off to conserve batteries. All hands not immediately required for duty withdrew to their bunks to lie quietly, breathe slowly, and conserve oxygen. Not even the one toilet for the fifty-seven crew could be flushed; the pumps would create too much noise, and in any event could not function against the great external pressure beyond 90 m depth. Such was the scene as U-548 listened to her intended victim turned hunter overhead. The sound of the destroyer circling the U-boat's position at high speed was clearly audible throughout the Boat. And then came a new sound, one the crew had not encountered before: the high-pitched, undulating turbine-like sound that made Zimmermann suspect a towed decoy against acoustic torpedoes. He was hearing Cat Gear. Surrounded by all the sounds of a concerted search, the crew of U-548 waited for a depth-charge attack, which ought to have occurred but which quite inexplicably never materialized. Their would-be attacker, HMS *Hargood*, with a completely inexperienced crew, faded away to the north, having neither attacked, dropped scare charges, nor even switched on asdic. Within a couple of hours, Zimmermann's hydrophones picked up two distant fading contacts, which he identified as destroyers streaming torpedo decoys. If we judge by the often erratic patrol track of the next few days, Zimmermann would seem not to have had the slightest idea where the best hunting might now be found. Nor could he navigate accurately. Fog obscured the coast, and the radio beacons upon which his predecessors in 1942 had relied had now changed frequencies and signals. He therefore shaped course for the well-defined bottom contours of a point south of Cape Race, in order to position his U-boat and then navigate by depth-sounder. Thus, by sheer chance, his dead-reckoning wanderings southeast of Newfoundland brought him into the path of Escort Group C-1.

The group consisted of six Canadian warships: the frigate HMCS *Valleyfield* (LCdr D.T. English, RCNR), and the corvettes HMCS *Halifax* (Lt M.F. Oliver, RCNR), *Frontenac* (LCdr E.T.F. Wennberg, RCNVR), *Giffard* (LCdr C. Peterson, RCNR), *Edmundston* (LCdr R.D. Barrett), and *Fredericton* (LCdr J.E. Harrington, RCNVR). Under the tactical command of the Senior Officer, Commander J. Byron, RNR, who was riding in HMCS *Valleyfield*, and was affectionately known as "The Brain," it had departed Londonderry on 27 April 1944 with the seventy-five ship westbound convoy ONM-234. The convoy crossed the Atlantic without incident, HMCS *Fredericton* picking up its only straggler on 3 May and proceeding independently with her to Newfoundland. The uneventful crossing to Halifax continued to the Western Ocean Meeting Point (WESTOMP) some 200 miles south of Cape Race, Newfoundland, where at 1736 hours local time on 6 May the convoy was passed to the Western Local Escort Force, HMCS *St. Boniface*, Senior Officer. Escort Group C-1 now zigzagged northward for St John's in line abreast 4000 yards apart in the order (left to right) *Halifax*, *Frontenac*, *Valleyfield*, *Giffard*, and *Edmundston*. The latest enemy disposition reports placed the nearest enemy submarine about 150 miles "east or south of Cape Race." But, as C-1 had now passed on responsibility for its convoy to W-4 Group, so a surviving officer observed, quite "typically everyone's thoughts had turned to getting to Newfy-John for a bit of a lay-off."[32] At 2000 hours local time (2300 GMT) Lt Ian Tate in *Valleyfield* took over a watch that "had all the prospects of being a most pleasant one, with only ice to bother about by way of immediate dangers." Both the captain and the Senior Officer "looked very weary, particularly the Captain [who] had been up on his feet almost continuously with the fog ... for forty-eight hours just prior to handing over the Convoy." Now, however, the weather was clear, the moon bright with a light sea running.

The Senior Officer's final order to cease zigzagging at 2330 (GMT) led subsequent investigators to infer a degree of laxness that did not exist in fact. The subsequent Board of Inquiry, in this case a far more casual and informal investigation than the written records would indicate, might have thought otherwise if Lt Tate had mentioned the substance of a conversation he had overheard between the Senior Officer and the captain on the bridge. Looking down into the troughs of the waves they could see dangerous growlers, "great masses of water-logged ice," which were obscured when looking forward into the wind and the darkness. Thus, they reasoned, the sudden appearance of a growler among zigzagging ships might necessitate a sudden and independent evasive "zig" at the very moment when the antitorpedo manoeuvring pattern actually called for a "zag" and cause risk of ships colliding. And in any event, the enemy disposition reports seemed too vague to be of any real concern. The Senior Officer was doubtless equally worried by something which, though reported initially, was inexplicably filtered out of later reports to higher authority: the radar equipment of both HMCS *Valleyfield* and *Frontenac* (on the latter's beam), unreliable throughout the voyage, had now become completely defective.[33]

On this night, Lt Tate observed that *Valleyfield*'s "RX/C was as unreliable as ever." This was in theory an excellent type of radar, but in practice a "lemon." In this case it had even failed to "paint" a large iceberg along a known bearing and within a range of 3 miles; on another, its bearing of the nearest corvette on the beam was $30°$ in error. Lt Tate managed to keep an eye on the farthest ships on either side of the formation by resorting to the notoriously bad SW1C radar, although it was their job to keep station on him in the senior ship. In actual practice, therefore, the ship had no tactical radar. The sea was filled with icebergs and growlers, useful camouflage for schnorkels and periscopes. Indeed, there were so many echoes cluttering the radar screen that steering a straight course could only increase the equipment's efficiency.

Ironically, the ships had a tactical advantage of which they were unaware: the U-boat's defective Wanze frequency-scanning radar warning device was insensitive to their radar beams. Thus the five ships of C-1 steamed directly into U-548's path – not zigzagging, partially blind, and not streaming Cat Gear. And, of course, had they streamed anti-Gnat Cat Gear in contravention of normal practice prior to gaining contact with an enemy submarine, the decoy's noise would have seriously impaired asdic detection. The vital blind spot where U-548 would accidently emerge lay precisely in the overlapping zones the radars of *Valleyfield* and *Frontenac* would otherwise have covered. None the less, in Tate's words at the time, "everything [else] seemed in order ... the ships in company appeared to be keeping quite good station, and it looked like clear sailing to the Crow's Nest [officer's club in St John's] the following evening." Oblt. zur See Zimmermann was also feeling happy during Tate's watch. Admiral Dönitz had just signalled personal congratulations on the birth of a daughter (KTB).

Zimmerman's U-548 was proceeding on the surface in "moderate visibility with bright moonlight" (KTB) at 2300 hours, when it sighted a rapidly moving shadow fine on the bow. Unaware of any escort formation, he dashed forward to the classical advance position until he identified his target as a "USA escort." HMCS *Valleyfield* began to close the range despite Zimmermann's maximum speed, thus forcing U-548 to attack somewhat earlier than anticipated. Fearing the moonlight, Zimmermann crash-dived in a spiral descent for a submerged attack at periscope depth and ran toward his target. Only now did his hydrophones reveal the sounds of other escorts. Standing at an extremely tight firing angle of 5 degrees at 2332 hours, Zimmermann fired one of the new T-5 Zaunkönig acoustic torpedoes at *Valleyfield*'s bow, now 1500 m distant. Zimmermann immediately dived deeper and sheered off to starboard. This was a routine evasive action to protect himself from his own torpedo which might potentially turn on him if his depth and noise level corresponded with that of the target calibration. A disciplined routine had meanwhile prevailed aboard *Valleyfield*, where the asdic ratings now carried out their precautionary searches 80° either side of the bow, and the asdic loudspeaker pinged away comfortingly on the darkened bridge. Suddenly, Lt Tate noticed the pointer on the Captain's Bearing Indicator hover around "Red 65." This indicated that the hydrophone operator below decks had apparently heard something unusual 65° on the port bow, and so trained the oscillator in the direction of the sound in order to investigate more closely. The loudspeaker immediately began emitting a high-speed ticking noise, almost a steady hum. All this took but a few seconds. Before the hydrophone operator could report the contact, or the officer-of-the watch react to the Bearing Indicator, Zimmermann's torpedo tore into *Valleyfield*'s boiler room after a run of 3 minutes and 12 seconds. It was now 2335 local time on 6 May 1944. In Lt Tate's words,

a terrific explosion shattered the calm night air. It hit amidships, port side, and stopped us in our tracks. I looked back to see bits of twisted metal flying skywards in all directions. The noise was awful – the roar of escaping steam, tearing metal, churning water, and crashing superstructure. [Lt Cashman] "Guns" [Mason] rang the Action Station bell, to snap those who were momentarily stunned out of it, and I rang up the Engine Room to tell them to get out. Too late, I afterwards found out ... Looking aft again, I could see the mainmast staggering about as the after half of the ship wallowed. She had broken in half with the force of the explosion! Luckily, the boilers never blew up. Cries and shouts could vaguely be heard above the din, as the after part began to settle a little by the head. All this happened in a split second.

Within seconds of the explosion, the severed halves of the vessel began twisting into the sea in opposite directions. Tate held on to the now almost horizontal binnacle to keep from being thrown over the side as the captain, followed by the navigator, Lt "Jaker" Warren, emerged from the chartroom and ordered the crew to abandon ship. As Warren recalled:

She was rolling over so far it was simply a matter of stepping off the bottom into the water. Everything was very orderly. There was no panic. It took the front half about a minute and a half to go down. She reared up steeply, almost vertical, like a horse shying away from a snake, and wavered a couple of times. For a few seconds we thought it was going to topple over on us, and swam away as fast as we could.

Sucked downward, Lt Tate burst to the surface to watch the final seconds of the bow section. Reporters subsequently inflated his terse reflections into an uncharacteristic expression of bravado. In the words of the slick journalistic account: "It was like something in a horror movie, or a bad nightmare. I did a Johnny Weismuller out of there with the fastest spurt of swimming in my life. I managed to get clear, but passed out. My lifejacket saved my life."[34] Other survivors, as well, alluded to images from the movies as a measure of the unreality of their experiences.

Following the swift separation and sinking of the forward section of *Valleyfield* in approximately 90 seconds, survivors of the cataclysmic explosion struggled to abandon the vessel's shattered remains and to survive the freezing sea. The stern held for about 5–6 minutes longer. During these last precarious moments three ratings ran aft in order to withdraw the primers (pistols) from the depth charges. Whether lessons had been learned from the fate of the torpedoed HMCS *Charlottetown*, which had died on her own explosives, thus killing many crewmen in the water, or whether it was spontaneous initiative, is not clear. However that may be, the three men – Leading Seaman Donald Henry "Dave" Brown of Windsor, Able Seaman M.E. "Merv" Woods of Montreal, and Able Seaman David Edgar "Dave" Brown of Lulu Island, British Columbia – sacrificed themselves in a courageous but needless endeavour. Unknown to them, *Valleyfield*'s charges had been fitted with the new Mark VII and

Mark IX pistols, and would only explode at depths greater than 300 feet. This meant in fact that the depth charges were virtually harmless. Such ironies are inherent in war. The gallant men received posthumous honours.

Conditions below decks must have been chaotic and terror filled for many. Not one man escaped the Stoker Petty Officers' or Engine Room Artificers' Mess. Only one seaman came up from below; Cdr Byron failed to get out of his cabin in the fore part of the ship. Several sailors lost their footing on the steeply canting decks and hurtled to their deaths deep in the torn interior. Some managed to escape the writhing vessel, only to face the frigid temperature of an oil-covered sea. Thus, Steward William Daubs, who had been asleep in the after overflow mess when the explosion knocked him out of his hammock, landed on the catwalk over the engine room and later floated clear on a tightly lashed "seven seas" hammock. Ordinary Telegrapher Richard Snider was literally flushed out of the hatch of the flooded bow compartment. Dressed in his one-piece "zoot suit" weather gear, which saved his life despite severe exposure, Yeoman of Signals Irving J. Kaplan bolted out of the escape hatch and walked over the ship's bottom into the sea.

As the stern went down, crew in a Carley float roused themselves into singing "For She's a Jolly Good Fellow." Some of the singers would be dead within the half hour. The grim joviality, an ambiguous mix of pride and tenacity, of gallows humour and despair, drew men together. Less than one-third of the ship's company had managed to abandon ship. The icy sea lay thick with oil, wreckage, hammocks, lifebelts and all sorts of debris. Men hunched on overcrowded Carley floats, crowded waist deep in scramble nets hung between floats, or clung desperately to the sides. Others floated away unconscious. Many succumbed. Two men – Lt John Carleton "Tony" Flath of Medicine Hat and Signalman Victor Albert Ward of Montreal – choked to death on the oil that clogged their beards.

The crew of U-548 could meanwhile hear the sounds of *Valleyfield*'s death. It had begun with the hiss of the torpedo leaving the tube, was signalled by a "very loud muffled explosion," followed by the abrupt silencing of the victim's engines and screw noise. Sounds of "powerful bursting and cracking" were accentuated by "1 minute and 32 seconds [of] sustained roaring, hissing and cracking of bulkheads." They could hear "large parts of the ship crashing on to the sea bed at 70 m" depth, and gained "the impression as though the destroyer [sic] were falling right on top" of them (KTB).

The remaining vessels of C-1 were slow to respond. An assumption that the Senior Officer had intended to "engage in some exercises" at about this time, as Tate recalls, may have been in part responsible. Nevertheless, at 0235 GMT, 2335 local time, the moment when the sinking officially occurred, the officer of the watch (OOW) aboard HMCS *Edmundston*, 4 miles off *Valleyfield*'s starboard beam on the wing of the formation, had heard an explosion that his asdic operator reported. But as the explosion had not seemed particularly violent, he paid little attention to it. *Frontenac*'s OOW noticed a pall of black smoke over *Valleyfield*, but "wasn't surprised" as it had been his "experience that after dropping charges the boiler room usually makes smoke." Thinking that *Valleyfield* had attacked a contact, he "didn't at the time entertain thoughts of there having been a torpedoing." However, even 5 minutes later when *Edmundston*'s radar operator reported that *Valleyfield* had apparently dropped out of station and was difficult to detect, *Edmundston*'s OOW made three false assumptions: that the ship had left station in order to investigate a subsequently doubtful contact well astern; that she had dropped a depth charge; and that she would doubtless regain station in due course.[35] Had that in fact been the case, the subsequent Board of Inquiry reasoned, *Valleyfield* would certainly have signalled her A/S contact and intentions. And in any event, the OOW of the *Edmundston* should have concluded that unless proven otherwise, an explosion always spelled trouble. *Edmundston* should have investigated immediately. With the loss of *Valleyfield*, the commanding officer of HMCS *Edmundston* automatically became Senior Officer of Escort Group C-1. Yet, as HMCS *Giffard* – on *Valleyfield*'s immediate starboard beam at 4000 yards – was the first on the spot and the first to obtain a complete picture of events, it was she who assumed temporary tactical command. Reaction, however, was less than immediate.

HMCS *Giffard* had seen the blast column rising to twice the height of *Valleyfield*'s bridge but only twigged to a problem after having failed for some minutes to raise *Valleyfield* by visual signal and radio telephone. Only when actually investigating the frigate's last known position, did she sight the calcium flares of its survivors. *Edmundston* had heard the explosion, but, in the captain's words, had paid "no particular attention" to it. *Giffard* advised the group of the sinking and ordered Operation Observant. As the ships moved into position, Zimmerman's crew in U-548 heard "three high-speed destroyer sounds" overhead as their U-boat escaped slowly along the bottom toward the southwest, listening to the "very loud, sustained shrill tone of the circular saw" (KTB) emanating from the Cat Gear the Canadians had begun to stream as defence against further acoustic torpedoes. Zimmermann discerned the search and anti-Gnat technique at every stage, noting especially how the escorts "sporadically switched off their [Cat Gear] drogues, presumably in order to be able to listen with hydrophones" (KTB). Closing the target's position, *Edmundston* fired Hedgehog ahead-throwing A/S bombs in 50 fathoms despite the proximity of survivors in the water. Officer in Charge Tactics in Ottawa judged the attack an excellent move under the circumstances. It was vital to destroy the one U-boat Canadian authorities knew to be in the area. D/F would indeed track it for some three weeks after the event. The first "depth charge" attack struck at a "medium range" as U-548 touched bottom in 83 m, where it lay quietly for almost three hours (KTB). During all this time, it heard no asdic. On two occasions, however, "destroyers with circular saws" crossed directly overhead while "several series of detonations" occurred in "the deep water" below the ledge on which U-548 was resting. At 0318 local time, U-548 lifted off the bottom and headed dead slow in the direction of Halifax. "Random aerial bombs" and "destroyer noises" faded into the distance; U-548 surfaced at 1100 hours to find a barren sea (KTB).

Once *Giffard* had apprised *Edmundston* (now Senior Officer) of the situation, she detached from the A/S search and turned at high speed to pick up survivors. Her approach at first encouraged *Valleyfield*'s men, only to cast many into feelings of desperation when she turned away again to carry out a sweep of the wreck site. Lt Tate recalled: "I'm afraid that as she went out of sight some of the boys who were pretty far gone, gave up." Correctly judging the urgency of the rescue mission, LCdr Peterson finally edged *Giffard* among the flotsam again. *Giffard*'s position, the Board of Inquiry subsequently recognized, "was an unenviable one." On the one hand she "was the only ship [able] to prevent the escape of the submarine," but at the same time remained the only one available "to pick up survivors who could not be expected to survive much longer in waters of this temperature." At risk to his own ship, *Giffard*'s captain stopped engines as scramble nets, ropes, and ladders were lowered over the side. Someone even passed a fire hose overboard in order to pull Yeoman Kaplan from the sea. CERA Norman Fraser (Edmundston, New Brunswick) saved many of the numbed, oil-blinded survivors by lowering himself into the water in order to secure them with lines. The survivors "were so smeared with oil that it was almost impossible to grab hold of them," he mused, "especially the ones with no lifejackets." Indeed, "some were so oily you couldn't even take hold of their hair."

Medical assistance was scarce. The Escort Group's only medical officer, Surgeon-Lieutenant Clarence E. Evans, who had given up a good practice in Timmins, Ontario, to join the service, had been transferred to *Valleyfield* by sea boat just prior to the sinking to attend a case of suspected appendicitis. He was lost at sea. *Giffard*'s 21-year-old sick bay tiffy, Leading SBA Howard N. Bailey of Saint John, New Brunswick, was apparently the only man aboard with any knowledge of first aid, a fact the Board of Inquiry noted with grave concern. It urged basic medical training for all seagoing personnel. Commenting on his hurried work in a ship darkened against U-boat attack, Bailey recalled the difficulty of getting survivors below deck for treatment with his four stretchers, and of administering morphine and sulpha. *Giffard's* upper deck was itself now covered with oil and grime. As Bailey recounted:

Most of them were dazed, cold and suffering from shock; others in a state of collapse, some unconscious and with internal injuries from the explosion. Of the five dead which *Giffard* brought in, two died within four or five minutes of being taken aboard. The others had apparently died from exposure. The oil made identity very difficult. Sometimes it was hard to tell whether a man was dead or alive. For a while we thought the Navigating Officer [Lt Warren] was dead.

Altogether, the survivors had been in the water from 40 to 90 minutes. *Giffard's* small sea boat was meanwhile pulling through oil and debris in search of survivors.[36] It rescued eight, and helped more to the scramble nets. "And cold and half-conscious though most of the survivors were when we pulled them inboard," Lt Ralph Flitton remarked, "quite a few distinctly muttered 'Thanks, fellows!' or 'Nice going, boys!'" When the sea boat's crew returned after more than an hour of back-breaking effort, they were so physically exhausted and soaked in black Bunker B diesel fuel that they could no longer hold their oars. At 0330 GMT on 7 May, about one hour after the *Valleyfield* had gone down 50 miles southeast of Cape Race, *Giffard* sent her "Secret Emergency" message: "Valleyfield torpedoed and sunk 46°03′ N, 52°24′ W." At 0630 GMT (0330 local) she signalled that she had picked up thirty-eight survivors and five dead, and was returning forthwith to St John's. No explanation for the delay in signals is forthcoming. By the time HMCS *New Glasgow* joined to assume Senior Officer, U-548 had long since left the zone. *Valleyfield* had been a happy ship. As Coder Thomas J. Siebert (Saskatoon, Saskatchewan) reminisced in hospital: "We had a great bunch on board, officers and ratings ... When I get another ship I hope she's as good as *Valleyfield*." In the muted affidavit of Lt Warren and Lt Tate before the Board of Inquiry: "We regret deeply the loss of our Captain ... our Senior Officer [and] our fellow officers and men. They were fine leaders and good shipmates."

Of *Valleyfield's* total complement of 163, only 38 survived. The majority of these were younger than twenty-five years, and had been at sea for less than a year. None had ever been torpedoed before, and few had even seen action. Despite their shock and trauma, they were assessed by medical authorities ashore as an "exceptionally stable" group. A combined funeral for the five victims whose bodies had been recovered was held in the Chapel of RCN Barracks, St John's, on 10 May 1944.[37] In the old Newfoundland tradition, horse-drawn hearses with top-hatted drivers carried the flag-draped coffins to the Joint Services Cemetery on Black-marsh Road. A long retinue of naval personnel followed, with the naval band playing the moving harmonies of Chopin's Funeral March.

All in all, May 1944 was a quiet month for the Canadian Navy in home waters. As LCdr A.G.S. Griffin, RCNVR, wrote in his monthly operations report, "the unfortunate sinking of HMCS *Valleyfield* arising from a daring attack by an obviously skilful U-Boat captain was the only loss to HMC ships engaged in A/S warfare."[38] Indeed, she was the only frigate to be sunk, and the first Canadian escort lost since the sinking of HMCS *St. Croix* (LCdr Dobson) on 23 September 1943 by a T-5 acoustic Zaunkönig from U-305 (Bahr) in the North Atlantic.

The Board of Inquiry into the sinking of HMCS *Valleyfield* urged the view that the first duty of an escort group unhampered by a convoy was to attract, seek out, and destroy U-boats. Escort Group C-1, it observed, seemed to have relaxed its vigilance, a danger easily befalling fatigued ships' companies detached from their convoy duties and heading home. Though it found no evidence of negligence aboard HMCS *Valleyfield*, the Board of Inquiry argued that "Channel Fever" had adversely affected watch-keeping standards in the group as a whole. Slow reactions to *Valleyfield*'s plight were a case in point. The Senior Officer's decision to cease zigzagging was judged imprudent, especially since a U-boat was known to be in the area (albeit about "150 miles south or east" of Cape Race), and weather conditions were deemed extremely favourable for an attack. As we have seen, however, the Senior Officer had had reasonable grounds for his decision that the Board of Inquiry seems not to have considered. A point the Board of Inquiry did not address, but which was sharply discussed at senior levels and subsequently published in the confidential RCN-RCAF *Monthly Operational Review* for July 1944, concerned radio communications. The radio log of HMCS *Giffard* revealed the seemingly widespread practice of commanding officers to regard either HF or VHF "R/T" (radio telephony) as a convenient telephone line. Examination of *Giffard*'s radio log revealed that only two of the signals sent on the naval general operational band of 2410 kc/s need actually have been sent. Indeed, as the C-in-C CNA observed with some rancour, "the belief exists in HM and HMC ships engaged in the Battle of the Atlantic that the principles of [wireless telegraphy] silence in no way affect the use of R/T." It was, therefore, vital to remind commanding officers, as he had done frequently in the past, of "the undoubted use [which] the enemy makes of these seemingly harmless transmissions." Admiral Murray concluded "that in this particular case the U-Boat could gain a very good idea of the course of C-1 Group from the signals made, and this, together with the fact that ships were not zigzagging, may well have contributed to the regretted loss of HMCS *Valleyfield*."[39] There is indeed ample German evidence to support Admiral Murray's contention that U-boats D/F'd the so-called "gossip lines" or "yack circuits." But nothing in the thorough War Diary of U-548 suggests that Kapitänleutnant Zimmermann had had the slightest inkling of the presence of either *Valleyfield* or the Escort Group until he glimpsed a shadow in his periscope. It was an entirely fortuitous encounter that would have been in no way altered had C-1 been operating strictly "according to the book."

Dense fog harried U-548's continued patrol toward Halifax, though it proved no obstacle to the RCAF in its persistent air attacks. The best defence under the circumstances lay in submerged passage, a decision that led to one of the eeriest incidents in its cruise when a fast convoy and escorts passed directly overhead with minimal hydrophone warning. U-548 had now been on patrol for forty-seven days, but had not managed to contact BdU since its final weather report twenty-three days earlier on 16 April. Zimmermann's sixty-five word coded broadcast now provided terse details: his first acoustic torpedo failure, the sinking of a "destroyer" (actually the *Valleyfield*), the lack of traffic off St John's, heavy patrols by destroyer groups, active daylight and twilight air surveillance, and constant fog and ice. Understandably, he neglected to mention having been caught off guard by the fast convoy. In any event his broadcast had already been long enough. Shore D/F stations had located him, and Naval Operations had begun to vector air and surface units toward him. Zimmermann's War Diary itself reveals that "the D/F of our transmissions was good" (KTB); for barely two and a half hours after he had commenced transmitting, "twelve aerial bombs close astern" shook the submerged U-boat cruising 205 miles SSW of Cape Pine. This was quite an extraordinary achievement, for the U-boat had by now progressed 15 miles in dense fog beyond the transmission position. Sounds of "destroyers" and "distant aerial bombs" marked its passage. Curiously, Canadian documents reveal none of these incidents, though USN forces from Argentia might have carried out the aerial attacks.

Zimmermann patrolled zone CB 27–28 some 215 miles due south of Halifax and 300 miles east of Cape Cod from 10 to 17 May 1944. His purpose was to control "the shipping routes New York-Bermudas, Halifax-Cape Race, and then to stand off Halifax during the nights of the new moon" when it would be particularly dark. BdU's reasons for deploying both U-548 and U-107 south of Halifax were clear: U-boats had not occupied this most vital area of the U.S. Atlantic seaboard for some "considerable time" and German on-site Intelligence was out of date. Zimmermann experienced many isolated attacks on re-entering Canadian waters, and remained convinced that Canadian forces had uncannily homed onto him without his having exposed himself or offered overt provocation. He may, in fact, have wandered into a series of coordinates provided by the running detection of his colleague Heinz Bielfeld in the type IXC-40 U-boat U-1222. Bielfeld had left Kiel for Canadian operations on 13 March and was to operate largely south of Nova Scotia from April to June. Like U-107, he would do little more than conduct unsuccessful attacks on escorts and convoys before returning home. Apart from isolated reports of U-boat activity off the southeast coast of Newfoundland, subsequent RCAF sighting reports correctly indicated the probings of U-548 and U-1222 toward Sable Island, and southwest towards George's Bank. Surfacing on 19 May 1944, some 14 miles southeast of the East Halifax lightship, Zimmermann could see a "very bright glow which illuminated the whole horizon" to the northwest (KTB). The lights of Halifax, 30 miles away, had been a reliable beacon for German submarines since their first arrival in 1942. Bielfeld advised BdU of air patrols by day in the Halifax area, the use of searchlight aircraft at nightfall, and generally inexperienced patrol vessels.[40] U-548 concurred.

Not until 22 May did U-548 hear the sounds of battle after U-1222's double salvo had exploded harmlessly beyond the independent tanker SS *Bulkoil* and triggered a counter-attack by HMCS *Agassiz* escorting convoy HHX-292. Aircraft and the corvette HMCS *Norsyd* joined the counter-attack after Zimmermann had intercepted the tanker's radio report advising that she had herself attacked a surfaced submarine with gunfire 65 miles south of Halifax. "That can only have been Bielfeld in BB 7850" who has been "blessed with these bombs," Zimmermann mused. His pun "*Bombensegen*" ("blessing of bombs") instead of the more usual "*Bombenregen*" ("rain of bombs") reflects the gallows humour that pervaded the German submarine service. Bielfeld survived the protracted search by the Canadian ships, strengthened by HMCS *Burlington* and the escorts of W-1, but never arrived home. His U-1222 was sunk with all hands on 11 July 1944 near La Rochelle in the Bay of Biscay by RAF Squadron 201.

Canadian authorities knew from various sources that U-boats were operating in their zone. They had located Zimmermann's U-548 on 4 June and correctly construed that it was homeward bound after operating off the southeast coast of Newfoundland; they estimated two U-boats patrolling the Halifax Approaches during the second week of June. U-107 had, of course, betrayed her presence in the *Lark* incident. Canadian D/F stations continued to play a key role, as for example when they fixed a U-boat transmission in the vicinity of the Sable Island Bank where U-107 was operating. The fix triggered a concentrated, combined A/S search by Canadian and U.S. forces. Task Group TG-22.6, consisting of the carrier USS *Wake Island* and five destroyer escorts, was despatched to the area where it was joined by the Bangors HMCS *Truro* and *Brockville* from Sydney. HMCS *Amherst*, en route from Halifax to St John's, was diverted to join the new Task Group now designated W-13. Unfavourable weather prevented *Wake Island*'s aircraft from operating for most of the time. A fruitless search continued until 21 June when W-13 proceeded to St John's. Such rapid responses were typical of the period, and reflect the high commitment of defence forces that even scant U-boat opposition provoked. Canadian D/F stations later located U-1222 without incident on 1 July after what observers estimated as a "briefer stay [than U-107], perhaps not longer than a fortnight." They also located Kapitänleutnant Steen's Halifax-bound minelaying U-233 and correctly construed the general area of its tactical mission.

On 13 June 1944, one week after the Normandy Invasion, to which we will return shortly, U-107 stood off the Baccaro Bank about 50 miles southeast of Cape Roseway, Nova Scotia. This was very near the spot where U-754 had been sunk on 31 July 1942. Here it received BdU's "Exclusive" coded message for "Lauterbach [U-539], Krankenhagen [U-549], Wermuth [U-530], Tillessen [U-516], Hellriegel [U-543], Niemayer [U-1233], Simmermacher [U-107], Bielfeld [U-1222], to be deciphered exclusively by the Commanding Officers of the named Boats only" (KTB). The message ordered these Lorient-based U-boats to calculate their withdrawal from their operational zones so as to allow sufficient fuel not only to reach Lorient, but if necessary the Norwegian base of Bergen as well. BdU implied, therefore, that the Biscay ports might have to be closed, and that he was now forced to regroup. Instead of the shorter, great circle "southern" route home to France via the Azores, the U-boats now had to contemplate retracing the tougher and longer northern route of their pre-Biscay predecessors to Germany and Norway. This would lead through the high regions of the North Atlantic, through the Iceland–Faroes Gap into the Norwegian Sea, and then southward off the Shetlands to the Norwegian coast. The signal augured the beginning of the end.

German naval preparations for the long-expected Allied invasion of Fortress Europe exceed the scope of this account, as indeed does an examination of the conflicting views of General von Runstedt and the more astute (though utterly disregarded) Field Marshal Rommel. A comparison between German situation estimates and the record of Allied deception operations would show that all the German commands had been more or less misled. Von Rundstedt remained convinced of an assault on the Pas de Calais, whereas Rommel grew convinced of the correct target of Normandy only once the invasion had begun in earnest. Suffice it to say that the D-Day landing on 6 June 1944 caught the German navy entirely off guard as well. The German naval force in the invasion sector consisted of but one small assault craft, a few motor torpedo boats, and six schnorkel-equipped U-boats.[41] Notwithstanding its unpreparedness, the German Naval Staff insisted that the *Kriegs-*

marine had in fact done "everything possible at sea that lay in its weak powers to disrupt the approaching landing units."[42] Within twenty-four hours of the D-Day landing, thirty-six U-boats managed to leave their Biscay bases, eighteen of which formed a Biscay patrol group. The sortie was brief. Fearing that "extremely powerful enemy air deployment will in time lead to heavy damage and losses," BdU on 12 June ordered all non-schnorkel U-boats to return to the safety of the bunkers. Admiral Dönitz considered the patrol group's further deployment to be in any event of no useful value, as he did not expect enemy landings in the Biscay. At the same time, however, he was preparing both himself and Hitler for the eventuality of withdrawing all his western U-boats to Norway.[43]

U-548 and U-107 returned to Lorient in late June beneath the intense Allied air superiority over the Biscay that seriously damaged U-548. Like Zimmermann, Simmermacher reported personally to BdU who had now withdrawn to Berlin; his crew went on leave.[44] The Allies broke through at Avranches during their absence, thus cutting off the whole Brittany hinterland and preventing the crews from returning to their U-boats. They eventually re-mustered in northern Germany aboard the new type XXI U-boat U-3013, which, however, never undertook a single combat patrol. On 7 August, BdU staff minuted the fact that American advances into Brittany necessitated the rapid conversion of all French-based U-boats into schnorkel boats. Crews of U-boats not combat-ready would be returned to Germany by sea and posted to the new class of submarine on which the German navy continued to place its tenacious hopes.[45]

The month of August saw the removal of U-boats from the French bases and the self-destruction of the Biscay ports. U-107 was lost on 16 August 1944 (KTB). She was one of ten U-boats sunk, while escaping, by the Second and Third Escort groups and RAF Squadron 201.[46] By 31 August, bomber raids had shattered the northern bases where some of the western-based U-boats were heading, causing severe damage to the principal shipyards of Howaldt, Germania, and Deutsche Werke. This loss was far more critical than it may at first appear, for the new type XXI U-boats were being built in prefabricated sections at a number of different locations. Not uncommonly, some thirty or forty similar sections might be stored side by side at one spot awaiting assemblage or transport. Thus, as BdU recognized, a single carpet bombing attack could in effect destroy thirty to forty submarines.[47] In addition, the fleet-in-being itself required urgent updating and repair; many U-boats lay exposed alongside. Significantly, however, the shipyards Howaldt, Germania, and Deutsche Werke in Kiel continued to produce submarines, and were included in the new building program for the type XXIII.

Despite every sign of crumbling fronts, and despite the obvious significance of his own order to send U-boats immediately into combat or to shift them to Norwegian bases, Admiral Dönitz continued to hold out to his navy the promise of ultimate victory. This promise hinged on the tenuous expectation of advanced technology, and on the steadfast will to fight. As he signalled on 26 August 1944: "The U-boat war will continue in the old spirit and with new means."[48] But the old spirit was dying, and the new means arrived far too late to determine the course of the war.

CHAPTER EIGHT

After Normandy

The first schnorkel-equipped type IXC U-boats that gradually became operational in the ports of western France during June and July 1944 provided unprecedented endurance survivability against overwhelming Allied air superiority. Operational Intelligence in London had quickly recognized that the "Snort" had profoundly "affected the balance of power between hunter and hunted," for now the U-boat could "remain submerged for up to ten days without presenting any target detectable by radar or visually except at close range."[1] In fact, the U-boat's underwater endurance was several weeks. BdU intended to assign the boats to as many distant stations as possible: in the Canadian-American coastal zones, in the Caribbean, and off the west African coast as far as Guinea. His purpose remained unchanged from the opening days of the Battle of the Atlantic: tie down Allied naval forces in zones as far removed from the European theatre as possible.[2] On 15 November 1944, banner headlines of the Nazi party's newspaper, *Völkischer Beobachter*, proclaimed the strategy a success. Claiming Allied sources for its information, it tallied Allied commitments to the U-boat threat: a quarter-million people directly involved in Anglo-American convoy escort and protection, 50 aircraft carriers, 110 destroyers, 400 destroyer escorts, 150 large sub chasers, and 250 smaller ones. "If U-boats were withdrawn from the oceans of the world," it asserted, "the enemy would be able to free numerous new Divisions with hundreds of cannon for the Western front." This alone justified the heavy U-boat loss.[3]

Towards the end of July the Allies had broken out of the Normandy bridgehead and forced BdU's hand. Loss of his French bases effectively shortened his U-boats' range, for their sole access to his preferred target areas now lay via the lengthy northern route. The Boats would run from the north German ports and Norway into the North Atlantic through the Rose Garden and Iceland–Faroes Gap. Under normal conditions U-boats carried sufficient fuel and supplies for limited sojourns in the assigned operational zone of four-to-five weeks' duration. But intense Allied air surveillance of the North and mid Atlantic rendered German re-supply missions next to impossible by restricting long-range operations to virtually the area between Newfoundland and Cape Hatteras. One by one, the Boats slipped through the A/S cordons. Schmoeckel's U-802 and Petersen's U-541 patrolled the St Lawrence unaware of each other's exact presence. Steen's minelayer U-233 eluded the RAF's Norway blockade, only to be sunk south of Sable Island by ships of U.S. Task Group 22.10 under the carrier USS *Card*.[4] Zinke's U-1229, carrying an agent to the Gulf of Maine, was sunk south of Newfoundland by aircraft of USS *Bogue*. The next two U-boats destined for the Canadian operational zone, Stellmacher's U-865 and Claussen's U-1226, were in all likelihood lost in the Iceland–Faroes Gap due to schnorkel failure.

The schnorkel, as Operational Intelligence had noted with some satisfaction when reading deciphered Enigma traffic, was a mixed blessing. Many U-boats in the early weeks were lost by uncontrollable flooding. Carbon-monoxide poisoning was not uncommon. It sometimes even led to crew deaths, as was the case with Marienfeld's U-1228 prior to its Canadian mission. In the long run, however, as Enigma traffic proved, the German navy remained convinced that the device had "made it possible for U-Boats to operate with success and reasonable impunity in narrow channels and inlets where formerly they could not have hoped to survive."[5] The St Lawrence, and to some extent the Nova Scotia coast, was a case in point. Ackermann's U-1221 completed its Nova Scotia patrol, only to be sunk during an air raid on Kiel harbour on 3 April 1945. Kneip's U-1223 returned from the St Lawrence, but was destroyed during an air raid off Wesermünde on 23 April 1945. The other eight U-boats of this type – U-1228 (Marienfeld), U-1230 (Hilbig), U-1231 (Lessing), U-806 (Hornbostel), U-1232 (Dobratz), U-1233 (Kühn), U-190 (Reith), and U-889 (Braeucker) – completed operations and survived the war. Though decryption of German routing instructions had specifically alerted the Allies to the arrival off Halifax and Cabot Strait of U-1221 and U-1223, they easily eluded forces from the U.S. escort carrier *Core* and shore-based aircraft equipped with MAD (magnetic anomaly detectors).

German successes in the Canadian zone remained slight during the summer and fall of 1944. None the less, U-boat warnings derived from Enigma, D/F, false sighting and contacts, and the apprehensions of Allied Intelligence that Dönitz's submarines were rallying, kept Canadian forces tense. Constantly worsening weather over Newfoundland and the maritimes led to decreasing air surveillance from September through December. During this time Eastern Air Command recorded no more than two authenticated sightings and one attack.[6] Had the U-boats been able to co-ordinate their patrols and concentrate on choke points in strength, their score would have been significantly higher than HMCS *Magog* and *Shawinigan* and the merchant ships they destroyed. Yet, given conditions in the European operational zone, submariners were not unhappy with the largely peaceful scene Canada provided. The longer they remained in Canadian waters, they felt, the better their chances for surviving the war. Yet lengthy cruises in enemy waters far from support bases at home sometimes caused mental distress. In one case the pressure led to desertion on the high seas.

Against this background, and with encirclement of the Biscay U-boat ports complete, Kurt Petersen's U-541 departed Lorient on 6 August 1944. Five days later he received amplifying orders to set course for the North American coast. As Petersen recalls: "We were all happy when we put to sea, for Lorient was already encircled by Allied troops and we understood nothing of the land war. But the war at sea we understood well."[7] Petersen had made his mark early as a competent, tough-minded U-boat skipper after having put his U-541 into service at the Hamburg-Finkenwerder docks on 24 March 1943. Only in later years did he allow himself to reveal the tensions his disciplined bearing had kept resolutely in check during his youthful years in command. *U-Klapperstorch* (the stork Boat), as his crew dubbed their U-boat on the birth of their captain's first son in 1943, sported a ship's badge depicting a flying stork on her conning tower. It reminded them of family ties ashore, and the bonds of fellowship at sea. After trials, training of crew in the Baltic, and time alongside for arming, Petersen undertook his first operational cruise. He had at the time, he recalls, "a really first-class crew" aboard. The Chief Engineer and NCOs were all seasoned and experienced people. He himself had had several trips on a VIIC U-boat in the North Atlantic and the Mediterranean, and in 1942 had trained submarine watch-keeping officers with the II U-Boots-Lehrdivision in Pillau. He had distinguished himself on his first operational sorties in command through 9 January 1944 by his "exemplary, commanding *sang-froid*" in a running battle with an antisubmarine group, and was credited with having sunk four destroyers.[8] His second tour, from 24 February to 22 June 1944, brought him no tactical success, despite his persistent search, and his attempt to attack convoy DC-5125 in May. Enemy traffic was scarce. The *Serpa Pinta* incident, in which in surface-raider style he stopped the Portuguese liner carrying refugees to the United States and Canada, and removed two American citizens while letting one Canadian free, contributed nothing to his tonnage war. However, it revealed the impunity with which U-boats felt they could still deal with unarmed neutral commercial vessels proceeding on the high seas according to international law.[9]

On 24 August 1944, BdU radioed Petersen's precise operational zone:

the Gulf of St Lawrence, with a special focus on the river mouth, known familiarly in German circles as *der Schlauch*, between Pointe des Monts and Cap à la Baleine. Schmoeckel's U-802 was by this time some 220 miles south of Burin Peninsula, Newfoundland, and would precede Petersen into the Gulf. BdU's inordinately lengthy intelligence signal reminded both commanders that German U-boats had not occupied the zone since 1942, and that they could therefore expect to snatch great opportunities for surprise attacks from these heavily frequented waters. He did not mention the clandestine winter forays of U-536 and U-262 in 1943. Yet he enjoined caution, for the improved technology of aircraft with newer detection devices could now more easily drive U-boats from the Gulf as they had done two years earlier. Indeed, Schmoeckel discovered that the concentrated air surveillance south of Newfoundland meant that "pure Biscay conditions" prevailed here as well (KTB). BdU then recapitulated the largely correct information German Intelligence sources had provided. Thus he advised U-boats to expect four leaver convoys per month from England escorted to "the dispersal point" just north of Cabot Strait in BB 5165. From here, he signalled, ships would break off for Westen, Cornerbrook, and Sydney. Four England-bound joiners would then run the reciprocal route each month. His commanders should expect to meet St Lawrence–Belle Isle convoys, as well as small units of coastal traffic linking St Lawrence ports with Halifax and New York. Particularly important, the "very heavy traffic" ran "invariably in small, weakly defended convoys." Naval countermeasures were "relatively meagre and unexercised." He drew attention to the characteristic layering in the Gulf that caused "unfavourable asdic conditions" for the Allied defenders.

In all, it is remarkable that the U-boats could not exploit the situation, even though commercial traffic was much lighter than BdU anticipated. Nor were Canadians able to plot U-boat deployments on the basis of Enigma, for, as Operational Intelligence discerned, the German's increasing use of "one ship cipher for transmitting the more important operational orders to U-boats" led to a "corresponding reduction of Special Intelligence intercepts."[10] Indeed, wireless communications generally had been reduced, which accounts for the fact that U-802 and U-541 remained incommunicado, even where they could have lent each other support.

The technical aspects of operations in the St Lawrence constituted a new experience for both Petersen (U-541) and Schmoeckel (U-802). As Petersen explains:

We didn't know the water conditions in the St. Lawrence, but very quickly ascertained that conditions obtained here which greatly favoured our sojourn ... Water density increased markedly from the surface to greater depths. On the top was the fresh water of the river, and below the salty Atlantic water had probably been pushed underneath it by the tides ... And in order to lie dead with stopped engines at any particular depth of water, we didn't need to employ the so-called hover gear which would keep us at a pre-set depth by automatically flooding and pumping a few litres of water. The gear was used in operational areas in order to conserve energy and to make as little noise as possible when we were, so to speak, at "lurking stations." Here, however, the water layerings bore us; they also had the great advantage that A/S vessels could detect us either not at all, or only with great difficulty, for the asdic sound waves were deflected at varying depths. Thus we felt as secure as in the bosom of Abraham.

As the first U-boat to enter the Gulf with an attack role since 1942, Schmoeckel intended to maximize the schnorkel in order to exploit every chance for surprise. Having surfaced for a cursory weather observation on 27 August 1944 some 175 miles east of Sable Island, he dived almost immediately for a prolonged operation, from which he would not re-surface until six weeks later. Skirting the French islands of St Pierre and Miquelon, he entered Cabot Strait on the Newfoundland side, and observed the striking backdrop of "the mountains" – Table Mountain, rising abruptly to an elevation of 1900 feet, and the lesser Sugar Loaf. In comparison with the surveillance he had encountered "on the open seas," patrols in the Gulf were "extraordinarily light" (KTB). Ironically, false U-boat sightings and asdic reports ranging from Cap Chat to Ste-Anne-des-Monts and Newfoundland had decoyed the patrols away from the path of U-802.[11]

Petersen betrayed his first approach to Canadian waters en route to Cabot Strait while surfaced during the night of 28–29 August some 60 miles east of Sable Island. When an unidentified low-flying aircraft flew innocently across his stern, Petersen "dived unnoticed," but transmitted the curious signal that he was "being attacked by aircraft" (KTB). It was the beginning of a series of clues to shore D/F stations that the immunity of the Gulf was about to be broken again. Other aircraft triggered his Fliege radar warning device on 1 and 3 September, alerting him to the fact that ASV-equipped aircraft were apparently on his trail. Canadian naval authorities were by this time certain that two U-boats had begun operations in the Canadian area: "one in the Gulf of St. Lawrence [and] the other moving westwards along latitude 44." Significantly, although radar and D/F had actually contacted U-541, the assumed presence of U-802, as has been seen, derived from entirely false information. Canadians deemed a third U-boat (possibly Kneip's U-1223) to have entered the Canadian area on 13 September, and to have reached its patrol off Halifax on 26 September, and yet a fourth (possibly Ackermann's U-1221) to have entered the area northeast of Flemish Cap on 22 September. By the end of the month, this U-boat was estimated in the vicinity of Cabot

Strait moving northwest. Its presumed course suggested Gulf targets. Thus it was that thinly scattered defence forces braced themselves for what looked like a new assault in strength.

Petersen's U-541 touched the periphery of its assigned operational zone when 60 miles southwest of Tête de Galantry, St Pierre Island, on 3 September. But, "since the element of surprise" that he assumed Schmoeckel to have enjoyed no longer existed, he had to grasp "every chance right away" (KTB). After a relentless and deadly game of cat and mouse with the lone tanker SS *Livingston* en route from Halifax to St John's, during which he fired faulty torpedoes and then chased the startled vessel along her radically evasive course to within 1200 m, his 40-knot Gnat tore into her engine room, breaking her apart some 66 miles east of Scatarie Island Light. The attack initiated a massive, though fruitless, search. HMCS *Shawinigan* picked up fourteen survivors in the only lifeboat that escaped. The master of the *Livingston* later reported having seen but a single U-boat, whereas the other crew members insisted on having seen three.

RCAF aircraft commenced a barrier patrol during the afternoon of 3 September from the northern perimeter in Cabot Strait between St Paul Island and Cape Ray, Newfoundland, running southeastward in an 80-mile swath extending 200 miles to seaward. HMCS *Rivière du Loup* searched the area of the sinking without result from dawn on 4 September. Only then did three Fairmiles depart their base in Sydney in an attempt to seal off the western access into the Gulf. Twenty-six hours after the SS *Livingston* had sunk, Escort Group C-6 commenced a search running southeast some 60 miles southward of the scene of the attack. The group, consisting of HMC ships *Eastview* (Senior Officer), *Ste. Thérèse*, *Thetford Mines*, *St. Lambert*, *Peterborough*, and *Cobourg*, was joined on 6 September by HMCS *Tillsonburg*. But U-541 had departed the scene in a northwesterly direction as soon as SS *Livingston* had sunk, and by the time the Canadians had responded, was well inside the Gulf some 22 miles northeast of Bird Rocks. At the time of the counter-attack, Schmoeckel's U-802 was approaching the river, having passed northwest off Bagot Bluff, Anticosti, to the sound of an inexplicable series of "several powerful depth charges every ten seconds" for over three hours (KTB). Reasons for the Canadians' delayed response are unclear. Nor is it clear why they falsely assumed that U-541 would retreat seaward rather than press on into the St Lawrence.

Schmoeckel's plan called for operations close to the mouth of the St Lawrence. Here he hoped to "control all traffic proceeding either up or down river" (KTB). Little of interest emerged from the mists for days. Confining itself to the river mouth from 6 to 15 September 1944, U-802 would perch at periscope depth on a solid water layer. Here at "lurking stations" with engines stopped, it had a clear periscope view of the tactical zone without betraying its presence to enemy hydrophones. Ironically, Schmoeckel's own hydrophones had become defective, thus making him dependent upon visual contact. But by now the closing of the HX-ON summer cycle had made September sailings very irregular. Eastbound HX (fast, medium, and slow) convoys terminated with the New York departure of HXF-310 on 21 September; westbound ON (fast, medium, and slow) convoys terminated with ONF-255 departing Liverpool on 22 September. A new slow convoy service departing Halifax was inaugurated on 3 October. The winter schedule for North Atlantic convoys came into operation on 26 October, with HX and ON departures every five days, and SC and ONS departures every fifteen days. By contrast, coastal convoys were organized and sailed according to NSHQ's appreciation of the U-boat situation in the Canadian coastal zone.[12] Had the U-boats blockaded Halifax as provisionally planned, they might have succeeded in at least cornering the fast, independently routed special convoys like the SS *Queen Mary* (convoy TA-144) and the *Île de France* (convoy TA-149), which quite typically crossed the Atlantic unmolested throughout the war.

Petersen's sense of peace was shattered almost immediately on surfacing 28 miles south of South Point, Anticosti, during the night of 7–8 September. The "blaring volume" of his Mücke and Fliege search radars warned him that U-541 was being virtually bombarded by radar waves that seemed to emanate from a shadowy "auxiliary aircraft carrier" 3 miles distant. Petersen none the less thrust ahead to engage at full speed, despite the undoubted threat. The murky darkness under low, overcast skies obscured the target: the as-yet-unseen corvette HMCS *Norsyd*, which was closing him at full speed on a radar bearing. Her triple-expansion, four-cylinder engine could develop 2760 horse power, propelling her at 16 knots. Her armament comprised one 4-inch gun, one 2 pounder pom-pom, two single-mounted 20-mm oerlikon guns, depth charges and Hedgehog. This time, however, the encounter was too abrupt, and the range too close, to bring the powerful Hedgehog ahead-throwing mortar into play.[13]

Just as Petersen's U-541 was about to fire a T-5 acoustic Gnat at the very large vessel (which he had assumed to be the only target in sight), *Norsyd* suddenly opened fire with her forward deck gun. Petersen and his bridge watch could see her muzzle flash and hear the fall of shot. Five star shell burst just astern of U-541, "illuminating the surface as bright as day" (KTB). By this time, "the destroyer," as Petersen identified his opponent, had attained "20 knots" on an almost parallel course to starboard; she fired automatic weapons from a range of 300 m, as U-541 veered sharply to port, dived, and fired the Gnat. Only on surfacing much later, did Petersen discover the scars that the raking fire of *Norsyd*'s guns had carved into his conning tower, fortunately after all his men had gotten below.

The whole sequence, from *Norsyd*'s radar contact to U-541's shot, had lasted but 4 minutes. *Norsyd*'s hydrophones tracked the torpedo along its 11-minute, 52-second run until it exploded harmlessly beyond. The "powerful detonation with subsequent sounds of sinking" (KTB) caused Petersen to credit himself with a kill. For the next couple of hours the crew of U-541 felt harassed – not so much by the repeated depth-charge patterns, which kept a healthy distance, but by the harrowing sound of the searching vessel's Cat Gear. Petersen recalls the traumatic experience with practised understatement: "We could hear an unpleasant, loud circular-saw-like noise which cut us right to the quick. We had the feeling that the U-boat was being sawed in half." He was still uncertain of the sound's origin, either a new type of asdic, an undisclosed offensive weapon, or anti-Gnat defence. Operational authorities escalated the hunt by diverting the Norwegian minesweeper *King Haakon VI* and the four frigates of EG-16 from Cabot Strait, and scrambling the RCAF. The four frigates of Group W-13 patrolled the area between St Paul Island and Cape Ray in order to prevent U-541's suspected escape to seaward. At the same time, the 71st M/L Flotilla from Sydney and the 79th from Gaspé patrolled a line from Cap des Rosiers (Gaspé) to South Point (Anticosti), to block off the Gaspé Passage and prevent U-541 from entering the river. HMCS *Magog* later joined W-13 from Halifax. The fruitless search continued until the forenoon of 10 September. By skirting close off Bagot Bluff, Petersen slipped through the cordon, and spent the next two nights on the bottom before advancing into the St Lawrence.

Unaware of Petersen's presence, Schmoeckel in U-802 could only assume from the escalated air surveillance over the river mouth that he himself had been detected, and that Canadians had "perhaps picked up [his] schnorkel with shore-based equipment" (KTB). Only when summarizing his patrol on the homeward leg, did he express the suspicion that another U-boat had preceded him into the St Lawrence (KTB). By 13 September 1944, Petersen's U-541 had schnorkelled to within 9 miles of Great Cawee (Île du Grand Caouis), a barren granite island rising 134 feet out of the river off the northern shore between the mouth of Rivière Pentecôte and Rivière aux Rochers. Fixing his position by the Cawee Light and that of Egg Island (Île aux Oeufs), the narrow, low granite island 14 miles to the southwest, he began his inshore patrol. It led him to Pointe des Monts off the river mouth on the northern side of the "gap" (*Schlauch*), past the sandy "brightly illuminated beach of Trinity" (KTB). Petersen may well have expected some coastal ships in the comfortable anchorage of Baie de la Trinité. The generally low, wooded shoreline from Rivière Pentecôte to Pointe des Monts, backed by hills rising from 900 to

1240 feet, presented no navigational hazards. Indeed, by following the 20-fathom line, he could skirt all dangers about 1.5 miles from shore in complete safety. Only occasional hydrophone contacts interrupted the tranquillity of the cruise. Intending to drift southeastward, as the current charts and navigational instructions had indicated, U-541 "stopped on a water layering at 30-m depth in order to save [electrical] current and hear better" (KTB). Petersen was in for a surprise, for on surfacing hours later, he found himself 20 miles upstream, 7 miles NNE of Matane Light, where U-132 had patrolled over two years earlier in July 1942. As he observed with some consternation, U-541 had been "thrust into the gap by the prevailing tidal current in the opposite direction from that which the Pilot Book had described."

The frigates of W-13 had meanwhile undertaken a routine patrol of the Gaspé Passage on 14 September when they inadvertently fell into the torpedo range of U-802. Assuming a convoy following astern of the sweep, U-802 tried to slip through the screen. Asdic sounds surrounded it as the formation zigzagged around its base course in full view of Schmoeckel's periscope. "Suddenly a destroyer turns bows on at full speed, making black smoke" (KTB). Incorrect though his assumption was, Schmoeckel could only conclude in that split second that HMCS *Stettler* had gained asdic contact and was commencing her attack. Precisely similar shifts in formation under similar tactical conditions would lead to the sinkings of HMCS *Clayoquot* in December 1944 and HMCS *Esquimalt* in April 1945. Pressed by the apparently threatening frigate slicing through an "absolutely smooth, leaden sea [at approximately] 20 knots" (KTB), Schmoeckel hastily fired a T-5 acoustic Gnat at a range of 500 m. An "explosion," in the words of the Canadian report, "believed to be a torpedo, occurred 40 yards astern of HMCS *Stettler* in the ship's wake."[14] The crew of U-802 heard their torpedo explode, followed by "the sounds of sinking," and credited themselves with a kill. Lying under protective layers at a depth of 170 m eight minutes after their attack, they listened in safety to the counter-attacks as "destroyers" crossed overhead. U-802 rounded Cap de la Madeleine by late afternoon on 15 September, and let itself "drift eastward with the prevailing set of the Gaspé stream" (KTB).

In the days following his inadvertent penetration of the gap to Matane on 13 September, U-541 gradually withdrew along the Gaspé Peninsula. Like U-802, it passed Cap de la Madeleine and Cap des Rosiers, and reached a position midway between Heath Point (Anticosti) and Bird Rocks. Here both its gyro and magnetic compasses became unserviceable. With the exception of a couple of inbound "destroyers" – they were in all likelihood frigates – it rarely saw or heard any traffic. In fact, "as a result of the strong water layering, the range of the hydrophones [was] not great enough" to permit the U-boat to "bear on to a fast target at periscope depth and still be able to fire" (KTB, 18). This was precisely Schmoeckel's experience.

On 20 September 1944, Schmoeckel in U-802 and Petersen in U-541 stood but 54 miles apart south of Bagot Bluff, Anticosti. One could speculate on what might have happened tactically had they supported one another in the gap, or what might have happened socially had they met in this quiet Gulf sector so far from home. Petersen was celebrating his twenty-eighth birthday, "safe as in the bosom of Abraham," as he had described the Gulf, submerged at "lurking stations" on a firm water layer. To mark the occasion, the U-boat's surgeon Dr E. Messmer (later professor of medicine at the University of Heidelberg) described their experiences in a piece of doggerel verse entitled "Der Schnorchel," set to the hit tune "Lilli Marlene."[15] Ironically, this sentimental song about the German soldiers' stereotyped sweetheart Lilli Marlene who waited hopelessly for her war-bound lover "underneath the lamplight by the barrack gate" was popular in both Axis and Allied camps. Indeed, sheet music for piano and guitar with both English and German lyrics was not uncommon in Canadian homes. The haunting melody revealed a romantic nostalgia for normalized human relationships, and hinted at a touch of *Weltschmerz* common to combatants on both sides. Dr Messmer's rendition, however, masked the tender feelings and deep-seated anxiety behind its intentionally trivialized emotions and occasionally ribald juvenilia. The gallows humour of seamen in a hostile environment pervaded the evocation of everyday experiences. It divested the conditions in which they found themselves both of danger and pathos. Thus, "Der Schnorchel" betrays a quizzical admiration for the disarmingly naive "local strategic thinkers" in Canada who didn't seem to realize that there was a war on. It expresses a longing for further operations in the peaceful St Lawrence where navigation was easy and U-boats had a good chance of survival. It laments the passing of youth, and the missed opportunities. Its self-conscious bravado lauds the monotonous diet, the claustrophobic living conditions in foul air and diesel fumes without seeing daylight for weeks on end. It extols the smells of garbage, unwashed bodies, grease and cooking that pervaded the U-boat. One verse chronicles the difficulty of firing the well-culled garbage out of the torpedo tube. Two others parody the effects of cruising under schnorkel. This was a problem many submariners recorded. Whenever the "snort" dipped beneath the surface due to slight variations in cruising depth, it would cause a sudden, intense and often painful suction throughout the U-boat. Momentarily deprived of their external intake and exhaust, the diesels would draw ravenously from the interior of the U-boat and exhaust their fumes inside. The suction, according to the boisterous lyrics, made submariners bald. Shipboard poets aboard U-Dobratz (U-1232) even claimed it drew fillings from their teeth. The cohesiveness of the U-boat "family" throughout the whole service never let spirits flag. The submariners' own admiral, "Papa" Dönitz himself, epitomized their deep-grained fellowship. The jocular final verse of "Der Schnorchel" reflects personal devotion to one of the most charismatic leaders in German naval history:

Dear Papa Dönitz
Have mercy as we plead.
Grant us please a brand new Boat,
That's all we really need.
Then we can hit the road once more
And add more shipping to our tonnage score,
With you, Lilli Marlene.

It seems unlikely that the plea of war-weary submariners for a new Boat reflects any genuine desire to continue the battle, either with or without the new type XXI.

U-541 departed the Gulf on 21 September, passing 10 miles northeast of Bird Rocks via Cape Anguille, Newfoundland, and through the middle of Cabot Strait. During the next two days, it patrolled a north/south line some 65 miles east of Scatarie Island. Germany's loss of its French bases had caused Schmoeckel (U-802) to reduce his operating days in the Gulf to ten. He now faced an extended cruise home via the Iceland Passage and Norway. He now schnorkelled southward into Cabot Strait, passing 7 miles off St Paul Island on 23 September, and continued southeast through the deep Laurentian Channel between the deep-sea ledges of Banquereau on the west and St Pierre Bank on the east. Petersen's inability to intercept a "large passenger freighter of approximately 12,000 tons" (KTB) illustrated the urgent need for the new high-speed submarines on which Dönitz placed all his hopes. Five of Petersen's torpedoes against two targets failed, despite sound firing data.

Both U-541 and U-802 had for technical reasons remained out of touch with an anxious BdU who repeatedly called for situation reports. On-site information was crucial to his plans for deploying new Boats to the North American zone. Fear of being D/F'd prevented the Boats from broadcasting while crossing the Newfoundland Banks on the homeward leg, where they would have to surface in order to repair antennae. In Schmoeckel's account, it was tantamount to suicide to surface in an area where "no U-boat gets through on the surface without an air attack" (KTB). In his case, he feared that his anti-aircraft weapons would malfunction after six weeks of submersion. Schmoeckel's silence in particular caused BdU "grave concern" on 9 October, for U-802 had last signalled a position report when outbound on 13 August. Naval Staff continued to plot U-802's tracks by dead reckoning, and calculated according to assessed fuel reserves alone that it must now be reaching Norway. If it did not appear shortly, they would declare U-802 missing.[16] BdU still anticipated the return of U-1229 after three months of silence. In this case he waited in vain.[17]

U-1221's intrusion into the Canadian combat zone on the first operational cruise for both U-boat and the majority of the crew must have been a topic of shipboard discussion. The crew doubtless inferred the close proximity of the coast, even though only crossing the southern tip of the Newfoundland Banks far out to sea. There seems no other explanation for the only recorded case of a submariner deserting on the high seas by leaping overboard. Ackermann's War Diary reveals that on 24 September a certain Able Seaman Emil-Heinz Motyl had been upbraided for repeatedly falling asleep while on look-out duty. For this he received "very hard work punishment" (KTB). Whatever the special causes of the fatigue that triggered the sequence of events, the crew had apparently always disliked Motyl. The captain regarded him as being of "weak character and a loner." The dynamics of life aboard a U-boat demanded an extraordinary degree of cohesion, community, mutual support, and an element of psychological intimacy unknown in other classes of vessel, or indeed ashore. Even barring ideological differences, the life of an outsider would have been hell. "On the second day, [having] washed and put on fresh clothing" to present himself to the captain on the bridge, according to the custom of "men under punishment," Motyl slipped aft, cigarette in hand, to the "Winter Garden" anti-aircraft deck where on this particular day the gunners were not closed up. Like all the crew, he was wearing his life-jacket. Nothing seemed amiss until a look-out saw him leap – 200 miles SSW of Sable Island. Immediate recovery attempts in the pre-dawn darkness and sea state 3 failed.[18] U-1221 dived at first light and continued to Nova Scotia. The subsequent discovery of Motyl's torn and discarded personal papers lying among the garbage seemed at first to support that initial hunch that he had committed suicide, a conclusion that a later shipboard investigation rejected. As far as U-1221 was concerned, Motyl had deserted the flag and in all likelihood had been dragged into his U-boat's screws.

The combination of false submarine sightings and actual encounters in the Cabot Strait and Gulf areas had made the Canadians wary throughout the whole area. Every hint of U-boats had to be checked. This necessitated diversion of coastal convoys and full-scale searches from Carroll Point, Labrador, through the Belle Isle Strait, and into the Gulf. The searches again confirmed Dönitz's principle that even the presumed presence of U-boats took initiatives out of the enemy's hands by forcing him to commit resources to defence. In this case, it placed a severe burden on

NOIC Sydney who exercised operational control of all escorts in the Gulf. Petersen had meanwhile stoutly refused to acknowledge BdU until well clear of the Canadian inshore zone. When he eventually broke radio silence on the Newfoundland Banks, Canadian D/F stations and A/S countermeasures reacted much faster than he had anticipated:

About two hours [after having broadcast] we heard weak signals on our radar warning devices ... Seconds after we had dived, bombs exploded in our vicinity. The Boat was shaken and the periscope developed a leak. From my perspective the Canadian defences had reacted and operated magnificently. Swift detection of our radio transmission, good evaluation with precise position, good attack by aircraft with sparing and rational use of radar. If we had dived but a few seconds later, the bombs would possibly have hit us at the beginning of the diving manoeuvre.

Surface vessels vectored on to U-541 had meanwhile been pounding into heavy, often violent seas, which ultimately forced C-in-C CNA to abandon the hunt before his ships had reached their search position. Thrashed by force 8 winds, a screaming gale that amassed long, heavy swells with waves sometimes breaking at a height of 40 feet, HMCS *Restigouche* (LCdr David W. Groos, RCN) clawed her way into the storm. Just before dawn on 4 October 1944, the violent seas sweeping over her decks tore depth charges from their rails and washed a man overboard (Chief Petty Officer G.S. Jewitt, RCNVR). Abandoning hope of finding him after a relentless, three-hour search, the ship returned to Halifax.[19]

U-1221 (Ackermann) and U-1223 (Kneip) had meanwhile been operating in their respective zones off Halifax and in the Gulf of St Lawrence since the end of September. Whereas U-1221 managed only to miss troop ships and a cruiser, U-1223 torpedoed the River-class frigate HMCS *Magog*. By mid October, Operational Intelligence had detected an outward-bound 740 tonner "proceeding toward the Canadian area" in pursuit of the "German policy to maintain two or three U-Boats with the object of distracting and possibly reducing A/S forces" in the North Atlantic and European zone.[20] Canada's priority commitments in the mid-Atlantic zones and the Channel Approaches precluded any further concentration of inshore defences.

Whether by miscalculation or equipment failure, Ackermann had a luckless patrol. From the onset of his cruise in Bergen, Norway, he was plagued by a series of malfunctions – gyro compass, hydrophones, schnorkel, search radar, and echo sounder. The unreliability of his principal tools made him very cautious. He therefore betrayed none of the aggressiveness and drive that the former Chief of Operations and new BdU, Admiral Godt, had come to expect of his commanders in the early days of the war.[21] His patrol period off Halifax covered the usual convoy traffic, as well as the special movement "Monsters" SS *Île de France* (convoy AT-156) and SS *Mauretania* (convoy TA-151), and the cruiser HMCS *Uganda*. He sighted at close range the Free French auxiliary FFS *Toulonnaire* just outside Halifax. German *B-Dienst* was monitoring Allied transmissions and passing Allied sighting reports to U-1221 via the plotting room of BdU. Such reports implicitly urged caution upon Ackermann, even where they suggested that he himself remained largely undiscovered. One early German decryption had relayed the report of an "English unit" that had sighted "a surfaced U-boat in the Halifax area" (KTB). This would have been Kneip's U-1223. Ackermann's attack against the troop ship SS *Lady Rodney* (convoy JHF-36), escorted by HMCS *Burlington* and *Westmount*, failed when his FAT (surface-seeking angular course) torpedoes missed the target. As Ackermann faithfully recorded, "in my zeal for combat I forgot to turn on to the correct attack course." He had also underestimated the target speed. Unaware of Ackermann's presence within 3000 yards of *Lady Rodney*, the escorts reported hearing three underwater explosions astern of her as she passed 48 miles SSE of the Sambro lightship. Fearing drifting mines, HMCS *Thunder*, *Canso*, and *Bayfield* carried out an ultimately fruitless sweep until 24 October. As the Submarine Tracking Room had estimated no enemy submarines in the area at the time, despite D/F and cryptographic reports, naval authorities ruled the cause of the explosions as "undetermined."[22]

Ackermann's situation report of 30 October, rebroadcast on at least two more occasions due to poor reception in Germany, and finally submitted by telex on arrival in Flensburg on 5 December, provided promising details for the missions of U-806 and U-1232. In short, so he advised, the Germans could expect "small convoys every four days" between Cape Roseway and Le Have Bank, "exercised" escorts by day when principal convoys pass, weak defences, and easy navigation. The Canadian inshore zone "promised success for the deployment of several U-Boats" at once (KTB). But Dönitz had no wolf packs to spare. Even individual Boats were becoming scarce, and were already under tremendous pressure. Admiral Godt's criticism of Ackermann's patrol remained: "It is inadequate simply to locate traffic without taking all measures to attack it" (KTB). Kneip (U-1223) had meanwhile exploited the few chances he had.

The five-month-old HMCS *Magog* (Lt L.D. Quick, RCNR) had departed her base in Sydney on 13 October in company with the frigate HMCS *Stettler* in order to rendezvous with convoy GONS-33. This was a twelve-ship Gulf section of a slow convoy from the United Kingdom. An RCAF Catalina provided close convoy escort with the frigate HMCS *Toronto* from EG-16, the Support Group authorities had deployed the previous summer in response to earlier U-boat intrusions.[23] The escort had been instructed to provide support into the St Lawrence until crossing the meridian of 68° W longitude near Pointe Mitis Light. Here they were to detach and rendezvous with Quebec–Sydney convoy QS-97 for the return journey down river. Kneip in U-1223 watched 5 miles off Pointe des Monts Light in the river mouth on 14 October as a "destroyer" – it was actually the frigate *Magog* – drew into his sights broad on the bow at 6000 m, and at an incredibly low escort speed of 7 knots. Visibility was good despite low overcast skies, but the escorting Catalina discerned no hint of the impending attack. At 1325 GMT, as *Magog* was zigzagging in Station "Fox" on the starboard of the westbound convoy, one of Kneip's double-spread acoustic Gnats ripped into her stern after a run of 2 minutes 5 seconds and sheered off 60 feet of her after section. A second Gnat detonated astern.

Three of *Magog*'s men died instantly in the explosive impact that blasted several others overboard.[24] Some young sailors survived under circumstances they termed nothing short of miraculous. Nineteen-year-old Engine Room Artificer George Gordon "Gorde" Hunter, RCNVR, of Winnipeg recalled at the time "standing on the gun platform" at the moment of impact, when "the whole quarterdeck lifted up and folded over the top of [his] head," coming to rest on the gun that saved his life. Beside him, Hunter recalls, lay the mangled body of Petty Officer Thomas Davis; the blast had cut him in half. Twenty-year-old Electrical Artificer Harold Robertson, RCNVR, of Preston, Ontario, was just leaving the electrical stores, a compartment below the waterline when the torpedo hit: "I came right through a steel bulkhead and landed in the water. There was a steel deck above me, below me, and a steel wall all around me. Even though I was injured I figure I am mighty lucky to be here." Twenty-three-year-old Chief Petty Officer Alfred Lapsley, RCNVR, of Toronto was in his workshop in a corresponding position to Robertson's on the opposite side of the ship: "The explosion jammed the door of my shop, but lifted the deck open right overhead. I was below the waterline, and in a moment was in a mass of water and oil. I managed to climb up and out, and came back over what had been the bottom of the ship ... I was so covered with oil my own mother wouldn't have known me."

A few minutes after the initial explosion, a second torpedo detonated about 50 yards off *Magog*'s port quarter. HMCS *Toronto*, patrolling in Station "Dog" 1 mile ahead of *Magog*, sighted what appeared to be a periscope. She immediately opened fire with her 4-inch and oerlikon guns, and ran in to attack with depth charges. Below, Kneip's U-1223 heard the explosions and the scream of the "circular saws" as the Canadians streamed anti-Gnat Cat Gear. None of the ships gained A/S contact. Despite imminent threat of further attacks and the ship's succumbing to her massive damage, *Magog*'s damage control parties strove coolly and self-assuredly to save the ship. They had all undergone rigorous damage-control training at HMCS *Somers Isles*, the navy's new work-up base in Bermuda. It therefore seemed almost a matter of routine when Chief Stoker Norman Howes of Saskatoon donned breathing apparatus and anti-flash gear to enter the burning boiler room and quell the blaze, or when the shoring party under Lt (E) B.F. Larson of Vancouver struggled to prevent the engine-room bulkhead from bursting.

One-half hour after the initial attack, HMCS *Toronto* sent her medical officer, Surg.Lt Léon Beicque of Outremont, Quebec, aboard *Magog* in a motor boat. Then, while running in to take the listing ship in tow, she lowered her whaler to rescue the three men blown overboard. Within 10 minutes, however, *Toronto* picked up a U-boat contact and saw a torpedo track heading for her starboard bow. She broke off the tow to carry out a series of ultimately fruitless Hedgehog attacks on a contact in 600 feet of water some 3 miles off Pointe des Monts Light. It may well have been Kneip who had followed the current tactical doctrine of escaping into shallow waters. Aircraft dropped sonobuoys, while EG-16 undertook fruitless antisubmarine countermeasures until the evening of 15 October, when it broke off action in order to reinforce Quebec–Sydney convoy QS-97.[25] Meanwhile, "with great physical stress and extreme care for the patients," according to a medical report, a small sea boat's crew undertook the hazardous task of transferring the seriously wounded from the *Magog* to a waiting Catalina flying boat. Wind and a running sea, in the words of the report, made the job "physically impossible." Gorde Hunter, now a Victoria newspaper columnist, recalls the harrowing experience of laying strapped immobile in a Neil-Robertson stretcher and being lowered over the *Magog*'s ravaged side to the small boat surging and pitching below. One slip of the crew, he justifiably feared at the time, would most certainly send him plummeting helplessly into the depths. Once loaded through the "blister" hatch of the Catalina, they were flown to Mont Joli, whence other aircraft transported them to the Montreal Neurological Institute. Other ships had in the meantime pursued suspected contacts during the next days, while the tug *Lord Strathcona* relieved HMCS *Shawinigan* of her tow and took *Magog* to Quebec City.

Magog was paid off to Care & Maintenance on 20 December 1944. This meant little more than that she was not to be allowed to deteriorate further pending a decision on her disposition. Escort requirements for the war against Japan and Germany urged the view that both *Magog* and the similarly damaged frigate HMCS *Chebogue* in the UK should be rebuilt. The Admiralty in London opposed their repair, and they never saw service again. A Board of Inquiry judged *Magog*'s loss "the result of the hazards necessarily undertaken in convoy duty." She was sold for scrap in 1945.

Long periods of enforced radio silence forced BdU to rely on a variety of sources for information on the progress of the war at sea. Sometimes these sources were third or fourth hand. Such was the case as BdU awaited situation reports from Petersen, Schmoeckel, and Kneip. On 21 October 1944, the German naval attaché in neutral Sweden reported accounts that had reached the previous day's Swedish newspapers via London. Although reflecting tactically inaccurate data, they seemed to reveal the Canadian attitude towards the U-boat sorties. According to the press, U-boat warfare had revived on the Canadian coast after "not a single vessel" had been attacked since September. Canadians had apparently blamed the recent attacks on "suicide U-boats." These submarines, the report ran, had been driven out of their French support bases by the Normandy Invasion. No longer able to re-supply or repair, they were now content to carry out their desperate "pirate patrols" until they were either sunk or captured. BdU had earlier received an Allied press report of a four-day U-boat attack on a convoy off the Canadian coast that claimed one ship sunk. Whatever the precise details of these attacks, he now could safely assume that his three U-boats (U-1221, U-1223, and U-1229) were still active on station.[26] He still refused to give up U-1229 for lost. The success of the schnorkel had increased BdU's confidence in his U-boats' enhanced durability in battle, for he had lost only six U-boats to enemy action in October.[27]

Kneip's U-1223 may well have penetrated more deeply up river immediately after her attack on *Magog*. For, while awaiting Quebec–Sydney convoy QS-99 off Pointe au Père on 23 October, HMCS *Truro* and *Digby* executed several depth-charge attacks against a firm submarine contact over a period of three hours. Kneip would, therefore, have distinguished himself by having penetrated more deeply into the St Lawrence than any other U-boat. He would have exceeded U-69's record of 1942 by some 15 miles. However that may be, *Truro*'s contact eluded them, then wandered back into their asdic field, and escaped once more in a slow northeasterly direction. But on 2 November Kneip struck again, though Canadian authorities were still uncertain of the U-boat's presence. The 10,000-ton Vancouver-built SS *Fort Thompson* was proceeding independently some 6 miles off Matane en route from Quebec to Sydney with a cargo of grain for North Africa when two explosions ripped open her hold. No one aboard could tell whether she was the victim of enemy action or bursting boilers. Convinced by now that the last U-boat had left the St Lawrence after the *Magog* incident, operational authorities at first attributed the *Fort Thompson*'s damage to a mine, and consequently deployed a minesweeper. Their reasons derived from deductions by Naval Intelligence. For when shore D/F stations intercepted the departure report of U-1221 east of Newfoundland, Intelligence ascribed it to Kneip's U-1223. On this advice, Operations redeployed Gulf escorts outside the now supposedly free Gulf, thus leaving the St Lawrence virtually without defences. Naval personnel subsequently recovered bits of metal from the *Fort Thompson*'s hold that they identified as components of a German torpedo. Yet the explosion must have been severe (or the discipline aboard lax) for seventeen crew members immediately launched a lifeboat into the stream. Finding themselves without oars, they were content to drift ashore on Matane Beach. This gave rise to the curious rumour among local residents that a ship had sunk with all hands. In fact, forty-five officers and crew had remained on board keeping her afloat until help arrived.[28] Not until fifty-eight days later, on 30 December 1944, did back-page newspaper stories spread the fiction that this was "the first known torpedo attack in the river since 1942."[29]

It had served the navy's purposes for the public to learn (albeit belatedly) that SS *Fort Thompson* had been the first torpedo victim in the St Lawrence. Naval Information Services released no news of the *Magog* incident until six months after the event, though indeed the reasons for withholding such news for so long may have lost their rationale. A front-page story in the *Halifax Herald* (18 April 1945) announced that a "Hun U-Boat [had] Struck Far up Gulf of St. Lawrence," and obliquely suggested that there had been more than one of them pursuing "a renewal of their warfare on Canadian river shipping."[30] Unlike the *Ottawa Journal*, which avoided the political issue of Quebec's illumination, the *Halifax Herald* hinted that continued pressure by U-boats justified the dim-out regulations that had gone into effect along the St Lawrence on 7 April.

Eastern Canadian newspapers received the official text sufficiently quickly to attract their customers by "hot news" releases. Western Canadian papers, however, did not. The petulant complaint by the editor of the obscure weekly, the *British Columbian*, sheds some light on the relationship between press and naval news sources. Irritated by the fact that Canadian Press (CP) and British United Press (BUP) had carried the wire story of *Magog* on 18 April, the date of the official release, whereas he himself had not received the script and photographs until five days later, he charged the non-existent office of "Director of Public Relations (Navy)" with damaging his business by obliging him to print stale news. Not only should air mail service between Ottawa and New Westminster, British Columbia, not require the three days it had actually taken, he intoned, but "in view of the date of the *Magog* incident and the fact that it was known by word of mouth in many places in Canada, there seems no reason why mailing the release should be delayed until the last moment."[31] A postscript expressed the hope that he would be given "more leeway when the *Skeena* story breaks." Here he indecorously alluded to the supposedly secret circumstances of HMCS *Skeena*'s loss on 25 October 1944, when she dragged her anchor in a gale and was wrecked on Videy Island near Reykjavik, Iceland, with the loss of fifteen lives.[32] Official secret or not, the press was itching to publish the now well-known story, which in fact would not be released until 16 May 1945.[33]

The Director of Naval Information admitted in reply that he had been keeping the *Magog* story "on ice for some months" under instructions from Naval Intelligence to withhold all stories of damaged vessels until they had been returned to service. Though *Magog* was now out of the war for good, he let the British Columbia editor infer that authorities had released her story in April 1945 in order to sway the public in support of a government regulation for which there would otherwise have been no apparent need: "In view of the ... announcement ... that a dim-out would be put into effect immediately on the St. Lawrence, it was decided to break the *Magog* story so as to lend emphasis to the necessity." This was indeed a rather lame excuse, for proposals concerning the dim-out had long since become public knowledge. The *Montreal Daily Star* had even announced as front-page news on 1 May 1944, "St. Lawrence Dim-Out Asked by Macdonald." That this wartime measure was at least one year in the making is all the more surprising in light of the U-boat activity on the river since 1942. In deference to the British Columbia editor, the Director of Naval Information was now "trying to prevail on the powers-that-be to release the *Skeena* story."[34] The dim-out was, in any event, too little too late. U-1223 left the Gulf operational zone for home on 21 November 1944, five months before the regulation came into effect. All returning U-boats now ran the gauntlet of Allied strike groups. French ports and the English Channel route were closed. The Shetland zone was proving more impenetrable, and the Allied air defences over the Iceland–Faroes Gap was a cause for increasing German anxiety. To pass further north courted either exhaustion of fuel or even disaster beneath the ice. Yet this was the route that Petersen (U-541) chose on learning from Naval Operations in early October 1944 of a heavy concentration of antisubmarine vessels in the Iceland–Faroes Gap together with intensified air surveillance. Information in the *Sailing Directions* decided him on a passage of the Strait of Denmark between Greenland and Iceland. He hoped to round Iceland at 67° N latitude, and then cross over to Norway and, if all went well, a sheltered port. Navigation handbooks suggested that the route was easily navigable at this time of year. As things turned out, the advice was wrong:

Rounding the northwest corner of Iceland on a course for North Cape we quickly came into winter weather. Driving snow became thicker and the number of growlers mounted, and they got bigger. We reached the point when we could proceed no further on the surface, for a U-boat is no icebreaker. Batteries were up, and still trusting the navigational handbook's advice that no icebergs had been seen in this zone and season in a hundred years, and that a solid cover of drift ice had never been observed, we advanced beneath the ice. We were in good spirits, particularly as we could head east [for home waters] after having dived. I had the crew measure the sea temperature constantly. It dropped well below $1.5°$ C below zero. Condensation froze on the inside; electric heating couldn't be switched on [as we needed to] save power. It was ice cold in the Boat and absolutely still. Most of the crew slept, unaware of the situation in which we found ourselves. They probably thought "the Old Man will get us through" (the "Old Man" – that was me with my 28 years!). If the sea temperature drops below $0°$ C it's a sign of solid ice cover, or the near proximity of an iceberg. Both could be fatal. Ice cover makes surfacing impossible, and we could ram an iceberg. We had escaped the danger of heavy A/S surveillance, and had traded it for another. I can't say which is greater. The powers of nature had it within themselves, and could be dreadful and unpredictable.[35]

During a hurricane on an earlier patrol a powerful breaker had smashed across the U-541 bow, tearing the 3.7-cm gun clear off its mount: "These unleashed forces are indescribable. Here, however, it was the ice, the cold, the silence, the eerie awareness of sitting completely powerless beneath the ice. We had the sensation of being crushed by an invisible force. At such times one feels very tiny and powerless." When the batteries had reached half-strength, Petersen decided to surface in order to check his situation. With engines stopped, U-541 slowly rose centimetre by centimetre as anxious questions prickled along the captain's nerves. At such times command is very lonely. The Boat emerged amidst a vast expanse of ice, in the only ice-free hole for miles. It was barely large enough to contain the U-boat, but they were safe. A sense of euphoria gripped the crew. Diesels now sprang to life, hands turned to clean ship, and the cook went to the galley; the Boat was aired, bilges pumped and batteries charged, and they obtained their final assurance by an astronomical sight. Once more clear to dive, U-541 continued her journey beneath the ice, and reached home.

Earlier that month two more U-boats, U-1228 and U-1231, began moving across the Atlantic for the Canadian combat zone. U-1228, a 750-ton type IXC/40 commanded by Oberleutnant zur See Friedrich-Wilhelm Marienfeld of the graduating class of 1938, had completed her trials and work-ups in April 1944. According to the not-always-reliable "Report of Interrogation of the Crew of U-1228 which surrendered to the USS *Neal A. Scott* on 11 May 1945," Marienfeld was a crack torpedo shot.[36] During torpedo trials in Pillau, he allegedly received a high score of "7," equivalent to about 98 per cent hits. On completion of tactical exercises based in Gotenhafen, U-1228 returned to the Howaldt Werke for Hamburg for a one-month refit. A rubber-coated schnorkel was fitted as defence against the Allies' suspected infra-red detection devices. The latter was actually of no use whatever, as the Allies had only been deceiving the Germans into thinking that they had infra-red detectors. The red lights that Germans reported seeing on Allied aircraft were meant to decoy the Germans from detecting the Allied use of centimetric radar. The report on interrogation of survivors would lead us to believe that U-1228 returned from her very brief first patrol because of a bomb-damaged schnorkel. However, the U-boat's recently discovered War Diary reveals quite a different picture: near disaster through carbon-monoxide back-up in the schnorkel caused by careless workmanship in the shipyards, exacerbated by a bombing attack from an RAF Sunderland.[37]

U-1228 departed Bergen on 12 October 1944 for the second operational mission. She was a potentially powerful weapon. Her six tubes (four forward and two aft) fired a total of fourteen torpedoes (six acoustic T-5 Gnats, and eight T-3 LUTs); two twin 20-mm guns on platform 1 and her 3.7-cm gun on platform 2 provided anti-surface and anti-air protection. She carried the latest Hohentwiel anti-aircraft and anti-surface radar with mattress antenna. But poor workmanship prevented realization of her full potential. Marienfeld's shipboard technical personnel required eight days of the Atlantic crossing to rebuild the schnorkel head, which even then would not function properly. They had to exploit every available moment when surfaced to work on the bridge as the parts were too large to get down the hatch. Badgered by a series of other technical failures – gyro, echo sounder, rudder, 3.7-cm cannon, search radar, and surface radar – Marienfeld found his personnel having to cannibalize one piece of equipment in order to service another. All this time the U-boat was required to transmit weather reports. The importance of these reports for military planning in Germany may be gauged from an unprecedented message flashed to U-1228 on 4 November after a lengthy period of radio silence: "Marienfeld – signal weather report tonight, [they] are urgently required for the defence of the empire." This is the first such plea on record.

Kapitän zur See Lessing's type IXC/40 U-1231 had departed Kiel-Wik via the Skagerak, Horten, Christiansand, and Bergen on 5 October 1944 for a lack-lustre patrol, which eventually led him into the mouth of the St Lawrence west of Pointe des Monts. Lack of success, he ruefully noted on his return to Flensburg on 5 February 1945, derived from two frustrating circumstances: scarce commercial traffic in the Canadian operational zones, and the fact that targets he had either actually sighted or else picked up by hydrophones were always well out of range. This first operational patrol faced debilitating problems – unfamiliarity with new equipment, and the harassment of a variety of technical failures. The War Diary records, however, only one case of carbon-monoxide poisoning, and one instance when the "electro-motor engineer and two stokers became temporary casualties." The crew soon developed "great confidence in the schnorkel and felt absolutely safe." They in fact felt even more secure than many of their predecessors. For as defence against suspected infra-red detection, the whole hull of U-1231 had been coated with a protective rubber skin. On the whole, this "unsatisfying" mission depressed the crew's spirits considerably, particularly when they learned that Kapitän zur See Dobratz in U-1232 enjoyed such brilliant success operating in the very same zone off Halifax in January 1945. Lessing likened his apparently helpless tactical fate to that of a drifting mine waiting for something to bump into it.

Once Marienfeld (U-1228) had reached quadrant BB 9641 south of Newfoundland on 11 November 1944, BdU relayed Petersen's (U-541) situation report concerning prospects in the Gulf. Marienfeld seems to have been pleased. And so "I follow my teacher from [the] Pillau [submarine training school] into the same area," he noted in his War Diary. He would now take all precautions so as to "get into the operational area unnoticed" (KTB). During the early hours of 13 November, its upper deck bathed in moonlight, U-1228 encountered its "first enemy contact on the American [sic] Coast" (KTB). Without any prior warning, both the hydrophone operator and the officer of the watch at the air-target periscope simultaneously reported a close contact off the port bow that rapidly developed into a "shadow with single funnel and mast, and tall bow wave" heading southwest (KTB). Canadian Fairmiles, or *PC Boote* as Germans called them, using the American identifier, were noted among German submariners for their ability to make close approaches undetected on a near bows-on course. This particular *PC Boot*, as Marienfeld identified it (though it may have been the American Coast Guard cutter USS *Sassafras*), had proven the point again by passing harmlessly within 50–100 m of its enemy. Its failure to attack confirmed that Canadians really were as weak and unpractised as earlier reports had stated. On 14 November, Marienfeld reviewed the situation report of Petersen (U-541) and Schmoeckel (U-802) and reached his tactical decision: "Operate in quadrant BB 59 [Cabot Strait] as recommended by Petersen until the first success, and [only] then penetrate into the Gulf after the expected defence and security of traffic in the coastal zone" had been decoyed to the scene of his successful action (KTB). Following the advice of his former teacher led Marienfeld to cause the most serious Canadian loss of the month.

The safety of his own vessel demanded that he undertake urgent, and probably lengthy, repairs to his schnorkel before engaging the enemy. He therefore shaped course to pass 15 miles off the Channel Head and Rose Blanche lights, in order to enter what his *Sailing Directions* assured him to be "the least inhabited" area, Connoire Bay. Here, in any event, would be "the most favourable place to approach the coast at night without an echo sounder" (KTB). From 23 to 24 November Marienfeld seems to have enjoyed the scenery while cruising at periscope depth: the coast flushed in the "most beautiful and splendorous sunshine," as he passed 4 miles off Burnt Island; then "Cains Island Lighthouse" with the "Barasway waterfall" under cloudy skies. He passed 5 miles off La Pointe Bay, saw Ireland and Affer islands, but stopped 5 miles south of the haven of Connoire Bay when his gyro failed. His technicians completed repairs in surprisingly short order. Then, wending his way submerged through a tiny fishing fleet, Marienfeld once "again set course westward for Cabot Strait" during the dark morning hours of 24 November 1944.

The Flower-class corvette HMCS *Shawinigan* (Lt W.J. Jones, RCNR) had left Sydney Harbour on 23 November with USCG *Sassafras* for routine patrol in the Gulf. *Shawinigan* was an experienced ship. She had survived the U-boats' "happy hunting" season in the St Lawrence during 1942, had rescued victims of U-517 and U-541, and had spent months on the gruelling "triangle run" between New York, St John's, and Halifax. Like all corvettes of her class, the 205-foot-long *Shawinigan* displaced 950 tons and was modestly armed: two depth-charge rails and four throwers, asdic, a 4-inch gun forward, and a 2 pounder pom-pom aft. Her machine-guns had been replaced by six 20-mm oerlikons. In the course of refit she had also acquired two radar sets, one of them the newest and most sensitive 120-cm type 271 with higher definition and increased range to 20 nautical miles. Few ships in the local force enjoyed such an advantage. The additional equipment necessitated increasing her complement from five officers and sixty-one men to six officers and seventy-nine men.

At 0830 GMT on 24 November 1944, while U-1228 moved westward into their track, *Shawinigan* and *Sassafras* were signalled to discontinue their patrol in order to escort the ferry SS *Burgeo* from Sydney, across the Cabot Strait, to Port aux Basques, Newfoundland. This was a scheduled SPAB convoy like that in which the ferry SS *Caribou* had been sunk by U-69 in October 1942. The ships joined the *Burgeo* at 1015 GMT and arrived in Port aux Basques without incident at 1800 GMT the same day. *Sassafras* then detached while *Shawinigan*, having arranged to rendezvous with *Burgeo* at 1015 GMT next day for the daylight return to Sydney, undertook an independent patrol in the Cabot Strait. Marienfeld was the last man to see her.

Marienfeld's revised tactics now called for his remaining "outside the Gulf" after his first attack, "particularly as according to Petersen and Schmoeckel the Gulf traffic stops after a U-boat has been noticed" (KTB). This and equipment problems may account for Marienfeld holding back to the south even when searching for his first target. At 0145 on 25 November 1944, in "brightest moonlight, very good visibility and light sea," Marienfeld observed through his periscope the "coast, magnificent to see in the moonlight," picked up Sugar Loaf Mountain, and noted "the glow of Cape Ray Light on the horizon." Five minutes later, U-1228's hydrophones detected ship's propellers.

The sighting of a "zigzagging destroyer, base course northeast, range 3000 m" at 0220 shattered the idyllic scene in quadrant BB 5512. It took less than 10 minutes for Marienfeld to position U-1228 for a deadly shot with a T-5 acoustic Gnat. Aiming at the target's stern from 2500 m, Marienfeld fired at 0230. Two minutes later, the sounds of the torpedo merged with those of *Shawinigan*. The torpedo struck at 0234, raising a 50-m high blast column, heavy with showers of sparks and flame, which rapidly dissipated into thin clouds of smoke. Almost as soon as the torpedo had hit, *Shawinigan* "was gone" (KTB). "Great rushing sounds and crackling" immediately filled Marienfeld's hydrophones as the shattered hulk plummeted into the depths. At 0235 six of *Shawinigan's* primed depth charges exploded. Or else, as Marienfeld added, they might have been "scare charges of other escorts nearby" (KTB). U-1228 departed at a depth of 120 m "in order to stand outside Cabot Strait at evening schnorkelling" (KTB). Canadian records urge the view that *Shawinigan* was entirely alone in the strait at the time, and take no account of USCG *Sassafras*. Though U-1228 saw no evidence either of wreckage, survivors, or escorts, the Boat heard "various screw noises in shifting directions" as early as an hour and a half after the sinking. The earliest hydrophone contact even seemed to stop overhead. Whether *Sassafras* had attacked, or was even in the vicinity, remains unclear.

The *Burgeo* should have put back into Port aux Basques when *Shawinigan* failed to emerge from the mist and fog at the rendezvous next morning. Thinking perhaps that the escort might not be far off and would appear any moment, her master proceeded to Sydney alone, quite contrary to convoy instructions. He maintained strict radio silence. Thus not until after his arrival at 1757 GMT did Canadian authorities become aware that the corvette was missing. By this time a gale had blown up, grounding RCAF aircraft and seriously hampering the search by EG-16. NOIC Sydney advised C-in-C CNA he would have to await a moderation in the weather before augmenting EG-16 with all available Fairmiles in search of wreckage southeast of a line from Sydney Approaches to Port aux Basques. This would follow the direction of the prevailing current. Evidence of the disaster drifted southward as the storm subsided. On 26 November the Western Isles trawler HMS *Anticosti* discovered the first pieces of evidence 28 miles due east of Cape North, Cape Breton Island (42 miles southwest of Channel Head): one unmarked Carley float and small pieces of scattered wooden wreckage. Sixteen miles further south of Channel Head, near where *Shawinigan* had gone down, HMCS *Springhill* recovered three bodies. She transferred a total of six bodies to HMCS *Truro* on 27 November before continuing her search. HMCS *Gananoque* recovered another unmarked float on 29 November, some 75 miles south of Channel Head and 30 miles to the east of Flint Island. Nothing else remained.

A Board of Inquiry convened at Sydney on 30 November 1944 heard evidence from all possible sources. Yet the only real evidence were the macabre findings of EG-16 and the belief of the master of the SS *Burgeo* and of some Newfoundland fishermen that they had heard explosions at sea. The board considered it improbable that the ship had been destroyed by exploding boilers, magazines, or depth charges except in consequence of torpedoing. It ruled out a drifting mine. The disconsolate circumstances of *Shawinigan*'s fate only reached Canadian authorities in general outline when Marienfeld and his Chief Engineer, Friedrich Asmussen, recalled the situation before Allied interrogators after U-1228's surrender in May 1945. For the moment, the case remained undetermined.

Navy Minister Macdonald's first press release on 7 December 1944, the night on which the House of Commons was to vote on conscription, did not dispel the aura of mystery. Headlines of the late edition of the *Ottawa Journal* proclaimed "Canadian Corvette Sunk with All Crew – Five Drown, 85 Missing on Shawinigan." The newspaper went on to contradict itself in the text on numbers lost and bodies found. Though the minister had "revealed no details" (he didn't have any), the incident provided the occasion for reviewing the vessel's achievements against "Hitler's undersea raiders" who doubtless had sunk her on her last "operational duty in the North Atlantic." She was "the ninth corvette and the nineteenth [Canadian] warship whose loss [had been] announced by the RCN this war."

Marienfeld's failure to thrust on into the Gulf simply because of technical defects in gyro and schnorkel, and in consequence to head home early despite authorization to operate off Halifax, angered BdU. Though BdU's wrath seems unfair under the circumstances, it was doubtless symptomatic of his frustration at having to witness the decreasing effectiveness of his fleet. As usual, Rodger Winn in the Operational Intelligence Centre in England was reading the German Enigma signals, and noted with a hint of commiseration that Marienfeld had been "sharply rebuked for [his] allegedly excessive caution."[38] Dönitz addressed the problem of recalcitrance on 14 December 1944 in Standing Order no. 199. This unequivocal signal to all commanding officers – which Winn of course read – reviewed Marienfeld's experience and his reasons for remaining outside the Gulf. But it insisted that caution in this case was wrong. Spurning all excuses, Dönitz set the tone for the final weeks and months of the U-boat war: any commanding officer who pressed home the attack "whatever the risk" would always be right.

CHAPTER NINE

U-Boat Christmas

The Submarine Tracking Room in Naval Service Headquarters, Ottawa, had, early in December 1944, developed a fairly clear picture of recent U-boat operations in Canadian waters. Information filtering to NSHQ from Ultra, as well as through ships and commands on the basis of D/F fixes, sightings, and attacks, provided evidence of what one official regarded as "an increase in enemy submarine activity in the Canadian Coastal Zone."[1] Estimates had correctly placed four U-boats in the area on 1 December, roughly corresponding to the patrol zones occupied by U-1228 (Cabot Strait), U-1231 (Gaspé), U-1230 (Gulf of Maine/Bay of Fundy), and U-806 (approaching the eastern limits inbound). NSHQ tracked general U-boat movement towards Halifax on 4 December, the departure of one U-boat (U-1228) from the zone on 5 December, and circumscribed the area of highest risk as lying within 60–200 miles of the coast.

Lessing's U-1231 had passed deep into the Gulf towards the end of the previous month, while Marienfeld's U-1228 hunted HMCS *Shawinigan* in Cabot Strait. Having passed through the river mouth, U-1231 had sighted little more than a "saw mill in full operation," a wireless station on the snow-covered north shore by Pointe de Manicougan, and then picked up the lights of Matane and Ste Félicité. Lessing had experienced the ignominy of observing three FAT (surface-search angular contact) torpedoes bounce off the hull of an utterly oblivious freighter he stalked during one night within 6 miles of Les Méchins. Even his careful attack on HMCS *Matapedia* escorting Quebec–Sydney convoy QS-107 off Cap Chat had failed. All his torpedoes were duds. It was therefore no disappointment when BdU directed him to Halifax. Coastal convoys, as he might have suspected, were now winding down. The last Sydney–Quebec convoy of the season (SQ-97A) sailed on 7 December, and the final Quebec–Sydney convoy (QS-109) on 13 December. Dejected by faulty equipment and badgered by a constantly icing schnorkel, Lessing had long since considered departing for Halifax in response to Ackermann's promising report. His operations off Nova Scotia would do little more than confuse the patrols searching for Hornbostel's U-806.

Hilbig's U-1230 had fared significantly better during these days. Returning northbound to operations off the southeast coast of Nova Scotia from the Gulf of Maine where U-1230 had landed two agents, the Boat accounted for Canada's first victim of the month. At 1000 GMT on 3 December it sank the 5458-ton Canadian National Steamships vessel SS *Cornwallis* 10 miles southwest of Mount Desert Rock in the Gulf of Maine. *Cornwallis* had been proceeding independently from Barbados to Saint John, New Brunswick, with a full cargo of sugar and molasses. Five survivors were subsequently landed at Rockland, Maine. U.S. authorities initiated an intensive air-and-surface search with two large task units (22.3 and 22.4). Yet, in the whimsical words of a naval summary, "though several contacts were made and two attacks carried out, there is no indication that the U-Boat was inconvenienced."[2] The almost immediate arrests of Hilbig's spies made sensational news. As reported in the *Halifax Herald* and others, both Roosevelt and Churchill had regarded Hilbig's exploit as "yet another indication that the menace of Germany's underseas fleet is real and continuing."[3]

Vigilance at sea was, however, curiously counterbalanced by a relaxation of military organization ashore. The army's Atlantic Command, which had been created in August 1940 as part of the joint U.S.–Canada defence scheme (covering Quebec, Nova Scotia, the St Lawrence Waterway, New Brunswick, and Labrador) was now being disbanded. Local commanders were to resume command of their own districts as in peacetime. Atlantic Command had previously liaised directly with RCAF and the navy on all aspects of coastal defence. It had controlled all the infantry regiments stationed at vital ports, as well as the heavy coastal artillery batteries and anti-aircraft units. Now, however, with the Allies advancing deeper into Europe and the Battle of the Atlantic in hand, enemy landings on the Atlantic coast seemed quite unlikely. Indeed, the landing of the agents Langbein in the Bay of Fundy and von Janowski in the Baie des Chaleurs in 1942, the establishment of the German weather station in Labrador in 1943, and the attempted rescues of German prisoners of war by U-262 and U-536 that same year proved to be the closest that German forces ever came to actually establishing a bridgehead on Canadian soil. As for the war in Canadian waters, the sinking of the SS *Samtucky* on 21 December, and of HMCS *Clayoquot* just off Halifax on Christmas Eve 1944, served as a poignant reminder that any relaxation of one's guard was premature.

Kapitän zur See Klaus Hornbostel today describes the first and only operational cruise of his type IXC/40 U-boat U-806 as probably quite typical of the last phase of the war.[4] Built in the Seebeck-Werft in Bremerhaven-Wesermünde and commissioned on 29 April 1944, the U-boat was up to date in all respects. It had both schnorkel and the most modern Hohentwiel radar. The Hohentwiel (*seetakt*) was originally designed for the Luftwaffe in 1943 as a surface-vessel search radar, and was developed in five different versions in order to meet the requirements of different combat environments. In essence, Hornbostel's model was designed to enable U-boats to detect both surface vessels and aircraft, giving both bearing and range in all weather. It detected destroyers at 4–5 km, surfaced U-boats at 3 km; small 1500-ton coastal ships were picked up at 6 km, and 6000-ton ships at 10 km. Aircraft, depending upon their size, altitude and direction of flight, could be detected between 9 and 40 km.[5] By the same token, the British type 271 10-cm radar, which few Canadian warships carried, was capable of detecting a schnorkel target at ranges of 4000–5000 yards in seas of state 3 or 4.[6] The type 271 radar fitted in Canadian ships detected schnorkels at significantly shorter ranges.

Theoretically, at least, the tactical advantage lay entirely with the German submariners in Canadian inshore waters. As it turned out, however, the dockyard workmanship in Germany was no longer up to previous standards. Just before departure, for example, both the Hohentwiel and the radio direction finder became unserviceable. There was always a struggle with the radio antennae and insulation, a factor that rendered signal traffic in the operational zone complicated, if not impossible. Thus, where the War Diary of BdU records the despatch of signals to U-806, it nowhere mentions having received any replies until the submarine's task was completed. In fact, neither BdU nor the German Naval Staff learned of Hornbostel's success off Halifax until 19 January 1945. This was six weeks after U-806 had entered the Canadian operation zone, and four weeks after it had sunk HMCS *Clayoquot*. Other defects came to light early and increased in frequency as the mission wore on. The malfunctioning schnorkel rod system would force the U-boat to leave its operational area prematurely. Such technical problems Hornbostel attributed to the inexperience of shore personnel.[7]

Incomparably more serious in retrospect were the difficulties encountered in working up the crew. As in earlier years, of course, the individual sailors were trained for submarine duty in special courses; the crew was then trained as a unit with its own U-boat. But they lacked in-depth sea experience and hands-on practice in the U-boats. This was particularly true of the senior ranks in U-806. Captain Hornbostel, himself a qualified surface gunnery specialist, had only recently retrained for watch-keeping duties. He had been assistant gunnery officer aboard the *Scheer* during its encounter with Captain Fogerty Fagen, VC, in *Jervis Bay*. Yet he had no actual submarine sea time as such, other than his formal training as submarine watch officer, followed immediately by a command qualifying course. By the end of the war sailors were being mobilized so quickly that he was not even allowed the custom, previously accorded CO-designates, of understudying an operational U-boat skipper during an actual mission. On completion of his classes, he underwent work-ups with his new Boat and crew in home waters, and set off on his first solo sortie, which would last over four months.

Other submariners experienced similar fates. U-806's Executive Officer, Gerd Koppen, for example, was a retrained minesweeping officer; the Chief Engineer had just completed his first course; and the NCO navigator was a former army signalman who had never been to sea. None of them had any first-hand sea experience. If all these young people had not possessed such remarkable character, Hornbostel reflects today, and if the three decisive technical NCOs (diesel, electromotors, radar/radio/hydrophones) had not had broad experience in submarines, the journey of U-806 would have ended less happily. Yet their volunteer-reserve ("Wavy Navy") opponents in the encounter off Halifax were perhaps scarcely better prepared. The captain of the ill-fated HMCS *Clayoquot* is a case in point. A former bank clerk, LCdr Craig Campbell, RCNVR, assumed command on 26 July 1944. He exemplifies the rather rapid training of the civilians who swelled Canada's tiny professional navy, which numbered 1819 personnel and thirteen ships in 1939, to some 90,000 personnel and 400 warships by 1945.[8] Rapid expansion plus arduous times – or, in the words of the naval toast, "a bloody war and sickly seasons" – transformed a landsman into the rough facsimile of a master mariner in short order.

U-806 departed Kiel on its sole operational mission on 14 October 1944, and touched in at the usual Norwegian staging points of Horten and Christiansand before passing into the North Atlantic through the so-called Rose Garden in the Iceland–Faroes Gap. Prevailing heavy seas caused the inexperienced crew considerable difficulty (KTB). Hornbostel's orders indicated only a temporary operational zone in the North Atlantic where he would report weather. BdU had apprised Hornbostel that the assessment of the enemy's operational intentions demanded "absolute clarity on the large weather picture" and that therefore "constant weather reporting was of the utmost importance." BdU had now positioned four U-boats so as to filter the prevailing eastbound weather pattern: Hechler's U-870 at 19° W on a great circle route between the Biscay and Cape Cod (BE 4545); Lange's U-711 at 24° W to the far west of Ireland (AL 4469); Dobratz's U-1232 at 35° W, east of Cape Farewell; and Hornbostel's U-806 at 35° W in mid Atlantic.[9] Regular weather broadcasting from relatively constant patrol stations exposed the U-boats to detection by Allied D/F stations. Yet Dönitz's instructions insisted that the "importance and seriousness of the task requires the application of all measures to get radio signals through," whether by exercising evasive routes, feints, or use of a variety of radio frequencies.[10] Not until 13 November did BdU direct Hornbostel to the general area off Nova Scotia, and not until 30 November did he specify Halifax. That day he assigned Dobratz's U-1232 and Marienfeld's U-1228 to operate as circumstances might warrant in precisely the same quadrant. Marienfeld, as we have seen, declined the directive.

By midnight GMT on 13 December, as Lessing's U-1231 lay off Egg Island some 30 miles northeast of the Sambro lightship, U-806 completed its outbound track of 4400 nautical miles and reached naval quadrant CB 2225, "off Halifax" (KTB), a position actually 65 miles southeast of Sambro Island Light. Schnorkelling as frequently as possible, U-806 began to stake out the field and orient itself to the Canadian inshore zone. Occasional hydrophone contacts interrupted an otherwise colourless routine as U-806 approached the coast. At 0423 GMT on 15 December, Hornbostel made landfall from the northeast and noted "the first sighting of Egg Island Light" (KTB). Throughout his sojourn off Halifax, Hornbostel could navigate by night and day solely by coastal pilotage with the aid of such illuminated beacons. BdU received similar observations from U-1231 in the St Lawrence. An hour and a half before sighting Egg Island, in fact, Hornbostel had seen Halifax itself "clear as a bright glow over the horizon" (KTB). He had rather expected such an important naval and convoy base to be disciplined by black-outs, or at least by dim-outs. But Haligonians had proven somewhat petulant on this issue and preferred their light.

The familiar glow of Halifax, recognized by German submariners since their first approaches in 1942, served as a constant point of reference during the operations of U-806. Equally useful was the famous Sambro lightship situated at the southern extremity of the swept channel for convoys heading overseas or to Boston. Its bright red hull had for years proclaimed the name "Halifax" in large white letters, and had left both Allied and Axis mariners in no doubt as to their location. The East Halifax lightship rode at anchor in the immediate vicinity, 7.8 miles to the northeast. Designated "Isolde" by the Germans, after the girl-friend of Gerd Koppen, the Executive Officer of U-806, it could be seen on this misty day at a range of 6 miles. It could also be recognized by "the rattling of her anchor cables" (KTB). Hornbostel suspected that "Isolde" marked a steamer route for night passages. In fact, he had discovered the eastern end of the swept channel for convoys heading to Newfoundland. The convoy separation lanes thus indicated concur almost precisely with those traffic separation lanes marked on present-day nautical charts.

Canadian authorities had placed other deep-sea navigation marks at points where shipping would converge in the approaches to Halifax. These Hornbostel entered on his DR plot and named after the fashion of the East Halifax lightship. The marker buoy "Klaus" (named after himself) rode 11.5 miles SSW of the Sambro lightship; buoy "Karla" (named after his wife) 8.3 miles closer in; and buoy "Elfriede" (named after the Second Officer's girl-friend) 8.5 miles ESE of the East Halifax lightship. The crew of Captain Kurt Dobratz later resisted the temptation of taunting their peaceful adversaries by hanging signs on these buoys in order to advertise the fact that the "grey wolves" had arrived. They even considered pinching "a bloody great lightbuoy as a victory trophy" if only they could have gotten it through the conning tower hatch.[11] They needed such navigational aids and therefore left them alone.

The naval signal station on Chebucto Head provided a special reference point for both Hornbostel and Dobratz. They correctly identified it as Radio Camperdown, and regularly observed it communicating "with vessels by bright signal lamps" (KTB). However, neither Dobratz nor Hornbostel realized that it also housed a passive hydrophone station. Kapitänleutnant Paul Ackermann (U-1221) had meanwhile informed BdU from his Halifax station during one of BdU's cipher "conversations" that U-boats could only expect tactical success directly off Halifax. These "conversations," as Dönitz termed them, were a rapid series of cipher-signal exchanges between BdU and a U-boat commander that provided on-the-spot immediacy, and communication of conditions that actually obtained at the time of transmission. The "conversation" with Ackermann assured BdU that the zone promised safe hunting. They could expect "meagre, tired [Allied] surveillance." Significantly, Ackermann insisted that conditions were favourable for the submarine's "GHG" multiple hydrophone sensors, and that escorts ran without asdic.[12] This amplified his earlier signal that had attracted Lessing (U-1231) to the area. BdU passed Ackermann's observations to Hornbostel on 10 December by cipher *Funkschlüssel-M* and implied that Hornbostel would hold all the cards in any confrontation with the Canadians. Assured of success, he ordered Hornbostel to "press close to the harbour" ("*dicht ran an den Hafen*"). BdU thus envisaged the simultaneous operations of four U-boats off Halifax.

Knowledge of the U-boats' general presence did not solve the Allies' defence problem. For, whereas it had proven possible to plot with a certain degree of accuracy the positions of U-boats approaching or leaving the zone, they eluded detection once on their patrol station. As the Director of Operations Division advised the Chief of Naval Staff in November 1944: "The schnorkel has reduced the possibility of sighting to a minimum, and the only way in which the positioning of a U-Boat is likely to be fixed is by offensive action on its part."[13]

U-boats found navigation in Canadian waters uncomplicated in good visibility. Yet such conditions were rare in winter. Mist, ground fog, snow, rain, and generally very poor visibility predominated. In such constraining circumstances, submarines relied on Canadian radio aids, and upon their own echo sounders and hydrophones. The procedure often courted danger. Thus, while patrolling submerged off the Sambro lightship in swirling arctic sea smoke, U-806 suddenly detected approaching propeller noises, which swelled in intensity and actually crossed directly overhead. Indeed, a paravane of a passing minesweeper had caught the U-boat's steel cable net guard, which ran from conning tower to bow, and snapped it off with a resounding crack. Through his periscope, Hornbostel observed a second minesweeper stop, recover the dangling paravane, and proceed innocently on its way. "All around the U-boat," Hornbostel's War Diary reveals, pulsed "constant hydrophone echoes of ships with "rattling drogues" (*Rasselboje*) and "escorts with asdic" (KTB). The "rattling drogues," as Hornbostel called the Canadian-built Cat Gear anti-Gnat noise-makers, which the warships towed, dominated the underwater acoustic field. Contrary to Ackermann's earlier report, Hornbostel quite rightly believed asdic to constitute standard equipment in escort vessels; but he incorrectly assumed that it was simply switched on and left running as a scare mechanism even when no U-boats were expected. Hornbostel gained the impression of passivity from the fact that attacks frequently failed to materialize even after asdic beams had struck the U-boat's hull. In actual fact, however, when no attack was in progress, asdic sounds always indicated an active precautionary search. The instrument was never simply left unattended in the hope that its audible pulses would frighten an assailant away. Not infrequently, however, an operator simply failed to interpret his asdic correctly. Danger prevailed in good visibility as well, for while travelling at periscope depth Hornbostel repeatedly experienced the uncanny ability of Fairmiles to approach "head on at very close range" without being heard. They could become very "unpleasant" indeed (KTB).

Hornbostel appears to have been bolder than the more solicitous Lessing (U-1231) who, for understandable technical reasons and suspected shortage of fuel, held back to the Sable Island area. As it turned out, the Chief Engineer's miscalculation of fuel reserves had caused U-1231 to turn home. Once the error was discovered, however, Lessing backtracked to Halifax, having lost six patrol days in the process. Encouraged by official German news bulletins on the Ardennes offensive, which reported that "our massive attack begun on 16 December south of Aachen was advancing well," the U-boats rallied for inshore sorties. Such situation reports exerted a telling impact on crew morale. As the War Diary of Lessing's U-1231 reveals, there was now "great joy in the Boat."[14]

U-806 did not need long to reconnoitre almost the whole Halifax operational area, its traffic routes, and salient points. Characteristic of the zone were the ubiquitous "rattling buoys," so-called by analogy with the German "GBT" acoustic buoys (*Geraüschboje Tiefton*) used as defence against acoustic mines. Sometimes these drogues seemed to be towed by escorts; at other times they seemed anchored. The "screeching circular saws" were even more confusing and unnerving. Hornbostel assumed that these were towed by larger escorts like corvettes, frigates, and destroyers. Whether these sounds emanated from anti-Gnat devices or active detection equipment was never clear to the U-boat skipper. Both sounds, as far as can be ascertained, emanated from anti-Gnat devices: the 3-ton "Foxer"-towed array employed by British and American ships, and the very much lighter Canadian Cat Gear, which the RN began to adopt in February 1944 as the "Unifoxer." Adhering to current A/S policy at the time, *Clayoquot* was not streaming her Cat as U-boats were not expected in the area; HMCS *Transcona* immediately streamed hers once the attack began, and survived.[15] But, as will be seen, the situation was far more complex than this. The incident fuelled the running debate on precisely when and under what circumstances warships should resort to these anti-Gnat devices.

The voyage of HMCS *Clayoquot* to her fateful encounter with U-806 had begun with her launching on 3 October 1940 at Prince Rupert Drydock in Prince Rupert, British Columbia.[16] Launched as HMCS *Esperanza*, the Bangor minesweeper was renamed and commissioned on 22 August 1941. After several weeks of trials and work-ups, she sailed under the command of the career naval officer LCdr G.A. Thomas, RCN, with her sister Bangors HMCS *Quinte* and *Ungava* via the Panama Canal in order to support the hard-pressed Escort Group in the Atlantic struggle. *Clayoquot* reached Halifax via Bermuda on 14 November 1941 and commenced operations with the Local Western Escort Force in January 1942. She faced her first chance of attacking a U-boat on 16 February while escorting the thirty-two-ship convoy SC-70 with five other escorts. In extremely severe weather, with a frozen sea of pancake ice stretching from Jeddore Head (some 40 road miles from Halifax) to approximately 50 miles to seaward, she failed in attacking Kapitänleutnant Zimmermann's U-136, to which the corvette HMCS *Spikenard* had fallen victim six days earlier. The crew later caught sight of their first U-boat off the East Halifax lightship on 8 April 1942. HMCS *Chedabucto* had been about to conduct a depth-charge attack when its submerged target suddenly surfaced 1700 yards ahead. The unidentified U-boat escaped an otherwise unavoidable ramming when *Chedabucto's* steering gear jammed.[17] *Clayoquot's* involvement in rescue operations after the sinking of HMCS *Charlottetown* on 11 September 1942 presaged the almost parallel action she herself would experience on Christmas Eve 1944.

The tactical situation developed a threatening visage towards noon GMT on 20 December 1944. After a tour of 4831 nautical miles, U-806 stood 9 miles off Chebucto Head. Her "GHG" multiple hydrophone array revealed a variety of machine noises (propellers and pistons), which seemingly disappeared northeastward from Cape Sambro in the direction of Portuguese Shoal. Dispiriting, chilling weather prevailed, with perhaps one of the most paralysing natural enemies in the Battle of the Atlantic: thick fog. Wartime statistics reveal a heavy monthly toll of Allied shipping through collisions and groundings in reduced visibility in Canadian waters. The constant, cloying fog complicated attack and defence alike. Together with the strong currents in the area, it jeopardized the U-boat's navigation. The combat situation in this inhospitable attack zone remained like any other: the advantages of one opponent had to be played off against the disadvantages of the other. But here off Halifax, the U-boat seemed to hold a certain purely technical advantage.

On 20 December 1944, Hornbostel's U-806 struck upon the old acoustic anomaly: piston noises passing close along the coast, gradually fading into the all-pervasive and continuous sounds of a "rattling buoy" (KTB) off Chebucto Head. Cruising at periscope depth, U-806 saw a "PC boat" emerge from the mists, only to fade into the puzzling rattling close to shore. In German usage, "PC boat" designated American high-speed anti-submarine vessels. In this case, however, U-806 was dealing with Canadian Fairmiles. Lessing's U-1231 had meanwhile experienced similar acoustic anomalies from Emerald Bank to Cap Canso and Country Island. Lessing had even found them right in Chedabucto Bay itself, into which a navigational error had led him in a snow storm.

Schnorkelling shortly after midnight on 20 December, U-806 picked up the propeller noises of a patrol vessel. Then came the eerie "circular saw" whose nerve-cutting screech was soon dominated by an incisive "ping ping," as the opponents' asdic enveloped the U-boat's hull. The patrol vessel passed without attacking. No other vessel had yet come so close to contacting the U-boat. In the course of events, U-806 espied a number of isolated merchant and warships working their way through the ground fog in choppy seas. Hornbostel had few illusions about Canadian state-of-the-art technology. His reconnaissance patrol, which had first thrust westward toward Chebucto Head, now formed a long flat curve southward until it stood approximately 4 miles from the Sambro lightship. This would soon become the focal point for further action.

Hornbostel's first strike on the evening of 21 December 1944 triggered a series of events culminating in a massive A/S search. Running at periscope depth, he observed at 1947 GMT a "steamer belonging to a small convoy of four Liberty ships in two columns" (KTB). It was the 9-knot convoy HHX-327 forming up for departure. U-806 immediately went to action stations and one minute later fired a double salvo from a range of 1500 m. It missed. Hornbostel had "recognized too late that the convoy, coming from the southwest," had turned "northward around the Sambro lightship" (KTB). At 2004 GMT he fired a T-5 Gnat curved shot at the port aft steamer. She was the 7219-ton freighter SS *Samtucky* on bare-boat charter from the U.S. Maritime Commission to the British Ministry of Transport. The acoustic torpedo struck her 2 minutes 21 seconds later. Seeing "the stricken Liberty ship stern low in the water" with a single corvette standing by, Hornbostel fired the coup de grâce. It exploded on target after a run of 8 minutes 53 seconds. The lengthy run suggests it may have been a LUT (*Lageunabhängiger Torpedo*) or FAT (*Flächenabsu-chender Torpedo*) surface-search loop-track shot. Hornbostel now expected a short, sharp reaction because of his close proximity to Halifax. He therefore slipped away temporarily to the east.

Canadian interpretations of the event seem to have been at first somewhat confused. The Merchant Casualty Report recorded the *Samtucky* as sunk.[18] The Monthly Operational Summary recorded that, although "seriously damaged and in a sinking condition, the vessel, with the aid of her own engines and tugs despatched from Halifax, was able to return to port and was beached at McNabb's Cove" on 22 December.[19] The *Samtucky* was eventually refloated and remained in service until at least 1948.[20] Although interrogation of the master and later examination of the damage by divers urged the view "that the damage was caused by an enemy torpedo," the immediate buzz in the port of Halifax suggested that she had struck a drifting mine. The navy faced the uneasy task of mobilizing a minesweeper during the holiday season.

Canadian naval authorities had apparently granted Christmas leave to as many personnel as possible. The commanding officer of HMCS *Clayoquot*, Acting LCdr Craig Campbell, still recalls having been in Chester, Nova Scotia, a small town 80 km from Halifax, on the day of the *Samtucky* incident. Enjoying a glass of rum by the fireside, he was abruptly summoned back to Halifax to prepare his ship for immediate departure. But only one-third of his crew was ready for duty aboard. The other two-thirds were on leave and had either to be recalled or temporarily replaced. Time being of the essence, Campbell augmented from the manning pool and shifted ship forthwith to French Cable Wharf in order to fit the Oropesa minesweeping gear. This posed a problem, for up to now the Bangor minesweeper *Clayoquot* had served exclusively as an escort vessel. Nobody on board had any real experience with the equipment that was being hastily installed. With neither experienced personnel nor a worked-up crew, Campbell put to sea with his minesweeping manual quite literally in hand.

Hornbostel's escape route meanwhile followed a broad southwestern track, then turned northeast to curve 25 miles south of Jeddore Head and then to Egg Island. Here he stood within a few miles of Lessing's U-1231. Unaware of each other's presence, they followed their own plans. Lessing hopelessly chased a 3000-ton freighter at full surfaced speed off Sheet Harbour and finally gave up in disgust. U-806's broad loop led back to Chebucto Head where its hydrophones tracked a variety of distant targets. This was the same "heavy traffic before Christmas" that Lessing had observed.[21] In Hornbostel's case, however, an attack opportunity developed on 22 December. His triple salvo aimed at a "merchant vessel and zigzagging Flower-class corvette" off Egg Island failed. Two of the torpedoes proved faulty, and the third was damaged by a jammed retractor rod, but the explosion signalled his presence.

Technical failures throughout the mission intensified the kind of feelings of tactical isolation that Dönitz strove to overcome throughout the war. His personal touch bolstered the camaraderie on board and the sense of community throughout the service. His leadership style filtered throughout the command and often expressed itself in personal messages to individuals of all ranks. Thus, on 22 December, the Fifth U-boat Flotilla congratulated Hornbostel on the birth of his son back in Germany.

A subsequent laconic signal advised U-806 that "Hilbig" (U-1230) was perhaps in the area. Later, on 23 December, Hornbostel intercepted a signal assigning a contiguous patrol to U-1232. As recorded in his War Diary, "that means that U-Dobratz can be expected out here with us" (KTB). Maintaining radio silence, Hornbostel awaited his two experienced colleagues: Kapitänleutnant Hans Hilbig (U-1230), whom BdU expected off Halifax by 20 December after his clandestine operation in Maine; and Kapitän zur See Kurt Dobratz (U-1232) who after the *Clayoquot* incident attacked five ships out of three convoys in the Halifax area, for a total of 26,904 tons.[22] The C-in-C CNA suspected that two U-boats were operating while events surrounding *Clayoquot* and convoy XB-139 unfolded off Halifax. This suspicion influenced later tactical decisions and sheds light on many apparent inconsistencies in asdic results and methods of attack against the supposed lone assailant, which the escorts themselves thought they were hunting.

Since its attack on SS *Samtucky* on 21 December, U-806 had reconnoitred the whole inshore patrol zone. After over 5000 miles on patrol, it stood by noon GMT on 24 December in the vicinity of the Sambro lightship. It was surrounded by constant hydrophone echoes, and plagued by the puzzling "circular saws and rattling buoys" (KTB), whose sounds emanated from well beyond visual distance. Lessing's U-1231 was meanwhile spending its "Christmas on patrol in the sixth year of the war" (KTB) off Egg Island and Jeddore Rock. Lessing had just intercepted a message ordering Dobratz's U-1232 to occupy the Halifax area, but had decided to "stay here anyway as there's room enough" at the inn and he was soon to move off anyway (KTB). U-1230 remained silent.

Early on 24 December 1944, C-in-C CNA ordered an Escort Group consisting of the frigate *Kirkland Lake* and the Bangor minesweepers HMCS *Clayoquot* and *Transcona* to "sanitize" the route of convoy HJF-36 by executing a routine antisubmarine sweep. The code jargon indicated an independently routed "Monster," the 8194-ton troop ship SS *Lady Rodney* en route from Halifax to St John's. The three escorts were then to accompany convoy XB-139 to Boston. Screened by the corvette HMCS *Fennel* (LCdr K.L. Johnson, RCNVR) and the Bangor HMCS *Burlington* (Lt J.M. Richardson, RCNVR), SS *Lady Rodney* passed through the gates at 1324 GMT. Lurking off the Sambro lightship at periscope depth, U-806 spotted the first of "three Flower-class corvettes" (KTB). This was actually the frigate HMCS *Kirkland Lake* with the two Bangors *Clayoquot* and *Transcona* proceeding from seaward in line abreast from the "Monster" patrol. Soon the Bangors lay visible, broad on the U-boat's bow at 3500 and 4000 m respectively. At 1433 hours, U-806 sighted "ahead a convoy of about eight ships [actually the twelve ships of convoy XB-139] in broad formation, departing Halifax" (KTB). Hornbostel now stood outside the charmed circle to port, and led on to the port lead escort at a range of 400 m. At action stations 1 minute later, U-806 sighted broad on the port bow a "fourth corvette" – probably HMCS *Fennel* – at 1800 m.

The swiftly changing combat picture becomes obscure at this point. Two converging escort groups and two converging convoys were leading on to the same marshalling point. Inconsistencies between German and Canadian time frames obscure the picture even further. Be that as it may, one can imagine the tactical situation schematically as an inverted and elongated horseshoe, the upper left point of which marked Chebucto Head. Thus, the left side would cover the initial convoy route on the present-day traffic-management lane, and (a feature that U-806 could not possibly have construed) would curve northward around the Sambro lightship to the convoy rallying point. According to this scheme, U-806 stood at the open upper end of our imaginary horseshoe, her stern pointing to shallower waters, while the bow zone was encircled by enemy ships. Shortly after Hornbostel's attack, Escort Group 27 would be ordered to leave its inbound convoy with the HOMP (Home Ocean Meeting Point) and provide close antisubmarine support. In effect, therefore, EG-27 would tactically seal off the open end of the stylized horseshoe. But from Hornbostel's viewpoint, the situation seemed by no means as threatening as this. Assuming that convoy XB-139 and its escorts would hold their base course of 145° (T) for a while longer, he would not have inferred the horseshoe-shaped patrol line that threatened to encircle him. In all other respects, his firing position compared with that of three days earlier during the attack on SS *Samtucky*.

At 1430 hours (1030 local time) on 24 December 1944, as convoy XB-139 passed buoy no. 1 in the swept channel out of Halifax, the Escort Group was steaming in line abreast at 1000 yard intervals: HMCS *Kirkland Lake*, *Clayoquot* in the centre, and *Transcona*. When the group reached the lower curve of the narrow "horseshoe," just 2 miles from the Sambro lightship, the escort commander signalled by flag hoist the order to take previously assigned positions on the convoy. By naval practice, all ships acknowledged receipt of the Senior Officer's signal by repeating his flag hoist on their own halyards, or in this case by hoisting an answering pennant. This could sometimes be a time-consuming process, especially in low visibility or when winds were unfavourable and flags hung limp or askew. Once all ships were flying his series of flags, the Senior Officer would "execute" the signal by hauling his hoist down. Thus ships could manoeuvre while maintaining absolute radio silence. According to ACIs (Atlantic Convoy Instructions), ships would proceed at full speed to their assigned stations, reducing to 12 knots on arrival, and immediately commence zigzagging. Hornbostel watched the activity without understanding its intent.

When the signal was executed, *Clayoquot* may have reacted somewhat more quickly than the others; she had to get to the other side of the convoy. Or possibly she responded in timely fashion where the others were slow. This gave Hornbostel the sudden and distinct impression that *Clayoquot* had detected his presence and was pulling out of line to commence her attack. In fact, *Clayoquot* was unaware of U-806, but was crossing its track. U-806 now "counter-attacked" in self-defence by firing a T-5 Gnat acoustic torpedo, and then dived to 50 m in order to escape its own shot. Sixty-nine seconds later, Hornbostel heard the hit and brought U-806 to periscope depth to observe its effects. A desolate image emerged, a broken ship on grey seas. Hornbostel saw a "corvette sinking quickly with only the aft superstructure towering out of the water ... Another corvette [actually the Bangor *Transcona*] alongside its stricken comrade [while] the other one [HMCS *Fennel* of convoy HFJ-36] shows a high stern sea" (KTB), as she thrust ahead at full speed. Hornbostel still recalls the sight from the periscope of U-806. He had gained the impression that *Clayoquot* lay broken in two, her mast staggering forward, and the forward and aft superstructures slowly inclining inward toward one another. In fact, the powerful Gnat had blown the Bangor's stern to the vertical.

Down below "in the cellar," the crew of U-806 was excited. So, too, were the Canadians. Inexperience and tension on both sides led to inaccuracies when recalling or recording events. The Canadians were never clear, for example, whether the Bangor had been struck from her port or starboard quarter, a fact that would have enabled them to surmise the direction of attack.[23] They agreed, however, that the weapon was a Gnat. Two almost simultaneous explosions – the first from the torpedo itself and the second from the magazine of spare charges stored on the quarter-deck – blasted the whole stern section into a vertical position against the hatch of the after officers' cabin. The blasts peeled back the whole quarter-deck like the lid of a tin can and tossed the minesweeping winch over the mast on to the forecastle, together with pieces of depth charge that landed on the bridge. Jagged fragments of depth charge passed through the galley skylight on to the stove where Petty Officer P. Dorion was just removing the ship's company's dinner. The fortuitous timing of the attack saved lives, for the majority of the ship's company had mustered up forward for their daily issue of grog before the noon meal.

Blowing heavy clouds of steam in a holocaust of noise, and spewing smoke from her stern, the ship listed severely to starboard and had to be abandoned immediately. As the steam subsided, the Executive Officer caught sight of two officers, Lt Paul Finlay and Slt William Munro, RCNVR, trapped in the twisted after cabin. Thrusting their bloodied heads in turn through the scuttle through which they could not hope to squeeze to safety, they shouted desperately for axes to chop or pry their way out. Rescue tools lay long since under water. The young men were left to their grisly fate. Other trapped men managed to escape by the narrowest margin. Caught in the aftermost section of the engine room, Stoker Peter Bewzak of Kapuskasing, Ontario, writhed his way the last seven feet to safety through a tight ventilator shaft. Two sailors saved many lives by chopping the whaler's falls. Survivors of the explosion quickly abandoned ship in an orderly and disciplined manner. All but four officers and four seamen got clear before *Clayoquot* went down at 1351 GMT in position 44° 24′ N 63° 24′ W, about 3 miles off Sambro lightship.

The 27-year-old captain of *Clayoquot*, A/LCdr Craig Campbell, was the last to leave the ship. Seated on the bilge keel as his men pulled clear on rafts, he slipped into the sea and breast-stroked to safety. A flash of fortuitous recollection refocused an event that may well have saved him from serious injury or death. Some time previously he had sat over drinks in Halifax Admiralty House with "Deck" Gregory, a survivor of the HMCS *Charlottetown* sinking in 1942. Casually illustrating the impact of exploding depth charges upon swimmers on the surface, Gregory had produced the Ronson lighter he had carried in his back pocket as he floated on his back in the St Lawrence. It was "thin as a dime" and bent to the shape of his hip. The blast had caused serious internal injuries to those floating belly-down. A stoker from *Clayoquot* would die this way. Now himself escaping his destroyed vessel, Campbell watched her go down. Suddenly reminded of the Ronson, he quickly rolled on to his back to take the powerful thrust of *Clayoquot*'s primed depth charges. He then swam to his men, who by this time clung to rafts and debris. Spirits were none the less high. The irrepressible Coder Alex Batt of Islington, Ont., typified the mood when shouting an imaginary news bulletin from his Carley float: "Flash! Canadian Minesweeper Destroys German Torpedo!" The whole sequence had lasted nine minutes.

HMCS *Transcona* had been proceeding on orders to pick up survivors when she intercepted the radio call of a freighter claiming to have attacked the surfaced U-boat with automatic weapons. The scenario sounded too incredible. It was, in fact, completely discounted by the subsequent Board of Inquiry, though Campbell remembered hearing machine-gun fire. But *Transcona* now dropped her four Carley floats as she sped past the survivors at full speed. As in other temporarily aborted recovery operations, the seemingly inexplicable break-off of a promising rescue operation cast many of *Clayoquot*'s survivors into a state of anxious disappointment.

The War Diary of U-806 proves that *Transcona*'s priority had been correct. As Hornbostel recorded amidst the sudden confusion:

1345: Port lead vessel (6000 tons) passes me on reciprocal course at range of 300 m to port. Torpedo shot no longer possible.

1346: Four depth charges (aerial bombs?), powerful machine-gun fire (passing vessel or aircraft).

1346: Shot from tube VI at lead vessel of second column (4000 tons). Detonation after 3 minutes 57 seconds. Noises of sinking not heard since U-boat stands directly beneath the convoy.

Hornbostel clearly recalls the machine-gun fire: he could see the spatter of shells as his periscope dipped beneath the sea; unusual "echoes" appeared on his sounder.

The swirl of water caused by a diving U-boat could betray the precise point of submersion for as long as 5 minutes. Had *Transcona* not been distracted, the subsequent action might have turned out differently. Directly after the explosion on board *Clayoquot*, all escorts immediately commenced anti-Gnat tactics by streaming Cat Gear. The protective measure seriously impinged upon asdic and hydrophone operations by causing more noise than the machinery of U-806. Thus it was that the torpedo Hornbostel fired at 1346 GMT did not home on to the screw noises of the targeted merchantman, but on *Transcona*'s chattering Cat Gear. Its harmless explosion just astern the gear explains why Hornbostel heard no sounds of sinking. What the Board of Inquiry could not possibly construe was that *Transcona*'s Cat Gear had inadvertently decoyed a torpedo and saved a convoy vessel. The fact that *Transcona* herself had actually "survived the attack" remained, theoretically at least, an irrelevant surmise of the board.[24] Hornbostel had never attacked her anyway.

At 1347 hours the hard-pressed U-806 dived to a depth of 60 m in soundings of 75 m, and headed for the greater security of shallower waters towards the shore where Canadians would not expect it. Passing directly beneath the convoy, he heard six "fairly distant" depth charges. Moving "dead slow" to reduce noise emission, so slowly by electromotors that the U-boat just barely responded to its diving planes and rudder, U-806 came to rest on the sea bottom in 68 m. It had reached a point 4 miles southeast of buoy HC on the present-day traffic-separation lane. That U-806 subsequently heard so many patrol vessels passing within threatening proximity did not derive from Canadian countermeasures having surrounded him. It in fact lay directly beneath the principal escort route in the Halifax Approaches. In effect, most vessels would have to pass over it in order to reach the search zone. An hour later, Hornbostel heard by hydrophone "twelve patrol vessels, both turbine and piston propulsion, departing Halifax" (KTB). In the course of events, he felt the impact of 100 distant depth charges. Again, contrary to Ackermann's earlier assertions, Hornbostel noted with chagrin: "all destroyers and corvettes have asdic (partly individual impulses, partly crackling), only a few carry the saw" (KTB).

HMCS *Fennel* had meanwhile observed the hit on *Clayoquot*, then heard the explosion astern *Transcona*, and ordered the loaded troop ship SS *Lady Rodney* (convoy HJF-36) to return to the safety of Halifax escorted by HMCS *Burlington*. After swift circumspection, she assumed *Transcona*'s rescue duties. Since *Kirkland Lake* was now sweeping south of the sinking, and *Transcona* to the west, *Fennel* moved northward toward the position of sinking in order to close the triangle. *Fennel*'s captain was concerned about the effect of the 36° F (2° C) water on the men in the sea and made all haste. Encouraging him on by their lusty singing of "O Come All Ye Faithful," and the irreverent "Roll Along, Wavy Navy," *Clayoquot*'s survivors rallied as *Fennel* dropped floats and sent her whaler. A crumpled telegram found in Campbell's oil-soaked jacket on *Fennel*'s deck served as an ironic reminder of transience in war: "Congrats on your new command – may God bless your ship and all that sail in her – Mother and Dad." *Fennel* took the seventy-six survivors to Halifax, and with minimal time-lag resumed the search for U-806. Canadian authorities later praised the initiative, acumen, and dash of *Fennel*'s captain.

C-in-C Canadian Northwest Atlantic had been kept current on all phases of the action. Ciphered signals flashed between commands in Halifax, Ottawa, the USN Commander 10th Fleet, the escort commander, escort groups of convoys XB-139 and HJF-36, and finally even EG-27. Under orders from C-in-C CNA, the frigate *Kirkland Lake* (Cdr N.V. Clark, OBE, RD, RCNR) assumed tactical command of the escorts of convoy HJF-36 (*Fennel* and *Burlington*) and XB-139 (*Transcona*). His task force would expand. About 30 minutes after the sinking, at 1108 local time, Operations ordered two Fairmiles on standby (ML 114 and 116) to the scene. Seven minutes later, the Halifax-based minesweepers *Westmount* and *Nipigon*, and the corvettes *Galt*, *Pictou*, and *Kenogami* received orders to hasten to sea. It took about an hour to recall all crew. This was remarkably swift. Two minutes later, all escorts of EG-27 inbound with convoy ON-271 northeast of Sable Island were briefed by cipher and ordered in support of the counter-attack. According to time of sea readiness, these were joined by five more Fairmiles (ML 051, 094, 099, 112, and 117), the corvette *Arrowhead*, the frigate *Lasalle*, and three British Western Isles trawlers, HMS *Anticosti*, *Manitoulin*, and *Ironbound*.

Designated W-12, the quickly formed task force now consisted of twenty-one ships. The first "secret immediate" executive signal from C-in-C CNA ordering *Kirkland Lake* to take the ships under her orders was radioed a full hour after this senior ship had already anticipated it and taken action on her own initiative. The signal's perfunctory flourish to "hunt [the U-boat] to destruction" needlessly defined a goal that had quite obviously preoccupied the Senior Officer since the action began. Under the most difficult and frustrating asdic conditions, *Kirkland Lake*'s highly experienced captain had competently co-ordinated the converging ships in their search and attacks. No one could have functioned better under the circumstances. Senior naval authorities would soon slight him, despite his effective command. Almost a further hour after having authorized *Kirkland Lake*'s assumption of tactical command, Cdr Clark's British superior officer on the Canadian staff, Captain "D" in Halifax (A/Captain W.L. Puxley, RN) provided an irritating example of the "imperial" attitude towards the "colonial" navy, an effrontery with which many Canadians frequently had to struggle. He signalled the assignment of the shore-based British staff officer, A/S Training, to assume tactical command. Thus it was that, four hours after the sinking of HMCS *Clayoquot*, a Fairmile delivered Commander Aubry, RN, aboard *Kirkland Lake*.[25] The imaginable thoughts of Commander Clark, RCNR, are not recorded.

Below in U-806, as Hornbostel recalls, "anxious stillness" had prevailed since minute 32 of the action when his Boat first touched bottom. All noise-producing equipment was switched off and energy consumption reduced to a bare minimum. All off-watch crew lay in their bunks and breathed through *Kalipatronen* CO_2 exchangers. But, "since the U-boat [lay] directly on the route from the firing position to Halifax," Hornbostel's War Diary notes, it was "frequently crossed overhead." During this time, U-806 registered 100 depth-charge explosions, punctuated now and again by the individual impulses and crackling noises of asdic beams from the "destroyers and corvettes" (KTB) passing overhead. A "circular saw" occasionally screeched through the water. Technically speaking, the Canadian ships had long-since detected U-806, for their asdic beams constantly tapped and pinged along its hull.

Whether the U-boat was lying in a dip in the sea bed, so that asdic "painted" a deceptive silhouette, or whether it presented so narrow a silhouette that the detection beams found scarcely identifiable striking surfaces is not clear. In any event, false echoes in this region were notoriously difficult to discriminate, whatever the training level of antisubmarine personnel. Certainly, asdic performance in the European theatre since D-Day had urged the view on Operational Analysis that "the U-Boat which operates inshore with great caution is a difficult target for asdic to detect."[26] The principle applied equally to the Canadian coastal zone, where "the high reverberation intensity ... increases as soundings get less." Experience confirmed the view that "tidal variations and layering add to the difficulties of identifying and at times even detecting a bottomed U-Boat." Equally significant, perhaps, is the fact that Canadians simply did not expect a U-boat to operate in such shallow waters. They certainly did not expect it on the bottom of the Halifax Approaches route. The conventional Allied wisdom held that U-boats escaped to deeper waters after an attack. But the very fact that U-806 was not detected, despite the unnerving asdic-accentuated criss-crossings of patrol vessels overhead, persuaded Hornbostel to remain quietly on the bottom until the hubbub subsided by nightfall. Waiting out this test of nerves in helpless passivity, Hornbostel recalls, drew his crew together in a highly disciplined bond of community. The cook cheered the crew with cold meals and Christmas cake.

Kirkland Lake passed on an interpretative situation report at 2040 GMT on 24 December: the U-boat had in all probability lain on the bottom after the sinking of *Clayoquot* and could be expected to escape the operational area during the night of 24–25 December by schnorkelling. In this light, the Task Force should establish a 10-mile "Observant" on Sambro lightship, advancing northward along the U-boat's presumed course. *Kirkland Lake* clearly counted on the fact that the U-boat had already been submerged for seven hours and that foul air and reduced electric power would force it to the surface to recharge batteries and obtain fresh air. U-806 had actually been submerged for fourteen hours. By 25 December the Canadians did not have a single ship at immediate readiness. The twenty-one ships in the Task Force W-12 still seemed inadequate, for among all available vessels, *Kirkland Lake* alone possessed the 144Q asdic capable of ascertaining a target's depth.[27] Besides, as the Staff Officer A/S reported, an ad hoc collection of patrol vessels created further difficulties. For "with the number of ships of different classes operating, codes lose their usefulness since all ships do not carry the same ones, and it was found necessary to come down to the lowest common denominator – viz. plain language."[28] Naval Reservists of today's navy with experience in Gate Vessels might take small comfort in the fact that little has changed in forty years. Sent in naval jargon, such messages might at first confuse the enemy, but their meaning could be deduced by close attention to tactical procedures. Two such signals read:

241845Z/12/44: From Literate to All Literates: Stream harmonicas.

242345Z/12/44: From Literate to All Literates: Our best method is by knacker
particularly after the moon has set.

Transmitted according to "date/time/group" at 1845 GMT on 24 December 1944, the first executive signal from the Officer in Tactical Command in *Kirkland Lake* ("Literate") ordered all ships under his command ("All Literates") to stream the anti-Gnat Cat Gear ("Harmonicas"). The next one, issued the same day at 2345 GMT, advised the expediency of a passive hydrophone search ("knacker"). Throughout the night Canadian ships heeded this advice more in the breach; their continued use of asdic provided U-806 with clear indications of where its best escape route lay. Thus, at 2339 local time, U-806 lifted from the bottom and set course into deeper water, running dead slow 10–20 m over the bottom. It headed southward – not to the north as W-12 expected. As *Kirkland Lake* had correctly assumed, U-806 had to begin schnorkelling as quickly as possible, in order to replenish air and charge batteries. Yet Cdr Aubry had not anticipated that, despite its pressing need, U-806 would refrain from schnorkelling until clear of the patrol area. Twenty-one more hours would elapse before Hornbostel felt he had removed himself far enough from danger to expose his schnorkel mast. The Staff Officer A/S Training had reckoned neither with Hornbostel's stamina and endurance, nor with distance.

Hornbostel's underwater journey proved as effective a defensive measure as lying on the bottom in the Halifax Approaches. Moving slowly and silently throughout the night, U-806 had little option but to second-guess the Canadians' strategies of search and attack on the basis of her hydrophone contacts and asdic sources. Thus the cool, reflective, and decisive Hornbostel correctly construed the circular search patterns around his firing positions; he quickly grasped the Canadians' principle of expanding the radii of the circles according to the U-boat's estimated direction and speed of advance. But the patrol vessels were crowding so close to one another, he observed, that they could not avoid crossing over him, despite his attempts at evasive action (KTB). For ten exhausting hours, from 0200 until 1200 (GMT), U-806 heard "all around us destroyers and corvettes, most with the 'saw', all with asdic, frequently five to seven hydrophone contacts at once" (KTB). As his War Diary records, U-806 was crossed over directly six times during the Observant. On one such occasion, a "destroyer switched off his 'saw' directly overhead such that asdic impulses rang throughout the Boat" (KTB).

During the long night, Hornbostel recorded his observations on Canadian defence. The insubstantial Canadian response to his attack on SS *Samtucky* forced the conclusion that local forces had not anticipated U-boats in the Halifax Approaches. Later events proved the correctness of this conclusion. Subsequent outbound patrols summoned to the *Clayoquot* sinking had failed to interpret the asdic contacts deriving from the bottomed U-806 simply because the very idea of a U-boat lying on the swept channel was unthinkable. This is a salient example of combatants falling victim to their presuppositions. The swift reaction to the *Clayoquot* incident, Hornbostel concluded, revealed the stand-by readiness of ships on immediate notice, for it had only taken one-and-one-quarter hours for the first half-dozen steam-driven patrol vessels to reach the patrol sector 15 miles off Halifax. In point of fact, however, three fortuitous elements had given him the mistaken impression of preparedness: the chance readiness of a few Fairmiles, the hasty departure of larger ships on cold engines, and the proximity of converging convoys and reconnaissance groups. In summary, Hornbostel recorded, though the A/S response was "well organized, [the] destroyers and corvettes [were] unpractised, for the U-boat wasn't even detected a single time" (KTB). His situation report to BdU on 20 January 1945 reported "insignificant A/S defence in advance of and with convoys both prior to and after" his having been noticed.[29]

At 1300 GMT on 25 December 1944, Hornbostel's U-806 headed for quadrant BB 7765, "in order to catch up on Christmas celebrations" (KTB), having listened every hour of the day and night to the depth charges of increased surface surveillance. When at 2305 GMT the submarine began to schnorkel, after a total of forty hours without a breath of fresh air, temperatures were so low that both periscope and schnorkel iced up. The chill rapidly spread through the Boat. Hydrophone conditions were not nearly so good as those west of the Sambro lightship, where U-806 had been able to hear up to a distance of 15 nautical miles. It is not surprising, therefore, that on 26 December the U-boat bottomed once more in order to rest the crew and hold "Christmas celebrations in the forward compartment" (KTB). It is no longer certain of what these celebrations consisted. Hornbostel merely recalls a "get-together of the whole crew in quiet conversation." They had just received a reflective message from Admiral Dönitz.[30] Couched in the pejorative hyperbole of national-socialist jargon, which strained after the expression of an uncompromising steadfastness and zeal, it elevated banalities to a parody of the sublime: "My U-Boat Men! At the front and at home we celebrate the sixth Christmas of the war in tough-minded resolve, in unconditional devotion and in fanatic faith in our Führer. On this day my thoughts link me with you especially, my old and new submariners fighting far from the homeland and celebrating the age-old German feast. Dönitz."

The crew of Lessing's U-1231 had meanwhile celebrated a quiet Christmas in 30 m of water off Egg Island. Inshore navigation became somewhat problematic, as Lessing observed coastal navigation lights switched off on 25 December. The recent loss of *Clayoquot* had triggered the Department of Transport into executing its defence plan "Instructions to Lightkeepers." Lessing's War Diary entry constitutes but the second time that a U-boat records such an occurrence. Dobratz (U-1232) would note a similar phenomenon off Halifax in January 1945. U-1231 took up patrol between the East Halifax and Sambro lightships in blowing snow, which prevented the Boat from identifying the source of sounds of the antisubmarine attacks against U-806. On 27 December, it inadvertently wandered into the periphery of the Canadians' search zone. Seeking out targets on Emerald Bank, where Escort Group 27 was now hunting, Lessing again heard distant detonations, but faced no direct attack. "There's never been so much going on all the time as the day before yesterday and today," he mused (KTB).

One week after *Clayoquot* had sunk, the *Halifax Herald* broke the news that a "Navy Ship [had fallen] Victim of Sub."[31] The navy's own *Avalon News* explained that *Clayoquot* was the third minesweeper and the twentieth Canadian warship lost in the war.[32] The announcements gave little indication of Canadian countermeasures, which, as the War Diary of U-806 reflects, though "well organized," remained unsuccessful for two interrelated reasons: extremely poor asdic conditions, and inexperience. Yet other equally important incommensurables were involved. Why, for instance, had W-12 let itself be distracted by certain "undoubted" contacts that it claimed to have detected, probed, and attacked? And how could an aircraft's sighting report some 30 miles from Hornbostel's bottomed position in the Halifax Approaches lure W-12 southeast to intercept a supposed schnorkelling U-boat? The use of *Pillenwerfer* (anti-asdic bubble decoys) alone would not have caused such well-intended tactical errors. C-in-C CNA in time suspected the presence of a second enemy submarine. We can exclude U-1231, U-1232, and U-190 on the basis of their own navigational and tactical data.[33] Whether Hilbig's U-1230 had inadvertently wandered into the early part of the action and become the "innocent" target of W-12, which thought it had now caught the long-sought killer, remains an open question. According to BdU's dead-reckoning estimate, U-1230 stood (on 8 December 1944) in operational quadrant CB south of Halifax and could have been in the vicinity on 24 December. It advised BdU by 3 January 1946 that it had commenced the return home "from the USA coast."[34] It could equally well have meant Canada.

The fact remains that, at 1341 GMT on 25 December, some twenty-four hours after the sinking, an RCAF Liberator on routine patrol 30–40 miles southeast of U-806 surprised a "schnorkelling U-Boat" heading west at 4 knots, which it claimed to have photographed and then bombed. The photographs seem no longer extant. The Liberator reported "two hits," followed by "oil bubbles and wreckage." Throughout the day, ships of W-12 were gradually relieved by others until the task force was eventually disbanded. *Kirkland Lake* investigated the scene of the air attack but, like ships of Escort Group 27, which had fruitlessly searched Emerald Bank, found no trace of a U-boat or a kill. Canadians intercepted German Enigma signals on 26 December, but could not obtain a D/F fix because of insufficient coordinates. The action over, Canadian units undertook new missions. The sum of the action remained: one torpedoed merchantman beached, one Bangor minesweeper sunk, eight men lost, and one U-boat forced off and pressed under. Hilbig (U-1230), Lessing (U-1231), Dobratz (U-1232), and Hornbostel (U-806) survived the war.

"U-Dobratz" remained clear of the Halifax action until New Year's Eve. It had departed Kristiansand-Süd, Norway, under escort on 12 November 1944 in company with U-870 (Hechler) for weather duties, and, after heavy storm damage in violent seas, crossed Flemish Cap on Christmas Eve. This salient deep-sea ledge, Dobratz observed, provided an admirable reference point for shaping one's course across the Newfoundland Banks. He noted a marked shift in ocean temperature, a gradual flattening of ocean swells, and, in the event of high barometric pressure, calm weather for repairing his damage without fear of enemy surveillance before entering the actual operational zone. He was crossing the Banks by 26 December, and by noon was steering on the "southeast corner of Sable Island" with the aid of Canadian radio beacons. For U-1232, the year 1944 ended not with a bang but a whimper. His long-range submerged attack in bright moonlight against a four-ship escorted convoy failed. All the torpedoes of his salvo were duds.

On 31 December 1944, when U-806 stood 20 miles southeast of Western Head (BB 7734), Lessing's U-1231 some 40 miles south of Sable Island (BB 8792), and Dobratz's U-1232 was running inbound 75 miles east of the Sambro lightship, the Admiral Commanding U-boats broadcast his New Year's message: "Greetings to all U-boat crews facing the enemy. I am with you in my thoughts. The year changes, but our watchword remains the same! 'Attack, let 'em have it, sink ships!' *Sieg Heil!* Admiral Commanding U-boats." Hornbostel's War Diary records the message without comment.[35] Dobratz did not even bother to record it. Lessing seems to have made it a centre-piece. His U-1231 was enjoying a New Year's mood despite the twenty depth charges it had heard throughout the day. "A ration of punch" issued just before midnight led to "congenial chit-chat in all compartments." More solemnly, Lessing gave a "New Year's address followed by the oath of allegiance and '*Sieg Heil*' to our Führer" (KTB). He then read the message to the crew. Dönitz's New Year's message reached the U-boats the next day:

Men of the U-Boat Arm! The past year has shown us that with the new Boats we can once more fight. The striking power of our Service will be strengthened in the coming year by new Boats. It's up to us to give them full effect. On this New Year's Eve let us vow to commit ourselves unconditionally and relentlessly in the struggle for the freedom of our people. *Heil* to our beloved Führer! [Signed] Ob. d.M. [Supreme Commander of the Navy] and BdU.

It is significant that the texts of such messages were only occasionally preserved by U-boat War Diaries and communications records. In another light, it is even more significant that in the majority of cases such sloganeering was considered not worth recording at all.

Germany's naval collapse, and ultimately its total capitulation, was imminent. It had been signalled as early as May 1943 by the crucial shift in the Battle of the Atlantic; it was rendered irrevocable by the loss of French bases after the Normandy landings of June 1944; it was sealed by the Allies' massive daylight bomber raids against key naval, industrial, and civilian targets at home. Ironically, one of BdU's final War Diary entries for New Year's Eve records the loss of further type XXI prototypes through heavy daylight raids on the Hamburg docks.[36] BdU staff would no longer bother to maintain a War Diary after 15 January 1945.

CHAPTER TEN

Black Flags

The German navy's rhetoric of battle, as 1944 faded, belied the worrisome strategic reality of increasingly reduced U-boat strength, and the gnawing fear that the Allies would soon become aware of the emaciated striking force of the U-Boat Arm. As early as October 1944, BdU had been concerned by the fact that "when the U-boats at present in operational areas leave, the number in the Atlantic will have reached the lowest figure in about three years."[1] At the beginning of October there were forty U-boats in the North Atlantic: four outbound, twenty-eight homeward bound, and a mere eight actually on patrol and waging war. Of these eight, four were operating in the English Channel, one off North Minch, two off Halifax, and one in the St Lawrence. Thus, contrary to traditional assumptions, the infrequency of U-boat incursions into Canadian waters during this period does not reflect a relaxation of German interest in the zone. Quite the contrary. The operational figures actually reveal that Canadian shores held a very high priority, almost equal to those of the UK. Germany's resources were stretched thin. BdU advised his staffs that the Allies' discovery of Germany's weakness was only a matter of time. Once discovered, he reflected, they could expect the Allies to redistribute their antisubmarine forces accordingly, and to reassign these naval and air forces to offensive operations against European targets and German shipping.

The German Naval Staff advised Grand Admiral Dönitz as late as January 1945 that pressures exerted by his U-boats, whether real or imagined, were now tying down 560,000 Allied personnel directly in A/S warfare, convoy duty, and dockyards.[2] Clearly, these personnel (and their equipment) might otherwise be deployed elsewhere. It was thus imperative to increase the number of available U-boats as quickly as possible in order to maintain this pressure. Given the demands in other theatres, redeployment of existing units offered an almost untenable solution. The only meaningful option lay in increased U-boat production. Indeed, the combat experience of both the type VIIC U-boats and the IXC U-boats like U-517, U-541, U-1221, and U-1223 in the Gulf of St Lawrence urged the necessity of even more rapid production of what would undoubtedly have been Dönitz's panacea: the new type XXI. Whereas the older Boats had proven unable to overtake and destroy important targets, the new designs developed a submerged speed in excess of between 16 and 17 knots.[3]

These were the "new U-boats" that BdU's New Year's message had promised. Under active development for the past two years, they were the ultimate submersible, capable of operating below the surface without recourse to frequent resurfacing or use of the schnorkel. They provided extended range, fire power, and manoeuvrability. BdU may for the moment have felt some slight respite in planning his covering ruse in order to gain time for his submarine production plans. German *B-Dienst* had managed to decipher parts of an Allied "Commander Task Group" secret directive instructing Allied A/S units to expect increased U-boat activity in coastal waters during the coming winter months.[4] Imaginary forces, as Dönitz knew, could exert as much pressure on Allied defences as a real assault on Allied supply lines – provided of course that the pretence could be maintained. It was necessary to allow the Allies to corroborate their suspicions. The largely successful German ruse of deployment in strength placed grave demands on U-boat crews.

The fears of Allied strategists soon became public knowledge. President Roosevelt's "State of the Nation" address of 6 January 1945 confirmed an increase in U-boat activity. Newspapers in Canada, Britain, and the United States picked up the "fact" with a degree of undisguised fascination. A joint communiqué issued by Churchill and Roosevelt in London and Washington on 9 January spoke of "renewed activity" of U-boats, reported increased loss of merchant shipping, and hinted at the enemy's improved submarine technology. Indeed, the communiqué viewed the landing of enemy agents in Maine as "yet another indication that the menace of Germany's underseas fleet [was] real and continuing." Hilbig's U-1230 had thus produced a significant propaganda effect, even though his agents had failed. Allied press conferences, like that given by Admiral Jonas H. Ingram, Commander-in-Chief U.S. Atlantic Fleet, sparked speculation about U-boat strength and tactics, while journalists fed the public on inferences and opinions divulged by a variety of "reliable sources." Triggered by Admiral Ingram's press conference, the *Halifax Herald* (12 January 1945) even pondered the possible threat of submarine-launched V-2 "robot bomb attacks on cities of North America's Atlantic seaboard." The *Ottawa Journal* (9 January 1945) had, however, hastened to assure its readers of ultimate Allied victory on the seas "despite the admitted fact that new and improved devices have made it harder for us to take countermeasures." These devices – the Gnat acoustic torpedo, the radar detectors, and above all the schnorkel – gave the public much cause for fantasizing. Thus, an article in the *Ottawa Journal* date-lined London, England, on 15 January proclaimed that "new deep-breathing Nazi subs" could remain submerged for up to thirty days at a speed of 10 knots. As we have seen, these were modest estimates of the schnorkel's capacity for extending submerged operations, even though underwater speed rarely exceeded 7 knots. "High officials in Britain, Canada and the United States," newspapers unrealistically reported, expected 200–300 such U-boats to operate in the North Atlantic, "in packs of twenty to twenty five."

The production of new U-boats that the stirring New Year's messages from German Naval Headquarters had promised was in the long run fraught with insurmountable difficulties. The Allies were by now bombing shipbuilding facilities and docks in bold daylight raids. They were cutting off supply lines of raw materials, and destroying railroads and factories. The War Diaries of BdU and the Naval Staff poignantly document the relentless destruction of their military and industrial resources. The French ports had long since been closed to U-boat operations. Now even the northern bases in Germany and Norway were utterly exposed to massive daylight bombing raids. By mid November, air raids against the Ruhr had gutted five principal railheads, thus reducing transport of coal and raw steel to unacceptable levels. Raids had destroyed or heavily damaged 80 per cent of all steel mills, had reduced gas production to 40 per cent of capacity, and seriously constrained the allocation of war material and propulsion fuels.[5] The latter had already taken a 25 per cent cut the previous September.[6] Despite having mustered sufficient shore staff to commence the new construction program, shipyards could not meet production quotas because of constant bombings and lack of material. The German Naval Staff understated the situation in early December as quite simply "bad."[7] Even those prototypes of the new type XXI U-boat managing to emerge from Germany's strained resources were struck down before they could put to sea. A November daylight raid against the shipyards of Blohm and Voss in Hamburg damaged the new U-2527 by a direct hit and blocked U-2526 on the same slip. A daylight raid on the same Hamburg docks on 31 December 1944 completely destroyed U-2532, and severely damaged U-2515.[9] January raids destroyed U-2530 and U-2537, and sank U-2523, U-2524, and U-2534. Remarkably, these last three were recovered, and two of them later recommissioned. It is a tribute to German initiative and energy that such U-boats had been built at all. While the Grand Admiral struggled with strategic problems attendant upon what he termed the "momentary shrinking of the whole Navy," through energy cut-backs, sinkings at sea, and destruction of ships in harbour and facilities ashore, his staffs tried to cope with the urgent pressures for increased war production in the now hopeless emergency armament program (*Rüstungsnotprogramm*).

Notwithstanding such debilitating obstacles, Admiral Dönitz advised Hitler on 28 February 1945 that the "U-boat can once more fight and be successful in areas under the strongest [Allied] surveillance in which for years it has been unable to even survive ... With the complete submersible [type XXI] a turning point has been reached in the war at sea."[10] Though Dönitz had counted on the first new types entering the war on 17 March 1945, it was not until 30 April, one week before Germany's capitulation, that U-boat ace Kapitänleutnant Addi Schnee took the first type XXI on patrol.[11] As Salewski observes, "This was the crowning achievement of two years of intense effort ... of the genius of U-boat architects, the upbeat to a renewal of the 'Battle of the Atlantic.'"[12] What would have happened if this extraordinary submarine, against which the Allies had no defence, had been developed much earlier? This seemingly pointless rhetorical question is vital. For, as Saleweski has argued, it "contains the historically legitimate question as to the sense and nonsense of the conduct of the German U-boat war after the collapse in May 1943." Against this background, Kapitän zur See Kurt Dobratz's U-1232 held lonely vigil off Nova Scotia's shores.

During the first two days of January 1945, Dobratz's U-1232 observed traffic patterns while lurking some 4 miles off Sambro lightship. The world seemed at peace. In the words of the U-boat's one-page daily newspaper *Der Zirkus* (*The Circus*), hardly anyone could have believed it possible to be able "to run about all merry and gay on the upper deck at the very front door" of Halifax.[13] Dobratz's opening bids for combat attracted no attention whatever. His first Gnat attack failed against one of five vessels of EG-16 on routine patrol 20 miles southeast of the Sambro lightship, though "two successive detonations" convinced him that he had sunk a destroyer (KTB). Not suspecting any U-boats, the Canadians blamed the explosion on the fortuitous bomb that an RCAF aircraft had dropped 2 minutes earlier without prior warning.[14] Next day, his triple salvo exploded harmlessly astern the lone troop ship, *Nieuw Amsterdam*, which had departed Halifax 90 minutes earlier. Taking little or no notice of the detonations, the ship continued her course to the UK. Both the scream of a "circular saw" and the width of the miss convinced Dobratz that she had been towing a "noise maker" on a 1000 m line (KTB). Canadian records do not corroborate this point and provide no clues as to whether or not anyone surmised a U-boat's presence. Dobratz would have caused widespread political turmoil in Canada if he had sunk this ship, for she was carrying NRMA "zombies" to England. These much maligned "walking dead," so called by their more "patriotic" countrymen for having enlisted for home defence only under the National Resources Mobilisation Act, had now been mobilized for overseas service under the authority of an order-in-council of 23 November 1944. Many of them had embarked against their will. Many had deserted rather than go overseas, a fact the Nazi party newspaper *Völkischer Beobachter* picked up with considerable satisfaction. German Naval Headquarters regarded Canadian news of the "desertions" as proof that Canadians no longer wished to be exploited in fighting a British war. In the meantime, however, Dobratz widened his patrol in unharried style around the East Halifax lightship; fixing by the reliable lights of Egg Island and Jeddore Head. Events took a drastic turn next day.

AT 1600 GMT on 4 January 1945, Dobratz sighted the 8-knot Sydney–Halifax convoy SH-194 rounding the shoal waters off the present-day Egg Island bell buoy. Consisting of the tanker *Nipiwan Park* and the two merchantmen SS *Polarland* and *Perast*, it was escorted by the single corvette HMCS *Kentville* and one RCAF aircraft. *Kentville* patrolled ahead of the convoy, doubtless sweeping with asdic in the conventional manner 80° either side of the bow, while the three ships followed in line abreast. The tanker rode in the centre for greater protection. Standing in the classical tactical position in advance of the oncoming convoy, Dobratz followed the "school-book" technique learned in submarine training: let *Kentville* cross overhead, and then pop up well astern to take the undefended targets close on a broad angle. Firing a T-3 contact torpedo from a bow tube, Dobratz struck the 1591-ton tanker *Nipiwan Park* at 1657 hours. Though he claimed to have seen her break in half and sink, the stern was eventually towed to port. When Dobratz's next shot against the leading steamer failed, he thrust between the two remaining ships and the shattered tanker, and 10 minutes later torpedoed the 1591-ton *Polarland*. She sank in about 20 seconds after he had observed her "literally fly into the air and burst" (KTB). The explosion galvanized the remaining *Perast* into violent evasive action. Below in the depths, the crew of U-1232 hung to the voice-pipes as their captain coolly narrated the course of events.[15]

Dobratz immediately headed for the dangerous shallows of the coast, while *Kentville* "circled the site with [her] circular saw" and – by Dobratz's account – actually passed right over U-1232 "several times" (KTB). As a commentator in U-1232's one-page daily newspaper facetiously reported: "A pattern of depth charges really ought to [have] followe[ed], but ol' buddy-boy of an escort quite rightly said to himself 'Better safe than sorry' and took care not to lob anything into the water ... He respected us too much to dare switch off his clatterbox [Cat Gear]." Escort Group 16 reached the scene within two hours. Supported by corvettes, Bangors, and Fairmiles despatched from Halifax, it conducted an extensive though fruitless search. Dobratz actually observed four of the ships "combing the area with saws." Like *Kentville*, they too crossed right over his Boat. HMCS *Burlington* and M/L 116 collided during these manoeuvres, holing the minesweeper and extensively damaging the Fairmile's bow. Running dead slow at a depth of 60 m in soundings of 80 m, Dobratz crept northeastward parallel to the coast. Two days later, American authorities placed U.S. Task Groups 22.9 and 22.10, consisting of four destroyers each, under Canadian operational control in order to scour the area until 8 January. TG 22.9 then left for Boston and TG 22.10 for Argentia, leaving Dobratz to enjoy his "magnificent operational area" under "peacetime traffic conditions" (KTB). His ultimate goal lay at the entrance to Halifax harbour.

Dobratz first, however, followed the coast northward as far as Cape Canso until near-freezing ocean temperatures iced up his periscope and schnorkel and forced him to turn south. Regaining a landfall, he noted "all navigation beacons on the coast extinguished," a fact he correctly attributed to his recent attacks. U-boat records suggest that this marked but the third occasion on which Canadians disrupted their navigational hospitality by darkening their shores, at great risk to safe navigation of friendly shipping. (As we have seen, however, Department of Transport planning had anticipated control of lighthouse illumination since 1939.) Normal peacetime conditions returned five days later; the move signalled to Dobratz the reopening of coastal routes to merchant traffic. No Canadian records provide any details. The cursory observations of U-1232 while lurking off the Sambro lightship concurred entirely with those of U-806: Allied convoys and independent vessels held stubbornly to the unwavering routes via the two lightships to Chebucto Head. Here lay the choice location for a U-boat attack, for at this point outbound and inbound ships would steam in single column. Merchant masters would therefore be concentrating on manoeuvring in close quarters, on keeping or taking station, and on the passing of visual signals. Few, if any, could be primarily preoccupied by thoughts of a submarine attack.

Awaiting larger game while positioned on the outbound track, Dobratz let frequent escorts pass. On 12 January he witnessed the departure for Naples of the 18,000-ton hospital ship *Llandovery Castle*; her pressure wave rocked U-1232, which lay directly beneath her keel. On 14 January he settled into the "best firing point, 2 miles due east of Sambro Light," where the convoys "have to maintain a tight and rigid route between shoals and banks and cannot escape" (KTB). In soundings of 50 fathoms he felt safe from asdic. On sighting "an inbound convoy, large ships in line ahead" (KTB), he commenced a bold attack that in 13 minutes destroyed three major vessels from Boston–Halifax convoy BX-141 and won him the Knight's Cross.

Like every convoy that sailed throughout the war, this twenty-ship convoy under Convoy Commodore LCdr T.B. Edwards, RCNR, in SS *Athelviking* was the product of far-reaching organization and care. Ships had to be unloaded and reloaded with utmost despatch; repairs and replenishments had to be facilitated, masters and communicators briefed by naval staffs on the forthcoming voyage, escort and support groups assigned, and in every case a variety of precise coded messages sent. The safe and timely departure and arrival of each convoy depended upon meticulous attention to disparate and sometimes conflicting circumstances. Could vessels loading molasses or grain be ready to sail with those loading coal, general cargo, and gas? How long could one hold back ships with spoilable foodstuffs until convoy and escorts were ready to sail, or should one permit them to sail alone? Would harbour movements of ships carrying explosives and ammunition encumber the preparations of oil tankers? Could these clumsy vessels all be marshalled in close-quarter manoeuvres in limited visibility and sea room during long periods of radio silence, and with crews speaking different languages? Which routes were safest, and how sound was the Naval Intelligence on which such decisions were based? The NCSO in Boston set the process in motion as the units of convoy BX-141 prepared for sea. At 1558 GMT on 10 January, he had issued his "Advance Sailing Telegram Part I." This informed respective authorities in the U.S. and Canada of the name, speed, cargo, and ultimate destination of each ship in the convoy. Some ships in this coastal convoy would terminate in Halifax. For others, BX-141 was a "feeder," linking to other convoy systems in the Gulf and to Europe. Thus New York promulgated an amendment to the signals of NCSO Boston that the escort oilers *British Honour*, *British Freedom*, *Glarona*, and *British Commodore* were being sailed to connect with convoy SC-165 for the UK.

At 2043 GMT on 11 January, Boston sent its "Convoy Sailing Telegram Part I" to Commander 10th Fleet, British Admiralty in London, Naval Services Headquarters in Ottawa, C-in-C CNA in Halifax, USN New York, and Naval Officer in Charge, Saint John, NB. It indicated the convoy's route by a series of coordinates, gave speed of advance, estimated time of departure (ETD) Boston, estimated time of arrival (ETA) Sambro lightship, and named the escorts. Departing point "Mike" near Boston's present-day traffic-separation zone, convoy BX-141 would advance eastward 35 miles across Stellwagen Bank to point "Nan," where it would commence its loop northward to "Oboe" and complete its ocean passage at point "Peter," 20 miles south of the Sambro lightship. At 1756 GMT on 12 January, Boston signalled "Sailing Telegram Part II." This contained the final revised list of ships and their destinations, number of ships and columns, the name of the convoy commodore and that of his ship. An hour later, at 1859 GMT, an addendum to "Advance Sailing Telegram Part I" updated ship requirements on arrival in Halifax: some would need water and fuel, others minor repairs.

Much like a platoon commander forming a gaggle of recruits into an effective platoon for efficient command and movement, the NCSO Boston had had to organize his motley collection of merchant ships into columns. He had had to design a diagram for his floating platoon, determine the position each ship should have, assign them their stations, instruct them how to form up. Guiding principles insisted that ships proceeding out of harbour single file in constrained waters should be able to form up in quickest sequence with due regard for their speed, manoeuvrability, and cargo. Flash cargoes like aviation gasoline should not sail beside explosives. Highly vulnerable vessels should not be exposed on the flanks of the "platoon." Less volatile cargoes like *Athelviking*'s molasses and the *Empire Kingsley*'s general cargo could maintain the flanks. Columns should form so that ships could eventually break out of formation in quickest sequence, "peel off" by columns if at all possible, and lead on to assigned berths in the terminal harbour, or sheer off neatly to join other convoys without encumbering other vessels. Thus spread out in a broad front of eight columns, BX-141 advanced at 7.5 knots through a choppy, distasteful sea with two escorts, HMCS *Westmount* and *Nipigon* sweeping ahead. Those like the grain carrier *Pacific Skipper*, which could not keep up because of engine failure, were left to fend for themselves along a predetermined "straggler's route." Nineteen ships of BX-141 arrived in a body off Chebucto Head on 14 January 1945, as U-1232 waited.

Three ships of EG-27 (HMCS *Meon*, *Coaticook*, and *Ettrick*) had joined BX-141 and her escorts at 2300 GMT on 13 January. *Levis* and *Lasalle* had remained in harbour with bottom damage after having run aground the previous day. Fourteen hours and 100 miles later, the convoy began the slow manoeuvre of forming a single column for the routine passage up the swept South Channel on course 290° past Chebucto Head. HMCS *Meon* assumed station "Able" at the head of the column. When the action began, she was already signalling by light to the Port War Signal Station close abeam. HMCS *Ettrick* assumed station "Peter" on the shoreward side of the convoy column. *Coaticook* took station "Fox" to starboard of the column, while *Westmount* brought up the rear in station "Sugar." Ships in the screen were zigzagging with Cats streamed. HMCS *Nipigon* was now far astern with the straggling SS *Pacific Skipper*. Steaming at 500 yard intervals, the convoy now presented an exposed flank 4.5 miles long.

Approaching from the east on a course of 210°, Dobratz in U-1232 took bearings of the first ships in the 8-knot column.[16] The first ships in his sights now stood at a range of 3500 m. Dobratz had placed himself in "precisely the right spot for firing" and only needed to "reduce the range by advancing full speed ahead" (KTB). In short order he stood inside the screen. At 1035 local time he fired a T-3A torpedo from 700 m at the third ship in line, the escort tanker *British Freedom*, as she bore 125° from Chebucto Head at 4 miles. He watched it strike her abaft the engine room 48 seconds later, "break apart and sink over her sternposts" (KTB). Following directly astern of her, the SS *Martin van Buren* now immediately increased speed to 10.5 knots and swung out to starboard. Dobratz watched her movements as she closed the wreck of *British Freedom* and then swung to port to regain station. Dobratz altered course forwards, and at 1041 hours fired a T-5 Gnat acoustic torpedo at 900 m from dead astern. The torpedo struck 80 seconds later port aft about 70 feet forward of her screws. Dobratz observed her "very quickly take on a port list up to the guard rails, and sink" (KTB). The explosion caused ships to pile up like a traffic jam. The seventh ship in the column, the 8779-ton *Athelviking* had by now overtaken the ship next ahead to starboard. As LCdr Louis Audette in *Coaticook* observed: "When the first attack took place she [*Athelviking*] put her helm hard-a-port, then starboard again, and finally to port again, crossing the convoy's line of advance to the western edge of the channel." As she continued her swing to port right through 180°, almost completing a full circle towards her original course, Dobratz fired a T-5 Gnat from 1500 m.

The crew of U-1232 heard the tell-tale explosion 127 seconds later, followed by "persistent powerful sounds of bursting and sinking" (KTB). Though the *Athelviking* in fact remained afloat for seven more hours, Dobratz immediately credited himself with a "tanker sunk" (KTB). LCdr Audette witnessed some of the results:

The torpedoings, ugly and effective as they might be, were not spectacular: the usual puff of smoke from the victim's funnel and the muffled explosion heard only by the nearer ships. At the time of the attack, the leading ship was in the vicinity of No. 1 Buoy. The weather was rather choppy and nasty. As all this happened, I was hunting an asdic contact to starboard of the convoy and dropped a few depth charges. The message of the first victim was passed up the line by V/S [visual signals and radio plain language on emergency band] to the Senior Officer. *Meon* immediately called *Ettrick* and me to join him; we used No. 2 Buoy as a datum because, by the worst of bad luck, visibility closed right in with heavy fog at that very moment.

The sinkings would indeed have been more spectacular if Dobratz had destroyed the *Joshua Slocum* and the *Mobile City*. They carried explosives and ammunition. Having despatched *Athelviking*, Dobratz now turned towards the stern of the nearest ship, a mere 400 m away as

Coaticook's depth-charge patterns crept inward. *Coaticook*, *Ettrick*, and *Meon* had entered the convoy column in order to commence an "Observant" search focused on No. 1 Buoy. Meanwhile, *Westmount* and *Nipigon* set about diverting the remaining ships to the East Channel.[17]

Dobratz's tactical picture suddenly shifted. In the final seconds of calculating his next target data, he observed HMCS *Ettrick* close abeam to his intended victim and bearing down upon him bows on. Triggered by the first explosion and torpedo traces, HMCS *Ettrick* (LCdr E.M. More) had run among the ships astern of the ship flying Pendant 11 at the head of the first column, and had dropped in succession five charges set at 100 feet and 50 feet. His choice of a shallow pattern was particularly astute. *Ettrick* had just thrown her third pattern when, as Dobratz recalls, the awe-inspiring power and determination projected by her bow perspective, thrusting full bore towards him, filled his periscope sight. Expecting to be rammed and depth charged while facing "two enemy on one Gnat firing track" (KTB), Dobratz was gripped by a split-second struggle between discipline and instinct: to fire his Gnat at dangerously close range, or else dive and escape. He fired. Close enough to distinguish the details of the American flag on the Liberty ship's stern, U-1232 then sheered off and dived. It had not quite reached 13.5 m when *Ettrick* drove right over its bridge. LCdr More felt his ship "heave as if over a mud bank," and at first attributed the movement to an underwater explosion.[18] The magazine-handling crew below decks reported hearing a "dull boom as if the ship had touched a shoal" but the engine-room staff heard nothing over the sound of the engines. Subsequent leaks and a damaged propeller convinced Operations that she had indeed "struck a submerged object near *Athelviking* at 1352 GMT."[19]

Dobratz himself had no doubts as to what had transpired. The impact had bent the attack periscope, spun him around wildly in his periscope seat, and smashed glass and gauges. U-1232 lurched brusquely on to its beam, and became suddenly bow heavy before righting itself. The crew hunched beneath *Ettrick*'s fourth and fifth depth charges and heard her screeching Cat Gear snag their forward net guard 15 seconds after she had passed. One hundred seconds later, sounds of their torpedo exploding "with subsequent bursting of bulkheads and clearly distinguishable sound of sinking" penetrated all compartments of U-1232. *Meon* reported having heard a torpedo cross her from west to east at this time. There is no record of any ship having been hit. This final shot must have struck an earlier victim that was already breaking up. Much later, Dobratz assessed the U-boat's damage: ripped bridge combing and gashed port side, forward net guard torn off, and the attack periscope, bridge torpedo sights, and FuMB anti-radar antenna smashed.

U-1232 hugged the shore by dead reckoning at 30 m depth to the west of the swept channel. Ironically, survivors' reports of having seen the U-boat on the west side corroborated EG-27's incorrect hunch that it had fired from shoreward, and drew them from the eastern sector where they had been searching. Naval Operations in Halifax later verified that the survivors had been in error, and that U-1232 must in fact have fired from the east. This caused the ships of EG-27 to shift the hunt again. Thus, while Dobratz sought refuge in the west by passing directly beneath the merchant ships, the escorts moved to the east. Once close inshore, he set course southwards at 40-m depth with 20 m below the keel. He and his crew counted sixty-six depth charges, and heard numerous asdic "pings" and the gravel sounds of the asdic beam rasping along the U-boat's hull. By 1622 hours they had rounded Outer Bank and gained the open sea. After midnight on 15 January, and after 134 depth charges and aerial bombs had punctuated his departure, Dobratz shaped course towards the 41st parallel of latitude, along which his route would curve homeward.

Antisubmarine operations against U-1232 on 14 January had faced a difficult task of seeking out the enemy amidst confused and unmanoeuvrable merchant vessels in restricted waters. Escorts also faced the question of disposing of the torpedoed hulks. Initial damage reports, as *Meon* radioed C-in-C CNA, suggested that all three ships could be salvaged if tugs could be sent immediately. But in fact the explosions proved too severe. Both tankers eventually sank. The *Athelviking* stood "stern on the bottom and bow floating at a very high angle in the channel" and had to be sunk by the guns of HMCS *Goderich*. EG-27, now joined by the frigates HMCS *Strathadam* and *Buckingham*, undertook vigorous sweeps while the "weather deteriorated badly: snow, sleet and fog made station keeping difficult, and combined action on contacts quite hazardous." In heavy darkness, HMCS *Buckingham* ran right across the towing hawser of the derelict *Martin van Buren* and narrowly avoided collision. Adverse weather conditions prevented the tug *Foundation Security* from finding the helpless Liberty ship, which now drifted ashore between Ketch Harbour and Sambro Ledge. While DEMS guns aboard *Martin van Buren* could be salvaged, together with all her deck cargo and some of the gear stowed below, the remainder of the cargo and the ship itself was a total loss. The severity of the weather caused other casualties during the period of the search. Thus the Greek SS *Odysseus*, a straggler from convoy SC-165, stranded on Cape Sambro in low visibility and was also abandoned as a total loss.

Meanwhile, more warships joined the hunt for U-1232: HMCS *Border Cities*, *Oakville*, *Napanee*, *Goderich*, and *Westmount*. They executed sweeps and attacks from the harbour entrance close inshore to the open sea; they boxed an area of 25 square miles around No. 1 Buoy, which they combed without result. During the late evening of 14 January, all ships formed a broad frontal search line abreast at 1-mile intervals. As LCdr Audette recalled, they "began sweeping at 8 knots in foul weather and no visibility at all," while Support Group C-4 swept on their reciprocal course from Egg Island. The convergence of these two forces increased "the traffic and confusion [of a] highly exhausting night." By this time U.S. Task Group 22.10 was escorting a special movement of vessels from Argentia to Norfolk, and was diverted by U.S. authorities to assist EG-27 until the morning of 23 January. Now well clear of the attack zone, Dobratz's U-1232 attempted to transmit a situation report to BdU. During the four hours of intermittent transmissions that day, caused by radio problems and poor reception in Germany, the Allies D/F'd him northeast of the Labrador Basin and abandoned the now-pointless search.[20]

Berlin's public military broadcast (*Wehrmachtsbericht*) on 26 January 1945 inflated Dobratz's success to "three tankers and three freighters for a total of 43,900 tons, and a large destroyer" (KTB). U-1232 heard this with considerable satisfaction. Significantly, the broadcast for some reason neglected to mention that U-1232 had attacked convoys "bound for England and France" at their Canadian source. But, of course, the public euphoria in Germany about the "happy hunting" time of 1942 had long since faded into the reality of a country on the brink of defeat. Dobratz wrote one final navigational note on the Canadian coast as he removed further eastward: he had received "loud and clear" radio direction signals from the East Halifax and Sambro lightships at 1100 nautical miles, and Sable Island at 1050 (KTB). They had proven to be excellent homing beacons for the U-Boat Arm.

What was the outcome of this skirmish in the Battle of the Atlantic? It was more than shipping sunk. HMCS *Coaticook*'s encounter three days later revealed the numbing reality of men facing a sudden, harsh, and often anonymous death. As her captain, LCdr Audette, recorded:

I stopped and picked up [a] body – alas, it was a body and not a man ... that of a red-headed young lad in his twenties, probably a casualty from one of the three ships torpedoed on Sunday 14 January; it was perfectly preserved though the lifejacket had a beginning of marine growth on it which indicated that it had been in the water for some time ...

When the body had been hoisted on board, I came down from the bridge to the quarterdeck [and] gave orders to search the body for identification; a large number of the ship's company had collected on the quarterdeck, all looking thoroughly pale and impressed by this close personal brush with death. There was ... a definite reluctance to touch the cadaver; to shame the lads, I strode quickly to the body and began to unzip the "zoot-suit;" immediately, Number One [the Executive

Officer] and other willing hands took over and I was spared a task for which I had no more relish than any of the others, whether or not they were aware of it. There was no identification of any kind on the poor devil.

... with Naval Honours from my ship and from the Group, all ensigns half-masted, I read a burial service over the lad and committed his body to the sea. I read a service entirely drawn from the Old Testament, ending up with the R.C. phrase of committal because I knew not whether he was a Jew or gentile, Protestant or Catholic. In the early shadows of evening, with the rough ill-dressed sailors, the other ships closed-in to the close order in line abreast, the ceremony was impressive. It was the ungilded tribute of seafarers to one more victim of the sea and the war: for many hours afterwards, my ship was quieter than usual as the men's thoughts turned to more serious things; however, the sailor's mind soon found its way back to its normal channels.

Dobratz's U-1232 sighted the snow-covered Norwegian coastline on 15 February 1945. Reports of collapsing fronts had raised searching questions in the crew's mind as to whether they could actually expect to be able to pierce the tightening Allied screen and reach home in northern Germany. Now U-1232 patrolled somewhat anxiously back and forth off "Point Krista," the code name for the rendezvous position where German escorts would meet returning U-boats for the short surface dash through the controlled minefields to harbour. A dilatory patrol vessel finally arrived after an uncustomary delay, exchanged recognition signals and beckoned shoreward. The unseamanlike procedure and manner rankled. In the old days smart professional escorts met the U-boats; a hearty welcome with senior officers, military band, and bouquets greeted them as they came alongside. Times had changed. Now a scrofulous little shallow-draught vessel guided him in – and led him right onto a reef. After 8000 miles, Dobratz's U-1232 perched ignominiously in shoal waters with a damaged rudder and awaited a tug. The event, he recalls, was a sign of the times. Neither bands nor bouquets would welcome him back. U-1232 came home at the end of a tow rope. Unabashed, flying five pennants to mark its kills, and with a hand-painted "Halifax" splashed across its conning tower, U-1232 managed the final stretch alongside on its own power. This had been her first and final tour.

News of U-1232's daylight attacks off Halifax in mid January did not reach the Canadian public until 10 February 1945. In a back-page story date-lined Halifax and entitled "Six Ships Sunk off Nova Scotia by Long-Range U-Boats," the *Ottawa Journal* explained: "Long-range German submarines made a desperate attempt to cut the Allied North Atlantic lifeline at its western anchor this winter by daringly sniping at convoys bound into and out of Canadian ports, and torpedoed a Canadian warship and five merchantmen within a period of twenty-two days off the Nova Scotian coast." Though this information on the predations of both U-806 and U-1232 had been withheld from the public for over three weeks, the attacks themselves had immediately provoked anxious reflection in official Ottawa circles with regard to at least one national issue: the transport overseas of 16,000 NRMA "zombies." The political implications of the movement of largely unwilling men may well have prompted an unguarded comment on U-boat warfare, which in turn had further repercussions both at home and abroad.

General A.G.L. McNaughton had recently been withdrawn from military command and appointed to Cabinet as Minister of Defence for the Army. He was charged, among other things, with effecting the rapid reinforcement of men and material overseas. Yet, because he was not an elected minister, he would have no voice in the next session of Parliament if he did not soon acquire a seat.[21] The Liberal caucus therefore decided that McNaughton contest the forthcoming by-election in the traditionally safe Ontario riding of Grey North. This time, however, the seat was hotly contested on the issue of NRMA mobilization for overseas service, and the apparent ineptitude of both McNaughton and the King government in dealing with conscription. More army officer than politician, and in any event preoccupied with his new ministerial duties, McNaughton held back from the campaign until the very last. When he did appear, he offered his excuses. He had remained in Ottawa, he told a gathering in the Orange Hall of Shallow Lake, a small town some 10 miles northeast of Owen Sound, Ontario, because of his pressing preoccupation with a large draft of army reinforcements. Only now could he explain his absence from the campaign, for the troops had already arrived safely in the UK. It was essential, he emphasized, to keep information about troop movements out of the press, "despite the wild and careless demands of certain newspapers" for news. His brash innuendo may well have disenchanted a few reporters, and in any event reflected a certain political naiveté.

McNaughton's reference to troop movements focused, of course, directly upon a crucial issue that had long plagued the King government and from which McNaughton hoped to gain some points in the election campaign. But in explaining himself, McNaughton doubtless drew on his secret information about U-1232's attack on convoy BX-141, and expressed a view that quickly became international news. His priority in remaining in Ottawa until the very last moment was sound, he explained, because "today the North Atlantic is, as it hasn't been for months past, alive with German submarines ... We are having ships sunk day by day." This sweeping claim was published in the *Ottawa Journal* for 25 January 1945, two weeks before any public announcement of submarine activity off the Nova Scotia coast had appeared. Headlined "Atlantic Alive with U-Boats," it flew in the face of the conventional wisdom that the Allies had now virtually won the Battle of the Atlantic. News from Shallow Lake, Ontario, hit London, England, where an editorial in the *Daily Mail* for 26 January expressed the "shock to the British people to learn from Gen. McNaughton, Canada's War Minister, that 'the Atlantic is alive with U-Boats.'"

If McNaughton's statements were justified by the facts, the *Daily Mail*'s editorial continued, then "it is very odd and disquieting also that the news should have been given to the British and American people, not from their own naval sources but from Defence Headquarters in Canada."[22] If the mother country felt slapped in the face by the supposed indiscretions of one of its colonial governments, it felt equally betrayed by "the absurd secrecy about important war developments which ruled in Whitehall." Canadian naval officials remained non-committal about the veracity of McNaughton's campaign speech. As late as 14 February, an *Ottawa Journal* article headed "Navy Minister Denies Ships Being Sunk Day by Day in Atlantic" quoted Navy Minister Angus L. Macdonald's press conference assertion that McNaughton's statement was "definitely untrue."[23] There is no evidence that the U-boat issue played any substantive role in McNaughton's decisive defeat by the Progressive-Conservative candidate John Bracken in the 5 February by-election.[24] Yet newspapers like the *Halifax Herald* for 27 January 1945 recognized political expediency behind the minister's claims. A cartoon entitled "Maybe They Don't Gag the Right People" caricatured the Grey North campaign: three figures named "Press," "Public," and "Radio" sit in a darkened room gagged with kerchiefs marked "Censorship" and "Penalties for Loose Talk," while outside on the hustings a wildly gesticulating McNaughton stands on his "political stump" proclaiming "The Atlantic is Alive with Subs." By 2 February, newspapers were none the less linking this assertion with claims of "neutral and underground sources" that the "Nazis are sending out 200 U-Boats" to continue the Battle of the Atlantic. On 10 February 1945, Naval Information Services disclosed sufficient details of U-1232's rampage to permit newspapers to publish human-interest accounts of convoy BX-141. Now that "the lid of censorship" had been "lifted from the complete stories of the U-Boat assaults for the first time," papers like the *Ottawa Journal* could apprise readers of the extent of German penetration into Canadian waters: "For weeks before the Nazis struck, the undersea raiders had prowled around the North Atlantic seaboard ... They were 'getting their bearings' on convoy lanes or possibly picking out targets for V-weapon [rocket] bombardments ... It was suspected [that] the primary target of the Germans were the speedy, closely guarded troop ships with their human cargoes." Such news tacitly vindicated McNaughton's indiscretion, though indeed much too late by five days to be of any help. The troop ship *Nieuw Amsterdam* – the only such ship to sail from Halifax during the month that McNaughton had sat in Ottawa – had indeed been attacked by U-1232.

The proliferation of actual and imagined U-boat sightings and contacts throughout the Canadian operational zone from February through April 1945 continued the impressions of intensified U-boat activity. Many of these sightings were summarized in official news releases that gave the impression that U-boats roamed almost with impunity from the Gulf of Maine to the Bay of Fundy, along the Nova Scotia coast and into the Gulf of St Lawrence. While Canadian authorities knew the U-boats' activity to be focused primarily on British coastal waters, there seemed perhaps no compelling reason for the Germans not to exert pressure on all points within their range. In fact, however, actual pressure along the Atlantic seaboard of North America remained fairly constantly lower than its earlier winter levels. U-1233 crossed the Canadian zone, followed by operational missions by U-866, U-879, and – at the very last – U-190 and U-889. No merchant ships were lost. Many suspected clues to U-boat operations led to full-scale searches and attacks with all the indications of a genuine quarry. Most of this action occurred in the general areas south of Sable Island, south and west of Cape Race, south of Nova Scotia towards the Gulf of Maine, and in the Halifax Approaches.[25] Uncharted former victims of U-boats, and of collision and weather, littered and scarred the sea bottom along principal routes, so that A/S attacks on supposed new contacts brought tell-tale oil and debris to the surface.

Contacts and sightings of whatever provenance always emitted an urgent ring of authenticity. All had to be verified, a task demanding the maximum commitment of both naval and RCAF resources until the very end of the war. Not all attacks were in vain. Thus, USS Task Group 22.14, at the time under the operational control of C-inC CNA, was en route to Halifax on 18 March 1945 to refuel, when the sonar of USS *Lowe* detected a bottomed U-boat in 60 fathoms, some 60 miles southwest of Sable Island, to the east of Emerald Bank. Hedgehog attacks produced a large quantity of oil and wreckage, official German documents, first-aid kits, deck planking, and the grisly remains of a desk with hair and flesh adhering to it. They had destroyed Rogowski's type IXC-40 submarine U-866.[26] There was, therefore, every reason for Canadians to believe that U-boats were preying close at hand when the Bangor HMCS *Esquimalt* proceeded on her fatal patrol from Halifax harbour to become the last Canadian victim of the U-boat war.

Oberleutnant zur See Edwin Reith, now a successful shipping magnate in the family business in Hamburg, had departed Christiansand, Norway, in the schnorkel-equipped IXC U-190 on 21 February 1945 under orders to control shipping off Sable Island and in the Halifax Approaches.[27] Commissioned on 29 September 1942 by Kapitänleutnant Wintermeyer,

U-190 now left its Norwegian base alone for its sixth and final mission. Besides the usual surface gunnery, it carried six T-3 LUT angular-search contact torpedoes and eight T-5 Gnat acoustic torpedoes. It was fitted with both the state-of-the-art Hohentwiel radar and the Fliege with Hela amplifier. The radar had been used by the Luftwaffe since mid 1943 and could detect a 3000-ton freighter at 13 km, and an aircraft (depending on its attitude and altitude) at between 9 and 40 km. BdU granted Reith very broad freedom of operations within the general assigned area as it was imperative that he be unhampered in responding to unanticipated shifts in the local tactical situation. Little substantive record of Reith's cruise remains, as he destroyed all official documentation prior to his surrender to HMCS *Thorlock* and *Victoriaville* on 12 May 1945. While it is likely that at least some of the suspected U-boat contacts reported in Canadian waters during the latter part of March and early April may in fact have derived from the movements of U-190, the Boat in all probability did not reveal its presence on the coast until 5 April when a U-boat (probably U-875) torpedoed the tanker SS *Atlantic States* outbound from Boston. The attack provoked a fruitless search by ships and aircraft of U.S. Task Group TG 22.15 (USS *Dionne*). Other units may have picked up U-190's trail as it shaped course toward Halifax. By mid April, Reith had presumably familiarized himself with the zone. Like U-806 and U-1232 before him, he withdrew to the choice tactical position by the Sambro lightship. On 12 April 1945, he received his last distinct ciphered message from BdU in Germany.

Reith's U-190 stood very much isolated and alone, for Hitler had by now issued direct orders for Germany to embark upon a path of self-destruction. He had, on 20 March 1945, ordered the destruction of all communications, industrial, shipping, and transportation resources that might be of use to the Allies. "The struggle for the existence of our people," the Führer urged, "forces us to exploit even within our own Imperial territory all possible measures to weaken the combat strength of our enemy and hinder his further advance."[28] Dönitz had committed the navy to providing all available ships to transport the retreating armies from the Baltic; Army Group North was totally broken and exhausted.[29] The Allies were thrusting over the Remagen bridgehead against weakening opposition. Heavy U-boat losses around the UK forced BdU to withdraw his U-boats "temporarily and in part from the English coast"; this permitted him to reassign four U-boats from arctic waters around Norway to "temporary" duty in the Atlantic.[30] Here they might at least be safe. German forces had exhausted the March supply of propulsion fuel after the first week. By early April, an insistent BdU had sent six type IXC U-boats to North American waters "in order to attack the England–America convoy route since reports from our agent indicate that the enemy has weakened his patrols in the Atlantic."[31] His agent may well have been the RCMP's "Johnny," covering for the double agent Janowski who had landed in New Carlisle, Quebec, in 1942, and was with British Intelligence in England. In any event, this apparent weakness of Allied patrols in Canadian and American waters awakened Dönitz's worst fears that his failure to exert pressure on North American inshore routes had enticed the Allies into redeploying their warships off European coasts. It was, therefore, imperative to re-exert that pressure in order to force at least some Allied naval units to withdraw and support the Atlantic convoys closer to their source. Whether U-190 or U-889, the last U-boats in the Canadian zone, had any idea that they were the linchpins in this operation is unclear.

The "renewed" U-boat assaults must have gained a degree of credibility, for Canadian newspaper reports date-lined Washington, 31 March 1945, and variously captioned "Nazis Embarking on Last Minute U-Boat Campaign," cited Allied naval sources as hinting that the "Germans today appeared to be making an eleventh hour effort to counteract the effect of Allied land victories by embarking on a new all-out submarine campaign."[32] One bit of evidence, something that had long served the Germans as a gauge of their effectiveness at sea, seemed to support the claim. British underwriters were reported as having increased the War Risk Insurance rate on cargoes to and from ports in North America. Navy Minister Macdonald himself confirmed the immediate and continuing threat when announcing on 3 April 1945 the misleading news that HMCS *Annan* had sunk a U-boat after a surface battle: "There is no reason to believe that Canadian coastal waters will be free of these underwater marauders. It may well be that we shall have submarine attacks in Canadian waters on an increased scale."[33] *Annan*, then with the 6th Support Group, had indeed sunk U-1006 (Horst Voigt). But the action had taken place over six months earlier on 16 October 1944 southeast of the Faroes, almost 3000 miles away from the Canadian coast.[34] Whatever the purpose behind this manipulation of news, other conflicting reports left little doubt that Germany's demise was clearly only a matter of time. By April 1945, massive daylight bombing raids were pounding the central and eastern German cities of Gera, Plauen, Halberstadt, Stendal, and Hof.[35] Allied press and officials talked openly of settling final accounts with Germany and of her unconditional surrender. Typically, headlines and by-lines in Canadian newspapers throughout the spring reflected victory. Perhaps this sense of euphoria rather than of ominous threat pervaded HMCS *Esquimalt* on her final voyage.

HMCS *Esquimalt* (Lt Robert Macmillan, DSC, RCNVR) departed Halifax alone during the early hours of 16 April with instructions to carry out a routine antisubmarine patrol in the approaches, and then rendezvous with HMCS *Sarnia* (Lt R.P.J. Douty, RCNVR) at 1100 GMT that day. Macmillan was an experienced officer. He had been captain of the converted minesweeper HMS *Skudd III*, on loan from Norway to the Royal Navy, when she was sunk in Tobruk harbour.[36] It is therefore difficult to account for the apparent lack of battle readiness in which *Esquimalt* now steamed. For, contrary to regulations, she was neither zigzagging nor streaming either of the two Cat Gear Mark II that she carried. This seems a rather striking omission, for the Board of Inquiry into the loss of HMCS *Clayoquot* off Halifax the previous December had urged the view "that the areas in the vicinity of swept channels offer excellent opportunities for the use of Gnat torpedoes." It had recommended, therefore, "that greater use be made of Cat Gear in those areas."[37] Besides this apparent neglect, *Esquimalt* had switched off her old-fashioned SW2C radar because the weather was clear. The 10–15 miles visibility, rising barometer, and a long, low swell augured a comfortable patrol. The asdic operator, routinely sweeping back and forth across the bows from 80° on the port side to 80° on the starboard side detected no contacts. Hydrophones seemed silent. There is little doubt, however, that the obsolete 128A asdic had located U-190. The difficulty lay in interpreting the data. Neither *Esquimalt*'s asdic rating, nor the officer of the watch, Slt B. Whitehead, RCNR (Vancouver), who subsequently died of exposure on a Carley float, realized their impact on the U-boat. The "ping" and "crackling" sound of their searching asdic emissions rasped along U-190's hull and alerted Reith and his crew to their imminent danger. As he recalled: "*Esquimalt* seemed to have picked us up, turned suddenly towards us and practically ran almost directly into my periscope." Reith just managed to turn his stern towards her and "fire a Gnat [acoustic torpedo] with angle zero [dead on to her bows], yet feared that the torpedo would not have time to cross the safety zone" before striking its target.[38] Like Hornbostel in U-806 before him, circumstances forced Reith to fire a "defensive" torpedo at close range. It was a bold and decisive move.

The torpedo tore into *Esquimalt*'s starboard side before dawn at 0935 GMT (0635 local), listing her heavily and sending her to the bottom in less than 4 minutes, with no opportunity to signal her distress by radio or flares. Reith put U-190 on the bottom in very shallow water, thus escaping the patrols that much later hunted along the 200-m sounding line. At this time, the unsuspecting *Sarnia* was patrolling off the East Halifax lightship expecting no contact with *Esquimalt* for another hour and a half. The delay was crucial, for despite calm seas and sunny weather most of those who survived the *Esquimalt* explosion would die of exposure.

Canadians had experienced a similar fate in distant waters the month previous on 17 March, 220 miles north of Cape Finisterre, when U-878 (Rodig) sank the lone minesweeper HMCS *Guysborough* en route from the Azores to Plymouth. Though the explosions of the two torpedoes neither killed nor injured anyone, forty-five died during the night on Carley floats, while eight remained unaccounted for. The U-boat was never detected.[39]

By the time 30-year-old Lt MacMillan reached his bridge, *Esquimalt*'s starboard side lay so deep that the whaler was flooded in its davits. Lack of care and maintenance (or lack of regular testing) prevented Carley floats on either sides of the ship from being released automatically. With considerable difficulty, four sailors cleared away four of the six, and thereby saved many lives. Only one man survived the engine room. Stoker Jack Ware (Sandwich, British Columbia) had quite fortunately opened an escape hatch in the dummy funnel just 20 minutes before the attack. He scrambled clear as the engine room filled with smoke. Slt Michael Kazakoff (Kamsack, Saskatchewan) had perhaps the narrowest escape of all. Trapped in his cabin by a "twisted mess of steel, with some glimmers of daylight shining through [and seeing] water a few feet away through one of the jagged holes" in the hull, the husky young officer forced himself through. Suffering lacerations and gashes over his whole body, he dragged himself through the ragged steel opening into the safety of the sea. The captain, the last to leave the ship and the only other officer to survive, remained aboard until the upturned bows began to slip beneath the sea. He stepped into the water and swam to a float.[40] Most of the men managed to escape the stricken vessel and cling to the four crowded floats in expectation of early rescue. Yet aircraft flying over the scene within minutes of the sinking took the survivors in yellow Carley floats to be fishermen, and paid no attention. Grave disappointment swept the dwindling number of survivors two and a half hours later when two minesweepers passed within 2 miles without becoming aware of their frantic calls and gestures. In the Battle of the Atlantic near-rescues such as these had frequently triggered the final stages of irrevocable exhaustion that ended in death.

Many men died in agony. Injured, scantily clad because of their hasty escape into the sea, and many without lifebelts, they clung desperately to each other and to rafts. On two floats lashed together, the captain led a small group of survivors in hymns and prayers. For many, survival was a lonely and hopeless struggle. As Able Seaman Frank Smith of Edmonton recalled after his rescue: "They kept up their determination to the last – until they could fight for life no longer and then, knowing death was coming, said goodbye to us and their families or girl friends."[41] So died Able Seaman Don White of Peterborough, Ontario, whose legs and arms had been broken in the explosion. Such was the death of Huntley Fanning of Drum Head, Nova Scotia, promoted to chief electrical artificer on the eve before the torpedoing; he was to have been married on his return from patrol. Others succumbed mutely in the grip of severe hypothermia. One jumped off the raft in a delirious attempt to swim ashore, only to become lucid for a brief moment and drown in his frantic effort to regain the raft. Detained by her A/S attacks, HMCS *Sarnia* came alongside almost seven hours after *Esquimalt* had gone down, and signalled Halifax the first news of the disaster. EG-28 and HMC ships *St Boniface*, *Burlington*, *Drummondville*, and *Kentville* scoured the area without result. Reith, who observed the action, recalls that the "Canadian search groups worked excellently [but] could not assume that instead of diving in deep water I went into 24 m and lay low." *Sarnia's* second signal reported having found twenty-four survivors and twelve dead on three Carley floats. She would "pick up further men from [the] Halifax Light Vessel" and return to harbour. The final toll would reach twenty-six survivors and forty-four dead. In a message whose civility masked its urgent tone, C-in-C CNA sought the assistance of his American counterpart: "In view of [the] sinking in Halifax Approaches this morning I should be grateful if I could retain control of TG 22.10 for two or three days."[42] After a fruitless search for U-190, USS *Buckley* and *Reuben James II* sunk U-879 (Manchen) with all hands by a Hedgehog attack some 120 miles southwest of Sable Island. "Human flesh and debris of German origin" authenticated the kill.[43]

The situation remained tense off Halifax in the closing days of the war. C-in-C CNA diverted the two "Monsters" SS *Britannic* and *Franconia* in order to "avoid enemy U-Boats" feared near Halifax.[44] The threat affected all deployments. On 29 April, U-548 (Krempl), which had sunk HMCS *Valleyfield* off Newfoundland the previous spring, sank two ships in the Gulf of Maine and was itself destroyed with all hands by the frigate USS *Natchez*.[45] Frömsdorf's U-853 scored the final U-boat success of the war off the North American coast. During the night of 5–6 May, a mere two days before Germany's unconditional surrender, it sank the 5353-ton U.S. freighter *Black Point* off Block Island, and was destroyed in turn with all hands by the USN destroyer escort *Atherton* and the frigate *Moberley*.[46]

The Board of Inquiry into the loss of HMCS *Esquimalt*, convened under the presidency of LCdr Desmond W. Piers, RCN, who at the time was commanding officer of the destroyer HMCS *Algonquin*, proved a serious disappointment to the Naval Board at Naval Services Headquarters, Ottawa. NSHQ was dissatisfied not only "with the manner in which the Board [of Inquiry] was conducted, [but also with] the inadequacy of the evidence adduced."[47] As inadequate as the board may have been, it none the less managed to uncover a muted litany of neglect whose roots, even as late as 1945, derived in large measure from Canada's pre-war policies of a national unpreparedness. Shortcomings in equipment, tactics, training, command and control in *Esquimalt* – though unexplored during the inquiry – hinted at a generality of problems in the fleet. *Esquimalt*'s asdic rating, as we have seen, had missed U-190 whose presence he had not remotely suspected. But not even the extensive bottom searches by ships of the Halifax Local Defence Force with asdic and echo sounder could locate *Esquimalt*'s hulk at the known position of 44° 26′ N, 63° 10′ W. (Insurance companies subsequently sought information on the exact position in hopes of not having to settle some of the life-insurance claims if the ship had gone down outside territorial waters.) Equally serious, it was claimed, was the fact that *Esquimalt* had switched off her radar set prior to U-190's attack. But the obsolete "SW2C with which [she] was fitted" was deemed incapable of "picking up a periscope." The naked eye, it was stated as evidence, had a better chance of seeing it. In view of the situation reports regularly issued by Naval Operations Halifax, one argued, *Esquimalt* ought to have anticipated U-190, and have zigzagged on evasive courses. In fact, however, it was physically impossible for her to receive current information and timely warning. The problem lay in shortages of personnel and limitations of equipment: as ships of the Halifax Local Escort Force were already required to monitor two important frequencies, they could not "therefore normally read [receive by radio] the situation report or the daily submarine report ... except when [carrying] additional telegraphists for training." As Macmillan himself told the Board of Inquiry: "We don't read the situation reports." The fact that a U-boat was known to be in the area caused him no real concern anyway, since "this has been the case on every patrol since I took over the ship" two months earlier in February 1945. Even without advance warning of the U-boat's presence, *Esquimalt*'s decision not to zigzag was deemed "contrary to very specific Halifax Patrol Orders." Yet the Board of Inquiry found no evidence that these orders had in fact been disseminated. And finally, despite the lessons provided by the sinking of HMCS *Clayoquot*, the board's investigations revealed "no Standing Orders for patrols on the streaming of [Cat] gear." NSHQ ultimately considered the findings of the Board of Inquiry "inconclusive," and therefore passed no judgment on a variety of obvious shortcomings ranging from planned maintenance of warships, to inspection of safety equipment and crew discipline. Significantly, C-in-C CNA subsequently enjoined his commanding officers in the understated style of the navy "to give their personal attention" to three basic points emerging from the board's preliminary findings: the necessity for (1) zigzagging in areas where submarines were known to be present; (2) routine inspection of equipment on Carley floats; and (3) wearing adequate clothing by officers and men twenty-four hours a day.[48] Again, the warnings were too little too late.

Naval Information Services withheld news of *Esquimalt*'s sinking until 7 May, twenty-one days after the event and one day prior to VE Day.

Under the banner headlines "Surrender Complete! Dönitz Orders All Huns Give up Unconditionally," the *Ottawa Journal* proclaimed the demise of the U-boat fleet and the loss of Canada's last naval action. Date-lined Halifax instead of the now unnecessary wartime rubric "An East Coast Canadian Port," the report explained: "Far-ranging Nazi U-Boats, making what may have been their last desperate stab for the crumbling Fatherland, last month crept close to the Nova Scotia coast and sank a minesweeper of the Canadian Navy." The *Halifax Herald* and others reported on 8 May 1945 that a "Nazi torpedo which struck without warning sent ... *Esquimalt* to the bottom of the North Atlantic." This was, according to the *Journal*, "the second time within a few months that daring German subs made their way through the Navy patrols to come practically within gunshot" of Halifax. Reports alluded to the sinking of HMCS *Clayoquot* and ships of convoy BX-141, but of course never specifically mentioned U-1232. They never dispelled the myths of marauding wolf packs off Canadian shores.

The cumulative effect upon Canadian maritime defences exerted by U-806, U-1232, and U-190 convinced the navy that Dönitz would by no means ease the pressure. A variety of seemingly authentic contacts and sightings confirmed its worst fears. This forced Canadians into the very defensive posture the Grand Admiral had envisaged, though indeed Canadian redeployment of resources would have occurred too little and too late for his taste. Canadian operational authorities recorded that the "opening of the river and gulf of St. Lawrence in the near future to a larger volume of ocean-going ships than in previous years, together with a shorter convoy cycle and an increasing number of U-Boats in the Western Atlantic, will entail the use of additional close escort and support groups."[49] NSHQ could only reinforce home waters at a minimal level by "withdrawing one corvette from each of the Canadian mid ocean groups." Given the threatening circumstances that then seemed to prevail, the navy was prepared to "accept a reduction from six to five ships." Anticipation of increased German pressure forced operational authorities to ponder an utterly dismaying situation. The two support groups EG-27 and EG-28 at the time allocated to C-in-C CNA were already trying to cover the Canadian coastal zone. But they could not do so effectively "even with the assistance that has been rendered by the US hunting groups." This crucial weakness despite joint Canadian–U.S. operations led NSHQ in Ottawa to request British Admiralty to release "for operations in Canadian waters" Escort Group 6, consisting of the frigates HMCS *Cape Breton*, *Grou*, *Outremont*, *Teme*, and *Waskesiu*. No longer required for its usual Murmansk runs, the group departed Londonderry for Halifax on 18 April 1945. C-in-C CNA now despatched the old Belle Isle Force consisting of HMCS *Preserver* and the 78th M/L Flotilla. The traditionally weak "striking force," as it was designated, arrived in Cornerbrook on 27 April, the day on which British forces entered the German port of Bremen.

The German navy was now facing its final hours. From early April 1945, RAF Bomber Command had been dropping hundreds of tons of bombs on the harbours of Hamburg and Kiel. It sank not only U-boats, but the heavy cruisers *Admiral Scheer* and *Admiral Hipper*, and the light cruiser *Emden*. Between 2 and 3 May, in principal harbours from Bremerhaven and Wilhelmshaven on the North Sea to Kiel and Bornholm on the Baltic, the Germans scuttled 118 U-boats.[50] Massed RAF attacks on the western Baltic from 2 to 6 May destroyed a further 60 U-boats, which were trying to escape to Norway. The fall of Berlin on 2 May caused the collapse of the Reich's capital and the removal of Naval High Command to Flensburg on the Baltic coast of the Schleswig-Holstein peninsula. On Adolf Hitler's death by suicide, Grand Admiral Karl Dönitz became head of the Nazi state. Dönitz had long since prepared for the eventuality of having to surrender unconditionally. Should that occur, he was determined that no war material fall into enemy hands. His desperate Plan *Regenbogen* (Rainbow) called for scuttling all his submarines. His commanders, of course, knew of the plan and awaited his executive signal. Yet, as Dönitz's Flensburg government negotiated the terms of surrender, it became apparent that his activation of *Regenbogen* would undermine certain securities he was attempting to obtain for his defeated people. The conditions of surrender expressly forbade him from sinking or damaging any of his ships. None the less, as conditions of the surrender gradually became known throughout his fleet, many naval personnel executed *Regenbogen* on their own authority, despite its illegality: sixty-seven U-boats sank to the bottom of the Flensburger Förde, Geltinger Bucht, Cuxhaven, and Eckernförde. Among them were submarines whose as yet unutilized advanced technology would have made them the pride of any navy: the type XXI, and the hydrogen-peroxide-driven Walther U-boats. Only twenty-six U-boats were actually patrolling on station at war's end. Three of these – U-190, U-805, and U-889 – were in Canadian waters. Eighteen U-boats were outbound on new assignments; among them the "Canadian" veterans U-802, U-1228, and U-1231 were heading for the United States.[51] Only four U-boats were returning home.

Canadian, Polish, and British troops occupied Emden, Wilhelmshaven, and Cuxhaven by 7 May. Two days later Germany's French bases in Lorient, La Rochelle, and St Nazaire fell. Yet German U-boat warfare, as NSHQ records noted, "continued unabated until the final surrender of Germany at 2201 GMT on 8 May 1945." On that day, Admiral Dönitz broadcast final instructions to his U-boat commanders. Under the terms of the unconditional surrender, they were to remain surfaced and immediately report in plain language on 500 kc/s their hull number and position to the nearest British, United States, Canadian, or Soviet wireless stations. They would subsequently transmit their position, course, and speed every eight hours while proceeding to the nearest designated Allied port. They would make all further signals in plain language at set times and frequencies, jettison all ammunition, and render torpedoes and mines safe. As a sign of surrender, they would fly a black or blue flag by day, and burn navigation lights at night. Dönitz expressly forbade them from scuttling or in any way damaging their Boats.

Canadian and Associated presses cabled news of the surrender from London, and provided translated texts of Admiral Dönitz's speech to the German nation and that of his foreign minister, Ludwig Schwerin von Krosigk. Surprisingly, Canadian newspapers regarded the speeches as back-page news. Dönitz urged his people to "face facts squarely ... The unity of state and [Nazi] party does not exist any more. The party has left the scene of its activities."[52] Yet many quarters continued to regard the U-boats with grave suspicion. As the *Halifax Herald* observed, "a considerable percentage of U-Boat crews are Nazi fanatics, and guerrilla action may continue after the declaration that the war in Europe is ended."[53] Certainly, the Canadian Navy could not relax its patrols until the seas were secure.

Prior to 8 May, as Canadian Operations reports of the day reveal, there was little activity in Canadian waters. Yet the navy believed, and newspapers reported, "that U-Boats in the [Halifax] area are likely to give themselves up at eastern ports rather than make the long trip back to Europe."[54] Canadians maintained continuous patrols off designated surrender points like Halifax, Shelburne, and Bay Bulls from 10 to 29 May. Six U-boats actually surrendered to North American forces during the next few days. Two of them, U-889 and U-190, became Canadian prizes. The other four fell to the Americans. Radio signals of U-805 on 8 May drew USS *Otter* and *Varian* from Argentia, Newfoundland, to intercept it 15 miles south of Cape Race on 12 May. USS *Sutton* and *Scott* intercepted Marienfeld's U-1228 some 350 miles due east of Cape Race on 11 May. Both U-boats were delivered to Casco Bay, Maine. USS *Carter* and *Muir* responded to the signal of U-858 some 325 miles south of Cape Race. After interception they passed it to USS *Pillsbury* and *Pope* for conduct to Delaware Cape where they arrived on 14 May. USS *Sutton* intercepted U-234 some 80 miles east of Flemish Cap and escorted her into Portsmouth, New Hampshire, on 19 May.[55]

Friedrich Braeucker's U-889 was the first of these U-boats to submit to Allied control. The 26-year-old captain, with his crew aged 19–33 years, had departed Germany via Norway on 5 April. After an uneventful patrol as a weather ship, he had been ordered to harass shipping off the port of New York. He had not fired a single shot in anger by the time Dönitz had signalled the capitulation. An RCAF Liberator on routine patrol from Gander, Newfoundland, sighted Braeucker's U-889 some 250 miles southeast of Flemish Cap on 10 May. Eastern Air Command relayed her sighting signal to C-in-C CNA, who in turn diverted Western Local Escort Group W-6 from inbound convoy SC-175. Prepared for hostility, the Liberator had meanwhile approached U-889 as she steamed due west at 12 knots through unkindly seas. On the aircraft's close approach the U-boat's crew hoisted the black flag of surrender and, in the words of one report, "kept waving their arms at the plane wildly" as a sign of welcome.[56] Group W-6, consisting of the Algerines HMCS *Oshawa* and *Rockcliffe* and the corvettes *Dunvegan* and *Saskatoon*, intercepted U-889 at 1951 GMT that day 175 miles SSE of Cape Race.[57] With W-6 at action stations and all guns bearing, HMCS *Oshawa* (A/LCdr J.C. Pratt, RCNVR) closed to loudhailer distance and through German-speaking ratings on her bridge ordered U-889 to set course for Bay Bulls, Newfoundland. Heavy weather prevented his sending a boarding party. W-6 then maintained station around their prisoner with all guns bearing until a couple of hours later, when *Oshawa* received orders to assign two ships to escort U-889 into Shelburne, Nova Scotia, while she and the remaining escorts rejoined their convoy. HMCS *Rockcliffe* and *Dunvegan* took charge.

As darkness tightened, Braeucker's signal lamps flashed a message in English to HMCS *Dunvegan*, the senior of the two Canadian escorts: "And so to bed. Have a good night." Like the watch officer of HMCS *Valleyfield* who had once signed off his log in the style of an eighteenth-century English novelist, so Braeucker's signalman had ended the day with a phrase reminiscent of Samuel Pepys' diaries. The two sailors might have had a greater cultural affinity than the events of the war would suggest. Twenty-four hours after the interception, the two ships passed their charge to the frigates HMCS *Buckingham* and *Inch Arran* of EG-28 some 140 miles SSE of Sable Island. Two RCAF Liberators carrying a party of newsmen and photographers overflew the westbound contingent for two hours as it passed 25 miles south of Sable Island on 13 May. Aerial photographs captioned "Still on the Prowl in the North Atlantic" and "U-Boat Surrenders at Shelburne – German Craft Taken over by Canadian Navy" hit the newspapers next day.[58] *Buckingham* and *Inch Arran* took over 100 miles east of Sable Island and during the subsequent transit carried out two Hedgehog attacks against a suspicious asdic contact. U-889's official surrender took place on 13 May 1945 off the Shelburne Whistle Buoy, 7 miles from the antisubmarine boom gates. As the *Halifax Herald* reported (14 May 1945):

Under an overcast threatening sky a twelve-man boarding party of the Royal Canadian Navy, accompanied by Captain G.R. Miles, Chief of Staff to the

Commander-in-Chief of the Canadian Northwest Atlantic, and a squad of RN submarine technicians, climbed onto the defeated enemy vessel and a few seconds later the White Ensign was hoisted at the undersea raider's flagstaff to officially mark the taking over of the craft.

Few others witnessed the brief ceremony: a flotilla of Fairmiles, a couple of RN frigates, and RCAF aircraft carrying a group of some thirty-five newsmen. Once U-889 was secured alongside, the *Ottawa Journal* could proclaim that "one of Germany's underseas demons of destruction lay harmless in Shelburne Harbour today."[59]

When Hans-Edwin Reith's U-190 reported to New York, Boston, and Cape Race its position as 42° 35′ N, 43° 05′ W at 1001 GMT on 11 May, Canadian authorities detached the corvettes HMCS *Victoriaville* (LCdr L. Hickey, RCNVR) and *Thorlock* (Lt John E. Francois, RCNR) from inbound convoy ON-300. Incorrect information about Reith's position and course at first put them off the track. Homing onto his radio transmissions, they sighted his steaming lights at 2303 GMT some 500 miles east of Cape Race.[60] Plain-language sailing instructions from the Flensburg government of Admiral Dönitz had directed him to release his crew from military service, and to regard them as civilians. British radio stations, German veterans insist, had repeated these instructions. Reith released his crew on the day of capitulation. Similarly, Klaus Hornbostel of U-806 recalls releasing his crew from the navy while alongside in Kiel; under direct Allied instructions he invited a core crew of these new "civilians" to ferry U-806 to the United Kingdom. In both cases the crews were to have been home within four weeks of having delivered their vessels. Memories still rankle at the fact that the Allies disregarded the terms that provided for the German crews' release, and held them as military prisoners of war.

By all accounts, therefore, the sailors aboard U-190 were civilians when HMCS *Thorlock* first went alongside at 2340 GMT on 11 May. Five minutes later, her boarding party under Executive Officer Lt R.O. Blackford went aboard. The Canadians dropped a grapnel hook and chain down her conning-tower hatch in order to prevent her from diving, and posted sentries throughout. This precautionary measure proved unnecessary, for the Germans offered every co-operation. As an understandably apprehensive Chief ERA, Stanley Dean, quipped at the time as he dropped down into the control room: "They just looked at me ... then saluted. I felt relieved. I had no gun." *Thorlock*'s Executive Officer went below with Reith to seize any ammunition or secret material and search for scuttling charges. He found nothing. Reith had followed his orders by jettisoning secret documents in weighted bags, and by disposing of all ammunition – even the acoustic torpedoes, which he regarded as a state secret. Blackford confiscated any remaining books, then locked up the wireless room and the captain's safe. He cleared all hands to the upper decks before signalling *Victoriaville*. The white ensign flew from U-190's mast at 0001 GMT on 12 May.

Victoriaville's boarding party arrived at 0040 GMT under the command of Executive Officer Lt Bud Burbidge. Within twenty minutes all Germans, with the exception of nine engine-room personnel and three upper-deck watch keepers, had been transferred to the corvettes for search, registration, and medical examination. Aboard *Victoriaville*, Hans-Edwin Reith signed a makeshift deed of unconditional surrender – the first official surrender of a U-boat to the RCN. By 0200 the contingent was steaming at 9 knots for Bay Bulls, Newfoundland, where it arrived at 0600 GMT on 14 May. With unrestrained literary zeal an American army correspondent recaptured an otherwise uneventful passage: "The Canadian crew [of U-190] found it difficult to believe that this hellish raider they had been fighting for years was now just another mechanical, steel monster, harmlessly nosing it's [sic] way toward the North Atlantic base, theirs to command at will."[61] Placed under the charge of an RCN party under the submariner Lt M. Wood, RNVR, U-190 now lay, in the correspondent's inflated phrase, "like a huge sea monster, barnacle-covered, rusty and salt-spotted." Having "entered Bay Bulls with her black flag of surrender flying," as the press reported, she now seemed suitably humbled. Indeed, as was publicly observed, "the black flag under which the U-Boats are making their meek way to British and Canadian ports is singularly appropriate for these piratical craft."[62]

HMCS *Prestonian* delivered the fifty-four prisoners to Halifax on 16 May where, on "one and the same day," as the Naval Intelligence Directorate minuted, "they were interviewed by pressmen and broadcasters, interrogated by NID, and handed over to the military."[63] Such interviews provided newspapers with columns of largely gratuitous fare in which innuendo and inference substituted for fact. Statements drawn from youthful and politically naive German sub-lieutenants out of touch with Germany after weeks and months at sea were interpreted as the undiscerning indifference of the German population as a whole. Yet despite the reporters' muted scorn, they seemed genuinely struck by the implicit tragedy of war as reflected in the enemy's unsullied youth: the "chubby faced and shaggy lot [were] young and inexperienced."[64] The skipper of U-889 (Braeucker) was quoted as wanting to remain either in Canada or in the United States after the war, for "Germany as a political interest is dead." As to whether he could adjust to a democratic political system, he apparently replied: "there is not such a big difference between your government and ours." He rose to the rank of captain in the post-war Federal German Navy.

There is no substance to the myths that boarding parties entering the surrendered U-boats found copies of recent Halifax newspapers and ticket stubs from local movie theatres. Canadian veterans still relish speculations that even up until the closing days of the Second World War, German submariners penetrated Canadian society with unrivalled bravado and ease. That such myths persist at all is a tribute to the tacit psychological warfare Dönitz's "grey wolves" had initiated in 1939.

The U-boat campaign officially ended at one minute past midnight on 4 June. At that time convoys at sea continued to their destinations un-blacked out, and burning navigation lights at full brilliancy. June brought the cessation of all convoys in the North Atlantic.[65] Escorted convoys had proven the safest means for conducting merchant traffic through enemy waters. Statistics of losses for convoys operating between North America and the United Kingdom (HX, SC, ON, and ONS) from 1942 to 1945 show that a very minimal number of ships had been sunk while under escort[66] (see table 8).

U-190 and U-889 were commissioned into the RCN in June 1945 retro-active to 14 May, the day on which Canadian and British crew commenced living on board. The service of HMC U-889 in the RCN was brief. Used as an experimental vessel because of her acoustic torpedoes and highly developed German GHG hydrophone array, she left Canada by inter-national agreement when the Tripartite Naval Commission meeting in Berlin in November 1945 decided to retain only thirty U-boats. These it divided among the UK, the U.S., and the USSR. U-889 was one of the ten allocated to the United States. An RCN crew sailed her to Portsmouth, New Hampshire, on 11 January 1946.[67] Canada retained U-190 as she was considered unoperational. Under the command of Lt D.M. Pope, RNR, the Canadian submarine undertook, during the summer of 1945, a ceremonial tour of the very river and Gulf that its sister ships had managed to close down. It visited the ports of Montreal, Trois Rivières, Quebec City, Gaspé, Pictou, and Sydney, and arrived in Halifax on 7 September for antisubmarine training duties until paid off on 24 July 1947 after having been commanded by Lt Rodney Johnston, RCN. Perhaps the most curious artefact of this phase of its service is the RCN commanding officer's rubber stamp – an oval shape superscribed "HMC S/M U-190," encircling a German eagle with a swastika in its claws.[68] Its iconography is revealing: the "monster from the depths" has now been tamed.

"Operation Scuttled" marked paid to U-190's account. Touted on two occasions in the press as an exercise designed to train inexperienced post-war recruits in the art of combined operations, it was in fact a final touch of rather raffish theatre.[69] Painted in bright red and yellow longi-tudinal stripes, U-190 was towed to the spot where it had sunk HMCS *Esquimalt*, and where at precisely 1100 hours on 21 October 1947 the tradition-bound RCN intended to celebrate Nelson's "glorious" Trafalgar

TABLE 8
Convoy Vessel Casualties, 1942–1945

Year	Ships convoyed	Sunk while under escort	Per cent sunk
1942	7,542	149	2.0
1943	9,196	125	1.4
1944	9,807	7	0.07
1945	3,835	5	0.2

Day victory over the French fleet in 1805 by pounding the empty hulk into the depths.[70] While the hapless "enemy" drifted, the "friendly" forces gathered for the kill: Tribal-class destroyers HMCS *Nootka* (Capt. H.F. Pullen, OBE, RCN), HMCS *Haida* (LCdr Frank B. Caldwell, RCN), and the Algerine minesweeper HMCS *New Kiskeard* (LCdr Breen P. Young, MBE, RCN). The Naval Air Arm provided a collection of "string-bag" aircraft: eight Seafires, eight Fireflies, two Ansons, and two Swordfish. The scenario, staged for twenty-four representatives of press and radio, called for a carefully choreographed sequence of battle escalating from airborne rocket attack to the grand finale of destroyer bombardment with 4.7-inch guns and a death blow with Hedgehog. The RCN's final sally against a German U-boat ended on much the same comic operatic note as its first foray against suspected invaders off Quebec City in 1939, when a "submarine diviner" had shared in the hunt. Almost before the ships had a chance to enter the act, U-190 pointed its bows into the air after the first rocket attack and slipped silently beneath the sea. And thus, the RCN press release announced with inflated pathos, "the once deadly sea raider came to a swift and ignominious end" – just 19 minutes after "Operation Scuttled" had begun.

Epilogue

German U-boat assaults on Canadian waters revealed the fallacies inherent in Canada's pre-war policies of national unpreparedness. Prior to both world wars, Canadian planners had failed to recognize the technological achievements of a potential foe whose capacity for waging war left little doubt as to his extraterritorial intent. When Canada finally awakened from her pre-war doldrums, she all too readily abdicated any nascent claims of national sovereignty and left the higher direction of the war to her alliance leaders. As was to be expected, the priorities of Great Britain and the United States in alliance warfare left Canada with little scope to assert herself even in her own territorial zone. But even such meagre resources as did become available were quickly siphoned off in support of overseas commitments. At the outset, Canada's preparations for home defence reflected an already outdated concept of war at sea. Whereas Germany's naval strategists on the eve of the Second World War had studied the documents of previous naval conflicts, Canada remained marvellously aloof from her own maritime past. Only when events had turned the day did she galvanize her forces. But, as we have seen, even as late as two years into the war, she had no comprehensive plan for deploying her burgeoning corvette fleet. Events in Europe had given her the undeserved respite to cope. Canada's opening gambits consisted of makeshift responses in terms of matériel, equipment, training, and operational hardware. It took anxious years to redress the balance, a process whose inadequacies persisted as late as 1945.

Had the German navy been able to strike the Atlantic sea lines of communication (and North American shores) in the strength and in the time frame that Admiral Dönitz had wished, there seems little doubt that it would have prevailed. Its ultimate failure to win the Atlantic war derives in large measure from a conflict of priorities inside German High Command itself. The German army insisted on the primacy of a land war (which Hitler could understand), whereas the navy saw Germany's future at sea (which he did not). Ignoring the strength of combined plans and operations, the army in effect started the war by pushing eastward before the navy was ready to move west. The navy was caught off guard when Germany invaded Poland, again when Britain responded by declaring war, again when Hitler refused to sanction the mining of Halifax harbour, and again when the Japanese attacked Pearl Harbor and shook the United States from its balancing act of belligerent neutrality and brought it officially into the war. Thus the U-boats could not attack in sufficient numbers, carried faulty torpedoes, and had to cope with a severe shortage of mines. However limited German resources were as late as 1942 in Operation Paukenschlag, the U-boats' extraordinary successes were encouraged by North America's virtually undefended shores. Combat developments in other areas punctuated the Canadian Navy's eventual ascendancy in strength: Allied decryption of German message traffic and the work of Operational Intelligence, development of centimetric radar, scientific tactical principles, gradual improvements in asdic, and, of course, the linchpin – long-range aircraft. All these developments underscore the vital importance of research and development, a concept that Hitler did not understand and therefore largely ignored in time of war.

U-boat operations in Canadian waters exposed attackers and defenders alike to situations they had not met before. Courage and tenacity marked both sides as they grappled with tactical and navigational problems peculiar to the Gulf of St Lawrence and the western Atlantic. Seamen laboured under severe physical and psychological pressure exacerbated by often faulty military intelligence and malfunctioning equipment. Chronic torpedo failures scuttled even the best-planned and best-executed U-boat operations, and threatened to undermine morale. Significantly, however, Admiral Dönitz's charisma kept his men fighting with utmost commitment until actually ordered to capitulate in May 1945. The highly trained submariners of the early months of the war encountered the seemingly unwary "peacetime" conditions of a rapidly mobilized Canadian Navy, which at first offered but a minimal counterthreat. Equally significantly, their combat-performance curves crossed one another around 1943: the Germans' strength declined because of their enforced deployment of largely inexperienced crews in hastily built U-boats, while Canadian technology and training improved and matured under duress. The year 1943, of course, marked the turning point of the Battle of the Atlantic: in a major reorganization, Canadians assumed command of the Canadian Northwest Atlantic with integrated operational-control centres; air supremacy closed over the infamous Black Pit in mid Atlantic, thus providing air cover for convoys from North America to Europe; increased Canadian escort and support groups with improved techniques and technology forced the U-boats back. The year 1943 was equally crucial for inshore waters. The ability of radar patrols to keep U-boats submerged and hence limit their range of action reduced in the long run the number of combat-effective U-boats; they discouraged lengthy patrols, and boosted Allied morale. Combined air/sea searches, such as against U-537 after it had planted its automatic weather station, virtually signalled the demise of U-boat supremacy.

Germany had realized for some time that Britain and the United States regarded Canada as a pawn that could be manipulated by diplomatic means and the weight of tradition to support high-level plans that they forged without her consultation. It knew, too, that Canada traditionally considered support of Britain a higher priority than her own home defence. This in large measure contributed to the peacetime conditions that U-boats encountered off Canadian shores. Canada's naval commitment to the eastern and mid Atlantic left but few ships for the defence of Canadian waters. Those that could be deployed faced the formidable difficulties of antisubmarine defence with inadequate and obsolete equipment. The politically motivated naval doctrine of "quality before quantity" argued, in effect, that small is beautiful, while masking pre-war recalcitrance and neglect. As in the First World War, this attitude launched unprepared naval forces against a foe who had given ample demonstration and warning of his technical capabilities and political intent.

Canadian naval forces required more ships for coastal defence than planners had ever envisaged. Nor had they understood the principle that it takes longer to build up a navy than it does an army or air force. Admiralty in London had advised the Borden government in 1917, for example, that a minimum of thirty-six steam-driven vessels were required to patrol "Canadian and Newfoundland" waters. Over twenty years later, a motley of thirteen ill-equipped hulls stood by for general duties. Nor was it realized how many surface forces were required to clear mines or hunt a submarine. St John's had to borrow minesweepers from Halifax in order to clear the field laid by U-220 in 1943; thirteen surface vessels hunted U-537 in a single combined air/sea search operation that same year, and twenty-one hunted U-806 in 1944. In each case these well-defined searches against a distinct single opponent drew upon more operational vessels than exist in the whole Canadian Navy today.

Even after the Battle of the Atlantic had ended, Canadian newspapers had continued to project the image of a supposedly incorrigible and unrepentant foe. On the eve of Germany's capitulation the Canadian press warned of an "untold number of German U-Boats still ... lurking in the North Atlantic, and [of] fanatical commanders [who] may strike one last blow before their fuel and food is gone." But Canadians need never fear, for "Canada's sheepdog navy of corvettes, frigates and other small craft will still maintain constant vigilance while shepherding the sprawling convoys across the ocean." The image of the sheepdog, a rather scruffy though always faithful beast, had always epitomized the Canadian Navy whenever the "wolf pack" seemed at the door. Politicians would soon legislate the amiable hound into lean years of toothless and decrepit retirement. But the German navy, which in Admiral Dönitz's words had "fought like lions," would rise from defeat under the leadership of such "Canadian" veterans as Paul Hartwig (U-517), Klaus Hornbostel (U-806), Klaus Hänert (U-550), Erich Topp (U-552), and Friedrich Braeucker (U-889) to become one of the strongest and most advanced navies in our NATO alliance.

Appendix

DER SCHNORCHEL (LILLI-MARLEN)

1 Auf dem Lorenzstrome
  in dem engen Schlauch
  da steckt ein alter Schnorchel
  die Nase frech heraus.
  Wo die dicken Dampfer gehn,
  da wollen wir dazwischenstehn
  mit dir Lilli-Marlen!

2 Und der Kommodore
  knurrt in seinen Bart:
  Die hiesigen Strategen
  sind von besonderer Art!
  Wenn wir auf Fernfahrt wieder gehn,
  Im Lorenzstrom nur wolln wir stehn
  mit dir Lilli-Marlen!

3 Und in der Zentrale
  da stöhnt der L.I.:
  Wo sind meine Haare?
  Der Schnorchel rupfte sie!!
  Glazköpfig kann man bald mich sehn
  mit Hut in der Zentrale stehn
  bei dir Lilli-Marlen!

4 Auch dem II W.O.
  dem wirds so langsam klar:
  Auch er war einst ein Jüngling
  mit schöngelocktem Haar.

Wehe, wie rasch die Zeiten gehn
die Glaze ist schon halb zu sehn
O weh, Lilli-Marlen!

5 Doch betont er oftmals,
was beträf sein Haar,
dass der Ausfall anfing
vom siebenzehnten Jahr.
Doch die Hauptschuld trägt an dem
der Schnorchel, der ihm unbequem:
mach Schluss Lilli-Marlen!

6 Und der alte Doktor,
der heilt nicht nur Weh-Weh,
er fummelt auch ganz gerne
herum bei der F.T.
Doch man sieht betrübt ihn stehn
Der Schlüssel 'M' will nicht mehr gehn
bei dir Lilli-Marlen!

7 Wo der I W.O. ist,
da geht es immer rund:
Das sind ja harte Töne,
das ist ein 'dicker Hund'!!
Um die Menage wärs geschehn,
würde er nicht nach dem rechten sehn
bei dir Lilli-Marlen!

8 Und in der Kombüse
da wühlt der Smut herum,
er haut mit seinem 'Bello'
die alten Dosen krumm.
Schmirgelnd, qualmend, kaum zu sehn
sorgt er für unser Wohlergehn
bei dir Lilli-Marlen!

9 Vorne pumpt der Minuth
raus den alten Mist,
doch trotz aller Mühe
gelingt es restlos nicht.
Da hilft ihm der I W.O.:
Den 'Dreckschuss' schiesst er als T.O.
mit 200 Kilo!!

10 In der Batterie da
     schlängelt Seibert sich,
     denn er ist 'Battriechef'
     und 'Ehrentheit' sein Siess.
     Sie lassen Gase zischend wehn
     aus der Batterie, das riecht so schön
     bei dir Lilli-Marlen!

11 Heimwärts fahren wir wieder
     nach langer Schnorchelei,
     da hat der alte Schnorchel
     für kurze Zeit mal frei.
     Doch wenn wir auch in Qualm vergehn
     Wir Schnorcheln
     bis wir nichts mehr sehn
     mit dir Lilli-Marlen!

12 Lieber Papa Dönitz
     erbarm Dich unsrer Not
     hör gnädig unser Flehn
     Gib uns ein neues Boot!!!
     Dann können wir auf Touren drehn
     drauf auf die dicken Dampfer gehn
     mit dir Lilli-Marlen.

(*Gemixt von* Dr E. Messmer *für "U-541" zum 20.9.44–Gewidmet dem Kommandanten*)

THE SCHNORKEL (LILLI-MARLENE)

As "mixed" for U-541 by Dr E. Messmer on the occasion of 20.9.1944, and dedicated to the captain. [Note: Messmer's curious term "mixed" has two possible origins: one in bartending, the other in submarine weaponry. Thus he either "concocted" the poem as one mixes a cocktail, or "fused" it as a torpedoman (German: *Torpedomixer*) fuses a torpedo.–MLH]

1 On the St Lawrence
    In the narrow spout
    Along comes an old schnorkel
    And lifts its cheeky snout.
    Right where the big fat merchantmen steam
    That's where we wait to pierce the screen
    With you, Lilli-Marlene!

2 Now the Convoy Commodore's
    Growling in his beard:

The local strategic thinkers
Are really rather weird!
But when we're sent on ops once more
We'll want nothing better than a St Lawrence shore
With you, Lilli-Marlene!

3 And in the control room
Ol' Chiefie groans aloud,
Where has all my hair gone?
The schnorkel's plucked it out.
Soon you can find me with a shiny bald head
standing with my cap on by the dials instead
Of with you, Lilli-Marlene.

4 Then the Second Officer
Soon becomes aware
That he was once a youthful lad
With golden locks of hair.
Alas how swiftly life's gone of late
We already see his balding pate.
Alas, Lilli-Marlene.

6 And the good old doctor
Can't only cure the clap.
He likes to fuss about a lot
With all our wireless crap.
But now we see him sad and grave
'Cause he can't make 'Cipher M' behave
With you, Lilli-Marlene.

8 Over in the galley
Ol' Cookie stirs about
Busting up the tin cans
To serve our dinners out.
Scrubbing while all smoked out, scarcely to be seen
He dishes up our haute cuisine
For you, Lilli-Marlene.

9 Forward in the torpedo room
Minuth pumps the shit.
Yet despite his efforts
He can't get every bit.
So along comes to help him the friendly XO.

He blasts out the muck shot like a tor-pe-do.
With a 200 kilogram thrust.

10 Homeward we go sailing
After schnorkelling weeks on end.
We'll give the schnorkel time out
Lest we all go round the bend.
Yet even should we gasp in thick black smoke
We'll never stop schnorkelling
Until we choke
With you, Lilli-Marlene!

12 Dear Papa Dönitz
Have mercy as we plead.
Grant us please a brand new Boat
That's all we really need.
Then we can hit the road once more
And add more shipping to our tonnage score
With you, Lilli-Marlene.

Artifacts of life in the Canadian Navy, 1939–45, found in miscellaneous files of the Directorate of History, Department of National Defence, Ottawa. In "The Swan Song of the Reservist," the hastily trained RCNVR spokesman who went to sea to win the war now faces demobilization. He satirizes the Regular Force, which to his mind had put on British airs, followed the social traditions of the RN, and stayed home. In "The Answer," ascribed to Real-Admiral Adams (ret'd), who was a seagoing member of the RCN, the Regular Force replies.

THE SWAN SONG OF THE RESERVIST
(or–Strange as it Seems, I Don't Regret Doing It)

The War is over, and we're in clover,
We leave the job to you;
This is no guff, it's safe enough,
We've shown you what to do.

With telescopes at proper slopes,
And hankies up your sleeves,
Just pace the decks of painted wrecks,
In jackets made at Gieves.

With brand new ships and salty dips,
With Half rings gained ashore,

Don't tell us how to do it now,
And how you won the War.

Oh – it's V.R.s for the V.R.s
And gins for the R.C.N.,
Who stayed ashore throughout the War
But now sail forth again.

The winter cruise and lots of booze
And awnings aft and fore,
Is all you'll do the whole year thru
Till you go back ashore.

To buxom gash with lots of cash
And scheming maiden aunts,
You shoot the flannel about the Channel
And the hostile coasts of France.

Lord God Almighty, you've never seen Blighty?
Where did that accent come from?
It must be schools and manning pools,
And draughts of the purser's rum.

From the V.R.s and the N.R.s
Here's a toast to the R.C.N.,
Come times of stress and deep duress
We'll take the strain again.

(Anonymous)

THE ANSWER TO THE SWAN SONG OF
THE RESERVIST (or – It's Strange)

With telescope at proper slope
And awning spread throughout,
We'll read again your short refrain,
What was it all about?

Yes I recall the stories tall
Made up in times of stress,
Of thrilling days and sailors' ways
Of cleaning up a mess.

The mess was not a pleasant lot,
Nor cooked by Axis men,
Its cause was ours we thank V.R.s
For bringing peace again.

The war is won and you're the one
Who always could be found.
You steamed your ships on all the trips.
And seldom ran aground.

Except now and then, and only when
The land was near at hand,
Or fog came down all dark and brown,
Or lookout wasn't manned.

It's nice to know that when the foe
Starts in to give the works,
That you'll come back and what you lack
We'll teach to all you jerks.

We'll teach again to all you men
That ships are things to know,
And how to drink, or do you think
That stuff will ever flow?

It will be swell to have you tell
Of how you sunk the Jap,
Of how you fought and beat the lot
While I just took a nap.

And as I slept I dreamed I kept
Teaching V.R.s all the day,
I wiped your nose, you stood in rows,
I wonder, did it pay?

From all us men in R.C.N.,
We hate to lose you now,
We'll never smile, but once a while
We'll laugh and take a bow.

But all the same what's in a name?
And who writes all this guff?

I'm not ashamed to be so famed,
I really wrote this stuff.

I'm proud as punch of all the bunch,
Of sailors old and new.

It will be swell to have y.
I wish you well and please don't tell
Of what you owe the few.

(K.F. Adams)

Notes

BA-MA	Bundes- und Militärarchiv, Freiburg, Federal Republic of Germany
BdU	Befehlshaber der Unterseeboote (Commander U-boats)
BfZ	Bibliothek für Zeitgeschichte, Stuttgart, Federal Republic of Germany
C-in-C CNA	Commander-in-Chief Canadian Northwest Atlantic
COAC	Commanding Officer Atlantic Coast
DHIST	Directorate of History, Department of National Defence, Ottawa
EAC, A/S	Eastern Air Command, Antisubmarine Report
FONF	Flag Officer, Newfoundland Force
KTB	Kriegstagebuch (War Diary, official records)
PAC	Public Archives of Canada, Ottawa
RCNMR	*Royal Canadian Navy Monthly Review*
Skl.	*Seekriegsleitung (German Naval Staff)*

INTRODUCTION

1 Kuenne, *The Attack Submarine*, 125. The spokesmen were Admiral Sir Arthur Wilson, RN, in 1902; Viscount Jellicoe in 1922; and Admiral Lord Fischer in 1941.

2 Tucker, "East Coast Patrols," cf. Bennett, *Naval Battles*, 246–63.

3 Marinedienstvorschrift Nr. 28, *Kriegserfahrungen der deutschen U-Boote im Weltkriege 1914–1918*, Oberkommando der Kriegsmarine, Kriegswissenschaftliche Abteilung (Berlin: Mittler und Sohn 1939). BA-MA: Sign. RMD 4/28. In actual fact, no completed historical analysis of the First World War U-boat war was available in 1939–41. Planned for five volumes, only two were completed. Dönitz therefore founded his strategic and operational concepts on experiences of former U-boat commanders.

4 *Ottawa Journal*, 19 March 1941, 24.

5 See KTB/U-117, BA-MA: RM 97/113. Navy Department *Submarine Activities*.

DHIST: "Operations in North American Waters," 1650–239A, in particular Senior Officer of Patrols HMCS *Guelph* to Captain of Patrols, Sydney, 13 August 1918; Department of the Naval Service, Naval Intelligence Report no. 5, 54–100, 1918, Naval Intelligence Records, 272–4. Sarty, "Silent Sentry," 306–24.

6 KTB/UB-156, BA-MA: Sign. RM 97/1130.

7 See "Brief History," DHIST: Niobe-8000, vol. 3.

8 For example, W.G.D. Lund, "The Royal Canadian Navy's Quest for Autonomy in the North West Atlantic: 1941–43," in Boutilier, *RCN in Retrospect*, 138–57.

9 Sarty, "Silent Sentry," 311, based on exchanges in PAC, RG 25, G–1, box 1161, file 558–1915C, Admiralty Colonial Office 7 November 1916, M. 09362/16, forwarded by Colonial Secretary to Governor of Canada 14 November 1916, and in PAC, RG 24, box 3831, NS 1017–10–1, W.1.

10 PAC, reel B–3444, PRO, Adm 116, N. 1400.

11 Kingsmill to Hose, 7 August 1918, DHIST: "Torpedo A/S General," 81/520, 1000–973, vol. 1.

12 Cf. McKee, *The Armed Yachts of Canada*, 46f.

13 KTB/UB-117, BA-MA: RM 97/1130. Dröscher listed the victims as "Aleda May" (31 ton), "William H. Starbuck" (53 ton), "Progress" (34 ton), "Reliance" (19 ton), "Earl and Nettie" (24 ton), "Cruiser" (28 ton), "Old Time" (18 ton), "Mary E. Sennet" (27 ton), "Katie E. Palmer" (31 ton).

14 The U.S. Navy Department monograph (99) claims the master's name as W.M. Reinhard.

15 Form S.A. (Revised June 1917), "Particulars of Attacks on Merchant Vessels by Enemy Submarines," DHIST: 1650-239/16A.

16 "Defence of Trade," PAC, MG 27, III, B5, N.37, file D-26. I am indebted to Marc Milner for bringing this document to my attention.

17 Milner, *ORAE Report*, 12.

18 Bacon and McMurtrie, *Modern Naval Strategy*, 148–9.

19 Cf. Stacey, *Canada and the Age of Conflict*, 261. Sunk in error by U-30 (Lemp).

20 E.g., *Ottawa Journal*, 18 September 1939, 3, and *Winnipeg Free Press*, 18 September 1939, 11–12.

21 *Ottawa Journal*, 14 October 1939, 1, and 17 October 1939, 1: "Two Air Raids on Scapa Flow Base – Official Story of Royal Oak Torpedoing."

22 "Combined Operations – 1939," *RCNMR*, DHIST: 1650–239/16B, vol. 2.

23 *Ottawa Journal*, 13 April 1940, 4.

24 Ibid., 3 October 1940, 17, and 25 October 1940, 8.

25 Ibid., 18 September 1941, 8 (construed from statistics of the Ottawa Bible Society claiming that Bible sales in Germany had declined from 250,000 copies in 1939 to 68,000 in 1940).

26 Ibid., 14 April 1941, 8.

27 Series entitled "The Issue in the Present War," published in Canadian newspapers. See, for example, *Ottawa Journal*, 28 October 1939, 2: "War against Nazis Crusade to Save Christian Civilization."

28 *Ottawa Journal*, 21 October 1939, 1: "Canada's Navy Plays Big Role Convoy System – Warcraft on Constant Duty Scanning Sea for U-Boats"; *Winnipeg Free Press*, 18 November 1939, 1: "Grey Vigil – Canada's Warships Alert for Raiders."

29 See Lamb, *Corvette Navy*; Easton, *50 North*, and Lawrence, *A Bloody War*.

30 Milner, ORAE *Report*.

31 *Montreal Daily Star*, 31 January 1940, 3: "Submarine Attack on This Side Ridiculed by Naval Authority."

32 Dönitz, "Aufgaben und Stand ...," *Nauticus*, BfZ, Sign. F 456.22. This edition went to press in November 1938.

33 *RCNMR*, no. 9 (September 1942): 65.

34 For example, Douglas, *Out of the Shadows*; Milner, OREA *Report*; and Sarty, "Silent Sentry."

35 *Victoria Daily Times*, 25 May 1940, 2.

36 For example, the quarter page ad in the *Ottawa Journal*, 14 June 1941, 6.

CHAPTER ONE

1 DHIST: 8000-St Laurent I (1937–43), NS. 1057-5-4.

2 Tucker, *Naval Service*, II, 7. The RCN had only thirteen vessels in commission: two destroyers, two minesweepers, and a training schooner on the East Coast; four destroyers, three minesweepers, and a motor vessel on the West.

3 *Leader-Post* (Regina), 20 November 1938, 11; *Montreal Daily Star*, 20 November 1939, 17.

4 Captain, DNO and T to DNIP, 4 April 1939, DHIST: 1650-239/16B, vol. 2.

5 See also Stacey, *Canada and the Age of Conflict*, 130.

6 *Ottawa Journal*, 5 November 1941, 1. Cf. the ostrich-like disclaimer of 19 March 1941 (16): "U-Boats on U.S. Side of Atlantic German Bravado."

7 KTB/U-111, BA-MA: Sign. PG/30107/1. Also KTB/Skl. 21.6.41; 7.7.41.

8 Beesly, *Very Special Intelligence*.

9 KTB/BdU, 20.7.41 (p. 170); 3.8.41 (p. 179); 14.8.41 (p. 187); 21.8.41 (p. 190); BA-MA: Sig. RM 87/4. See KTB/U-374, 20/10/41, BA-MA: Sign. PG 3046, case 10/4/.

10 KTB/U-208, 27.10.41. BA-MA: Sign. PG 30194-98.

11 KTB/U-109, November 1941, 15, BA-MA: Sign. RM 98/109. For the personal recollections of Bleichrodt's radioman see Hirschfeld, *Feindfahrten*, 132–84.

12 KTB/U-374, 16. Rohwer, *Seekrieg* (178–82) indicates deployments.

13 *Ottawa Journal*, 6 November 1941, 3: "Warns U-Boats Soon Operate near Nova Scotia."

14 Ibid., 18 November 1941, 13: "Reports U-Boat near Halifax."

15 Ibid., 20 November 1941, 26; 25 November 1941, 13.

16 Ibid., 25 November 1941, 13: "Two Canadian Corvettes Sink U-Boat in North Atlantic." Also 20 November 1941, 8: "Canadian Navy Does Its Job."

17 Stacey, *Canada and the Age of Conflict*, 337: "the Canadian government had no effective share in the higher direction of the war."

18 E.g., *Hansard*, 26 May 1938, 3264–8; *Globe and Mail*, 7 December 1937, 1: "Seize Island in Case of War"; and 17 December 1937, 6: "Getting Straight on Anticosti"; Frank Lowe, "The Canadian Island Nazis Tried to Grab," *Saturday Night*, 8 March 1952, vol. 67.

19 PAC, RG 24, box 2700, HQS 5199-1, V.1.

20 "Permanent Joint Board of Defence," document file DHIST: 82/196, vol. 1. The United States had, of course, the colour-coded "Rainbow Plans" anticipating potential war with various countries. Plan Black dealt with war against Germany, and Plan Crimson with war against Canada. The PJBD seems, therefore, to have adopted elements of the American scheme (see Stacey, 157).

21 Milner, *North Atlantic Run*, 34.

22 Director of Plans, to Chief of the Naval Staff, 21 December 1942, DHIST: m-11.

23 "Defence of Shipping – Gulf of St Lawrence": memorandum, NS 1048-48-22, DHIST: 1650-239/16B, vol. 1.

24 "Atlantic Convoy Instructions," NSS 1013-2-23, PAC, RG 24, vol. 3821, DHIST: 81/14, folder 1.

25 "United States Fleet Anti-Submarine and Escort of Convoy Instructions," FTP 233A, DHIST: 79/532.

26 *RCNMR*, no. 9 (September 1942): 61–2.

27 "Hints on Escort Work," part I (30 March 1943), part II (22 April 1943), part III (21 May 1943), part IV (8 June 1943), part V (16 July 1943) (DHIST: ADM 1/13749).

28 Minute sheet, 19 September 1943, attached to part IV, n. 27 above.

29 Milner, *North Atlantic Run*, 79.

30 See "Report of Proceedings, Director A/S and Booms," Halifax, 12 June 1940, DHIST: 81/542/1000-973, vol. 2.

31 "Modernisation of Armament and Equipment," DHIST: NS 8060, 4.

32 A/LCdr D.W. Piers, "Comments on the Operation and Performance of HMC Ships, Establishments and Personnel in the Battle of the Atlantic," 1 June 1943, PAC, RG 24, 3997, NS 1057-3-24.

33 "Defence of Shipping – Gulf of St. Lawrence – 1942 (short title – Plan GL2)," NS 1048-48-22, DHIST: 1650-239/16B, vol. 2.

34 Captain H.N. Lay, Director of Operations Division to Vice Chief of the Naval Staff, 19 February 1943, PAC, RG 24, 3997, NS 1057-1-21.

35 LCdr W. Redford, HMS *Salisbury*, "Report of Proceedings [convoy] QS 37," 26 September 1942, DHIST: Salisbury-8000.

36 Director of Operations Division, "Naval Aspects of the Defence of the Gulf

and River St. Lawrence," 11 December 1942, DHIST: NS 1048-48-22, vol. 1, 2.

37 "General Review and Report Upon Defences in the Gulf and River St. Lawrence Areas," committee formed under the direction of the Chiefs of Staff Committee, 30 January 1943, DHIST: 1650-239/16.

38 "Naval Aspects," n. 36 above, p. 2.

39 Vice-Admiral Percy Nelles, CNS, to the Minister of Defence, 7 October 1942, "Traffic in St. Lawrence River and Gulf," DHIST: NSS 1048-48-10, vol. 2.

40 Nelles, ibid., and Milner OREA Report, passim.

41 For this aspect of closure see Cdr Robert Thomas, "The Absolute Necessity: The Naval Defence of Trade in the St. Lawrence, 1939-1945," unpub. MA thesis, Royal Military College, Kingston, Ontario, 1982.

42 NCSO, HMC Dockyard, to NOIC, HMC Dockyard, Sydney, 15 October 1942, DHIST: 1650-239/16B, vol. 1.

43 Secretary of the Admiralty, to the Chief of the Naval Staff, Ottawa, 27 September 1929, DHIST: NS 1001-1-7, vol. 3.

44 See tracings in DHIST: NSS 1000-5-13, vol. 18.

45 Lt B.G. Jemmett, RCNVR, OIC Controlled Mining, to the Captain of the Port, St John's, 10 March 1942, attachment to FONF, Report of Proceedings, March 1942, DHIST: NSS 1000-5-20, vol. 1.

46 Ibid., p. 3. Jemmett refers here specifically to problems with the scow. His statement none the less reflects deeply rooted frustrations not only with the project, but with the inefficiencies of the naval "system."

47 Minutes of Subcommittee formed under direction of the Chiefs of Staff Committee, 23 February 1943, p. 5, DHIST: 1650-239/16.

48 Undated letter from Ropner, Ministry of War Transport, to Captain E.S. Brand, Director Trade Division, PAC, RG 24, box 6789, NSS 8280-166/16, vol. 4. Cited in Thomas (n. 41 above), 93.

49 Hansard, 8 June 1943, 3428. Cf. Thomas (n. 41 above), 88.

50 "Aircraft Detection Corps Organisation, Gulf and River St. Lawrence Areas – 1942 and 1943," appendix E, DHIST: 1650-239/16.

51 "Communication Requirements in the Area of the River and Gulf of St. Lawrence" [January 1943] appendix G, DHIST: 1650-239/16.

52 "General Review and Report Upon Defences in the Gulf and River St. Lawrence Areas," 30 January 1943, file S.22-1-17, DHIST: 1650-239/16.

53 See Watts, The U-Boat Hunters, 152f.

54 KTB/1 Skl., Teil B, IV (Juni-Dez. 1943), BA-MA: RM 7/98.

55 Minutes of the St Lawrence Operations Conference, 22-24 February 1943, DHIST: NS 1048-48-22, vol. 2.

56 Captain H.N. Lay, in minutes, ibid., p. 6.

57 "Proposed Naval Disposition, May 1943," and Chart D.o.D. 24 Ops Division NSHQ of 25 January 1943, DHIST: 1650-239/16.

58 Minutes, 22-24 February 1943, appendix A, p. 3 (n. 55 above).

59 RADM G.C. Jones, COAC Halifax, "Control of Navigational Aids – East Coast,"

20 July 1942 (with previous documents), DHIST: 181.002 (D68A), folder 2. Also DHIST: 83/662, "Extracts from the Evelyn Richardson Papers," Public Archives of Nova Scotia; and Transport Canada, Coast Guard, St John, NB, "Wartime Codes Used Between Saint John Lightstations and the Lurcher Light Ship."

60 Staff Officer (Plans) to Director of Plans, "St. Lawrence Defence Plan 1944," 10 March 1944, DHIST: 1650-239/16.

61 "R.C.A.F. Radar Anti-Submarine Measures in Gulf of St. Lawrence Area," NS 1037-2-6 (Staff), 22 May 1944, DHIST: 1650-239/16B, vol. 1.

62 *Monthly Review* of RCAF Ops – North America I, no. 11 (April 1944): 35–6, DHIST: 112.3M1009 (D101).

63 RCN Operational Research Report no. 24 (24 July 1944), DHIST: 1650-239/16B, vol. 2.

64 "Extract from the minutes of a meeting of the Cabinet War Committee held March 7th 1945," DHIST: 1650-239/16B, vol. 1.

65 C-in-C message to NSHQ, 26 February 1945, DHIST: 1650-239/16B, vol. II.

66 "Belle Isle Force," PAC, RG 24, box 11, 503, file 1-14-1.

67 "Belle Isle Force: 26 July to 21 November 1943," PAC, RG 24, vol. 11, 064, file 28-2-1B.

68 "1 Group RCAF to Eastern Air Command," 291745Z Jul 43, PAC, RG 24, box 11, 503, file 1-14-1.

69 "Belle Isle Force: 26 July to 21 November 1943" (n. 67 above).

70 "BIF 2," DHIST: 1650-239/16B, vol. 1. It was reissued with minor amendments on 15 August 1944.

71 C-in-C CNA, to NSHQ, 26 February 1945, DHIST: 1650-239/16B, vol. II.

72 "Plan for the Defence of the Gulf and Lower River St. Lawrence in 1945," DHIST: 1650-239/16.

CHAPTER TWO

1 Dönitz, *Memoirs*, 162. For a British view of "Drumbeat," see Beesly, *Very Special Intelligence*, 127–55.

2 Dönitz, *Memoirs*, 195.

3 KTB/BdU, 11 January 1942. BA-MA: PG 30302/3/.

4 U-66 covered zones CA 79, 87, and DC 12–13; U-123 covered CA 28, 29, 55, 53; U-125 took CA 38, 39, 62, 63: U-109 patrolled BB 7355–8575; and U-130 patrolled BB 51, 55, 57, 58.

5 KTB/BdU, 23 February 1942, BA-MA: RM 87/19.

6 KTB/BdU, 17 January 1942, BA-MA: PG 30302/3.

7 KTB/BdU, 24 January 1942, BA-MA: PG 30302/3.

8 BdU had 249 actually in service plus 15 just commissioned in January, for a total of 264. Five were lost in January, leaving 259.

9 KTB/BdU, 1 February 1942, BA-MA: RM 87/19.

10 KTB/BdU, 15 February 1942, BA-MA: RM 87/19.

11 Dönitz, *Memoirs*, 198.

12 Ibid., 202.

13 Beesly, *Very Special Intelligence*.

14 "Operational Intelligence Centre, Special Intelligence Summary, Week Ending 12 January 1942," Public Records Office, Kew Gardens, file ADM 223/15.

15 There were two offices responsible for torpedo production and testing: the civilian TVA (Torpedo-Versuchsanstalt) and the naval TEKA (Torpedo-Erprobungskommando).

16 Dönitz, *Memoirs*, 203. For the statistics see Rohwer, *Seekrieg*, 212. Hardegen's War Diary (33) notes ten ships for 66,135 tons. For a tabulation of Axis successes see Jürgen Rohwer, *Axis Submarine Successes 1939-1945* (orig. *Die U-Boot - Erfolge der Achsenmächte 1939-1945*). My account, based on the logs, occasionally disagrees with Rohwer.

17 Rohwer *Seekrieg*, 211.

18 NCSO Sydney, January 1942, DHIST: 1000-5-31, vol. 9.

19 FONF, Operational Report January 1942, 2, DHIST: NSS 1000-5-20, vol. 1.

20 Eastern Air Command Anti-Submarine Report, January 1942, 8, DHIST: 181.003 (D25).

21 Dönitz (*Memoirs*, 203) omits references to "the night of the long knives" and the Jews when citing this passage.

22 KTB/BdU, 4 February 1942, BA-MA: RM 87/19.

23 For an account of the sea-going tug *Foundation Franklin*, see Farley Mowatt, *Grey Seas Under* (New York: Ballentyne Books, 1974; orig. published 1958).

24 See Halifax Local Defence Force Monthly Report - January 1942 (DHIST).

25 Convoy HX-169 was escorted by HMCS *Saskatoon* and *The Pas*. Also, Staff Officer, Operations, Report of February 1942. Cf. KTBs of U-109, U-130, U-552, and BdU. Canadian records are vague on this point.

26 EAC, A/S, January 1942, 2, DHIST: 181.003 (D25).

27 EAC, A/S, January 1942, 8, para 32 and 33, DHIST: 181.003 (D25).

28 Not until 20 January did Hardegen (U-123) break radio silence to inform BdU of the earlier sinking of *Cyclops*. SS *Dayrose* was torpedoed 46° 38′ N, 52° 52′ W.

29 FONF Operational Report, January 1942, 1, DHIST: 1000-5-20, vol. 1.

30 EAC, A/S, January 1942, 2-8, DHIST: 181.003 (D25).

31 Reichssicherheitsamt, Amt III, SD Hauptamt, *Meldungen aus dem Reich*, Nr 254 (26 January 1942): 2; Nr. 255 (29 January 1942): 1 and 4, BA-MA.

32 With the exception of the Eck affair in which LCdr Heinz Eck of U-852 sank the lone Greek vessel SS *Peleus* (4695 GRT) in the Indian Ocean on 13 March 1944 and machine-gunned the debris and survivors in order to leave no trace of the attack, no case has ever been documented. Eck and his officers were executed after a British court martial on 30 November 1945 (see Dönitz, *Memoirs*, 263f., and Peillard, *Histoire Générale*, 345).

33 Rohwer, *Seekrieg*, 214; KTB/ U-754 records four ships for 16,876 tons (BA-MA: PG 30733).

34 FONF Operational Report, January 1942, 2. EAC, A/S, January 1942, 10, DHIST: 1000-5-20, vol. 1.

35 Easton, *50 North*, 85.

36 EAC, A/S, January 1942; also FONF Operational Report, January 1942, appendix IB, 3–4. U-754 was attracted by her lights (KTB).

37 EAC, A/S places her 7 miles off. FONF states 2 miles off. Median position 47° 47.3′ N, 52° 37′ W.

38 EAC, A/S, January 1942, 10, gives 46° 02′ N, 52° 22′ W. C-in-C CNA gives 45° 59′ N, 52° 38′ W. U-754's DR is compatible with the area.

39 Rohwer, *Seekrieg*, 216. EAC, A/S, January 1942, 10, positions the action 42° 02′ N, 57° 18′ W.

40 COAC, Report of Proceedings, Staff Officer Operations, February 1942, DHIST: NS 1000-5-13, vol. 10.

41 EAC, A/S, February 1942, 4, para. 13–14.

42 Canadian operational records (n. 39 above) mention the action briefly as "Shelled by S/M Atlantian and Opalia (escaped undamaged)."

43 Rohwer, *Seekrieg*, 218.

44 KTB/ U-656 places action at 46° 15′ N, 53° 15′ W.

45 FONF Operational Report, March 1942, DHIST: NSS 1000-5-20, vol. 1.

46 Canadian records do not corroborate (see EAC, A/S March 1942).

47 Rohwer, *Seekrieg*, 231. Convoy screen vectored USS *Leamington* on to target. *Leamington*, Aldenham, *Grove*, and *Volunteer* sunk it with all hands on 27 March 1942 SW Ushant.

48 According to Rohwer (*Seekrieg*, 247) it sank twelve ships (62,536 tons) in the Gulf of Mexico, by Cuba and Yucatan. Its success report was D/F'd, leading to destruction by an American Mariner flying boat of Squadron VP-74.

49 COAC, Report of Proceedings, Staff Officer Operations, March 1942; also EAC, A/S, March 1942, DHIST: 1000-5-13, vol. 10.

50 DHIST: biographical file: J 14023 Buchanan Charles Stewart; also, EAC, A/S, March 1942, 6, para. 11 and 12.

51 *Ottawa Journal*, 26 September 1942: "2 Ottawa Fliers in Bomber That Attacked U-Boats." The RCAF Personnel Assessment attests to Buchanan's "enthusiasm, coolness and courage [that] has set a high standard which is proving to be an ′ inspiration to others."

52 An RCAF Hudson of 113 Squadron eventually sank U-754 off Cape Roseway, NS, on 31 July 1942 after the U-boat had sunk a lone fishing vessel. Ironically, U-754 had just finished signalling "light air surveillance" when death struck.

53 EAC, A/S, January, February, and March 1942. Canadian and German records do not tally precisely. The secret police constantly reported the national mood in a secret mimeographed circular, *Meldungen aus dem Reich*. For its perceptions of "Drumbeat" see Band 12, Nr. 257: 6, Nr. 258: 1, and Nr. 259: 2. BA-MA.

54 See, for example, *Montreal Daily Star*, 1 April 1942, 11.

55 *Halifax Herald*, 4 March 1942, 9.

56 *Hansard*, vol. III, 1942, 2846 (28 May 1942). See also *Halifax Herald*, 29 May 1942, 1 and 4.

57 For example, the *Halifax Herald*, 6 March 1942, 2, and the *Montreal Daily Star*, 5 March 1942, 23.

CHAPTER THREE

1 Rohwer, *Seekrieg*, 240. The term "Battle of the St Lawrence" was first used officially in RCNMR (May 1943): 77. It has been picked up in popular accounts, e.g. Jacques Castonguay, "La Bataille du Saint-Laurent," *Perspectives* (n.d.) and in *Sentinelle, Revue des Forces Canadiennes*, (1982/4): 8–10.

2 EAC, A/S, May 1942, DHIST: 181.003 (D25).

3 The French *Aconit* sank U-432 on 11 March 1943; U-653 sank on 15 March 1943; U-564 on 14 June 1943 (in the Biscay); U-135 on 15 July; U-566 on 24 October 1943; U-593 on 13 December 1943 and U-455 on 6 April 1944 (both in the Mediterranean); U-333 on 31 July 1944.

4 Morison *Battle of the Atlantic* I, 288, places this action on 17 May 1942 some 70 miles south of Halifax; Rohwer (*Axis Submarine Successes*, 96) southeast of Yarmouth (43° 20′ N, 63° 08′ W).

5 U-588 was attacking convoy ONS-115 at the time (see Rohwer, *Seekrieg*, 240); EAC, A/S, May 1942, DHIST 181.003 (D25).

6 DHIST: 1650-239/16B, vol. 1.

7 COAC, Report of Proceedings, Staff Office Operations, April 1942, DHIST: NS 1000-5-13, vol. 11.

8 COAC, Report of Proceedings, Staff Office Operations, May 1942 (DHIST: NS 1000-5-13, vol. 11), refers incorrectly to Lanse Avalleau, and times the sinking at 0356 GMT in position 49° 20′ N, 64° 55′30″ W.

9 KTB/U-111, BA-MA: Sign. PG 30107/1. U-111 gave equal credit to a "sharp-eyed crow's nest look-out."

10 COAC (n. 8 above) indicates sinking in position 40° 32′ N, 63° 19′ W. Some records time the action at 0640 GMT.

11 COAC (n. 8 above).

12 *Le Soleil*, 15 May 1942, 2.

13 Director of Censorship, pamphlet, DHIST: 1650-239/16B, vol. 1.

14 *Montreal Star*, 13 May 1942, 1, and *Ottawa Journal*, 14 May 1942, 7. The map approximates the territory in Canadian Hydrographic Chart L/C 4001.

15 *Le Soleil*, 15 May 1942, 3.

16 Montreal Star, 13 May 1942, 2; *Halifax Herald*, 13 May 1942, 7.

17 *Halifax Herald*, 22 April 1942, 4; 9 May 1942, 9.

18 For this and the following, see "The St. Lawrence Incident," "U-Boat Tracking," DHIST: 1650-239/16B, vol. 1.

19 Ibid., p. 24.

20 KTB/Skl., 21 May 1942, BA-MA: RM 7/34.

21 EAC, A/S, June 1942, 3.

22 COAC, Report of Proceedings, Staff Office Operations, June 1942, DHIST: NSS 1000-5-13, vol. 12; EAC, A/S, June 1942, 2. *Mattawin* sank at 0120 local time in position 40° 15′ N, 66° 04′ W.

23 EAC, A/S, July 1942, 1.

24 EAC, A/S, June 1942, 2-3. The identity of the U-boat remains obscure.

25 Rohwer, *Seekrieg*, 252.

26 KTB/U-132, FT 1655/27/233, BA-MA: PG 30122.

27 Hessler, *U-Boat War* II, 19.

28 "Board of Inquiry – Loss of HMS/M P-514, 21 June 1942," PAC, RG 24, vol. 11, 930.

29 HMS/M P-514 sank in position 46° 32′30″ N, 53° 33″ W, off Cape Pine. "Narrative A: Canadian Participation in North Atlantic Convoys, Operations June 1941– December 1943," DHIST: NS 1886-147/1. For Dönitz, on exchange of recognition signals, see KTB/U-402, BA-MA: Sign. PG 30456, case 11/1.

30 FONF, Administrative War Diary, July 1944, DHIST: 1926-112/3.

31 EAC, A/S, June 1942, 1. See Watts, *The U-Boat Hunters*, 131-5. The ASV MK I was superseded by the ASV MARK II with a maximum range of 20 miles.

32 EAC, A/S, June 1942, 1.

33 Rohwer, *Seekrieg*, 262. Cf. Rohwer, *Axis Submarine Successes*, 107.

34 EAC, A/S, July 1942, 9-10. The Attack Report of Hudson 648 U at 2043 GMT on 7 July 1942 does not match the movements of U-132 even though the RCAF assessed a "good attack" in which the "U-Boat [was] probably given quite a shaking."

35 "Report of Proceedings, Convoy QS-15," DHIST: 81/520/8280, box 8.

36 *Hansard*, vol. IV, 10 July 1942, 4098.

37 *Hansard*, vol. IV, 13 July 1942, 4122-5.

38 *Le Soleil*, 13 July 1942, 3.

39 EAC, A/S, July 1942.

40 EAC, A/S, July 1942 (3), which notes torpedoing at 1810 GMT in position 49° 27′ N, 65° 12′ W; also "Report of Proceedings, Convoy QS-19," DHIST.

41 COAC, Report of Proceedings, Staff Office Operations, July 1942. Cf. *Ottawa Journal*, 14 October 1942, 2, DHIST: NS 1000-5-13, vol. 12.

42 *Ottawa Journal*, 14 October 1942, 12; *Le Soleil*, 14 October 1942, 3: "Un sous-marin ennemi attaque un convoi dans le St. Laurent." Also, Rimouski *Progrès du Golfe*, 16 October 1942, 3-4.

43 Rohwer, *Seekrieg*, 261; EAC, A/S, July 1942, 16. EAC reports sinking in 41° 40′ N, 66° 53′ W.

44 Rohwer, *Seekrieg*, 262.

45 EAC, A/S, July 1942, 1-3.

46 Ibid., 11.

47 EAC, A/S, 4 and 16. Rohwer, *Seekrieg*, 264, records U-132's sighting as on 29 July.

48 See EAC, A/S, July 1942, 13.

49 EAC, A/S, August 1942, 1–6.

50 "COAC to Senior British Officer, Western Atlantic, Re Walrus W.2793," 2 November 1942, DHIST: 181.003 (D 68A).

51 British United Press correspondent Beverley Owen, *Ottawa Journal*, 1 August, 1942, 1.

CHAPTER FOUR

1 Leslie Roberts, ed., "The Battle of the Gulf," *Canada's War at Sea* II, part I, *The Fighting Navy* (Ottawa, November 1944), 39–43.

2 *Sailing Directions. Newfoundland* (Ottawa: Department of Fisheries and Oceans 1980), 344f.

3 Morison, *Battle of the Atlantic* I, 330. For Canadian documentation see EAC, A/S, August 1942, 9. See also NCSO Sydney, "Activities During Month of September 1942," 2., DHIST: NSS 1000-5-21. EAC indicates position of sinking as $51°52'$ N, $55°30'$ W. Air cover arrived five hours later.

4 DHIST: 8000-Weyburn, and 8000-Clayoquot; amplified by letter to Hadley from Captain A.B. German, 2 May 1982. Weyburn sighted U-517 in position $50°16'$ N, $59°04'$ W.

5 EAC, A/S, September 1942, 10, para. 57.

6 FONF, Monthly Report for September 1942, DHIST: 1000-5-20, vol. 2.

7 DHIST: 1650/U-517. Rohwer's letter to DND of 9 May 1964 on file.

8 EAC, A/S, September 1942, 6, placed sinking at 0210 GMT in position $49°10'$ N, $66°50'$ W near Cap Chat. EAC claimed thirty-nine survivors and two killed. COAC, Operations, and Records of SOMC/Trade include HMCS *Vegreville* among escorts.

9 For a full account of what Hugh Keenleyside termed "The Great Yacht Plot" (*Weekend Magazine*, 23 March 1974), see McKee, *The Armed Yachts of Canada*.

10 COAC to C-in-C U.S. Fleet, "Analysis of U/Boat Attack on Convoy Q 33," 23 November 1942 (DHIST: 81/520/8280, box 8, QS 33). Explosions seem to have occurred at $49°12'$ N, $66°24'$ W.

11 Rohwer, *Seekrieg*, 276. Also Rohwer, *Axis Submarine Successes*, 12.

12 EAC, A/S, September 1942, 18. COAC, Operations, lists the position as $48°51'$ N, $63°44'$ W, at 2100 GMT.

13 *RCNMR*, no. 19 (September 1942): 18. This was broadcast in Spanish to North and South America.

14 For this and the following discussion, see EAC, A/S, September 1942, 8f. See appendix D, 25, for photograph.

15 Reprinted in McKee, *The Armed Yachts of Canada*, 143.

16 DHIST: 8000-HMCS Charlottetown.

17 See reports in *Montreal Daily Star*, 19 May 1942, 3–4; *Fort William Daily Times-Journal*, 21 September 1942; *Toronto Evening Telegram*, 18 September 1942; and *Halifax Herald*, 19 September 1942, 4.

18 "Report of the Loss of HMCS Charlottetown," submitted by LCdr G.M. Moors, RCNVR (DHIST: 8000-Charlottetown), cited passim; also 8000-Clayoquot.

19 DHIST: NS 18870-331/2, vol. 1, and NS C-11156-331/22, vol. 1.

20 See, for example, *Le Soleil*, headline story for 18 September 1942: "La corvette 'Charlottetown' a été coulée"; *Montreal Daily Star*, 18 September 1942; *Toronto Daily Star*, 19 September 1942.

21 NOIC, Gaspé, 13 September 1942, DHIST: 8000-Charlottetown.

22 For an account of the loss of *Ottawa*, see Schull, *Far Distant Ships*, 138.

23 See Schull, 135. News of *Oakville*'s U-boat capture in the Caribbean (Schull, 137) was not published until much later.

24 *Halifax Herald*, 19 September 1942, 6.

25 See "SQ-36" in "Operations North American Waters – Gulf of St. Lawrence," DHIST: 1650-239/16, together with associated ship files; also "Report of Proceedings – Q-063," 20 October 1942, re the U-boat attacks on QS-36, DHIST: 8280-HMS Salisbury; "Report of Proceedings of S.Q.36 and Q.S.35," in DHIST: 81/520/8280, box 10, SQ 36. Rohwer, *Seekrieg*, 276, notes the screen as "1 British destroyer, 2 Canadian corvettes, and in addition sweepers." Cf. Rohwer, *Axis Submarine Successes*, 123.

26 COAC, Staff Office Operations, September 1942, notes sunk at 1638 GMT in position 48°51′ N, 65°05′ W. See also SOMC/Trade, 31 December 1942.

27 COAC (n. 26 above) records attack at 49°10′ N, 67°05′ W. Cf. Rohwer, *Seekrieg*, 276: U-165 sank two ships for 10,292 tons and torpedoed one for 4570 tons.

28 EAC, A/S, September 1942, 9, records attack at 49°28′ N, 65°20′ W.

29 EAC, A/S, September 1942, 11–12. Appendix E of the document contains photographic enlargements.

30 *Hansard*, 13 July 1942, 4124–6.

31 E.g., *Ottawa Journal*, 14 October 1942, 26.

32 *Völkischer Beobachter. Kampfblatt der national-sozialistischen Bewegung Grossdeutschlands*, 18 December 1942: "U-Boote. Londons grösste Sorge."

33 Admiral Hartwig insists that aircraft sank Hoffmann in consequence of his exposing himself to D/F. Rohwer (*Seekrieg*, 277) claims he struck a mine.

34 Rohwer, *Seekrieg*, 230. Camouflaged as freighters and fishing vessels, the USS *Asterion*, *Eagle*, and *Atik* were deployed between 23 March and the beginning of April. Hardegen's U-123 sank USS *Atik* on 26 March 1942 in consequence of a gun duel.

35 COAC, Staff Office Operations, October 1942. Position: 48°47′ N, 68°10′30″ W.

36 E.g., *Ottawa Evening Journal*, 15 October 1942, 12.

37 E.g., *Le Soleil*, 24 November 1942, 3: "La grève se propage dans les chantiers maritimes à Lauzon."

38 EAC, A/S, October 1942, 3. The attack occurred at $47°07'$ N, $59°54'$ W.

39 For an account of air attacks on U-106 after detection by ASV, see EAC, A/S, October 1942, 4, para. 20.

40 EAC, A/S, reports contain no record of these attacks. Nor do either naval or trade records reveal which convoy this might have been.

41 E.g., *Ottawa Journal*, 10 December 1940, 13: "21 Missing and 18 Wounded." For an account of the *Saguenay* incident, see Schull, *Far Distant Ships*, 53–6.

42 *Ottawa Journal*, 17 October 1942. The SS *Tavernor*, named after the *Caribou's* skipper and his two officer sons, entered the Gulf service in 1962.

43 DHIST: 8000-Grandmère. See comments by Admiral L.W. Murray on the "Report of Attack."

44 U-69's War Diary notes the attack at 0821 hours in BB 5198, but does not indicate which time it kept. Assuming the practice of DSZ (GMT plus 2 hours) he fired at 0221 Atlantic Standard Time. Canadian records show *Caribou* was struck at 0640 GMT, or 0240 AST. Newspaper reports variously indicate 0220 a.m., 0340 a.m., and "shortly before 4 a.m."

45 DHIST: 8000-Grandmère, "HMCS Grandmère – Historical Summary," 27 November 1963. U-69's identity was unknown when this official summary was written. See also COAC, Staff Office Operations, October 1942.

46 *Halifax Herald*, 17 October 1942, 1 and 3, claimed twenty-two children aboard.

47 Commemorative address, 1965, by G.H. Basto, 8000-Grandmère.

48 E.g., *Ottawa Journal*, 17 October 1942, 1.

49 DHIST: NS 1000-H.

50 EAC, A/S, October 1942, 2 (para. 11), 3 (para. 12). COAC, Staff Office Operations, October 1942.

51 All stories appeared in front-page articles on 17 October 1942. *Ottawa Journal*, however, published it that day on p. 11. HMS *Viscount* destroyed U-69 with all hands in the North Atlantic on 17 February 1943.

52 *Ottawa Journal*, 20 October 1942, 1.

53 His apt but controversial address was widely reported on 19–20 April 1982.

CHAPTER FIVE

1 E.g., Kahn, *Hitler's Spies*; Beesly, *Very Special Intelligence*; Jones, *Most Secret War*.

2 General-major Lettow-Vorbeck, ed., *Die Weltkriegsespionage. Authentische Enthüllungen über Entstehung, Art, Arbeit, Technik ... auf Grund amtlichen Materials* (München: Justin Moser 1941); see in particular Ludwig Altmann, "Zur Psychologie des Spions," 37–42.

3 KTB/Skl., Teil A, 12 December 1942, 261, BA-MA: Sign. RM 7/43.

4 KTB/U-213, BA-MA: PG 3021/3.

5 Rohwer, *Seekrieg*, 241, indicates that U-213 was to lay mines in St John's, Newfoundland.

6 I am indebted to Chief Superintendent P.E.J. Banning, RCMP, Departmental Privacy and Access to Information Coordinator. Eric H. Wilson, "A Wartime Incident," *The RCMP Quarterly* 39, no. 4 (October 1974): 34–7, contains errors of fact. His claim, for example, that his father was stationed in Saint John during the Langbein incident and therefore had personal knowledge of the case is not corroborated by the officer's service record.

7 COAC, Report of Proceedings, Staff Office Operations, May 1942 (DHIST: NS 1000-5-3, vol. 11, 3.

8 *Hansard*, vol. 1, 1952, 305, in a speech by Dan Riley (L, Saint John-Albert). U-213 sailed for its second mission on 13 July 1942 and was sunk eighteen days later with all hands near the Azores by the sloops HMS *Erne*, *Rochester*, and *Sandwick*.

9 *Ottawa Citizen*, " 'Spy' Lived Not Far From Peace Tower," 15 March 1952.

10 For this and the following remarks, see KTB/ U-518, BA-MA: Sign. PG 30556, case 12/3.

11 *Montreal Daily Star*, 22 May 1942, 1: "Maine Hunts Nazi Spies – Foreign Agents Came from Canada."

12 E.g., *Ottawa Journal*, 29 June 1942.

13 Godbout to King, 15 July 1942, PAC, MG 26J1, reel C-6806, 276149-276149A; King diary, 18 July 1942. I am indebted to Dr W.A.B. Douglas for this reference.

14 *Halifax Herald*, 29 July 1942, 2.

15 *Le Soleil*, 10 August 1942, 1.

16 *Le Soleil*, 16 October 1942, 8.

17 COAC, Staff Office Operations, November 1942; FONF, Monthly Operational Report for November 1942, 2; DHIST: NS 1000-5-20, vol. 2.

18 EAC, A/S, 1942, 4.

19 Report of Proceedings, Captain of the Port (Schwerdt), 15 January 1943, 2: "Defence of Wabana, Bell Island."

20 *Toronto Daily Star*, 9 August 1945: "Gaspé Spy Bought His Life by Becoming Allied Spy." Also *Montreal Gazette*, 10 August 1945: "German Spy Captured in Gaspé Dodged Death by Work for Allies."

21 Harvison, *The Horsemen*. John Picton, "The Reluctant Double Agent: Mounties Got Their Man," *Sunday Star*, 4 October 1981, A10.

22 *Toronto Globe and Mail*, 10 August 1945: "Spy Captured at Gaspé Valuable Aide to Allies." Also *Montreal Gazette*, 10 August 1945: "German Spy Captured in Gaspé."

23 *Ubootshandbuch* III (Berlin: 1943), 95.

24 For a personal view see Harvison, 105–21. His details occasionally diverge from those of other records. For example, his claim that the agent landed "during a rainstorm" (109) does not agree with U-518's meteorological record.

25 I am indebted for the following to Chief Superintendent Banning, Ottawa, and Mr Malcom Wake, RCMP Museum, Regina, Sask.

26 According to RCMP records, Janowski remained on the beach until approximately 7 AM, began walking along the highway at 8:30, when he was picked up by a passing car, and arrived at the hotel "between 10 and 11 A.M.." Civilian witnesses, however, later recollected that the spy checked into the hotel around 6:30 that morning. These and other discrepancies render a completely reliable account of subsequent events impossible.

27 *Montreal Standard*, 20 May 1945: "No Medals for Werner."

28 The county sheriff, Gus Goulet, informed the press after the war that the agent "spoke pretty decent English and good French. But his accent was funny in both tongues ... I would have taken him for a German or a Dutchman," ibid.

29 *Toronto Daily Star*, 14 May 1945: "Quebec Spy Catcher Tells Own Story."

30 *Ottawa Citizen*, 16 May 1945: "Some Spy."

31 Staff Officer Operations to NOIC Gaspé, Report for November 1942, notes in part: "Every co-operation was given to the Quebec Provincial Police, Royal Canadian Mounted Police, and the investigating officer from NSHQ."

32 C.W. Harvison to the Officer Commanding, "Depot" Division, RCMP, Regina, 3 April 1963, RCMP Museum archives

33 *Newsweek*, 23 November 1942, 14. I am indebted to the RCMP for information on press leaks.

34 *Ottawa Journal*, 24 November 1942, 1 and 12.

35 KTB/Skl., Teil A, 24 April 1943, 470 and 533, BA-MA: Sign. RM 7/47.

36 *Montreal Star*, 29 July 1943: "Police Duties Emphasized – Col. Lambert Heard at Conference."

37 *L'Action Catholique*, 27 December 1943, with photo of Duchesneau.

38 See *Toronto Daily Star* (14 May 1945); *Ottawa Evening Citizen* (14 May 1945); *Montreal Herald* (14 May 1945); *Montreal Star* (14 May 1945); *Halifax Herald* (15 May 1945); *Montreal Gazette* (15 May 1945 and 16 May 1945); *Montreal Star* (16 May 1945); *Ottawa Citizen* (16 May 1945); *Montreal Standard* (20 May 1945); *Toronto Daily Star* (9 August 1945); *Montreal Gazette* (10 May 1945); *Toronto Globe and Mail* (10 August 1945).

39 The *Ottawa Journal* for 14 May 1945 featured the front-page story "Spy's Arrest in Quebec Is Revealed," whereas "Old-Type Dollar Catches Nazi Spy" only warranted p. 18 in the *Winnipeg Free Press* for 15 May 1945.

40 *Ottawa Journal*, 15 May 1945, 10: "Used Captured Spy to Lure Other Agents into Trap."

41 *Montreal Gazette*, 16 May 1945: "Duplessis Says Spy Captured by Vigilance of N.U. Appointee."

42 Rohwer, *Seekreig*, 290. COAC, Ops, November 1492, 4.

43 KTB/U-537, BA-MA: Sign PG 30569-576. See also Douglas and Selinger on the discovery of the weather station. Franz Selinger was the first to trace the location of WFL-26, and ultimately joined Douglas to lead an expedition to the site with the Canadian Coast Guard.

44 FONF, Operations War Diary, October 1943, 4, DHIST: 1926-112/3.
45 KTB/Skl., Teil A, November, 24ff., BA-MA: Sign RM 87/37.

CHAPTER SIX

1 Paul Carell and Günther Böddeker (*Die Gefangenen. Leben und Uberleben Deutscher Soldaten Hinter Stacheldraht* [Berlin: Ullstein 1980], 43) first described the scheme without indicating the source. My discussions with U-boat veterans confirmed the principles and practice of letter codes.

2 Franke to Hadley, 26 July 1982. Franke first offered his unpublished account dated 12 December 1981 to Ali Cremer for inclusion in the latter's memoirs (see Brustat-Naval, *Ali Cremer: U 333*).

3 For a German view of the sinking of the ex-P&O liner, which had been converted into an armed merchant cruiser, see Bekker, *Hitler's Naval War*, 41-8.

4 "Maps of areas in Canada apparently drawn by POWs, June 42/June 45," DHIST: 113.3 V1009 (D29).

5 See John Melady, *Escape from Canada*. Melady does not discuss "Magpie" or "Kiebitz."

6 Franke to Hadley, n. 2 above.

7 FONF, War Diary, April 1943, DHIST: 1000-5-20, vol. 3; Report of Proceedings, Staff Office Operations," April 1943, DHIST: NSS 1000-5-13, vol. 18. The attack occurred at 43° 25′ N, 56° 20′ W. Rohwer, *Seekrieg*, 345, incorrectly lists 25 April. See KTB/U-174, précis by BdU (Godt).

8 KTB/U-161, BA-MA: Sign. PG 30147/30148. Rohwer, *Seekrieg*, 385.

9 C-in-C CNA, Staff Office Operations, "Report of Proceedings," April 1943, DHIST: NSS 1000-5-13, vol. 18, 1.

10 EAC, A/S, Report, May 1943, 6-7, DHIST: 181.003 (D25).

11 NOIC Gaspé, War Diary, May 1943, part II, DHIST: NSS 1000-5-21.

12 For a variant see Harvison, *The Horsemen*, 137-43. Harvison erroneously placed the escape attempt at Grande Ligne, Que. Cf. "Prisoners of War and Internees, Mar/Oct 44," DHIST: 321.009 (D92). Carell's (42-54) racy and often fanciful account uses the *Kristall* magazine article without acknowledgment.

13 Rohwer, *Seekrieg*, 109. Despite having consulted Kretschmer, Terence Robertson (*The Golden Horseshoe* [London: Evans Press 1955]) confuses many aspects of the escape. For example he incorrectly identifies the rescue Boat as U-577, claiming it survived the war when it was in fact sunk on 9 January 1942.

14 "U-536," DHIST: 1650/U536, DHIST: 80/580/item 54.

15 *Kristall*, September 1945, n.p. About the calibre of *The National Enquirer*, it described the mission as "the wildest and most adventuresome story of the war," and caused consternation among the crew who saw in it a reawakening of German militarism.

16 Harvison, *The Horsemen*, 143.

17 Lett, "A Book and Its Cover," 30-1.

18 DHIST: Biographical File: "Piers, Desmond William." Typescript of an interview by Hal Lawrence, 7 January 1982, 163-70. Many of Piers's recollections are blurred, and confuse elements of the Janowski story with the narrative of U-536.

19 Harvison, *The Horsemen*, 140.

20 Piers, n. 18 above. The reasons for the British veto of a Canadian decision are not clear. The British had profited by capturing U-570 and commissioning it as HMS *Graph*.

21 Lett ("A Book and Its Cover," 20) observes that the forged document was in error, as it should have read "Coxwell Avenue."

22 I am indebted to Marc Milner for this description of his visit to Pointe de Maisonette, August 1984. For the following account, see "Weekly Intelligence Report," September 23-30 1943, 6, DHIST: 181.003 (D423).

23 R.J. Pickford, "Sub-Lieutenant Commando and Young Corvette Skipper," in Lynch, ed., *Salty Dips* I, 1-5.

24 G.M. Schuthe, "MLs and Mine Recovery," in Lynch, *Salty Dips* I, 83.

25 Piers could be confusing the incidents. He concludes his tapescript of the U-536 incident with the curious phrase "And that was the end of the spy hunt in Bay Chaleur."

26 KTB/ U-536, notes by 2 Skl. BdU Operations, BA-MA: PG 30574/3.

27 This version was borrowed approvingly and without acknowledgment both by Carell/Böddeker,52 (n. 1 above) and by the *Vancouver Courier Nordwesten*, 25 January 1979, 9 and 18.

28 As reported to BdU by Loewe, KTB/ U-536, BA-MA: PG 30569-76.

29 Carell, 54 (n. 1 above). *Courier-Nordwesten*, 13 January 1979, 9, and 25 January 1979, 9.

30 *Nene* became an RCN ship on 6 April 1944. See Macpherson and Burgess, *Ships of Canada's Naval Forces*. Dunn was relief skipper of *Snowberry*.

31 CO, HMCS *Snowberry* to CO, HMCS *Nene*, "Narrative of Attacks on U-Boat on Night of 19-20 November 1943," 24 November 1943, DHIST: 8000-Snowberry.

32 Loewe to BdU, January 1944, KTB/ U-536. Dr Freudenberg confirmed the details during discussions in June 1983.

33 Cited by Lt (SB) Peter MacRitchie, RCNVR, Office of Naval Information, story no. 2: "Account of destruction of U-536 by Nene, Snowberry and Calgary." Also CP News 1 February 1944, story by Ross Munroe from Ireland (DHIST: 8000-Snowberry).

34 Ruge, *Torpedo- und Minenkrieg*, 42.

35 U.S. Navy Department, *German Submarine Activities*, 139.

36 Ruge, 42. It is noteworthy that the American *Argonaut* of 1927 carried 60, and the British *Seal* of 1935 carried 120.

37 Tucker, *The Naval Service* II, 81.

38 Ibid., 21.

39 DHIST: 1650-239/16, message of 3 January 1940 to Admiralty, file 1028-3-1, vol. 2.

40 Ibid., letter of 24 July 1941, in file 8375-440, vol. 1.

41 Cowie, *Mines, Minelayers and Minelaying*, 147.

42 KTB/BdU, 30 November 1939, 263, BA-MA: Sign. RM 7/6.

43 KTB/Skl., 6 February 1940, BA-MA: RM 7/6.

44 Jones, *Most Secret War*, 120: "In fact, had they been laid in sufficient numbers and with sufficient ingenuity they could have brought our [UK] economy to a standstill."

45 KTB/Skl., Teil A, May 1942, 358–60, BA-MA: Sign. RM 7/36.

46 KTB/BdU, 19 May 1942, 119, BA-MA: RM 87/21. The German SMA mine was not ready until early 1942. This submarine-laid mine was designed for the vertical launching tubes of type VIID and type XB submarines. The "torpedo mine" (TMB and TMC) was for types II, VII, and IX submarines.

47 KTB/BdU, 19 September 1942, 67, BA-MA: RM 87/23. I have restricted my comments to the Canadian zones. BdU also minuted his intentions with regard to the Mississippi, Trinidad, etc.

48 Ranger B. Gill, La Scie Detachment, to Chief Ranger Whitbourne, Newfoundland Ranger Force, 16 August 1941, DHIST: FONF Operations Report, September 1941, file 1000-5-20, vol. 1. For a description of such contact mines see Cowie, 188.

49 DHIST: 1650-239/16, memo of 1 October 1942 in file 1037-30-2, vol. 1.

50 DHIST: 8660-Minelaying, 8000-Medicine Hat; see also Tucker, *The Naval Service* II, 81 and 117.

51 "Mining Operations – Halifax, June 1943," DHIST: NSS 1000-5-13, vol. 18.

52 "Summary of Naval War Effort, April 1st to June 30th, 1943," North American Waters, Ops, DHIST: 1650-239/16.

53 "Report on Mine Operations, 3/6/43 to 19/6/43," Senior Officer 112nd M.M.S. to the Commodore, Halifax, 20 June 1943.

54 C-in-C CNA, War Diary, 31 May 1944, part II, 2, DHIST: NSS 1000-5-13, vol. 22.

55 DHIST: Mine Disposal, 8670-440B, provides but scant details of this largely undocumented area.

56 "Report on Mine Recovery Operations – ML 053," Sub-Lieutenant G.M. Schuthe to Captain (ML), HMCS *Venture*, Halifax, NS, 11 June 1943, DHIST: Mine Disposal, 8670-440B. See also G.M. Schuthe, "MLs and Mine Recovery," Mack Lynch, ed., *Salty Dips* I, 79–83.

57 Commodore, Halifax, HMC Dockyard, to C-in-C CNA, "Loss of Five Mines, Controlled Mine Field, Halifax, N.S., 13 April 1943," DHIST: NSS 1000-5-13, vol. 18.

58 Commodore HMC Dockyard, Halifax, to C-in-C CNA, 15 May 1943, "Report on Mine Units Not Recovered," DHIST: NSS 1000-5-13, vol. 18.

59 "Minesweeping Operations – Halifax, June 1943," DHIST: NSS 1000-5-13, vol.

18; also C-in-C CNA, War Diary, Month Ending May 31, 1943, part II.

60 "Operationsbefehl St. John's," KTB/BdU, October 1943, 168–9, BA-MA: RM 87/31.

61 KTB/BdU, October 1943, 18. The mines were laid between 47° 23' N and 47° 54' N, and from the coast to 52° 17' W, (BA-MA: RM 87/31-32).

62 DHIST: 8660-Minelaying. Also NHS 1650/U-233. Tucker (*The Naval Service* II, 196) records discovery as 12 October.

63 Message of 13 October 1943, in file 1037-30-4, DHIST: 1650-239/16.

64 *RCNMR*, no. 26 (November 1943): 4.

65 Position 48° 53' N, 33° 30' W, on 28 October 1943.

66 DHIST: NSC 1926-112/3, vol. 1. Monthly Reports and Reports of Proceedings: HMCS Avalon, 8000-Annapolis.

67 "Report on the Interrogation of Survivors from U-233 sunk 5 July 1944," Navy Department, Office of the Chief of Naval Operations, Washington, 21 September 1944, 11. DHIST: 1650/U-233. BA-MA: KTB/U-233 vom 22.September bis 27.Mai 1944, prepared by BdU.

68 J.H.L. Johnstone, Director of Operation Research, to A/CNS, 22 August 1944, DHIST: 8660-Minelaying.

69 "Weekly Summary of Information Respecting Departmental Activities," Summary no. 230, Report no. 168, Ottawa, 30 March 1944, 6 (DHIST: 1000-5-19). Censors released nothing of U-220's work until after the war when back-page accounts announced "Mine-Laying U-Boats Tried to Close off St. John's, Newfoundland" (*Ottawa Journal*, 13 June 1945, 13).

CHAPTER SEVEN

1 FONF, Operations War Diary, January 1944, DHIST: 1926-112/3.

2 C-in-C CNA, Operations War Diary, January 1944, DHIST: NSS 1000-5-13, vol. 21.

3 "RCN [sic] Loch Class and River Class Frigates Taken Over by RCN," Naval Staff 225, 14 February 1944, NS 0-7-31, F.D. 1003, DHIST: 8000-Ettrick.

4 "Weekly Summary Information Respecting Departmental Activities," Report 160, 3 February 1944, DHIST: 1000-5-19.

5 "Special Intelligence Summary, Week Ending 8.11.43," Public Records Office, Kew Gardens, file ADM 223/18.

6 KTB/BdU, January 1944, BA-MA: Sign. RM 87/35.

7 KTB/Skl., Teil A, January 1944, 43, BA-MA: Sign. RM 7/56.

8 KTB/BdU, June 1944, BA-MA: Sign. RM 87/41; see also Beesly, *Very Special Intelligence*.

9 Anhang zum KTB/BdU, Januar 1944, 108, BA-MA: Sign. RM 87/35. Period I covered the forty months of the war up to the end of 1942, and reflects "normal losses," which BdU expected. Periods II (January–June 1943) and III (July–October 1943) reflect "relatively self-contained portions of 43" with

higher-than-usual attrition as the Battle turned against the U-boats.

10 KTB/BdU, Anlage, Juni 1944. In his capacity as OKdM, Dönitz advised Hitler on 29 June 1944 that while U-boat losses would continue to be heavy, it was "none the less of value" to send them to sea (see G. Wagner, *Lagevorträge*, 29 June 1944, 543).

11 Dönitz issued a special communiqué to all ranks under his command warning of a "major landing in Western Europe at any time" (KTB/Skl., Teil A, 10 April 1944, 220, BA-MA: Sign. RM 7/59).

12 BdU's review of submarine warfare 1 March–31 May 1944. See "Anlage zum KTB vom 7.6.1944 – Ubootslage 1.6.44," KTB/BdU, June 1944, BA-MA: Sign. RM 87/40.

13 KTB/U-107, 8 October 1940 – 23 July 1944, 99, BA-MA: Sign. PG 30103.

14 KTB/BdU, 11 August 1944, 63, BA-MA: RM 42.

15 KTB/U-543, BA-MA: Sign. PG 30551, case 16. Hellriegel's claims of two sinkings are uncorroborated. See C-in-C CNA, War Diary, 31 January 1944, DHIST: NSS 1000-5-13, vol. 21.

16 War Diary, part II, Month Ending 30 June 1944, DHIST: NSS 1926-102/1, vol. 1. Nothing corroborates U-107's claims of having sunk a destroyer.

17 Schmoeckel, letter to Hadley, 27 February 1982.

18 "Special Intelligence Summary, Week Ending 27.3.44," Public Records Office, Kew Gardens, ADM 223/21.

19 "U-854 – Interrogation of Survivors," DHIST: 80/582, item 64; also 1650/U-854. KTB/U-854, BA-MA: Sign. PG 30755, case 15/3. RCN-RCAF *Monthly Operational Review* (February 1944): 6–7, DHIST: 182.013 (D6).

20 RCN-RCAF *Monthly Operational Review*, "Summary of Training" (March 1944): 2 and 6, DHIST: 181.009 (D86).

21 See "Prisoners of War and Internees, Mar/Oct 1944," DHIST: 321.009 (D92).

22 FONF, Ops War Diary, February 1944, DHIST: 1926-112/3.

23 For the following see Summary Report, prepared by Historical Records Officer to Senior Canadian Officer (London), 31 March 1944, file C.S. 632-1, and FONF Operational War Diary, January–March 1944 (DHIST: NSS 1000-5-13, vol. 21).

24 For an account see Roskill, *The War at Sea* II, 209ff.

25 Macpherson and Burgess, *Ships of Canada's Naval Forces*, 94, incorrectly record that *Valleyfield* escorted an RN tug towing *Dundee*.

26 "Report of Proceedings – SC 154," Commanding Officer, HMCS *St. Laurent*, 14 March 1944, and "Detailed Report no. 3, Sinking of U-Boat," DHIST: 8000-St Laurent I; also "The Sinking of U-845," RCN-RCAF *Monthly Review* (April 1944): 14–15, DHIST: 182.013 (D6), and NSS 1650/U-845. The account in the text draws on an assessment of all available sources.

27 The RCN-RCAF *Monthly Review* (January 1944): 24–6 comments on the Double Foxer, the American FXR, and the Canadian Cat Gear. The latter was towed 200–300 yards astern depending upon the class of ship (DHIST: 182.013 [D6]).

28 RCN News Release, 3 June 1944, CP 10 June 1944 (DHIST: 1650/U-845). Further crew quotations from this source.

29 *St. Laurent*'s message 111522Z of March 1944 seems confusing in the light of subsequent manoeuvres: "Sub surfaced on Forester's port quarter dead ahead of St. Laurent at 1100 yards."

30 See Rohwer, *Seekrieg*, 446. Current views hold that despite their regular broadcasts no weather U-boats became casualties.

31 C-in-C CNA, Staff Office Operations, 31 May 1944, DHIST: 1000-5-13, vol. 22.

32 Lt Ian Tate, RCNVR, Senior Survivor, HMCS *Valleyfield*, to editor, *RCNMR*, 13 June 1944, DHIST: 8000-Valleyfield. See also "Board of Inquiry, Loss of HMCS Valleyfield," 10 May 1944, PAC, RG 24, vol. 11, 930.

33 For example, RCN-RCAF *Monthly Operational Review* (May 1944): 26: "all Radar sets were busily engaged during the dark hours with innumerable echoes, the vast majority of which were bergs" (DHIST: 182.013 [D6]).

34 RCN Press Release, 20 May 1944, DHIST: 8000-Valleyfield. Weissmuller was the macho hero of numerous Tarzan movies; he died in 1984 at the age of 79. The sinking reminded others of a similar scene in the popular propaganda movie *In Which We Serve*, starring Noel Coward.

35 "Report of Proceedings, HMCS Edmundston," 13 June 1944, DHIST: 8000-Edmundston.

36 Sea boat's crew consisted of Lt Ralph Flitton, LS Douglas Edgar, AB Donald Marks, Stoker Charles Coleman, Signalman Donald Bonnell.

37 Interred were Martin J. Hoffman (22), J.C.H. Therrien (26), Frank C. Reynolds (31), William C. Burton (26), and Archie W. Mills (37).

38 FONF, Operational War Diary, May 1944, DHIST: 1926-112/3.

39 RCN-RCAF *Monthly Operational Review* (July 1944), DHIST: 8000-Valleyfield.

40 Drawn from Bielfeld's situation report subsequently rebroadcast by control to U-107. See KTB/U-107, June 1944, 43, BA-MA: Sign. PG 30103.

41 Ruge, *Rommel*, 194.

42 KTB/Skl., Teil A, 6 June 1944, 118. BA-MA: Sign. RM 7/61.

43 G. Wagner, *Lagevorträge*, 589, v. 5, 6.

44 Simmermacher, letter to Hadley, 23 April 1983.

45 KTB/BdU, 7 August 1944, 27, BA-MA: Sign. RM 87/42.

46 Rohwer, *Seekrieg*, 466. Zeissler, *U-Boots-liste*, 20.

47 Wagner, *Lagevorträge*, 584, Abs. 1.

48 KTB/Skl., August 1944, 698, BA-MA: Sign. RM 7/63.

CHAPTER EIGHT

1 "Special Intelligence Summary, Week Ending 21.8.44," Operational Intelligence Centre, Public Records Office, Kew Gardens, ADM 223/21.

2 "Anlage zum KTB/BdU vom 7.6.44," 14, Abs. 3: "Entfernte Op. Gebiete einschl. Indischer Ozean," BA-MA: Sign. RM 87/40.

3 *Völkischer Beobachter*, 15 November 1944, 1: "Die Zwangsjacke des Geleit-

zugsystems" – "Eingeständnis über die Kräftebindung durch die U-Boote."

4 Rohwer, *Seekrieg*, 450. See also chapter six, "Clandestine Operations."

5 "Special-Intelligence Summary, Week Ending 23.10.44," 2, Operational Intelligence Centre, Public Records Office, Kew Gardens, ADM 223/21.

6 EAC, A/S, for October, November, and December 1944.

7 Petersen to Hadley. I am indebted to Kurt Petersen for detailed descriptions.

8 BdU Assessment, KTB/U-541, 24 March 1943 – 9 January 1945, BA-MA: Sign. PG/30577-30581.

9 KTB/Skl., Teil A, 26 May 1944, 464, BA-MA: RM 7/60; KTB/U-541, 26 May 1944, RM 98, case 13/2/30579/2. See *Ottawa Journal*, 31 May 1944, 1/4: "U-Boat Takes Two Americans off Liner."

10 "Special Intelligence Summary, Week Ending 18 December 1944," 2, ADM 223/21.

11 For this and the following discussion, see C-in-C CNA, War Diary, Month Ending August and September, DHIST: NSC 1926-102/1, vol. 1.

12 Ibid., Month Ending 31 October 1944, part I, 2.

13 Very lean data is provided in DHIST: 8000-Norsyd.

14 C-in-C CNA, War Diary, Month Ending 30 September 1944, 4, DHIST: NSC 1926-102/1, vol. 1.

15 Anthony Hopkins, *Songs from the Front and Rear: Canadian Servicemen's Songs of the Second World War* (Edmonton: Hurtig 1979), 148-9.

16 KTB/BdU, 9 October 1944, 33, BA-MA: Sign. RM 87/44.

17 KTB/BdU, 29 October 1944, 86.

18 Although pre-dawn local time, the U-boat functioned on Central European Time. It was therefore 10:10 AM when the incident occurred and quite a proper hour for Captain's Defaulters.

19 Deck log, HMCS *Restigouche*, October 1944, PAC, RG 24, vol. 7795; see also C-in-C CNA, Operations War Diary, Month Ending October 1944, NSC 1926-102/1, vol. 1, part I, 1.

20 "Special Intelligence Summary, Week Ending 16 October 1944," ADM 223/21.

21 See "Assessment," KTB/U-1221.

22 C-in-C CNA, War Diary, Month Ending 31 October 1944, part II.

23 DHIST: 8000-Magog. For the following discussion in the text, see also *Globe and Mail*, 18 April 1945 (1, 2, 13); *Winnipeg Free Press*, 18 April 1945 (4); *Ottawa Journal*, 18 April 1945 (5); amplified by my interview with Mr Gorde Hunter, August 1984.

24 Killed immediately were PO Thomas Davis (Toronto), O/S Gordon Eliot (Kingslea, Alberta), AB Kenneth Kelly (Arnprior, Ontario).

25 C-in-C CNA, War Diary, Month Ending 31 October 1944, DHIST: 1926-102/1, vol. 1.

26 KTB/BdU, 21 October 1944, BA-MA: Sign. RM 87/44.

27 KTB/BdU, 2 November 1944, 10, BA-MA: Sign. RM 87/45.

28 C-in-C CNA, War Diary, Month Ending 30 November 1944, part I.

29 *Ottawa Journal*, 30 December 1944, 19: "Vessel Torpedoed in St. Lawrence Returns to Service."

30 Cf. *Ottawa Journal*, 18 April 1945, 5: "Sub Hits Two Ships Last Fall Killing Three in St. Lawrence." This was obviously stale news.

31 Letter from R.A. McLellan, editor, 19 April 1945, in DHIST: 8000-Magog.

32 For an account see Schull, *Far Distant Ships*, 382f.

33 See, for example, the *Ottawa Journal*, 16 May 1945, 3: "Canadian Destroyer Lost in Fierce Gale off Iceland."

34 H.O. Howard, DNI, to R.A. McLellan, 24 April 1945, DHIST: 8000-Magog.

35 Petersen to Hadley, 22 February 1982.

36 Photocopy of document (NS 1487-716/733, vol. 1) in DHIST: 8000-Shawinigan, and in DHIST: 1650/U-1228.

37 KTB/U-1228, BA-MA: Sign. RM 98, case 16/1/PG 30863-68.

38 Special Intelligence Summary, Week Ending 18 December 1944, 2.

CHAPTER NINE

1 C-in-C CNA, War Diary, Month Ending 31 December 1944, appendix 8, A/S Operations Intelligence Report no. 135, DHIST: NSC 1926-102/1, vol. 1.

2 Summary of Information ... Respecting Departmental Activities, Summary no. 241, Report no. 179, 6 January 1945, file 1000-5-19.

3 *Halifax Herald*, 12 January 1945, 5. For an account of Hilbig's spy landings see Morison, *Atlantic Battle Won*, 330f.

4 Hornbostel correspondence with Hadley. See Hadley, "U-Boote vor Halifax."

5 M.DV., Nr. 960, "Betriebsanweisung Fu Mo 61 (seetakt) (Hohentwiel), BA-MA: RMD 4/960.

6 "Review of U-Boat Results in Inshore Waters, Period 1st July to 31st October, 1944," 29 November 1944, para. 12 (Public Records Office, Kew Gardens, ADM 205/36).

7 However, Captain Klaus Ehrhardt, formerly in charge of fleet maintenance and readiness in the Biscay, recalls that qualified personnel were always available even up to the end of the war, and that the U-boats were properly fitted by base personnel. These opinions reflect the divergent attitudes and expectations held by front-line operators and support base.

8 Schull, *Far Distant Ships*, 426.

9 It is not clear whether "U-Lange" mentioned in the signal refers to Hans-Günther Lange's U-711, which was sunk on 4 May 1944 during an air attack on Norway, or to Helmut Lange's U-1053, which was lost off Bergen on 15 February 1945 during deep-diving trials. Hechler's U-870 was destroyed on 30 March 1945 during a USAAF attack on Bremen.

10 KTB/U-806, 21, FT 1822/3/331.

11 From U-1232's daily newspaper *Der Zirkus* (Nr. 1, Jg. II, 3 January 1945). Sole extant copies in the possession of Dr Kurt Dobratz.

12 KTB/BdU, 28 November 1944, 78, BA-MA: Sign. RM 87/45.

13 A/Captain D.K. Laidlaw, RCN(T), Director of Operations Division, to CNS, "Protection of Shipping in the Canadian Coastal Zone," 21 November 1944, DHIST: NSS 1048-48-31.

14 KTB/U-1231, 19 December 1944, BA-MA: PG 30869-879a.

15 Missing gear deduced from entries in "Fighting Equipment Report," dated 20 March 1944, approved on 14 April 1944, DHIST: 8000-Clayoquot.

16 For this discussion, see DHIST: 8000-Clayoquot.

17 DHIST: 8000-Chedabucto.

18 Merchant Casualty Report no. 52, Week Ending 24 December 1944, entry no. 5A, PAC, RG 24, box 6890, NSS 18871.

19 C-in-C CNA, War Diary, Month Ending 31 December 1944, part I, 2.

20 See *Lloyd's Register 1948*, vol. II, code 73976. Thus the wreck symbol on charts of McNabb's Cove does not refer to her.

21 KTB/U-1231, 23 December 1944.

22 KTB/BdU, 20 December 1944, 61, BA-MA; Sign. RM 87/46. As will be seen, however, not all were sunk.

23 The Board of Inquiry concluded in error that *Clayoquot* had been hit from the starboard side, whereas the commanding officer of *Fennel* insisted correctly on part aft.

24 The Board of Inquiry attributed the explosion to *Clayoquot*'s primed charges ("Minutes of the Board of Inquiry – Sinking of HMCS *Clayoquot*, 27 December 1944," NSS 11156-443/10, PAC, RG 24, vol. 11, 930).

25 For an account of Aubry as a Lieutenant-Commander in command of HMS *Foway*, see Macintyre, *Battle of the Atlantic*, 42–3, 47–9.

26 "Asdic Detection of U-Boats Inshore," 30 October 1944, ADM 205/36.

27 *Kirkland Lake* to C-in-C CNA, 25 0934Z/1244, DHIST: 8000-Clayoquot.

28 Training Commander to Captain "D Halifax, Minute II, 30 December 1944, file D.026-1, PAC, RG 24, box 11,111, file 55-2-1/542.

29 KTB/U-806, 55.

30 KTB/U-806, 40, FT 1600/24/383.

31 *Halifax Herald*, 31 December 1944, 1.

32 *Avalon News*, February 1945, vol. 3, no. 2, 1 (published by the navy in St John's, Newfoundland).

33 During interrogation at St John's in May 1945, the captain of U-190 surmised that Dobratz's U-1232 had sunk *Clayoquot*.

34 KTB/Skl., 3 January 1945, 44, BA-MA: RM 7/68.

35 KTB/U-806, 44, FT 2133/31/386.

36 KTB/BdU, 31 December 1944, 92, BA-MA: Sign. RM 87/46.

CHAPTER TEN

1 KTB/BdU, October 1944, 14, BA-MA: RM 87/44.

2 KTB/Skl., 17 January 1945, 301, BA-MA: Sign. RM 7/68.

3 KTB/Skl., 25 December 1944, BA-MA: Sign. RM 7/66.

4 KTB/BdU, November 1944, 35, BA-MA: RM 37/45.

5 KTB/Skl., 17 November 1944, 367, BA-MA: RM 7/66.

6 KTB/BdU, 18 September 1944, 475, BA-MA: RM 87/43.

7 KTB/Skl., 9 December 1944, 203-9, BA-MA: RM 7/66.

8 KTB/Skl., 4 November 1944, 86, BA-MA: RM 7/66.

9 KTB/BdU, 31 December 1944, 92, BA-MA: RM 87/46.

10 KTB, 28 February 1945, cited in Salewski, *Seekriegsleitung* II, 496.

11 KTB/Skl., Teil A, 17 March 1945 (BA-MA: RM 7/70), records, however, "The first Type XXI U-Boat U-2511 (Schnee) departed on patrol today," 244.

12 Salewski, 497.

13 *Der Zirkus*, Nr. 1, Jg. II, 3 January 1944. Series in sole possession of Dr Kurt Dobratz.

14 C-in-C CNA, War Diary, Month Ending 31 January 1945, part I.

15 *Der Zirkus* (n. 13 above), Nr. 2, Jg. II, 4 January 1945.

16 L.C. Audette, unpublished memoirs (p. 28) states speed of advance of 9.5 knots. Manuscript in sole possession of L.C. Audette.

17 *Meon* to C-in-C CNA and Captain "D" Halifax, 141448Z/1/45.

18 SO, EG-27, Message 180226Z, January 1945, to C-in-C CNA, DHIST: 8000-Ettrick.

19 C-in-C CNA, War Diary Month Ending 31 January 1945, part I, para. 13.

20 Ibid. See also KTB/U-1232, 84.

21 Swettenham, *McNaughton*, vol. 3, 69-80.

22 See, for example, *Ottawa Journal*, 26 January 1945, 3: "McNaughton's Report on U-Boats 'shock' to People of Britain." *The Times* of London, which had been following the Grey North by-election through its Ottawa correspondent, merely headed a note "U-Boats in Atlantic: General McNaughton on Revived Activity," and quoted without comment the now famous line "North Atlantic ... alive with German submarines."

23 *Ottawa Journal*, 14 February 1945, 3.

24 Bracken subsequently urged that McNaughton resign, citing in part "the cause of the humiliating desertion of 6300 [NRMA] men after they had been warned for Service overseas." See, for example, the *Halifax Herald*, 14 February 1945, 3.

25 Summary of Information Respecting Departmental Activities for Month Ending 31 March 1945, summary no. 244, report no. 182.

26 War Diary for Month Ending 31 March 1945, part I, para. 21. Summary of Information ... Ending 31 March 1945 (n. 25 above).

27 In a letter to Hadley, 17 February 1982, Reith insists that he departed Kiel on 10 February 1945. The Allied "Interrogation Report" must be used with caution. NID Ottawa, 22 May 1945: "Report on Interrogation of some members of the crew of U-190," DHIST: 1650/U-190.

28 KTB/Skl., Teil A, 20 March 1945, 287, BA-MA: RM 7/70.
29 KTB/Skl., Teil A, 26 March 1945, 375.
30 KTB/Skl., Teil A, 29 March 1945, 422.
31 KTB/Skl., Teil A, 2 April 1945, 30, BA-MA: RM 7/71.
32 *Ottawa Journal*, 31 March 1945, 1.
33 See *Halifax Herald*, 4 April 1945, 5.
34 For an account see Schull, *Far Distant Ships*, 381-2; Rohwer, *Seekrieg*, 484. Also *Halifax Herald*, 4 April 1945, 13: "Navy Minister Warns of U-Boat Attacks on Coastal Waters."
35 KTB/Skl., Teil A, 8 April 1945, 131, BA-MA: RM 7/71.
36 See J.M. Ruttan, "Minesweeping at Tobruck," in Mack Lynch, ed., *Salty Dips* I, 85-99. Ruttan's recollection of hull numbers does not always concur with naval records.
37 "Minutes of the Board of Inquiry into the Loss of HMCS *Clayoquot*, 27 December 1944," file NSS 11156-443/10, PAC, RG 24, vol. 11,930.
38 Reith to Hadley, 31 March 1982. See "Interrogation Report" (n. 27 above): U-190 discerned itself "picked up by the asdic of a ship thought to be 800-1000 tons, which circled the U-boat and passed overhead two or three times."
39 "Summary of Information Respecting Departmental Activities ... 31 March 1945," summary no. 244 (n. 25 above). Rohwer, *Seekrieg*, 529.
40 RCN Release, 11 May 1945, NSHQ Information Section, DHIST: 8000-Esquimalt. Also A.G. Maitland, "Battle of Atlantic Survivors Remember," *Legion* (July 1982): 42. This nostalgic bugle-and-drum account must be used cautiously.
41 *Halifax Herald*, 8 May 1945, 1.
42 C-in-C CNA to C-in-C Lant, 161857Z April 1945.
43 C-in-C CNA, War Diary for Month Ending 30 April 1945, part I, para. 17. Cf. "Summary of Information Regarding Departmental Activities for Month Ending 30 April 1945," summary no. 245, report no. 183, 5: "four pieces of wreckage picked up would indicate that the U-Boat attacked was U-369." Also Rohwer, *Seekrieg*, 540.
44 Com 10th Fleet, to CTE 61.2, C-in-C CNA, 2311/17/4/45, DHIST: 8000-St. Laurent. See also Report of Proceedings, Halifax, section CU 66, Halifax Destroyer Group.
45 Rohwer, *Seekrieg*, 540.
46 Ibid., 554.
47 "Minutes of the Board of Inquiry into the Sinking of HMCS *Esquimalt*," with addenda, file 1156-442/18, PAC, RG 24, vol. 4109, and file S.8870-442/18, PAC, RG 24, vol. 6890.
48 AIG 409.0-398, DTG 201534Z, DHIST: 8000-Esquimalt.
49 Summary of Information, n. 39 above.
50 Rohwer, *Seekrieg*, 550.
51 U-1228 surrendered on 13 May 1945 in Portsmouth, New Hampshire; U-1231

on 14 May 1945 in Loch Foyle, Ireland: and U-805 that day in Portsmouth, New Hampshire.

52 *Ottawa Journal*, 9 May 1945, 19: "Dönitz' Address to German People."

53 *Halifax Herald*, 8 May 1945, 8: "Admiral Dönitz Orders German U-Boat Fleet to Cease Activity."

54 *Ottawa Journal*, 7 May 1945, 1: "U-Boat Surrender Possible at Halifax."

55 C-in-C CNA, War Diary, 31 May 1945, DHIST: NSC 1926-102/1, vol. 1.

56 *Halifax Herald*, 12 May 1945, 1: "Air Force Plane Takes First German Submarine."

57 "Brief History of HMCS *Rockcliffe*," 8000-Rockcliffe.

58 See *Halifax Herald*, 14 May 1945, 1 and 7. Also "Summary of Information ... summary no. 246, report no. 184, for Month Ending 31 May 1945, 9. *Dunvegan* and *Rockcliffe* intercepted U-889 at 43° 55′ N, 51° 36′ W.

59 *Ottawa Journal*, 14 May 1945, 12. U-889 arrived Halifax from Shelburne at 0758 GMT on 24 May 1945.

60 In position 43° 43′ N, 43° 07′ W. The following account is based on DHIST: 8000-Victoriaville, C-in-C CNA, War Diary, 31 May 1945; 1650/U-190; "HMCS Victoriaville – Report of Proceedings on U-190," CS [Sydney file] 165-20-C9, 8000-Victoriaville; also on my discussions and correspondence with Hans-Edwin Reith.

61 Sgt Frank Bode, *Yank* field correspondent, Newfoundland, typescript in DHIST: 1650/U-190.

62 *Ottawa Journal*, 14 May 1945, 1: "Another U-Boat Surrenders on East Coast." See also p. 8, "Notes and Comment."

63 NID 3 Ottawa, 22 May 1945, DHIST: 1650/U-190.

64 *Ottawa Journal*, 14 May 1945, 7. See also *Halifax Herald*, 17 May 1945, 3: "Hitler 'Did No Wrong' Submarine Men Contend." For this, reporters interviewed "two young Huns," Sub-Lieutenants Werner Müller and Ernst Glenk.

65 C-in-C CNA, War Diary, Month Ending 30 June 1945, part I, DHIST: NSC 1926-102/1, vol. 1.

66 Summary of Information ... For Month Ending 30 April (n. 43 above), 13.

67 "Brief History," 4, n. 1 (n. 57 above).

68 No original records of U-190 are extant. The whole file is listed as destroyed "in error" on direction of the Department of External Affairs. An unsigned historical note in DHIST file is all that remains.

69 RCN Press Release, no. 445, H.Q.A., 15 July 1947; RCN Press Release no. 562 H.Q., 18 October 1947, DHIST: 1650/U-190.

70 "Operation Order: Sinking of Former German Submarine U-190: Trafalgar Day, 21st October 1947," DHIST: 1650/U-190. Press handout similarly entitled.

Bibliography

BIBLIOGRAPHICAL SOURCES

The military archives of the Federal Republic of Germany, the Public Archives of Canada, and the Directorate of History, Department of National Defence, provide the researcher with a wealth of material. In writing this book I have benefited from the resources these institutions offer, and have examined more documents than can be conveniently accounted for here. The Bundes- und Militärärchiv in Freiburg, Germany, has given complete access to the once-classified War Diaries of naval commands, ships, and submarines, as well as to maps and charts, and to wartime directives on armament, communications equipment, technology, and personnel. Canadian sources have supported me with an equally wide range of documentation. Research is facilitated by locator books (*Findbücher*) and catalogues in Germany, cardex and catalogues in Canada. In the few cases where these proved inadequate, professional staff in both countries have shown an uncanny sense of divination in locating documents that eluded more orthodox approaches. I have in addition received documentation from the Public Records Office, Kew Gardens, as well as from the Operational Archives, Navy Yard, Washington, DC and from the Military Archives Division, National Archives and Records Service, Washington, DC. Over the years I have developed broad correspondence with German submariners, which, although not as yet constituting anything as formal as a collection of "Papers," may well do so in time.

My search for popular reactions to U-boat warfare concentrated upon German and Canadian newspapers. Wartime censorship confined newspapers to virtually the same official account of events, though their emphasis might differ. In Germany I chose both the conservative *Die Frankfurter Zeitung* and, at the other extreme, the Nazi party organ *Völkischer Beobachter.* For Canadian stories I focused primarily on the *Ottawa Journal*, because its proximity to the source of information at Naval Service Headquarters suggested its ability to scoop competitors. At the same time I remained especially sensitive to the francophone press, read representative papers across the country in search of local variations, and resorted on occasion to such relatively obscure journals as *The British Columbian* of New Westminster, BC, and *Le Progrès du Golfe*, of Rimouski, Quebec. Clearly, documenting all these sources would needlessly encumber the bibliography.

Full bibliographical details of principal government documents used in the text will be found in the notes for each chapter. Full details of selected published sources appear in the bibliography, thereby permitting an abbreviated notation in the notes themselves.

SELECTED SECONDARY SOURCES

Bacon, R., and McMurtrie, F.E. *Modern Naval Strategy.* London: Frederick Muller 1940.

Beesly, Patrick. *Very Special Intelligence: The Story of Admiralty's Operational Intelligence Centre in World War II.* London: Hamish Hamilton 1977.

Bekker, Cajus. *Hitler's Naval War.* Translated and edited by Frank Ziegler. London: Macdonald and Jane's 1974. Orig. publication, Oldenburg and Hamburg: Gerhard Stalling Verlag 1971.

Bennett, Geoffrey. *Naval Battles of the First World War.* London: Pan Books 1983. Orig. publication, London: Batsford 1968.

Boutilier, James A., ed. *RCN in Retrospect, 1910–1968.* Vancouver and London: University of British Columbia Press 1982.

Brost, Wolfgang. "Minenkriegführung gestern und heute." *Jahrbuch der Marine* 15 (1981): 20–8.

Brustat-Naval, Fritz. *Ali Cremer: U 333.* Berlin: Verlag Ullstein 1982.

Cameron, James M. *Murray: The Martyred Admiral.* Hantsport, Nova Scotia: Lancelot Press 1980.

Carter, David J. *Behind Canadian Barbed Wire: Alien, Refugee and Prisoner of War Camps in Canada 1914–1946.* Calgary: Tumbleweed Press 1980.

Clark, W.B. *When the U-Boats Came to America.* N.p. 1929.

Cooke, O.A. *The Canadian Military Experience 1867–1967: A Bibliography.* Department of National Defence, Directorate of History, Occasional Paper Number Two. Ottawa: Canadian Government Publishing Centre 1979.

Cowie, J.S. *Mines, Minelayers and Minelaying.* London, New York, Toronto: Oxford University Press 1949.

Dönitz, Karl. "Aufgaben und Stand der U-Bootswaffe." *Nauticus, Jahrbuch für Deutschlands Seeinterressen* 22 (Berlin 1939): 187–98. Translated anon. as "The Submarine and Its Tasks." *RCNMR*, no. 10 (April 1943): 33–9.

- *Memoirs: Ten Years and Twenty Days.* Translated by R.H. Stevens. London: Weidenfeld and Nicolson 1959. Originally, *Zehn Jahre und Zwanzig Tage.* Bonn: Atheneum-Verlag, Junker und Dünnhaupt 1958.

- *Deutsche Strategie zur See im Zweiten Weltkrieg: Die Antworten des Gross-*

admirals auf 40 Fragen. Frankfurt am M.: Bernard und Graefe 1970. Original-ly, *La Guerre en 40 Questions.* Paris: Editions de la Table Ronde 1969.

Douglas, Alec [W.A.B.]. "The Nazi Weather Station in Labrador." *Canadian Geographic* 101, no. 6 (December 1981/January 1982): 42–7.

Douglas, W.A.B. "Kanadas Marine und Luftwaffe in der Atlantikschlacht." Trans-lated by Friedrich Forstmeier. *Marine-Rundschau*, Nr. 3 (März 1980): 151–64.

Douglas, W.A.B., and Greenhous, Brereton. *Out of the Shadows: Canada in the Second World War.* Toronto: Oxford University Press 1977.

Douglas, W.A.B., and Selinger, Franz. "Oktober 1943–Juli 1981: Eine Marine-Wetterstation auf Labrador." *Marine-Rundschau*, Nr. 5 (Mai 1982): 256–62.

Easton, Alan. *50 North.* Markham, Ontario: Paperjacks 1980. Orig. publication, Toronto: Ryerson Press 1963.

Elsey, George M. "Naval Aspects of Normandy in Retrospect." In *D-Day: The Normandy Invasion in Retrospect*, edited anon., 170–97. Wichita: University Press of Kansas 1971.

Freyer, Paul Herbert. *Der Tod auf allen Meeren: Ein Tatsachenbericht zur Geschichte des faschistischen U-Boot-Krieges.* Berlin: Militärverlag der Deutschen Demokratischen Republik 1974.

Gallagher, Barrett. "Searching for Subs in the Atlantic." *United States Naval Institute Proceedings* 88, no. 7 (1962): 98–113.

Garner, James Wilford. *International Law and the World War* II. London: Longmans, Green & Co. 1920. For U-boat warfare, see chapters 30–37.

Granatstein, J.L. *Canada's War: The Politics of the Mackenzie King Government 1939–1945.* Toronto: Oxford University Press 1975.

Hadley, Michael. "U-Boote vor Halifax im Winter 1944/45 (I)." *Marine-Rund-schau*, Nr. 3 (März 1982): 138–44.

– "U-Boote vor Halifax im Winter 1944/45 (II)." *Marine-Rundschau*, Nr. 4 (April 1982): 202–8.

Harvison, C.V. *The Horsemen.* Toronto: McClelland & Stewart 1967.

Herwig, Holger H. *Politics of Frustration. The United States in German Naval Planning, 1889–1941.* Boston/Toronto: Little, Brown and Company 1976.

Hessler, Günther. *The U-Boat War in the Atlantic* I, *1939–41.* London: Admiral-ty, Tactical and Staff Duties Division 1950. BR 305(1).

– *The U-Boat War in the Atlantic* II, *January 1942–May 1943.* London: Admi-ralty, Tactical and Staff Duties Division 1952. BR 305(2).

Hirschfeld, Wolfgang, *Feindfahrten: Das Logbuch eines U-Bootfunkers*, Wien: Paul Neff Verlag 1982.

Hoch, G. "Zur Problematik der Menschenführung im Kriege: Eine Untersuchung zur Einsatzbereitschaft von U-Boot-Besatzungen ab 1943." Jahresbericht der Führungsakademie der Bundeswehr, 22. ASTO, Hamburg, 2 November 1981. Unpublished.

Hoyt, Edwin P. *U-Boats Offshore.* New York 1980.

Jones, R.V. *Most Secret War: British Scientific Intelligence 1939–1945*. London: Hamilton 1978.

Kahn, David. *Hitler's Spies: The Extraordinary Story of German Military Intelligence* London: Arrow Books, 1980. Orig. publication, London: Hodder & Stoughton 1978.

Kuenne, Robert E. *The Attack Submarine*. New Haven: Yale University Press 1955.

Lamb, James B. *The Corvette Navy: True Stories from Canada's Atlantic War*. Toronto: Macmillan 1979.

Lawrence, Hal. *A Bloody War: One Man's Memories of the Canadian Navy, 1939–45*. Agincourt: Gage 1979.

Lett, Stephen H. "A Book and Its Cover." *RCMP Quarterly* 39, no. 2 (April 1974): 30–1.

Lynch, Mack, ed. *Salty Dips: "When We Were Young and in Our Prime"* I. Ottawa: Ottawa Branch, Naval Officers Associations of Canada 1983.

Lynch, Thomas G. *Canada's Flowers: History of the Corvettes of Canada 1939–1945*. Halifax: Nimbus Publishing 1981.

Macintyre, Donald. *The Battle of the Atlantic* (1961). London: Pan Books 1983.

McKee, Fraser. *The Armed Yachts of Canada*. Erin, Ontario: The Boston Mills Press 1983.

Macpherson, Ken, and Burgess, John. *The Ships of Canada's Naval Forces 1910–1981: A Complete Pictorial History of Canadian Warships*. Toronto: Collins 1981.

Marinedienstvorschrift. *Handbuch für U-Bootskommandanten*, M.DV. Nr. 906. Berlin: Oberkommando der Kriegsmarine 1942.

– *Ubootschandbuch der Ostküste Kanadas* I: [Cape Breton, Nova Scotia, Fundy]. M.DV. Nr. 299. Berlin: Oberkommando der Kriegsmarine 1942. II: *Neufundland und Belle Isle Strasse*. Berlin 1942. III: *St. Lorenz-Golf*. Berlin 1943.

Melady, John. *Escape from Canada: The Untold Story of German POWs in Canada 1939–1945*. Toronto: Macmillan 1981.

Metson, Graham. *An East Coast Canadian Port ... Halifax at War 1939–1945*. Toronto and Montreal: McGraw-Hill Ryerson 1981.

Meyers, Reinhard. "Kanada und die britische Appeasement-Politik." *Zeitschrift der Gesellschaft für Kanada-Studien*, no. 2 (1982): 57–85.

Milner, Marc. *Canadian Naval Force Requirements in the Second World War*. OREA Extra-Mural Paper No. 20, Operational Research and Analysis Establishment, Dept of National Defence. Ottawa 1981.

– "Convoy Escorts: Tactics, Technology and Innovation in the Royal Canadian Navy, 1939–43." Paper presented to the Ottawa Military History Colloquium, March 1982.

– *North Atlantic Run: The Royal Canadian Navy and the Battle for the Convoys*. Toronto: University of Toronto Press 1985.

Morison, Samuel Eliot. *The Battle of the Atlantic, September 1939–May 1943.* In *History of United States Naval Operations in World War II*, vol. I. Boston: Little Brown and Company 1960.

– *The Atlantic Battle Won, May 1943–May 1945.* In *History of United States Naval Operations in World War II*, vol. X. Boston: Little, Brown and Company 1960.

Morton, Desmond. "The Military Tradition of the Canadian Forces: An Historian's Perspective." Paper presented to the 1982 Conference on the Canadian Military: Directions for Future Research, York University, 20 November 1982.

Peillard, Léonce. *Histoire Générale de la Guerre Sous-Marine (1939–1945).* Paris: Robert Laffont 1970.

– *La Bataille de L'Atlantique.* I: *La Kriegsmarine à son Apogée, 1939–42.* II: *La Victoire Des "Chasseurs" 1942–1945.* Paris: Editions Robert Laffont 1974.

Range, Clemens. *Die Ritterkreuzträger der Kriegsmarine.* Stuttgart: Motorbuch Verlag 1974.

Reche, Reinhart. "'Die Quadratur der Meere'–zur Umrechnung der Marine-Quadratekarte 1939–1945." *Marine-Rundschau*, Nr. 3 (März 1984): 120–2.

Rohwer, Jürgen. "Funkaufklärung im Zweiten Weltkrieg: Bibliographie." *Marine-Rundschau*, no. 10 (1980): 638–40.

– *Axis Submarine Successes 1939–1945.* Completely revised. Translated by John A. Broadwin. Annapolis, MD: Naval Institute Press 1983. Originally, *Die U-Boot-Erfolge Der Achsenmächte 1939–1945.* München: J.F. Lehmanns 1968.

Rohwer, J., and Hümmelchen, G. *Chronik des Seekrieges 1939–45*, Hrsgg. vom Arbeitskreis für Wehrforschung und von der Bibliothek für Zeitgeschichte. Hersching: Pawlak 1968.

Rohwer, J. and Hümmelchen, G. *Chronology of the War at Sea.* Translated from the German by Derek Masters. Vol. 1: *1939–42*: Vol. 2, *1943–45*, London: Ian Allan 1972, 1974.

Rohwer, J., and Jäckel, E., eds. *Die Funkaufklärung und ihre Rolle im Zweiten Weltkrieg.* Stuttgart: Motorbuch Verlag 1979.

Roskill, S.W. *The War At Sea 1939–1945.* I: *The Defensive.* London: HM Stationery Office 1954. II: *The Period of Balance.* London: HM Stationery Office 1965.

Ross, Tweed Wallis. *The Best Way to Destroy a Ship: The Evidence of European Naval Operations in World War II.* Manhattan, Kansas: MA-AH Publishing 1980.

Rössler, Eberhard. *The U-Boat. The Evolution and Technical History of German Submarines.* Translated by Harold Erenberg. London: Arms and Armour Press 1981. Originally, *Geschichte des deutschen Ubootbaus.* München: J.F. Lehmanns 1975.

– "Die Entwicklung von Primärelementbatterien für Torpedos und Kleinst-U-Boote in Deutschland." *Marine-Rundschau*, Nr. 6 (June 1982): 317–21.

Ruge, Friedrich. *Torpedo- und Minenkrieg.* München: Lehman 1940.

- "German Naval Operations on D-Day." In *D-Day: The Normandy Invasion in Retrospect*, edited anon., 149–69. Wichita: University Press of Kansas 1971.
- *Rommel in Normandy: Reminiscences*. Translated by Ursula R. Moessner. London: Macdonald and Jane's 1979.

Salewski, Michael. *Die deutsche Seekriegsleitung 1939–1945*. 2 vols. München: Bernard and Graefe 1975.

Sarty, Roger. "Silent Sentry: A Military and Political History of Canadian Coast Defence 1860–1945." Ph D diss., University of Toronto 1982.

Schull, Joseph. *The Far Distant Ships: An Official Account of Canadian Naval Operations in the Second World War*. Ottawa: Queen's Printer 1961.

Stacey, C.P. *Canada and the Age of Conflict*. Vol. 2: *1921–1948: The Mackenzie King Era*. Toronto: University of Toronto Press 1981.

Swettenham, John. *McNaughton, 1944–1946*. Vol. 3. Toronto: Ryerson Press 1969.

Tucker, Gilbert. "The Organizing of the East Coast Patrols 1914–1918." *RCNMR*, no. 23 (November 1943): 8–20. From The Canadian Historical Association, Ottawa, 1941, 32–40.

- *The Naval Service of Canada: Its Official History*. 2 vols. Ottawa: King's Printer 1952.

United States. Navy Department. *German Submarine Activities on the Atlantic Coast of the United States and Canada*. Office of Naval Records, Historical Section. Washington: Government Printing Office 1920.

Wagner, Gerhard, ed. *Lagevorträge des Oberbefehlhabers der Kriegsmarine vor Hitler 1939–1945*. München: J.F. Lehmanns Verlag 1972.

Wagner, Jonathan, F. *Brothers Beyond the Sea: National Socialism in Canada*. Waterloo, Ontario: Wilfrid Laurier Press 1981.

Watts, Anthony J. *The U-Boat Hunters*. London: Macdonald and Jane's 1976.

Welland, R.P. "To Catch a Submarine." *The Canadian Military Journal* 28, no. 7/9 (1962): 5–9.

Wellershoff, Dieter. "Minen und Minenabwehr gestern und heute." *Marine-Rundschau*, Jg. 75, Nr. 8 (1978): 509–19.

Werner, Herbert A. *Die Eisernen Särge*. München: Wilhelm Heyne Verlag 1980. Orig. publication, Hamburg: Hoffmann and Campe 1969.

Westerlund, Karl-Erik. "'Whiskey on the Rocks'–Der U-Boot-Zwischenfall vor Karlskrona." *Marine-Rundschau*, Nr. 1 (January 1982): 30–5.

Wicklung, Walter. "Whiskey on the Rocks." *Naval Forces: International Forum for Maritime Power* III, no. 1 (1982): 26–31.

Wilckens, Friedrich, "Meereseinflüsse bei der U-Boot-Ortung." *Soldat und Technik*, Jg. 3, Nr. 4 (April 1960): 165–6.

Zeissler, Herbert. *U-Boots-Liste*. Hamburg-Wandsbek: Selbstverlag 1956.

Index

This selective index excludes frequently occurring terms and geographical names unless of special importance.